They we
Americar
Pacific Northwest.
They came to stay.
Then they talked to
Fred Lockley.

# Conversations with Pioneer Men is...

"...fascinating. Full...of buffalo galloping across the prairie, prairie schooners, campfires of buffalo chips or sagebrush, frying antelope steaks, peaceful and warlike Indians, early schools, frontier missionaries, gold mining, encounters with grizzly bears, moonshine, ripoffs, legendary drunks and hard work."

*The Delta Paper*
Delta Junction, Alaska

"We started with two wagons and eight oxen. We got here with one wagon, drawn by an ox and a cow."

William M. Billyeau
Pioneer of 1852
Jefferson, Oregon

"When I came to this country in
1848 there were no roads and no bridges
and no ferries. There were Indian trails
and fords. I don't mean flivvers. I
mean shallow places where you could
cross the river."

Levi Bennett
Pioneer of 1847
near McMinnville, Oregon

# VOICES OF THE OREGON TERRITORY

## Conversations with

# BULLWHACKERS
# MULESKINNERS

## Pioneers, Prospectors, '49ers
## Indian Fighters, Trappers
### Ex-Barkeepers, Authors
### Preachers, Poets & Near Poets

## All Sorts & Conditions of Men

### By Fred Lockley

Compiled and Edited by Mike Helm

This book was first published in 1981 as **Conversations with Bullwhackers, Muleskinners, Pioneers, Prospectors, '49ers, Indian Fighters, Trappers, Ex-Barkeepers, Authors, Preachers, Poets & Near Poets & All Sorts & Conditions of Men.**

Library of Congress Catalog Card Number
81-50845

International Standard Book Number
0-931742-09-9

Published by Rainy Day Press
PO Box 3035
Eugene, OR 97403

## Conversations with Pioneer Men

Published in 1996

International Standard Book Number
0-931742-18-8

Printed in USA

Cover photo: Stephen Meek, Pioneer of 1847. Used by permissio
of the Oregon Historical Society.

"After all is said and done, people
are just folks, and if you feel a real
and sincere interest in them, and if
you are a good asker and a good listener,
you will be rewarded by getting good
human interest stories."

Fred Lockley
1871–1958

# Acknowledgments

I would like to thank the following people for their contributions to the publication of this volume of **The Lockley Files:**

**Chris Helm,** for spending much of her summer vacation in a tireless search for typographical errors.

**Philip Zorich,** formerly librarian in the Oregon Collection at the University of Oregon Library who has moved on to different pastures on the east coast, and **Liz Cooksey,** Phil's assistant who, in his absence, has assumed most of his duties in addition to her own, for introducing me to **The Lockley Files,** fetching them for me, volume after volume, until I had read through all 58 volumes, and for trusting me with them, each day, as far as the nearest working Xerox machine.

**Donald J. Sterling,** editor of the **Oregon Journal,** in Portland, Oregon, for his encouragement of this project at its inception, and to **Ed O'Meara,** associate editor of the **Oregon Journal,** for his research into the life and work of Fred Lockley and for his efforts to bring attention to the project in the pages of the **Oregon Journal.**

**Ben, Malindi, Polly,** and **Luke Helm,** for patiently foregoing those camping trips and for under-standing and explaining to their friends why their dad spent the summer in the attic.

The unnamed and unknown person or persons who clipped, pasted, catalogued and alphabetized those thousands of Fred Lockley's columns to create and preserve **The Lockley Files** so they could, in time, find their way into this book.

The reading public in the Pacific Northwest, who, by their acceptance of the first volume of **The Lockley Files, Conversations with Pioneer Women,** have made this volume possible.

# Table of Contents

"In the summer of 1852 I was working with a surveying party in southern Oregon. One morning we ran across two wagons loaded with flour standing in the road, with the mules lying dead in front of the wagons. Both of the teamsters had been killed. The Indians had broken out again. I decided that farming in Polk County was healthier than surveying in southern Oregon, so I came back to Polk County."

Uncle Sammy Burch
Rickreall, Oregon

1

"Have I any children? What do you take me for? That's a nice question to ask an old bachelor."

Frank Wilehart
Woods, Oregon

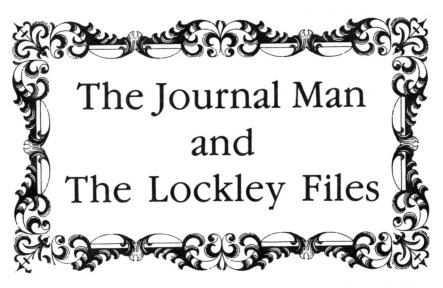

# The Journal Man
# and
# The Lockley Files

Fred Lockley was one of Oregon's pioneer newspapermen. He worked for newspapers in Montana and Kansas before coming to Oregon in the late 1890's, where he worked first for the **Capital Journal** in Salem. In 1905 he was in Pendleton, where he owned a 25% interest in the **East Oregonian**. Later, Lockley sold his interest in the **East Oregonian** and moved to Portland, where he worked for the **Oregon Journal**. He was known as "The Journal Man", and, for nearly 20 years, his column, "Impressions and Observations of the Journal Man", appeared daily on the editorial page of the **Oregon Journal.**

During his career, Lockley conducted more than 10,000 interviews with--as he once said in an interview with himself--"bullwhackers, muleskinners, pioneers, prospectors, 49ers, Indian fighters, trappers, ex-barkeepers, authors, preachers, poets and near-poets, and all sorts and conditions of men and women."

Today, 58 old, black, three-ring binders stuffed --perhaps by Fred Lockley himself, no one seems to know for sure--with yellowed copies of his interviews and observations turn slowly to dust behind two locked doors in the Oregon Collection at the University of Oregon Library in Eugene, Oregon. They are a rare treasure, an oral history of pioneer days in the Oregon Territory, recorded in the words of the people who walked to Oregon in the mid-1800's, or were born during those years in log cabins on their parents' donation land claims, and who lived to tell about it in the early part of this century.

This is the second of three volumes of oral history by Fred Lockley planned for the Oregon

Country Library. The first, **Conversations with Pioneer Women**, is a feminine view of life on the Oregon Trail and in the society building in the wilderness at its end. In this volume the pioneer men share with Lockley their stories of life on the Oregon frontier.

Mike Helm
July 10, 1981

"Mother and the rest of the children spoke Chinook as readily as English."

Robert C. Bonser
Scappoose, Oregon

4

# All Sorts
# &
# Conditions
# of Men

## VOICES OF THE OREGON TERRITORY

"The Indians who lived along the river gave us no trouble. They lived largely on fish, camas berries, and hazelnuts.

"The government decided to move all of the Indians to a reservation, so they were gathered up and, as it was late in the year, they decided to take them to the reservation the following spring. They issued rations to the Indians twice a week. The Indians would eat all that was issued to them the day it was issued and then for two days have nothing. The result of this was that more than half of them died that winter."

W. H. Cole
Umpqua, Oregon

# "Tell you about the time . . .

"*Tell you about the time when I was a stage driver,*" said Uncle Dave, as he tipped his chair back and tamped the tobacco into his corncob pipe with a calloused finger. "*I used to take pride not only in getting into the station on time, but getting in with my team in good shape. I remember on one trip, where I had a mountain run, I had to make a cut-off on a road I had never seen before. I let the check reins down so that when my horses went through the stream they could drink. The leaders came to the edge of the stream, put their noses down into the water, gave a terrified snort, jumped stiff-legged, and dragged the wheelers into the stream. They snorted worse than the leaders and went through the creek like a bullet out of a gun.*

"*I couldn't imagine what ailed my horses, so I got a passenger that was sitting up on the boot with me to hold the team while I went back to investigate.*

"*I lay down by the bank of the stream. The water looked clear and good. I stooped down to see if the water tasted all right, but the minute I got a mouthful I snorted worse than the horses and jumped back as if I had been shot. The water was nearly boiling hot. Fifty yards or so above, the water came out of a crack in the lava rock, steaming hot.*

"*There used to be a driver on that line that had driven up in Yellowstone Park in the early days. He told me about an experience he had that I have always kinda doubted. He said there was a wooden bridge over a creek that he had always used, but one time the bridge went out and he drove down the stream a little way until he found a place to ford.*

"*He said the stream was not over 100 yards*

7

wide, and, unknown to him, it was strongly impregnated with alum and some other kind of salts. He had four American horses on his team. The water was deeper than he thought, and in one place they went clear under and had to swim. When they came out on the opposite bank, what was his surprise to find that the water had shrunk his horses till they weren't any bigger than Shetland ponies.

"He asked the fellow that lived there about it. He told him he had started in with a good-sized team and after fording the stream for a week or ten days his horses had shrunk till they were no bigger than jackrabbits. I always kinda doubted it, though."

*Oregon Journal*
undated

# Benjamin Franklin Bonney
## Pioneer of 1845
## Mulino, Oregon

*Mulino is a village on the line of the Willamette Valley and Southern Railway between Oregon City and Mount Angel. Though Mulino is a very small dot on the map and has a population of but a few hundred, many interesting people live there. Among the interesting pioneers of the west living at Mulino is Benjamin Franklin Bonney. Recently while at Mulino I spent part of an afternoon with him.*

"Those old days are gone forever, and the present generation can never know the charm and romance of the old west."

"I was christened Benjamin Franklin. My father, Jarius Bonney, was born in New York state, October 14, 1793. His people were from Scotland. My mother, whose maiden name was Jane Elkins, also born in New York state, March 11, 1809. My mother was my father's second wife. He had five children by his first wife and nine children by his second. I am the second child of the second brood. I was born in Fulton County, Illinois, November 28, 1838. My father was a millwright, carpenter, cabinetmaker and cooper. When I was a boy flour sacks were not used, flour being shipped in barrels. My father ran a cooper shop and manu-factured flour barrels near what is now called Smith-field, in Illinois.

"There was so much fever and ague in Illinois that Father decided to move. He had heard of Oregon. One thing that decided him to go to Oregon was that he had heard there were fish in plenty there. Father was a great fisherman, and while he caught pike and redhorse in Illinois, he wanted to move to a country where he could catch trout and salmon. He put in his spare time for some months making a strong wagon in which to cross the plains. His brother, Truman Bonney, after talking the matter over with him, decided he would also go to Oregon. He had a large family.

"My father and mother, with their children, Edward, Harriet, Truman, Martha Jane, Emily, Ann, and myself, started for the Willamette Valley April 2, 1845. Over 3000 people started for Oregon in the spring of 1845. Presley Welch was captain of one of the trains. Joel Palmer and Samuel K. Barlow were his lieutenants. Samuel Hancock was captain of another train. Both trains started from Independence, Missouri. Another company with over 50 wagons started from St. Joe. The captain of the St. Joe wagon train was A. Hackleman. Still another wagon train left St. Joe under command of W. G. T'Vault. John Waymire was his assistant. Sol Tetherow was in command of still another wagon train.

"I was seven when we started for Oregon. I can well remember what a hullabaloo the neighbors set up when Father said we were going to Oregon. They told him his family would all be killed by Indians, or if we escaped the Indians we would starve to death, be drowned, or lost in the desert. Father was not a man to draw back after he had put his hand to the plow, so he went ahead and made ready for the trip. He built a large box in his home-made wagon and put in a lot of smoked and pickled pork. He had made over 100 pounds of maple sugar the preceding fall, which we took along instead of loaf sugar. He also took plenty of cornmeal. At Independence he laid in a big supply of dried buffalo meat and bought more coffee. I remember he bought two gallons of unroasted coffee, with the wooden pail thrown in for a dollar. He also laid in a plentiful supply of home-twist tobacco. Father chewed it and Mother smoked it. To this day I enjoy seeing some white-haired old lady smoking her 'Missouri Meerschaum', as we used to call the old corncob pipes in those days. It always reminds me of my mother.

"When we passed through Independence, back in 1845, it was the last trading point on the frontier. The Indians were camped all around and were anxious to trade buffalo robes for shirts, powder, lead, or firewater, preferably the latter. Father bought four finely tanned buffalo robes of the Indians. There were several stores at Independence and a number of blacksmith shops and wagon shops, as well as livery stables and hotels. At Independence we joined the Barlow wagon train. Barlow soon took command. In those days you could size a man up, but you can't do it any more: there isn't the opportunity. Barlow had good judgment, was resourceful, accommodating, and firm. One man in the company, named Gaines, had a fine outfit. He had six wagons and was well-to-do. He settled in Polk County.

"One of the things I remember very vividly was a severe thunderstorm that took place toward the middle of the night. The thunder was incessant, and the lightning was so brilliant you could read by its flashes. The men chained the oxen so they could not stampede, though they were very restive. Our tents were blown down and the covers were blown off the wagons and in five minutes we were wet as drowned rats. Unless you have been through it you have no idea of the confusion resulting from a storm on the plains, with oxen bellowing, the children crying, the men shouting and the thunder rolling like a constant salvo of artillery, with everything as light as day, and the next second as black as the depths of the pit.

"At Fort Hall we were met by an old man named Caleb Greenwood, and his three sons, John, 22 years old, Britian, 18, and Sam, 16. Caleb Greenwood, who originally hailed from Nova Scotia, was an old mountain man and was over 80 years old. He was a scout and trapper and had married a squaw. His sons were therefore halfbreeds. He was employed by Captain Sutter to go to Fort Hall to divert the Oregon-bound emigrants to California.

"Greenwood was a picturesque old man. He was dressed in buckskin, had a long, heavy beard, and used very picturesque language. He called the Oregon emigrants together the first evening we were at Fort Hall, and made a talk. He said the road to Oregon was very dangerous on account of the Indians. He told us that while no wagons had as yet gone to California, there was an easy grade, and crossing the mountains would not be difficult. He said Captain Sutter would have ten Californians meet the emigrants, and that he would

11

supply them with plenty of potatoes, coffee, and dried beef. He also said he would help the emigrants over the mountains to their wagons, and that to every head of family who would settle at Sutter's Fort Captain Sutter would give six sections of land from his Spanish land grant.

"After Greenwood had spoken the men of our party held a powwow that lasted nearly all night. Some wanted to go to California, while others were against it. Barlow, who was in charge of our train, said he would forbid any man to leave the train and go to California. He told us we did not know what we were going into, that there was great uncertainty about the land titles in California, that we were Americans and should not want to go to a country under another flag. Some argued that California would become American territory in time. Others thought Mexico would fight to hold it and that the Americans who went there would get into a mixup and probably get killed. The meeting nearly broke up in a riot. Barlow finally appealed to the men to go to Oregon and make Oregon an American territory, and not waste their time going to California to help promote Sutter's land schemes.

"The next morning old Caleb Greenwood, with his boys, stepped out to one side, and Caleb said: 'All you who want to go to California drive out from the main train and follow me. You will find there are no Indians to kill you, the roads are better, and you will be allowed to take up more land in California than in Oregon. The climate is better, there is plenty of hunting and fishing, and the rivers are full of salmon.'

"My father, Jarius Bonney, was the first one of the Oregon party to pull out of the Oregon train and head south with Caleb Greenwood. Truman Bonney, my uncle, followed my father. Then came Sam Kinney of Texas. Then came Dodson, and a widow named Teters, and some others. There were eight wagons in all that rolled out from the main train to go to California with Caleb Greenwood.

"The last thing those remaining in the Barlow train said to us was, 'Goodbye. We shall never see you again. Your bones will whiten the desert or be gnawed by wild animals in the mountains.'

"After driving southward three days with us, Caleb Greenwood left us to go back to Fort Hall to get other emigrants to change their route to California. He left his three boys with us to guide us to Sutters Fort. Sam, the youngest, was the best pilot, though all three knew the country as well as a city man knows his back yard. We headed

southwest.      I  never  saw  better  pasture  than  we
had   after   leaving   the   main   traveled   road.      Our
oxen  fattened  up  and  became  unruly  and  obstreperous.
        "After   two   weeks'   traveling   we   struck   a   desert
of   sand   and   sagebrush.      Breaking   the   way   through
the   heavy   sagebrush   was   so   hard   on   the   lead   team
of   oxen   that   their   legs   were   soon   bruised   and   bleeding,
so   each   wagon   had   to   take   its   turn   at   the   head
of   the   train   for   half   a   day,   then   drop   to   the   rear.
On   this   sagebrush   plain   we   found   lots   of   prickly
pear.      We   children   were   barefooted,   and   I   can
remember   yet   how   we   limped   across   that   desert   from
piercing   the   soles   of   our   feet   with   the   sharp   spines
of   this   cactus.      The   prickly   pear   also   made   the
oxen   lame,   as   the   spines   would   work   in   between
their  hoofs.
        "One   day   Sam   came   back   riding   as   fast   as
he   could   and   told   us   to   corral   the   oxen,   for   a
big   band   of   buffalo   were   stampeding   and   would
pass   near   us.      Whenever   oxen   smell   buffalo   they
go   crazy.      They   want   to   join   them.      We   got   the
wagons   into   a   circle   and   got   the   oxen   inside.
The   buffalo   charged   by.      The   Greenwood   boys   killed
a   two-year-old   bull   and   a   heifer   calf.      We   had
to   camp   there   for   a   few   hours,   for   our   guides   told
us   that   if   our   oxen   crossed   the   trail   of   the   buffalo
they  would  become  unmanageable.
        "It   is   an   odd   thing   that   when   oxen   smell
the   fresh   trail   of   the   buffalo   they   stop   and   paw
and   bellow   as   if   they   smelt   fresh   blood.      If   you
have   every   tried   to   stop   a   runaway   ox   team   you
know   what   hard   work   it   is.      I   remember   seeing
on   the   plains   a   stampede   of   oxen   hitched   to   a   wagon.
They   tried   to   stop   them,   but   they   had   to   let   them
run   until   they   were   tired   out.      Two   of   the   oxen
were   killed   by   being   dragged   by   the   others.      The
men   cut   the   throats   of   the   two   oxen,   bled   them,
and   we   ate   them,   though   the   meat   was   tough   and
stringy.
        "When   we   turned   off   the   Oregon   Trail   near
Fort   Hall   to   go   to   California   we   had   to   follow   the
lay   of   the   country,   for   this   was   before   the   discovery
of   gold   in   California,   and   there   was   no   road   then.
In   our   party   were   four   or   five   young   men   who   used
to   ride   ahead   with   the   Greenwood   boys,   sometimes
in   front   and   sometimes   by   the   side   of   the   wagons,
as  a  sort  of  bodyguard.
        "One   day   when   John   Greenwood   was   acting
as   pilot   an   Indian   suddenly   rose   from   the   sagebrush,
frightening   John's   horse.      John   had   a   fine   riding
animal,   one   of   the   best   I   have   seen.      As   it   reared,
John   jerked   it   savagely,   and   it   almost   unseated
him.      Several   young   men   laughed.      This   made   John

furious. He declared he would kill the Indian for scaring his horse. John took his gun from in front of his saddle and pointed it at the Indian. The Indian threw up his hands. The young men with John remonstrated with him and told him the Indian meant no harm, and not to shoot. One of the young men called the Indian to run. The Indian instantly obeyed and started to run away at full speed. This was too much for John, who drew a quick bead on him and fired, shooting him through the back. The Indian fell forward, face downward in the sand. The men on horseback there waited until the others rode up, but John rode on as fast as he could.

"My uncle, Truman Bonney, who was a doctor, examined the Indian, who was gasping for breath, and said he had been shot through the lungs and that it was a fatal wound. My mother took a quilt from our wagon and laid the dying Indian on it. She also brought him a drink of water, but he shook his head and refused to drink. We camped a mile or so farther on.

"Just about dusk Caleb Greenwood and his son Sam, who were escorting some other emigrants, rode into our camp. They had come across the Indian, who was still living. Caleb Greenwood had told Sam to shoot the Indian through the head to put him out of his misery, which he had done. They had then dug a hole in the sand and buried him. When Caleb Greenwood came into our camp he said, 'The man that killed that Indian must die.' He thought John Kinney had killed him.

"My father said, 'Your son John shot him.'

"Greenwood told the men of the party to meet and state the facts fully. When he found his son John had not shot in self-defense, but had shot the Indian wantonly, he said, 'I will act as judge of this trial. I order that the murderer of the Indian be killed.' He told the men of the party that whoever saw his son John was to shoot him on sight, as he would a wild animal. John, who was mounted on a fine horse, rode on as fast as he could and fell in with a Mexican. In a quarrel with a Mexican over a game of cards he was stabbed and killed, so our party did not have an opportunity to carry out the orders and kill him.

The fall we arrived at Sutters Fort there was a good deal of trouble about the coming of Americans to California. A Mexican officer named Castro brought up the question of the legality of foreigners coming to California without passports. The authorities at Mexico City had issued instructions that Americans from the Sandwich Islands could come to California even though their passports were not regular, but the emigrants who came from Missouri or who came from Oregon must have proper passports. The order, which was published in California on September 12, 1845, said the coming of American families from Missouri into California was likely to cause subversion of order and complicate the foreign relations of California as well as create much embarrassment, and as a consequence positive orders were issued that no more families should be permitted to come into California unless they became naturalized.

"Castro and Castillero came north to ask the American emigrants their intentions in settling in California. Castro explained to them that friendly relations had been broken off between the republic of the United States and the republic of Mexico. The emigrants promised that if they were allowed to remain until spring they would go away peacefully if the Mexican government would not permit them to settle. Fallejo was put in charge of the American settlers. He supplied them with provisions and did not require them to give bonds to keep the peace. Sutter himself was more than kind to the emigrants. He was anxious to build up an American colony there and he did everything possible for the Americans.

"In the spring of 1846 a Mexican officer with 30 soldiers came to the fort and announced that all Americans who did not care to become Mexican subjects must leave California. Late in April a meeting of the emigrants was called and the question was discussed. Most of the emigrants decided they preferred to go to Oregon rather than lose their American citizenship. Captain Sutter urged my father to stay and told him he would give him six sections of land, but he refused. Captain Sutter then gave him horses and wagons in exchange for his oxen.

"Captain Sutter wanted to have as many Americans settle there as he could get, and planned to furnish them land so they would raise wheat. He wanted to buy all the wheat from them, as he planned to sell it to the Russian government at Sitka, Fort Wrangell, and other points in Alaska. He was a man of real vision. The Russian government had given up the Russian settlements in California and the Hudson's Bay Company was retiring from Oregon to British Columbia, and Sutter believed he could exchange wheat for furs with Russia in Alaska and make a fortune. He probably would have done so if gold had not been discovered in California.

"While we were crossing the sagebrush desert, one of the men in our party named Jim Kinney,

15

who hailed from Texas, came upon an Indian.
Kinney had a big wagon and four yoke of oxen
to carry his provisions and bedding. He also had
a spring hack drawn by a span of fine mules.
His wife drove the mules, while Kinney himself always
rode a mule and had a hired man to drive the
wagon with the four yoke of oxen. Kinney had
long, black hair, a long, black moustache, and
heavy black eyebrows and was tall and heavy,
weighing probably 225 pounds. He had a violent
temper and was a good deal of a desperado.

"When he saw this Indian in the sagebrush
he called to the driver of his wagon to stop the
oxen. Kinney's wagon was in the lead that day,
so the whole train stopped. Going to the wagon
he got a pair of handcuffs and started back to
where the Indian was. Of course, the Indian had
no idea Kinney meant any harm to him. My father
said, "Kinney, what are you going to do with that
Indian?"

"Kinney said, 'Where I came from we have
slaves, and I am going to capture that Indian
and take him with me as my slave.'

"My father said to him, 'The first thing you
know that Indian will escape and tell the other
Indians and they will kill us all.'

"Kinney said, 'I generally have my way.
Any man that crosses me regrets it. I have had
to kill two or three men already because they did
not want me to have my way, so if you want trouble,
you know how to get it.'

"Kinney was an individualist and would not
obey the train rules, but he was such a desperate
man, and apparently held life so lightly, that no
one wanted to cross him.

"Kinney went to where the Indian was, jumped
off his mule and struck the Indian over the head.
The Indian tried to escape. He put up a fight
but he was no match for Kinney, and in a moment
or two Kinney had knocked him down and got his
handcuffs on him and dragged him to the hack.
He fastened a rope around his neck, fastened him
to the hack and told his wife to hand him his blacksnake whip, which she did, as she was as much
afraid of him as the men were. Then he told his
wife to drive on.

"He slashed the Indian across the naked shoulders with the blacksnake whip as a hint not
to pull back. The Indian threw himself on the
ground and was pulled along by his neck. Kinney
kept slashing him to make him get up until finally
the Indian got up and trotted along behind the
hack. For several days Kinney kept back of the

Indian, slashing him with the blacksnake to 'break his spirit'. After about a week or ten days Kinney untied the Indian and turned him over to his ox driver and told him to break the Indian in to drive the ox team.

"Kinney had a dog that was wonderfully smart. He had used him in Texas to trail runaway slaves. After two or three weeks he did not tie the Indian any more at night, as he said if he ran away the dog would pick up his trail. He would then follow him and kill him, to show the other Indians the superiority of the white man. He said he had killed plenty of Negroes and once had had to kill a white man who could not see things his way.

"After the Indian had been with Kinney over three weeks, one dark, windy night he disapeared. Kinney called the Indian his 'man Friday'. In the morning when Kinney got up he found the Indian had taken a blanket, as well as his favorite Kentucky rifle, a gun he had paid $100 for. He had also taken his powder horn, some lead, and three hams. I never saw a man in such a temper in my life as was Kinney. He was furious. Everyone in the train rejoiced that the Indian had escaped, but they all pretended to sympathize with Kinney, for they were afraid of being killed if they showed any signs of satisfaction.

"Kinney saddled his mule, took his dog that he had used to trail runaway slaves with, and started out on the track of the Indian. The wind had blown the sand in ridges and hummocks, thus covering the trail of the Indian. After hunting half a day in all directions, Kinney finally returned to the wagon train and we started on.

"At the foot of the Sierra Nevada Mountains we were met by ten Mexicans with a pack train conveying flour, potatoes, dried beef, and other provisions. We camped at the foot of the mountains several days, waiting for other emigrants who had turned off at Fort Hall to join us. After a day's travel toward the summit we came to a rimrock ledge where there was no chance to drive up, so the wagons were taken to pieces and hoisted to the top of the rimrock with ropes. The wagons were put together again and reloaded, the oxen which had been led through a narrow crevice in the rimrock, were hitched up, and we went on. Once more while crossing the Sierras we came to a rimrock ledge that could not be mounted, so we repeated the process of hoisting the wagons. It took us four days to reach the summit of the mountains. In going down the western side, toward the Sacramento Valley, the mountains were so steep in places that we had to cut pine trees and hitch them to the ends of the wagons to keep them from running forward upon the oxen.

"At the foot of the Sierras we camped by a beautiful clear ice-cold mountain stream. We camped there three days to rest the teams and let the women wash the clothing and get things fixed up. My sister, Harriet, who was 14, and my cousin, Lydia Bonney, daughter of my father's brother Truman Bonney, and myself and other boys of the party put in three delightful days wading in the stream. It was October, and the water was so low that in many places the sand and gravel bars were showing. On one of these gravel bars I saw what I thought were grains of wheat, but when I picked them up I found they were heavy and of a dull yellow color. I took one of the pieces, about the size of a small pea, into camp with me. Dr. R. Gildea asked me for it. That evening he came to my father and, showing him the bit of dull yellow metal I had given him, he said: 'What your boy found today is pure gold. Keep the matter to yourself. We will come back here next spring and get rich.'

"My father thought he was visionary and did not pay much attention to Dr. Gildea. Dr. Gildea asked me to pick up all the nuggets I could find. He gave me an ounce bottle and asked us to fill it for him. The next day we children hunted along the edges of the bars and in the crevices of the bedrock and soon filled his ounce bottle with nuggets ranging in size from a grain of wheat to a pea.

"When we arrived at the Fort Captain Sutter made us heartily welcome. He told my father that the fort would accommodate 12 families and that the first 12 families joining his colony would be furnished quarters. He furnished us quarters in the fort and also gave us plenty of fresh beef, potatoes, onions, coffee, and sugar. The families who joined the colony received regular rations in accordance with the number of children in the family. He gave all of the men work who cared for it. Some of the men helped break the wild Spanish cattle to the plow. The native method of farming was by means of crude plows drawn by oxen. Instead of ox-yokes the cattle had poles tied to their horns. They used rawhides for tugs and their method of plowing was to have a man lead the oxen and one walk on each side with a long sharp stick to goad the oxen.

"Captain Sutter engaged my father to make ox-yokes to replace the native outfits. Our men had a busy and strenuous job breaking the native cattle to plow. They would put one of our well-broken teams in front, then put a yoke of wild

18

steers in the middle, and a well-broken American yoke of oxen in the rear. In this way our men broke 20 yoke of oxen during the winter.

"There was a large cookhouse at the fort where we children liked to watch them do the cooking. They cooked here for the Indian laborers. In addition to the Indian workers there were a lot of Indian boys who were being trained to work. They had to keep getting new workers, as many of the Indians would die each winter of mountain fever. These Indian boys were fed in a peculiar way. They ground barley for them, made it into a gruel, and emptied it into a long trough. When the big dinner bell rang the Indian boys would go to the trough and with their fingers scrape up the porridge and eat it. In the middle of the fort was a big oven where the bread was baked. Nearby was a well, from which we all got water. At the east end of the fort there was a pile of oak lumber. Here the Indians and other servants were punished for any infraction of the rules. The man or boy to be punished would be strapped, face downward, to one of the logs and would then be flogged on the back with a five-tailed rawhide. Out near the gate a large bell was hung. One of the servants rang this every hour so the people would know what time it was.

"So many emigrants were crowded into the fort that winter that there was a good deal of sickness from what in those days was called mountain fever. Now it is called typhoid. A large number of the natives died of this disease, as well as many of the emigrants, mainly children. Among those who died was Dr. Gildea. He was the one who was going back the next spring with my father to get rich picking up gold nuggets at our camping place. He died January 22, 1846, and, as you know, two years later gold was discovered in the millrace at Sutters Fort. My uncle, Truman Bonney, who had gone north to Oregon, remembered where we children had found the gold, so he and some others returned to our old camping place to stake out claims, but the claims had already been staked, and it proved to be very rich ground.

"Those Americans who were unwilling to renounce their native country were required to move in the spring. We had always traveled by wagon, and it was a problem how to move our families and our possessions on horseback. In the party to Oregon there were 15 small children. Father and Mother were extremely anxious to go to Oregon, because my eldest brother and my sister Ann had died and were buried at Sutters Fort. Among the Americans, the single men who were unwilling to take the oath of allegiance to Mexico and wanted to stay in California, took to the hills, deciding to stay anyway.

"Among the young children to be taken to Oregon was my sister, Ellen Francisco, who had been born at Sutters Fort and who was only a few months old. There were no roads to Oregon, so the children would have to go on horseback. An old Scotchman solved the problem by making pack saddles with arms 15 inches high. He wove rawhide strands around the framework, making a regular basket. Two children could be placed in each of these pack saddles without any danger of falling out.

"I shall never forget the exciting forenoon we spent when we started from the fort. Many of the horses were not well broken, and when the children were put into these high pack saddles the horses would run and buck. At first many of the children set up a terrible clamor, but when they found they were not spilled out they greatly enjoyed the excitement. The mothers of the children were frantic. After running for miles the horses were rounded up by the Mexicans who were to accompany us on our way northward.

"Captain Sutter furnished each family a fat beef animal and also sent ten Mexicans with us to drive our loose stock and teach our men to pack. They were supposed to go with us about 250 miles, to where Colonel Fremont was camped. When we reached the camp we found Colonel Fremont had gone to southern California to join the American forces there. We camped at Fremont's camp while the Mexican killed our beeves and dried the meat. They told us we could follow the old Hudson's Bay trappers' trail northward to Oregon. After traveling a few days northward from Fremont's camp we came to a beautiful lake beside which was a clover meadow. We camped there for the night.

"The young man who took the horses out to pasture found near the lake an Indian girl about 8 years old. This little girl was perfectly nude, her long black hair was matted solidly, and she was covered with sores from head to feet. She could make only a pitiful moaning sound. Dr. Truman Bonney, my uncle, examined her and said she was suffering from hunger and that the flies had almost eaten her up. Nearby we could see where two tribes had fought. She had apparently crept to one side out of danger and had been left. She had been living on clover and roots and grass.

"A council among the men was held to see what should be done with her. My father wanted

"A council among the men was held to see what should be done with her...A vote was taken and it was decided to do nothing about it, but leave her where we found her. One of the young men in charge of the horses felt so bad about leaving her that he went back and put a bullet through her head to put her out of her misery."

to take her along.  Others wanted to kill her and put her out of her misery.  But father said that would be willful murder.  A vote was taken and it was decided to do nothing about it, but leave her where we found her.

"My mother and my aunt were unwilling to leave the little girl.  They stayed behind to do all they could for her. When they finally joined us their eyes were red and swollen from crying and their faces were wet with tears. Mother said she had knelt down by the little girl and asked God to take care of her. One of the young men in charge of the horses felt so bad about leaving her that he went back and put a bullet through her head and put her out of her misery.

"A few days later we came to an Indian camp. The Indians were living on dried acorn and crickets. The crickets were very large. The way the Indians prepared them was to catch the crickets, pull off their hind legs so they couldn't hop away, pile them in the sun and let them dry, then mix them with the acorns, put them all together in a stone mortar and make a sort of bread out of them. The squaws gave us children some of this black bread, which looked like fruit cake, but had a different taste. Some of us ate it, while others were rather squeamish about it and didn't care for it.

"That evening an Indian came to camp, bringing an Indian boy about 12 years old. Allan Sanders traded a pinto pony for the boy. He cut the Indian boy's long hair, bought him clothing from one of the other members of the party, and named him Columbus. The first night Columbus was very unhappy, but after Sanders had given him a sound thrashing he seemed more contented. He reached Oregon safely, but a few years later died of measles.

"A few days' travel northward from where Sanders had bought Columbus we were attacked by Indians. When night had fallen our party moved back into the brush about 50 yards from where we had camped. The men put the packs in a circle to protect the women and children. The nine men of our party who had guns crept out to the bank of the stream, where they believed the Indians would cross. When everything was still the Indians started to cross the stream. Our men gave them a volley, and the other men, who had cut clubs, with a loud yell splashed into the stream after the Indians, who broke and ran. Next morning we found plenty of blood along the trail where the Indians had gone, but we didn't find the bodies of any Indians.

"We reached the Rogue River Valley in southern Oregon early in June. I never saw a more beautiful valley. The grass-covered hills were dotted with deer and elk. The streams were full of trout, and there was not only plenty of wood and water, but there were many little open parks and prairies. Several of our party decided to settle there.

"Dr. John McLoughlin of Vancouver employed

my father to go to Champoeg to repair a gristmill there. He furnished Father with a bateau and eight Indian oarsmen to take his family to Champoeg. We landed near the old Indian landing, near where the monument to the provisional government now stands. We stayed there that winter while Father worked on the mill. The winter of 1846 was one of the coldest that the oldest settlers of Oregon could remember. Hundreds of wild cattle and Indian horses died because they could not get at the dried grass beneath the snow. In the fall of 1847 we moved to our donation land claim two miles east of where the town of Hubbard now stands.

"Among the pleasant memories of our stay in Oregon City are those of a playmate, a son of Colonel W. G. T'Vault first editor of the **Oregon Spectator**, the first paper published west of the Rocky Mountains. One day young T'Vault and I were walking along the streets of Oregon City when we met Dr. McLoughlin and Mr. Barlow. Barlow had a plane bit in his hand. Dr. McLoughlin put his hand upon my head and said, 'Don't you boys want to earn some candy? If you will go with Mr. Barlow and turn the grindstone while he sharpens that plane bit I will give you each a handful of candy.'

"As soon as Mr. Barlow pronounced the bit sharp enough we hurried back to Dr. McLoughlin and he gave us each a handful of plain candy hearts with mottoes on them. That was the first 'store candy' I had ever eaten, or, for that matter, had ever had in my hands.

"Another recollection of Oregon City is going with my cousin, Wisewell Bonney and young T'Vault to the building used as a mint. The men there would melt up the gold dust on a blacksmith's forge, pour it into molds, roll it through a roller, and keep rolling it until the bars were thin. Then they would stamp five-dollar and ten-dollar gold pieces out of the gold bars. These coins had the image of a beaver on one side and were called 'beaver money'. They manufactured about $30,000 worth of the ten-dollar pieces and $25,000 worth of five-dollar pieces. By accident they made them too heavy, so they were worth more than $5 or $10 respectively, so when the people got them they would melt them up or send them to the mint. That is why they are so scarce now.

"My uncle, Truman Bonney, settled at Hubbard. He was what was known in those days as a calomel and quinine doctor, as that is what he prescribed for everything that ailed people. My father died in 1854. Shortly thereafter my mother married Orlando Bidwell. Our claims joined A. R. Dimick's. John

Dimick, father of Grant Dimick, and I went to school together. The first time I ever saw the inside of a school house was when I was 14.

"In those days they used to have big times at the barn raisings. When Dimick's barn was built it was christened the Queen of French Prairie, because it was the biggest barn on the prairie. Neighbors with their ox teams came for 20 miles around to help. One incident of that barn raising I remember very distinctly. There was a man there named Zack Fields. He offered to bet anyone a five-dollar beaver gold coin that he could not raise his (Zack's) head from the ground by his ears. It looked as if it would be easy, but when a man put up a five-dollar piece, Zack greased his ears so the man's fingers would slip off, and Zack won the bet.

"Father paid $12 each and sent five of us children to school there. The teacher didn't have to know much about books, but had to be able to lick the big boys. I saw a teacher tackle George Dimick, who was 18. It was a battle royal, for George put up a hard scrap. The teacher wore out a six-foot hazel rod on him.

"I put in most of my time making cedar shingles. My father's donation land claim on the Pudding River bottom had 40 acres of fine timber on it. We split out cedar timbers for Ford's and Kiser's houses. We got $10 a thousand for the cedar shingles. People came from all over Mission Bottom and French Prairie to buy shingles off us.

"The first time I was married I was married to Catherine M. Thoads, who was 15 years old. We were married February 11, 1864, at Champoeg by Reverend T. B. Litchenthaer of the United Brethren Church. We had nine children, seven of whom are still living. You will know we shifted around a good bit when I tell you that these nine children were born in seven different houses. My second wife was Louise Coats. We were married at Tygh Valley, in eastern Oregon, by Reverend Roland Brown. My third wife was a widow with five children. Her name was Mrs. Emma J. Lamb. We were married at Oregon City by County Judge Grant Dimick, son of my former schoolmate.

"When I was a young man I worked as a carpenter and bricklayer. Then I got into a peculiar sort of business. I would take up a squatter's right on a piece of land, build a good house on it and sell it to someone who wanted to homestead the land. In 1861 I went to the Orofino mines in Idaho and had fair success. Some little time after the Civil War I decided to be a preacher.

For 11 years I preached on the circuit from Dufur, in eastern Oregon, to Goldendale, Washington. Later I preached in British Columbia, and still later I had a circuit in the Puget Sound country.

"When I tell my grandchildren about the old days, about the plains being dark with vast herds of buffalo, about the Indians and the mining camps, they look at me as if they thought I could not be telling the truth. Those old days are gone forever, and the present generation can never know the charm and romance of the old west."

Oregon Journal
October 16-22, 1922

# O. A. Waller
# Salem, Oregon

"When I was a boy Chemeketa—or, to give it its present name, Salem—was the favorite camping ground of the Indians. I have seen hundreds of Santiam, Callapooia, and Molalla Indians passing through Salem on their way to the mountains to pick huckleberries and get their winter's supply of jerked venison. In those days, of course, there were no fences in the country, and not nearly so much timber as there is now, and very little under-brush, for the Indians kept the small growth down by running fire through it."

Oregon Journal
January 22, 1924

# F. P. Walker
# Born on Joe Meek's Farm, 1852
# Portland, Oregon

"My father started for Oregon with a bunch of brood mares, intending to go into the stock business when he got to the Willamette Valley. The Indians stole all his horses and mares on the plains, so he had to hook up his cows to his prairie schooner."

Oregon Journal
January 5, 1927

# Butler's Fantastic Milch Cow

*In the '70s John Hailey owned the stage line between The Dalles, Oregon, and Kelton, Utah. One day John Hailey and his division agent stopped at Rock Creek Crossing in Idaho to buy a few tons of hay from a man named Butler, who had settled there two years before. Butler said to Hailey, "I can't spare you any hay. I need it to feed my own cattle."*

*"How many head of cattle have you?" asked Mr. Hailey.*

*Butler said, "When I settled here, two years ago, I had one yoke of steers and a milch cow. But by careful management I now have 35 head of stock, mostly calves and yearlings and young stock."*

*Hailey said, "You settled here two years ago, started with one milch cow, and now have 35 head of stock, mostly calves and yearlings? What will you sell me that milch cow for?"*

*Oregon Journal*
*January 12, 1933*

# A. G. Spexarth
# Astoria, Oregon

*Many men who became prominent in the business life of Oregon came to Oregon as soldiers. This is particularly true of troops quartered at Vancouver in early days. A. G. Spexarth, well known merchant of Astoria, enlisted at St. Louis at the close of the Civil War and served a year and a half in Montana. From Montana he came to Portland and arranged with Wah Kee & Co. to dry smelt for shipment to China.*

"I rented an empty loft over the Hopkins hardware store on the east side of Front Street. I bought seines and employed a number of Chinamen to do the seining and help dry the smelt. While my seines and equipment were stored in the loft a fire broke out, burning many blocks on Front Street, including the Hopkins store. All of my equipment, of course, was destroyed.

"I decided to purchase new equipment, but just at that time trouble that had been brewing with one of the partners of the Wah Kee Company over the price he was to pay for another man's wife broke out. The man who had contracted for the wife brought suit and Judge Matthew P. Deady ordered Tom Young to bring the parties into court. The marshal went to Wah Kee's place and either the Chinaman didn't understand what he wanted or distrusted the white man's justice; in any event, he refused to go. In the mixup the marshal killed the Chinaman.

"As he was prominent, his friends gave him the biggest Chinese funeral that Portland had ever seen up to that time. The religious services were held on Alder Street and there was plenty of roast duck and roast pig, with funeral offerings of all kinds. These were loaded into express wagons and, preceded by two brass bands, went down to the Stark Street ferry and thence to Lone Fir Cemetery. A big lot of Indians who happened to be in town went to the funeral, hoping to get in on the feast.

"The other members of the firm of Wah Kee were so upset by the death of their partner that they decided not to go into the enterprise of shipping smelt to China."

Oregon Journal<br>
February 10, 1933

# Matt Brown
## Pioneer of 1846
## Silverton, Oregon

"On October 15, (1846) exactly six months to a day from the time we left Missouri, we made our last camp and turned our oxen loose to graze on the site of what is now Silverton. My father took up 640 acres here."

Oregon Journal<br>
May 18, 1922

# Arlie B. Watt
## Amity's Oldest Native Son
## Amity, Oregon

"It took a lot of money to get oxen and a wagon and to outfit a family for the trip across the plains, so Father saw that his father would not be able to make it. Father refused to wait any longer, so, in 1844, with $2.50 in cash, a new pair of cowhide boots and a few fishhooks and pins, he started for Oregon. By the time he had reached Burnt River he had turned his $2.50 and his fishhooks over in numerous swaps till he had acquired a cow and a rifle. Food was short, so, with another young man, Father struck out ahead of the emigrant train across the Blue Mountains. The snow lay deep on the mountains, and they ran out of grub and traveled on their nerve. Near where Pendleton is now they met some Indians, to whom Father traded some gunpowder for potatoes. Father shot several grouse, so they let out a few holes in their belts and ate till the belts were tight. They went to the Whitman Mission, where they waited till the emigrant train came up."

**Oregon Journal**
September 20, 1923

# Franklin Pierce Wheeler
# Gold Beach, Oregon

"We lived at the bridge about 18 miles from Bend. We put in six years there, raising horses. I used to go to Albany every year with a four-horse team and bring a year's supplies. One winter the snow started to fall in November and it didn't go off till the following March. During that winter the mercury went down in the bulb till it froze. It froze more than the mercury, for I had 145 horses when the snow began falling, and when a chinook in March took the snow off I only had 60 head of horses left."

**Oregon Journal**
December 22, 1932

# Barnet Simpson
# Pioneer of 1846
# Portland, Oregon

"I'm not figuring on getting married or running for office, so I might as well tell you the exact truth about my age and anything else you care to ask me about. I was born in Platte County, Missouri, December 29, 1836, and was the youngest child of a family of 11. So as not to give a one-sided picture, I am going to tell you the things that are not creditable about myself as well as the things that are.

"For example, I might tell you my most vivid recollection of our trip across the plains in 1846. I was going on ten when we crossed the plains to the Willamette Valley. We crossed the river at St. Joe and camped for a few days to let the emigrants gather and to organize the wagon train.

"My oldest sister, Eleanor, married a man named John Anderson. Her son John was a year and a half older than I, in spite of the fact that I was his uncle. My father told me to look up a bridle that had been mislaid, so John and I started to look for it. While looking under one of the wagons John saw a stone jug. He pulled out the cork and smelled it, and said, 'This is whiskey. Did you ever drink any corn liquor, Barnet?'

"My father was a Primitive Baptist preacher and was very strict, so I had never tasted liquor. I confessed that I had never drunk any whiskey and was curious as to its taste. John tipped up the jug and took a swallow and handed it to me. I didn't like to be a quitter, so I took a swallow. It nearly strangled me, but I pronounced it mighty good.

"John thought it would be funny if he could get me drunk, so he suggested that we drink some more. We took a generous drink and then resumed our search for the bridle. We found the jug in the middle of the afternoon, and by 5 o'clock we had pretty finished what whiskey there had been in it. We went back every few minutes to take another drink. John would tip the jug up and pretend to take a big drink, and would pass it to me and urge me to drink heartily. By 5 o'clock I couldn't walk. I fell in a stupor.

"John had drunk enough to make him drowsy. He sat by the camp fire. He had a new hunting coat my sister had made for him. A spark jumped out on the tail of his new hunting coat and he was so fuddled he didn't notice it till someone saw the smoke, and by that time the whole back of the coat was burned off.

"They saw he was drunk and they knew I had been with him, so they began to look for me. Presently they found me, lying where I had fallen. They carried me to our wagon and worked over me all night. I foamed at the mouth and had convulsions and they thought I was going to die. The first thing I remember was along about 9 o'clock the next morning. I heard my brother Thomas, who was not going to cross the plains with us, telling Mother goodbye and saying, 'Don't worry, Mother. Barnet is going to pull through all right. Give him a tablespoon of whiskey every couple of hours till he sobers up.'

"I rolled over toward him and said, 'I have had plenty. I don't want any more. As long as I live, never another drop of whiskey will ever go down my throat.' That was nearly 80 years ago, and from that day to this I have never tasted liquor of any kind or description.

"My father, William Simpson, was born in North Carolina. My mother, whose maiden name was Mary Kimsey, was born in Tennessee. I don't remember what year my father and mother were married, but Ben was their first child, and he was born in Tennessee in 1818, when my mother was 21. Mother was born in 1797 and Father in 1793. Father was 53 when he started across the plains and Mother was 49. They were considered old people. They called Father 'Uncle Billy', and Mother, 'Aunt Polly'. My brother Ben, who was 28 when we started for Oregon, was elected captain of the wagon train. Ben married Elzirah Jane Wisdom in 1839, when he was 21. They had one son, John T. Simpson. She died not long after her baby was born. My brother married Nancy Cooper in 1843. When we crossed the plains in 1846, to Ben and his second wife, two more boys had been born-- Sylvester C. and Samuel L. Sam was a baby, having been born about six months before we started for Oregon. Sam, my nephew, was the author of the book of poems entitled **The Gold-Gated West**. I guess his "Beautiful Willamette" is his best known.

"Our whole family came to Oregon in 1846 except my brother Thomas, who did not cross the plains till 1852. Tom married Rosena Buff back in Missouri and decided to let us come out and see if we like it and if we did he would sell out and come.

"When we started across the plains all our neighbors told Mother what a dangerous trip it was and how we were sure to be killed by Indians or drowned or die of cholera or be run over by buffaloes. Mother, who had heard how they buried people who died while crossing the plains, in a blanket by the side of the road, decided she would be forehanded, so the winter before we left she carded and spun and wove a lot of cloth, dyed it and cut it up and made a shroud apiece for everyone in the family. No, we didn't get to use a single one of them. I think she cut them up after we got to Oregon and made clothes out of them. I was more interested in the hunting shirt she made for me than I was in my shroud.

"It will be 80 years ago next spring that we started with our ox teams and covered wagons for Oregon. We didn't have any particular trouble on our six months' trip across the plains. My brother Ben was captain of the train and he was the right man in the right place.

"The only fatality we had was one man killed. Two men went in together to come to Oregon. They pooled their resources and bought a wagon, a couple of yoke of oxen and supplies for the trip. They didn't get along any too well. One night the driver of the outfit lagged behind. They camped about three miles from the rest of the train. The next day the driver caught up with us. When they asked him where his partner was he said, 'The Indians must have killed him during the night. I buried him this morning by the side of the road.'

"We had not had any trouble with the Indians, so most of the folks in the train thought he had killed his partner for his share in the outfit. No, we didn't do anything about it. There was nothing we could do. We were in a hurry to press on to Oregon, and even if we had turned back and dug his partner up we couldn't have proved that some prowling Indian hadn't shot him, so we went on, but the man whose partner had been wiped out so mysteriously wasn't very popular with the rest of the folks in the wagon train.

"The last man to join our train before we pulled out for the long trip westward from the rendez-vous across from St. Joe was Uncle Ben Munkers. The train rarely had the same number of wagons in it two days together. It averaged about 100 wagons. Sometimes some of the party would straggle and drop back with another train, or hurry up and get ahead, later dropping back to join us. Lots of folks crossing the plains imagined the train ahead or the train back of the one they were in must have more considerate and congenial people in it. They usually found out they were mistaken when they dropped back or forged ahead to join the other train. Some folks always have good neighbors. Others always complain about having bad neighbors. I guess it is the people themselves more than the neighbors that are at fault.

"One incident of the trip that I greatly enjoyed was having a band of several hundred Indians draw up across the road and refuse to let us go on unless we would pay for passing through their country. They were nearly naked and all painted up. They danced and whooped and scared the women and the little children half to death. My brother Ben gave the word for every man able to bear arms to get his gun and march toward the Indians ready to shoot if they made any hostile move. They gave way and let us through, for they saw our men meant business.

"The chief, who spoke some English, said, 'You scare all our game away. Won't each man give us a present of a charge of powder apiece to prove you are our friends?' My brother told the men to pour out enough powder from their horns for a charge for each of the Indians.

"While they were doing this an antelope ran by. Half a dozen of the Indians leaped on their horses and took after it. They dropped it within 100 yards. They shot it with arrows. Most of the band were armed with bows, though some had guns.

"Did we have any fights on the plains? I saw only one. A woman claimed that another woman in the train was trying to vamp her husband. The lady who was doing the vamping had very abundant and beautiful hair, so the wife of the man who was more or less willing to be vamped sailed into her. It was a lively fight while it lasted. They pulled hair, scratched, yelled, and cried and fought like a couple of cats. The lady with the beautiful hair had a lot less of it when the fight was declared a draw.

"We had to stop one day to let a herd of buffaloes go by along the Platte. Two miles before they came to us we could hear a subdued roar like the sound of the surf at Newport. They fairly shook the ground. There were thousands of them. They ran along paying no attention to our wagon train, though our oxen were mighty restless at the smell, the sound, and the sight of them.

"All I need to do today, nearly 80 years later, is to shut my eyes and I can see the vast, empty plains with their rolling land waves. I can see the wagons come to a stop, see the children pile out of the wagons while the men folks unyoke the oxen and all the women scatter as soon as the train comes to a stop, to gather their aprons full of sun-dried buffalo chips to cook the coffee and bacon.

"What did we eat for supper? Bread cooked in a Dutch oven, or cornbread with coffee, bacon, beans, and dried peaches or apples. We had some cows along, so we usually had milk. Sometimes we had buffalo or antelope meat in place of bacon. Sometimes the women folks rustled sagebrush or willow wood in place of buffalo chips, but the chips made a quick, hot fire, and proved very satisfactory.

"I told you I saw only one fight while crossing the plains. Well, I'll stick to that statement, but there were a lot of fights I was in, but I was too busy fighting to stop and be an eye-witness to them. The Burnett boy was a year older than I, but I was a mite larger. My father, being a Primitive Baptist preacher, had taught me to turn the other cheek. My mother had also impressed upon me that boys who expect to be gentlemen don't settle their differences with their fists. The Burnett boy found he could lick me, so hardly a day went by that he didn't make my life a burden. I could hardly call my soul my own. He generally caught me where my folks wouldn't see us fighting. I put up a half-hearted fight, usually trying to avoid punishment more than to try to hurt him.

"One day my mother saw him licking me. She pulled him off of me and said to me, 'The time has come for you to take your own part. I want you to thrash this boy, and do a thorough job.' I could hardly believe my ears. I hesitated, and she said, 'You can take your choice. Either you whip this bully within an inch of his life or I will give you a worse licking than he ever gave you.'

"I knew my mother was a woman of her word, so I waded in, and what I did to that boy was plenty. After that all I had to do was double up my fists and scowl at him and he would beat it.

"One of the things I remember very distinctly is our stopping at Independence Rock. The men and women gathered around the rock and read the names of the emigrants who had registered during the preceding two or three years. Then they scratched their own names on the rock. Some of the men painted their names on with tar from the tar buckets that hung from the back axles of the wagons. I doubt if there are many left of those who wrote their names on Independence Rock 79 years ago. There are a few of us left, but when I call the roll of my former campmates who crossed the plains

33

with me in 1846, not many are here to answer the rollcall.

"You can't spend six months with a couple of yoke of oxen in a covered wagon crossing the plains without having lots of peculiar adventures and misadventures that stick in your mind. My father and Uncle Ben Munkers were the oldest men in the wagon train. My brother Ben, who was captain of the wagon train, let them take turns leading the train with their wagons, so they wouldn't have to swallow so much dust. If there was any wind the drivers of the wagons in the back swallowed their share of dust, for the oxen kicked up the fine alkali dust till the wagons were in a heavy fog.

"One day when my father's wagon was in the lead a couple of young Indians met us and one of them threw up his hand quickly as a signal for us to stop. This scared our oxen, and they bolted. They ran down the hill, turned into the river, and splashed through to the other side. The Munkers oxen also became panic-stricken and followed our wagon. Mrs. Munkers, with her son Jimmy, six years old, was riding on the front seat when the oxen bolted. She was a cripple. Wherever she went she had to carry her chair and, also, hobble on crutches. She was so frightened that she grabbed Jimmy up under one arm, reached back and got her camp chair under the other, jumped out of the wagon, as it was going full tilt, ran as hard as she could to a hundred yards or so, and then, realizing that she was a cripple and couldn't walk, she put down the chair and sat down.

"The oxen tried to climb the bank on the other side of the river, but the wagon turned over, so they got over their scare and waited for the men to come and fix things.

"Coming across the plains I usually rode one horse and led another, or rode and herded the stock. One day I was riding a big American mare and leading her mate. I went on ahead of the train, but finally decided I had better backtrack and join it. I rode back 12 or 15 miles without seeing any sight of the train. I finally came to another train and asked what had become of the Simpson train. The captain told me Simpson's train was about 10 miles ahead of them and I had better hurry if I wanted to get there before night. It was growing cold, so he loaned me a big coat, for I was in shirtsleeves. I retraced my way till I saw where our wagon train had left the road to camp on a small stream some distance from the road. It was about dusk. My mother was spreading the table cloth on the ground ready to serve supper. She said, 'Where have you been, Barnet? I haven't seen you since breakfast time.' My brother Ben had missed me and, being afraid something had happened to me, he and three other men had struck out to look for me. They didn't get back till long after midnight.

"When we came to the Sweetwater, Ben decided to have the train lay over Friday, Saturday and Sunday for washing clothes, repairing wagons and drying out supplies that had got wet. We had three preachers in our train. My father was a Primitive Baptist, Elder McBride was a Campbellite, and I have forgotten what the other preacher was, but each of them preached while we laid over on the Sweetwater.

"The ox drivers decided to get a little of the dust off, so they made up a crowd to go swimming. With my nephew John Anderson, who was about a year and a half my senior, I followed them and went into the shallow water. When the men had dressed and gone, John and I decided to learn to swim. John said, 'We can't learn to swim in shallow water, so we'll go where it's deep.'

"I said, 'Go ahead. I'll follow you. I don't care if the water is a thousand feet deep.'

"We had hardly got out into the current till John was washed into a deep hole. He called out, 'Give me your hand, quick, or I'll drown.'

" I started toward him, but before I got there the current had caught both of us and we were washed downstream. I can remember yet seeing John's head, first under water and then coming into sight again as he whirled round and round in a whirlpool. The next thing I remember I was washed up on a sandbar and John was climbing up the bank to go back to the train and tell Mother I was drowned. We made a solemn compact not to tell our folks about our narrow escape till we got to the Willamette Valley.

"When we got to Fort Hall, some of the folks in the train took the road to Sutter's Fort in California. Among them was my brother-in-law, Alva Kimsey. He came north to Oregon the following year. When gold was discovered at Sutter's Fort he took the back trail and returned, but he didn't have much luck.

"At Fort Hall my father exchanged all of the bacon and flour and cornmeal he could spare for an order on Dr. McLoughlin for a similar amount at Oregon City. This saved hauling this surplus across the Cascades. We came by the Barlow Route, which had just been opened, and it was a terror. I guess none of the emigrants who came down Laurel Hill with men pulling on the ropes to keep the wagons from running over the oxen will ever forget Laurel Hill.

"We wintered at North Yamhill. In the spring Father leased a place and put five acres in wheat. We had a big crop. My brother James and I tramped it out with oxen. In the fall of 1847 Father took up a donation land claim in the Waldo Hills. We had 18 inches of snow that winter. Father had no hay, so he fed our cattle boiled wheat. We lost all of them but one cow and three steers.

"I went to school in the winter of 1846 to Herman Higgins, a cooper. He was a son-in-law of Reverend Vincent Shelling, a Baptist preacher. Higgins taught school, as he was a cripple, and this was about his only qualification as a teacher. He used to make tubs and barrels during school hours. If we children laughed he would look up from his work and say, 'Larn your lessons. Tend to business there and larn your lessons.' I stayed overnight once at his home. They had no dishes and no furniture. We sat on the floor, and when it came time for supper his wife stirred up some dough and gave us each a sharp stick on which we put the dough and held it over the fire in the fireplace to bake.

"My first teacher in the Waldo Hills was Paul Darst. I was married June 12, 1853. I sold my 150-acre farm in the Waldo Hills for $600 and moved to Salem. I was sexton of the I.O.O.F. Cemetery there for 25 years."

Oregon Journal
March 18-20, 1925

# John Bentley
# Barefoot Pioneer
# Pendleton, Oregon

"I came across the plains from Missouri. We struck California in 1861. I drove an ox team all the way across. My shoes wore out somewhere near Green River, and I hoofed it the rest of the way barefooted."

Oregon Journal
January 27, 1921

# D. M. Taylor
## Pioneer of 1852
## St. Johns, Oregon

"What I have learned in the past 80 years has not been from books, but from life. I had but nine months' schooling, six of which was under Judge J. W. Whalley at Yreka, California. He studied law while teaching school, and later became a judge in Portland. Before he came to Portland I used to see him at Canyon City, where he and Joaquin Miller were in the law business together.

"My people came originally from England. My great-grandfather, Jesse Taylor, with his two brothers settled in Virginia. All of these married in Virginia and had large families. Most of their children were boys. My grandfather, named Jesse after his father, married in Virginia and had five sons and three daughters. He founded the town of Taylorville, Virginia. He owned a plantation and 60 slaves. He operated a wagon shop, blacksmith shop, harness shop and cotton gin, the labor being performed by his slaves. One of his five sons, Samuel, was my father, born February 4, 1807.

"My mother, Nancy Ann Phipps, was born December 8, 1814. On January 22, 1829, when Father was 22 and Mother 15, they were married. My brothers William, Jesse, and Noah, and my sister Jane were born in Virginia. Not long after the birth of their fourth child my parents moved to Terre Haute, Indiana, where eight more children were born—Preston, Sarah, David, Mary, John, Myself, Squire, and Mariah. In 1850 we moved to Rock Island, Illinois, where my youngest brother, Samuel, was born.

"In the spring of 1852 we started across the plains for Oregon. Father was elected captain of the wagon train. At Fort Laramie my brother Preston died of the cholera. This was on June 15. From then on it seemed there was hardly a day when there were not one or more funerals in the wagon train. Father died of cholera in the Black Hills. My sisters Sarah and Mary died within 12 hours of each other, when we struck the Snake River.

"My mother was very self-reliant and resourceful. At The Dalles she chartered a flatboat to take our family and goods to the Cascades. My brothers Will and Dave drove the cattle and horses down

37

the Indian trail to Portland. At the lower Cascades we took a boat for Portland. We reached Portland on October 23, 1852, and spent that winter in a four-room house made of clapboards at the corner of Third and Washington Streets. The Dekum building now occupies the site of our first home in Portland. We were short of money, so we lived largely on deer meat. My brother Will, who was a good shot, used to go out on the nearby hills and bring in a deer every few days. Occasionally we would buy a 30-pound salmon for 50 cents, for a change from the steady diet of deer meat.

"In April, 1853, a man named Ward got my mother to go to Tumwater, Washington Territory, to board the millhands. Mother built a large house at Tumwater and boarded 60 hands, half on the day shift, half on the night. We served meals to 60 at breakfast and supper and 30 at noon and 30 at midnight. We all worked. During the next two years there my mother cleared $3000.

"Tumwater was a sawmill town. The first mill there was built in the fall of 1847 by M. T. Simmons, B. F. Shaw, E. Sylvester, Jesse Ferguson, John R. Kindred and two or three other men, who were partners in the Puget Sound Milling Company. They used the mill irons that had been used at Fort Vancouver in the Hudson's Bay Company's mill. They sold the lumber at Nisqually. They also furnished the lumber for the barracks and officers' quarters at Steilacoom.

"In the summer of 1855, we moved to Yreka, California. My brother William decided to stop at Jacksonville. I was ten years old. He had me stay with him. Mother and the rest of the children went on to Yreka. In 1855 the settlers on Bear Creek went to Fort Lane on account of the outbreak of the Rogue River Indians. My sister-in-law, Eliza, had taken refuge in the fort. Indians were discovered gathering around the fort, so it was decided, because of the absence of the soldiers, who were out on a scouting expedition, that word would have to be sent to the volunteer company at Jacksonville. It was thought a boy might get through without danger, but if a man attempted it he might be killed by the Indians. I told them I would be glad to go to summon help if my sister-in-law, Eliza, would let me ride Flora, her racing mare. I was pretty sure no Indian pony could overtake this blooded mare.

"It was eight miles from Fort Lane to Jacksonville. I made the trip in good time, and the company of volunteers came back to the fort with me. The Indians had disappeared. Two days later the soldiers ran across them at Table Rock and had a fight with them.

"The next year I went to Yreka to join my mother. She had married Samuel Waymire, a brother of Fred Waymire of Polk County, Oregon. They were married in December, 1855. The next year, 1856, my half-brother, Jacob Waymire, was born, and in 1858, Mother gave birth to another son, Alexander.

"I lived at Yreka with my mother till 1858. I was 13 then, and plenty old enough to make my own living. I got a job learning the blacksmith trade with Frank H. Shimer. He paid me $5 a month, and I worked for him three years. He was father, mother, and teacher all in one. He took care of me when I was sick, and after our day's work in the shop he had me study and recite to him. Whenever he had a suit made for himself he had one made for me from the same goods. When he had the shoemaker make boots for him, he had a pair made for me. After I had worked about a year he used to let me do extra work evenings and keep the money for myself. After I had worked for him for three years, he sold his shop and went to Idaho.

"The man that bought the blacksmith shop wanted me to go on working at $5 a month, but I was 16 and knew I could earn more money, so I went back to Yreka and went to work for Fred Stine, who paid me $4 a day and board. Stine later moved to Walla Walla and became well known. I worked for him until 1863.

"On Christmas Day, 1862, my mother died of pneumonia.

"I doubt if our present standard of honesty and hospitality is as high as it was in the days when I lived at Yreka. Any traveler was welcome to stop overnight at a miner's cabin, and I have seen miners put their pans of gold dust out in the sun to dry by the cabin door, leaving them there all day and knowing that when they came back at night from work they would find them there, undisturbed.

"In the spring of 1864 I went to Canyon City. During the next two or three years I discovered that you can put more money into the ground than you can take out of it. I was getting $6 a day and board, working in a blacksmith shop there, and I put all of my savings into a claim in Marysville Gulch. I put $3500 into trying to find gold there, and never got anything back. In the spring of 1866 I went to the Elk Creek mines to see if my luck wouldn't change, but it didn't.

"I had a long talk with Captain William Martin, who came across the plains in 1843 and who succeeded

Peter H. Burnett as captain of the wagon train. I also talked with Barney Prine, founder of Prineville, and with Sol Durbin of Salem. All of these men had been greatly interested in the story of the Blue Bucket Mine and had talked to Herron and others of the party who had discovered the nuggets while on Meek's cut-off. These men told me that Canyon Creek was undoubtedly the stream where this gold had been picked up in 1845 and that the rich diggings near Canyon City and John Day were undoubtedly the site of the Blue Bucket Diggings.

"Canyon City more nearly resembles the district these lost emigrants described than any other place in eastern Oregon. Not only that, but it is the only place in eastern Oregon where nuggets of any size have been picked up in the bed of a stream. Canyon City is in a canyon on the headwaters of the John Day River. A young man picked up over $1100 worth of nuggets while the rest of his party were getting supper at Hog Point, near where Joaquin Miller's cabin was later built at Canyon City. Personally, I have no doubt whatever that the Canyon City diggings are the ones that were discovered by the emigrants under Sol Tetherow who took the Steve Meek cut-off in 1845 and wandered around for weeks before they finally got to The Dalles.

"While I was working at Andrew Lytle's blacksmith shop at Canyon City I became acquainted with Colonel Henry Dosch. I also met Marion Koontz, who runs a saddle and harness shop here in Portland. I also met Phil Metschan, who had a butcher shop in Canyon City. I was the best man at Phil Metschan's wedding. His son Phil Metschan, Jr., runs the Hotel Imperial here in Portland.

"I had some peculiar experiences at Canyon City. One night I was dancing with a girl in one of the hurdy-gurdy houses, when a big, husky German, six feet high and weighing about 195 pounds warned me not to dance with his girl again. The proprietor of the place had brought over six young girls from Germany to dance in his hurdy-gurdy house. For two bits you could dance with one of these girls, and you were supposed to treat her at the bar. The girl got half the money spent for drinks by her customers.

"I told this big German I would dance with any girl I wanted to. He began abusing me so I took off my coat and started for him. My chum, Mose Lyons, who weighed about 140 pounds, and who was a fighting son-of-a-gun, was standing near this big German. Mose was afraid the Dutchman would lick me. Quick as a flash, Mose caught the Dutchman on the point of his jaw with his fist and he went down and out. I dragged the Dutchman

40

off the dance floor and someone threw some water over him. As he came to, I said, 'Have you got enough, or shall I hit you again?'

"He said, 'I've got plenty for this time.'

"He never bothered me any more, and he told his friends I was quick as chain lightning and could hit as hard as a mule could kick. My friend Mose Lyons later went to Boise City and became chief of police and was shot and killed while arresting a man.

"My brother Squire died of pneumonia at Salem in 1867. That spring I started in business for myself, running a blacksmith shop at Olive Creek. In the fall of 1867 I went to Walla Walla and worked for Fred Stine, the same man for whom I had worked at Yreka, California, when I was 16. I worked for Stine from the fall of 1867 till the next spring, when I went to Waitsburg and bought a half interest in a blacksmith shop with G. W. Hull.

"On August 1, 1869, I married Miss Cornelia E. Redford, a daughter of Mr. and Mrs. William Redford of Walla Walla. Not long after my marriage I sold my half-interest in the blacksmith shop at Waitsburg and moved back to Walla Walla and went into the dairy business with my father-in-law. After a while I sold my interest in the dairy business and went to Wallula, where I bought Horace Juber's blacksmith shop. When D. S. Baker's railroad was built from Walla Walla to Wallula it killed my business, which consisted largely in shoeing horses for freighters and making repairs on their wagons. In the summer of 1875 I moved to Pendleton and opened a blacksmith shop there.

"My son Daniel was born in the fall of 1870. Two years later my son Samuel Jesse was born. My daughter Emma Elizabeth was born in Wallula in the summer of 1874. My daughter Grace was born in the summer of 1876 and when she was five years old was drowned in W. S. Byers' mill race at Pendleton. My daughter Maude was born on Christmas Day, 1868, at Pendleton. Three of my children are still living--Daniel W., Mrs. Fred F. Waffle, and Mrs. Maude M. Kent.

"At the outbreak of the Indian War in 1878 I took a contract from the government to shoe Indian ponies so the infantry could be mounted. I shod 300 wild Indian horses, and I certainly had a lively job of it. The Piutes and Bannocks had become excited by the Chief Joseph War in 1878. Buffalo Horn visited the Umatillas, the Cayuses, Walla Wallas, and various other tribes, who agreed to unite in a war to drive the whites out of the Inland Empire.

"In June, 1878, the Bannocks and Shoshones were joined by the Piutes under Chief Egan. The

41

had about 500 warriors. They started westward from Fort Hall to join the Cayuses, Walla Wallas and Umatillas. When word was brought to Pendleton by Major M. A. Cornoyer, early in July, the settlers from all around that district came into the cities. Pendleton, Weston, Milton, Walla Walla, and the other nearby communities were overcrowded with refugees. Pendleton had a population of about 150. Within a few days its population was doubled. We built a fort of cottonwood logs near where the Bowman Hotel now stands. Many of the women and children took refuge in the courthouse or the flour mill. For a while we had a very exciting time, but nothing came of it."

*Pendleton at that time had about 25 one-story buildings on Court and Main Streets. In the late '70s the only building of any pretensions in Pendleton was the courthouse, a two-story frame building. It stood in an open plaza, in the block now occupied by the People's Warehouse. Some distance out of town there was a three-story mill standing where Byers' flour mill was later built. When word was brought to Pendleton in June, 1878, that the Snake Indians and the Piutes under their war chief, Egan, were marching westward and would probably attack Pendleton, the citizens organized a volunteer company for defense. Dr. Frank Vincent, a dentist, was chosen captain. Wagons were stretched across Main Street for a barricade, and the women and children took refuge in Byers' mill.*

"At Umatilla City, as well as at Heppner, Milton and Weston, preparations were made to defend against the Indians. J. R. Foster & Co.'s stone warehouse, not far from Echo, became a fort in which the citizens of Butter Creek took refuge. J. L. Sperry, sheriff of Umatilla County, organized a company of volunteers to fight the Indians, who were reported to be near Ukiah, in the Camas Prairie country. Companies were organized in the Weston District, and recruits were secured at Pilot Rock. The various companies were combined under Captain J. L. Sperry, First Lieutenant J. Kirk, and Second Lieutenant William M. Blakely. William Lamar, T. S. Ferguson, J. C. Coleman, William Ellis, and R. Eastland were appointed sergeants. From Pilot Rock they marched south toward Camas Prairie, stopping at Willow Springs for dinner.
"The Indians attacked them there, and 13 of the volunteers jumped on their horses at once, each anxious to serve as a messenger to Pendleton to give the alarm. They were told that one messenger was sufficient, but all 13 insisted on serving as

volunteer messengers. The rest of the company took refuge in the shed at Willow Springs and stood the Indians off during the afternoon.

"William Lamar, a school teacher, was killed and the following volunteers were wounded: S. Rothschild, S. I. Lansdon, A. Crisfield, G. W. Titsworth, Jacob Frazer, C. R. Henderson, J. W. Salisbury, H. A. Howell, and Frank Hannah. Hannah received seven wounds.

"Professor William Lamar, who was killed, was engaged to be married to Dr. W. C. McKay's daughter. The Indians cut out his heart and roasted it over the fire in sight of the volunteers.

"That night when the volunteers attempted to retreat the Indians fired at them, killing Harrison Hale. Between midnight and daylight the volunteers marched northward six miles and were attacked six times.

"When Captain Sperry's company returned to Pendleton with their wounded, the citizens were thrown into a panic. Major Throckmorton, with 150 regulars from Walla Walla, marched to the relief of Sheriff Sperry and met his force near Pilot Rock and escorted it back to Pendleton. Troops were also summoned from Lapwai, Idaho. Major Throckmorton had a line of rifle pits dug from Foster's mill to the mouth of the Tutawilla. Lot Livermore, J. H. Turner, and J. A. Drake organized an additional company to guard Byers' mill from attack. J. A. Drake, who had seen service in the Civil War, was appointed captain. A volunteer company under Captain William Martin was posted along the Umatilla River, north of Court Street.

"On July 7 General O. O. Howard and Major Throckmorton, with their troops, met at Pilot Rock and moved southward toward the Indians. There were two companies of artillery, one of infantry, and seven of cavalry and a troop of scouts. The Indians were driven from the position they had taken and fled toward the Grand Ronde Valley.

"George Coggan, Fred Foster, and Al Bunker, while coming from Cayuse Station to Pendleton, saw some Umatilla Indians riding toward them, with the intention, so the Indians said, of warning them. Coggan and the others, thinking these Umatillas were hostiles, began firing at them. The Umatillas returned the fire, killing Coggan and wounding Bunker. Foster carried Bunker on his horse two miles and then placed him where he would be safe and hurried on into Pendleton.

"Colonel Miles, with his troops, marched to the agency to defend it. Snakes, Bannocks, and Piutes to the number of about 400 attacked them. Miles, with his single company of cavalry and a number of Cayuse Indian volunteers, charged the hostiles and defeated them. Umapine, whose father had been killed some years before by Chief Egan, went to see Egan and told him the Cayuse Indians would join them. Meanwhile, Umapine sent word to Major Cornoyer to bring a company of soldiers and capture Egan. Colonel Miles, fearing treachery on the part of Umapine, refused to let the soldiers go. Homeli, chief of the Walla Wallas, and a sub-chief of the Umatillas named Peo, with 40 Indians, volunteered to go instead of the soldiers and capture Egan.

"Umapine and Five Crows went to Egan's camp and asked him to come for a conference near Cayuse Station. He agreed to do so. Chief Egan had been shot in the arm, but when he got to the station he realized he was being betrayed, so he closed with Five Crows. Five Crows stabbed Egan through the heart and took his scalp. Umapine shot Egan's sub-chief and scalped him. The Piute warriors, hearing the firing, attacked Umapine and Five Crows, and the Umatillas under Peo came to Umapine's defense. In the fight that followed the Umatillas killed and scalped nine Piutes and took 18 women and children prisoners.

"Meanwhile, General Wheaton had come down from Walla Walla and taken command. Chief Homeli, with 80 young warriors of the Umatillas, Cayuses, and Walla Wallas, started out to locate the hostile Piutes. On July 17, he met and killed 30 hostile Indians on Camas Creek, scalped them and captured 27 women and children and a considerable number of horses. General Howard pursued the Indians, overtook them in Harney County, captured them and took them to Yakima, where they were placed on the reservation under Father Wilbur.

"William Blakely was a lieutenant in Captain John L. Sperry's company of volunteers that went out to fight the Indians in the summer of 1878. Blakely was cut off from Captain Sperry's company and brought the news of the defeat of the volunteers.

"After the defeat of Chief Egan and his Piute and Snake River Indians came what is known as the 'Sheep-eater War', the following year. My brother, Dave Taylor of Athena, father of Til Taylor, who was killed while sheriff of Umatilla County, served as deputy under Sheriff Sperry. When White Owl, Apes and Quintatumps were hanged for the murder of George Coggan, my brother Dave assisted Sheriff Sperry to hang them.

"I used to have some exciting times in the late '70's, when I was running my blacksmith shop at Pendleton. In those days Pendleton had a lot of practical jokers--men like Jim Turner, the lawyer;

"When some
cowboy or sheep-
herder or anyone
else drank till
he wanted to
fight they would
say, 'Mat Taylor
said he could lick
you with one hand
tied behind him.'
That would be
enough for the
fellow looking for
a fight. He would
come down to my
blacksmith shop
and begin to
swear at me, and
I would have to
stop my work to
lick him. In those
days I was strong
as a bull, and
pretty handy in
a fight, so gen-
erally I was able
to give them all they
needed. I never
looked for a fight,
and I never ran
away from one."

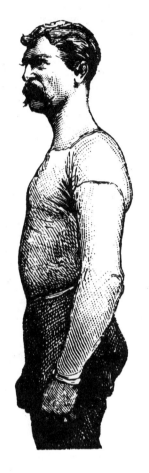

Ben and Bill Beagle, Judge Bishop, and a lot like
them. When some cowboy or sheepherder or anyone
else drank till he wanted to fight they would say
to him, 'Mat Taylor said he could lick you with
one hand tied behind him.' That would be enough
for the fellow looking for a fight. He would come
down to my blacksmith shop and begin to swear
at me, and I would have to stop my work to lick
him. In those days I was strong as a bull, and
pretty handy in a fight, so generally I was able
to give them all they needed. I never looked for
a fight, and I never ran away from one.

"I supplemented my earnings as a blacksmith
by teaching dancing. There was a man named
Bill Cotton at Pendleton, who had the bad habit
of getting drunk every so often and whenever he
was drunk nothing would do but he must have a
fight. One evening some of the practical jokers

at the saloon told him it would be a good scheme to go up to the dance hall and clean out Mat Taylor and his dancing class. Bill came up the stairs and began to be abusive. I threw him out into the hall. He invited me to come out into the street and get licked. When we were four steps from the bottom of the stairs he was so eager he couldn't wait till we got out, so he turned around and struck me.

"Shoeing horses for years had made me pretty strong in my legs, so I gave him a kick that lifted him clear off the steps. He lit on the sidewalk, on his face, and lit so hard it took the skin off one side of his face. He lost all desire to fight and, going back to the saloon, told them I had hit him with a broadaxe and nearly split his head open.

"I arrested Hank Vaughn seven different times and never had any trouble with him...He was as pleasant a chap as you would see in a day's drive, when he was not drinking."

"Whenever I could avoid fighting a drunken man I did so. I arrested Hank Vaughn seven different times and never had any trouble with him. My system was not to arrest Hank when he was drunk, but to wait till he had gone out to his home on the reservation and sobered up. He was as pleasant a chap as you would see in a day's drive, when he was not drinking.

"I knew Hank when he was a boy. He used to work in a blacksmith shop at Kelton, Utah. I first saw him at Canyon City. He wasn't over 17 at the time. He had been drinking and was having a dispute with a man. Hank pulled his gun and shot. The bullet hit the man high in the forehead, and glanced, going completely over the top of his head, cutting his scalp open. The blow of the bullet knocked him down. This was in the '60's.

"In 1867 Hank had got in with a bunch of rough characters who were running horses out of the country. Frank Maddock was sheriff of Umatilla County. He was given a warrant to arrest Hank for horse stealing. He found him and his companion camped on Burnt River near the Express Ranch. Maddock got the drop on them while they were asleep. He told them to throw up their hands. Instead of doing so the man with Hank grabbed Maddock's revolver, and in the struggle Maddock was shot under the eye. Though he lived for years, he eventually died of the wound. Maddock's deputy was also wounded.

"Hank came in later and surrendered voluntarily. He claimed he thought they were being held up and said he wouldn't have resisted had he known it was the sheriff. He was tried at Pendleton and was sentenced to a term in the pen. He always thought this was unjust, and possibly it was one of the reasons why he became a bad man.

"One time George Darvau and Gus LaFontain went on Hank's bond for $500. They became afraid Hank might leave, so they asked John Bentley, the sheriff, to arrest Hank, who was in town. They wanted to surrender him, so they would be released from their bond. Bentley said he would have the deputy sheriff get him. The deputy sheriff figured it wasn't worth being killed for $500, so he refused to arrest him.

"Darvau said to me, 'Mat, will you go and get Hank Vaughn?'

"I said, 'I will, for $20.'

"They dug down in their jeans and produced $10 apiece and handed it to me. I went over to where Hank was standing on the street and told him they wanted him at the courthouse in connection with his bond.    Hank said, 'Let's go in and get a drink before we go.'

"We took a drink, and then walked down to the courthouse, so Hank could see what it was all about.    Uncle John Bentley told him his bondsmen wanted to give him up, in which case he would have to either get a new bond or stay in jail.

"Hank said, 'I'll be back in a few minutes,' and he went out and got Bill Matlock and Tom Malarkey to go on his bond.

"I never carried a gun when I went out to arrest Hank.    I was afraid he would take it away from me.    One time when I went out to arrest him he asked me to stop for dinner.    After dinner I waited for him to shave and put on his good clothes, and he rode on in to Pendleton with me.

"I served as deputy sheriff at Pendleton for many years.    I worked as deputy under Sheriffs John A. Pruitt, Robert Sergeant, John L. Sperry and William Martin.    I also worked as a deputy under United States Marshals W. J. Furnish and S. L. Morse.    I had but nine months' schooling, so they never bothered me with clerical work. My job was to arrest people, and during the years I was deputy sheriff I had some pretty lively times."

*J. H. Sharon taught the first school at Pendleton. The school was located in what is now West Pendleton, then known as Marshall Station. The first term commenced on Washington's birthday, 1869. This school was broken up in 1873 by James H. Turner, a Missourian, who was one of the directors. He refused to admit colored children, so the school was closed.*

*The next school in Pendleton was held in the upper story of what was then the old county jail, but was later used as a city jail. The teacher was Abbie Lansdale, now Mrs. William Mays, probably as well known as any other resident of Pendleton.*

*Lot Livermore was the first mayor of Pendleton. Councilmen were William Beagle, Jerry DeSpain, J. H. Raley, Moses E. Folsom, J. B. Watson, and S. Rothchild.*

"In the spring of 1880 I moved on a farm north of Pendleton. Three years later I rented my farm and opened a restaurant in Pendleton. Pendleton was booming and I made big money. After running the restaurant a year I leased the Hotel Pendleton at $250 a month. When the railroad was built on east of Pendleton, there was a tremendous slump in Pendleton. Instead of making up beds in the hall I didn't begin to rent the rooms I had. I couldn't throw up my lease, for I had signed a bond, so I had to go ahead and run the hotel at an average loss of $10 a day till my lease was up. This took all of my ready money as well as the ten work horses on my farm, and when I was finally able to jar loose I was $3000 in debt. I went to work for Dave Horn as night clerk in his hotel. John M. Bentley was elected sheriff and appointed me deputy, so for two years I worked as deputy during the day and as clerk at the hotel at night, and was able thus to get out of debt.

"Bad luck, however, often comes in bunches, for the house on my farm burned down without insurance, and I lost my woodyard in a big freshet in the Umatilla River. I hired some men to cut wood for me. I had 100 cords in stovewood length, when along came the high water and next morning I didn't have enough wood to make kindling for my kitchen stove.

"After John Bentley's term as sheriff was up I was elected constable. The first case I had was to go to Milton to arrest 34 farmers who had destroyed a mill dam. A man named Mahanna built a flouring mill and turned the water out of the Little Walla Walla River into his mill race and, after using the water, turned back into the main Walla Walla River. Ninevah Ford, who had come to the Willamette Valley in 1843, settling in Polk County, protested, with others, against having prior water rights taken away. They brought suit against the owner of the mill, in which they showed they had used this water for many years for irrigating and that their crops would be ruined unless they could have the water.

"If you know anything about law, you know it's a slow and uncertain proposition. Pretty soon spring came, and the 34 farmers on the Little Walla Walla needed water badly. The mill owner refused to turn the water back into the Little Walla Walla, so Ford called a meeting of the farmers and led them to this mill and tore out the dam. Mahanna issued a warrant for malicious destruction of property. I was told that the farmers were armed with shotguns and would shoot any officer full of holes if he tried to arrest them. I knew it was foolish to take a gun with me, so I walked up to where Ford and the others with their shotguns were waiting for me and, picking up a dry mullein stock, shook it at Ford and said, 'I have come to arrest you, and all the rest of your outfit.'

"Ford looked at the mullein stalk and grinned, and said he guessed he and the other 33 farmers would have to surrender to such an exhibition of force as that. I told Ford that when I landed in Portland in 1852 I had heard of his 'goings on' and 'hell raising' in Polk County and had waited all these years for a chance to arrest him.

"I took them all down to Pendleton and at the hearing they were all turned loose. Three of the farmers were Germans and insisted that if they were under arrest I would have to furnish them board. I told them the only place I had any right to board them was the jail, and I would take them there, but they decided to buy their own meals.

"Mahanna jacked his mill up six feet so he could throw the water that he took from the Little Walla Walla back into the same stream, so that settled the trouble.

"About a week later I was given a warrant for the arrest of ten prominent sheepmen of Walla Walla for bringing their sheep across the state line without a permit. I wrote to one of them and gave him a list of the names of the others and suggested that he come on down to Pendleton and fix the matter up with the authorities. They had moved their sheep onto the summer range in Oregon and thus got into trouble with the law. They all came down, paid a small fine, and fixed the matter up.

"Once in a while I ran across people that you couldn't reason with. One day the depot agent got a telegram from the conductor saying there was an insane man on the train who had driven him into the baggage car and intimidated all of the passengers and he asked that an officer meet the train and arrest the crazy man. When I got on the train I found the crazy man had his six-shooter in his right hand and a big knife in his left hand. I took a deputy sheriff with me and told him that when I approached the crazy man from in front, for him to step up from the back and rap him over the head, but the deputy sheriff lost his nerve, so when I stepped up in front I had my hands full for the next five minutes. I disarmed him--that is, while I held him, Dick Kelly, the brakeman, took his knife and gun away from him. We found a card on this man saying he was apt to become violent and if trouble came up to wire his brother in the East. They wired his brother and held the crazy man in the county jail till his brother came and got him.

*Til Taylor, one of the most popular sheriffs Umatilla County ever had, was killed by prisoners in an attempted jailbreak at Pendleton. His brother, Jinks Taylor, was killed at the last Round-Up by being thrown from his horse. Their father, Dave*

50

"Once in a
while I ran across
people that you
couldn't reason
with. One day
the depot agent
got a telegram
from the conduc-
tor saying there
was an insane
man on the train
who had driven
him into the
baggage car and
intimidated all
the passengers
and he asked
that an officer
meet the train
and arrest the
crazy man..."

*Taylor, was a deputy sheriff of Umatilla County in the 1870s.*

"Up to 1918 there were five members of our family still living who had crossed the plains in 1852. Fourteen of our family have died in the past eight years, leaving me the only surviving member of the family. After my mother's death my younger brother, Andrew, left for California with a man named Cartwright. From that day to this we have never had a word from him. I advertised in numerous California newspapers but have never been able to get trace of him. Most of my old friends and neighbors in Pendleton are gone. However, among those still living are J. M. Bentley, Dave Horn, E. J. Summerville, William Blakely, J. E. Bean, Ed Murphy, Major Lee Moorhouse, Frank Neagle, J. V. Tallman, H. M. Sloan, J. H. Raley, C. H. Carter, J. A. Fee, Dr. J. W. Morrow and H. L. Hexter. Any time you meet any of these old-timers you can get a good story about Pendleton's early days.

"Some day when you are there ask some of them about early-day vigilance committees. One man killed by the vigilance committee near Pilot Rock I have always thought was innocent. His name was Stanley. He was a blacksmith and had worked for me at Pendleton. He was accused of harboring horse and cattle thieves, and, for all I know, he may have done so, but I am sure he didn't steal any stock himself. He was ordered out of the country but stood upon his rights and refused to go. A committee went out to bring him to Pendleton for trial. On the way from Pilot Rock to Pendleton they claimed he tried to escape, so he was killed. Personally, I doubt if he ever tried to escape.

"Poker Jim was a most unusual character. Another interesting man was Sheriff William Martin. A good writer could write a whole book about Til Taylor. He was one of the coolest men I ever saw, even if he was my nephew. He practically never used a gun, and rarely carried one, and yet he has arrested characters who had the reputation of shooting at the drop of the hat. Some day you ought to talk to some of the old-timers around Athena and get the real story of Hank Vaughn."

**Oregon Journal**
March 7-13, 1926

## Edwin J. Taylor
## Pioneer of Sauvies Island
## Sauvies Island, Oregon

"My brother and I used to hunt ducks for the market. The largest number we ever killed at one shot was 71. My brother and I crept up on a flock on the lake and each of us let them have both barrels. I don't know how many we killed, but we picked up 71.

"F. C. Barnes used to run a market in what had been an old church at the corner of Third and Washington Street (in Portland). He paid us $1.50 a dozen for teal, $3 a dozen for mallards, and from $6 to $7 a dozen for canvas back ducks. We used to kill quite a few deer here, too."

Oregon Journal
February 19, 1932

## David Caufield
## Oregon City, Oregon

"One of the first things I saw that made a vivid impression on my memory was Joe Meek cutting the rope that dropped the trapdoors for the five Indians who were being hanged at Oregon City for the Whitman Massacre. All five of the traps were sprung at once. A big crowd had gathered, from all over the Willamette Valley."

Oregon Journal
undated

## This Same Driver . . .

*"This same driver I was telling you about had been a miner before he took to driving a stage. He got blown up at Virginia City in the early days, and when he came out of the hospital one eye was gone, he was minus his teeth, and he was pretty badly scarred up. He got a glass eye and a double set of false teeth. The medicine the doctors had given him made all his hair fall out, so he wore a wig.*

*"One time in the '70s, during the Bannock War, the Indians stopped his stage and held a pow-wow whether they should kill him or not. He savvied their jargon, all right, so when he*

*heard them say they would scalp him he reached
up, took off his wig, and handed it to one of the
Indians. When the Indian looked at his glistening,
hairless head his mouth dropped open in astonishment.*

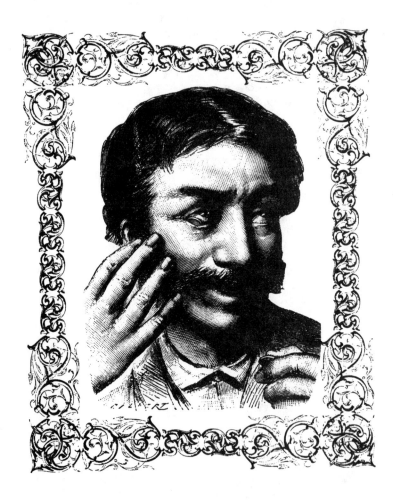

**"Then he reached up and took out
his glass eye and handed it to the Indian.
But this was too much...."**

*"He reached up, took out both sets of his
false teeth, and handed those over to him. The
Indian was too petrified to say anything.
"Then he reached up and took out his glass
eye and handed it to the Indian. But this was*

*too much. The Indian broke and ran, dropping
his wig and his teeth, and, as he put back his
false teeth and put on his wig he saw the last
of them going over the ridge like scared coyotes."*

*Oregon Journal*
*undated*

# Fred W. Christianson
# Tillamook County, Oregon

"Back in 1876, when Father started his dairy,
conditions in Tillamook County were very primitive.
Take the matter of transportation alone. My father
was a pretty good cooper, so he made his kegs
and firkins in which he packed the butter. He
shipped the butter to Sheridan--not on pack horses,
but on oxen. He had three oxen that he had broken
as pack oxen. They were very slow, but they could
carry large loads. He usually shipped about 250
pounds on each ox. At Sheridan he brought back
freight for neighbors--flour and sugar, hardware,
and all sorts of supplies. On one trip back into
Tillamook County he brought a rolling harrow and
on another trip one of the oxen carried an organ.
Ask any of the old pioneers of Tillamook County,
and they can tell you about Christianson's ox pack
train."

Oregon Journal
October 11, 1932

# Sam Brown
# Loganberry King of French Prairie
# French Prairie, Oregon

*I went out to the road, waited till Mr. Brown
drove up, gave him the high sign to stop, and
jumped aboard the wagon. He was driving a handsome
span of heavy horses. Standing in the bed of the
wagon and putting my hand on his shoulder to
keep my balance, I said, "What sort of man are
you? Are you as pleasant as your wife?"*

*He sized me up with a sort of who-in-h---
-are-you-and-what's-it-to-you? look and said, "Well,
that depends on what you want, whether I am pleasant
or not. What do you want?"*

*"I want to know about who took up this farm
first and about your father."*

*He still looked at me in a very guarded way
and said, "What are you selling?"*

*I said, "My name is Fred Lockley, and I
am not selling anything." I thought I was going*

to have a dead man on my hands for a moment, he was so shocked.

Finally he gathered himself together and said, "I have been so pestered with well-dressed strangers coming here to admire my place and then trying to sell me fertilizer or patent roofing or mineral paint, or something else, that every time I see a stranger I don't warm up till I know what he wants. It is so unusual to see a man that doesn't want to sell something that I hardly know how to act. I believe if a man should come to me and want to buy something and pay me money, in place of trying to find a new way of working me and getting some of my money, I wouldn't be able to resist inviting him to stay for a chicken dinner. Will you stay?"

*Oregon Journal*
*February 23, 1922*

## George Chandler
## Portland, Oregon

"We had no money, so Father decided to go on with one of our teams to The Dalles and get a job freighting supplies up to Auburn. He left me instructions to cut enough wild hay to winter our stock and also to get out logs so we could build a log cabin. Father hauled a load of flour on shares. He received one-half the load of flour for hauling the other half. As he came out of The Dalles he saw a settler who had a field of potatoes. Father traded one of his water kegs for two-thirds of a sack of potatoes. We kept these potatoes till spring and then cut the eyes out, ate the potatoes and planted the eyes and had a big crop of potatoes."

Oregon Journal
June 16, 1928

## L. D. Cates
## The Dalles, Oregon

"Father's baggage consisted of a pair of blankets, a carpetbag, and a six-shooter. He bought a steerage ticket (from Panama in 1852) for New York for $50. The first cabin ticket was $75."

Oregon Journal
November 29, 1927

# Captain Lloyd C. "Barview" Smith
## South Sea Trader
## Barview, Oregon

"What was I doing 50 years ago? Well, I am 76 years old. Fifty years ago I was 26. I was master of a ship in those days. I was cruising in the South Sea Islands, recruiting cannibals to take to the sugar plantations in the West Indies.

"We couldn't send our men ashore for fear the natives would rush them and take them inland to serve at some of their savage feasts as 'long pig.' The natives used to esteem 'white meat' as a great delicacy. We would send a boat to lie off shore. The native we had hired as interpreter would hold up a handful of bright cloth, some looking glasses and beads, a hatchet and a tomahawk or so, and the natives couldn't resist coming out to see the trade goods. We aimed to secure from 100 to 125 natives, for we were operating in small trade schooners.

"I can see it all plainly--the bit of fire on the beach, with the smoke curling up through the broad leaves of the palms, the naked natives standing on the beach like statues carved out of brown stone; the round, firm breasts of the women--for the natives of some of the islands, from swimming so much and living simply, are wonderfully graceful and handsome; the pile of yams, bananas and cocoanuts lying just above where the waves creep shoreward, to trade for beads and gewgaws; the natives splashing through the shallow water out toward our men in the longboat; the bright sunlight, the blue water, the dense green foliage just beyond the shore line.

"For years I was in that trade, getting natives for the plantations. They bought the natives for a three to five years' term, usually agreeing to pay them $90 for their services and promising to bring back those who were still alive to their native villages. You see, if you happened to drop a man on the wrong island the other natives either robbed him of all he had, as he was a stranger, or they ate him. Their methods are very direct.

"Sometimes a voyage would not be very profitable, as too many of the natives would die before you could deliver them. I remember on one trip I slid 35 of them over the rail. Maybe the food you give them doesn't agree with them, or they get the measles, or something else comes up that knocks the profit from the trip.

"Once I was transporting coolies from China

to British Guiana, and some kind of an epidemic hit them, and I threw 25 of them overboard before I could get it stopped. Their systems do not respond to medicine as a white man's does, or you don't guess what ails them right and give them the wrong medicine.

"We couldn't send our men ashore for fear the natives would rush them and take them inland to serve at some of their savage feasts as 'long pig'. The natives used to esteem 'white meat' as a great delicacy."

"For years I took naked islanders to Queensland, Australia, as contract laborers. I was in the trade for a long time between the New Hebrides and Australia, carrying natives. I also took natives from New Caledonia and coolies from China to the West

Indies. On one trip I took 525 coolies from China to the West Indies. I carried horses from Sydney, Australia, to Madras, India. During the score or more of years I was mate and master I made trips to New Zealand, Africa, Australia, India, Japan, China, the South Sea Islands, the Hawaiian Islands, the coasts of South America and a lot of out of the way places that are only dots on the map.

"I came from Japan to Portland in 1878. I met my fate in Portland, and married her--but that's another story and I have told you all I am going to."

Oregon Journal
July 6, 1920

# Jack London
# Sonoma Valley, California

*One time when I was a guest of Jack London's at his home at Glen Ellen in the Sonoma Valley --or the Valley of the Moon, as he loved to call it--he showed me a shallow dish carved out of ebony or some other hard, dark wood. He had secured it on account of its interesting history in the South Sea Islands.*

"When I heard the history of this ancient wooden bowl, I determined to secure it.

"On one of his trips to the islands a ship captain had come ashore to trade with the natives. He had given them rum, and when they had no suspicion of his purpose and were off their guard he had seized a number of the natives and had taken them aboard his ship. When their friends came out in their canoes to rescue them he had fired at the canoes and killed most of the natives. Some, however, had jumped overboard and swam ashore.

"For years the father of a boy that had been kidnapped and who had never returned, watched for the return of this ship. At last his patience was rewarded and the ship again came to the island. The captain, with an armed crew, came ashore to trade with the natives. The father, who had looked forward to this day, ambushed them, killing all but the captain, who was taken inland and eaten.

"To the father of the kidnapped boy was given the honor of cutting his throat and catching the blood in this bowl and drinking it as it flowed

59

warm from the throat of the struggling man.

"I had to pay much more than its real worth, in trade tobacco, but it was a treasured relic of the village.

"Yes, their methods are quite direct."

Oregon Journal
July 6, 1920

"To the father of the kidnaped boy was given the honor of cutting his throat and catching the blood in this bowl and drinking it as it flowed warm from the throat of the struggling man."

# Albert G. Walling
## Pioneer of 1847
## Rockaway, Oregon

"Most folks can describe what kind of house they were born in, and tell you something about their home town. I can't. They don't hold any 'old home' days or reunions at my birthplace. I was born in Wyoming, somewhere near the summit of the Rocky Mountains, June 24, 1847, at a place the emigrants called Mud Springs."

Oregon Journal
undated

# Robert M. Veatch
## Pioneer of 1854
## Cottage Grove, Oregon

"When I reached Feather River I was broke, save for a ten-cent shin-plaster which I was saving for seed. I camped near the cabin of a settler name Cochrane. He pronounced it Cowhorn. He invited me to stop with him. I refused. He urged me, so I said, 'I have only ten cents, and I never buy anything I can't pay for. What's more, your wife wouldn't want me in the house. I am alive with graybacks.'

"He said, 'Take your clothes off and lay them on a large anthill. Take a good swim in the river. In a few hours you can wear your clothes again.'

"I put my clothes upon a big anthill, and when I went to get them a few hours later the ants had eaten every grayback and everything that would become a grayback."

Oregon Journal
July 21, 1922

# Dr. William A. Turner
## Seaside, Oregon

"I was on horseback a few paces to the right and rear of General Miles when Chief Joseph came forward and started to hand his rifle to General O. O. Howard. General Howard motioned for him to hand the rifle to Colonel Miles. Chief Joseph handed his rifle to Colonel Miles, who took it, then handed it back to Chief Joseph and shook hands with him.

"I put in, in all, 15 years among the Sioux, Assiniboines and Mountain Crows. I am not going into the subject, but I will say that the more I saw of the relations of the white man and the Indian, the more sympathy I had for the Indians. In almost every treaty we have expected them to comply with its terms, but the white man has rarely done so if to his advantage to evade it. The white men have usually considered the Indians legitimate prey and have seen no wrong in defrauding them. The army officers and soldiers realized that most of the Indian wars were caused by the bad faith of white men. When trouble ensued through the fault of crooked or unscrupulous whites, the soldiers were called upon to punish the Indians."

Oregon Journal
May 8, 1935

# Lewis T. Thompson
## Indian Fighter
## Roseburg, Oregon

"We spent several days trying to round up and kill the Indians that had attacked our party of drovers and run off our stock in Northern California, but they had scattered, and while we found and destroyed some of their lodges, we couldn't find any more Indians. We never did get any of our cattle back, though I heard afterward that the settlers had rounded up about 50 of the 800 we had when the Indians attacked us.

"I was 19 when we had this Indian fight. For the next two or three years I worked on Truckee Flat, in Nevada, or drove cattle. When I was around 22 I came back to Cole's Valley. An old Frenchman on Brush Creek, just south of Humbug Mountain, in Curry County, had a big band of half-wild cattle. He sold them to cattle buyers at $10 a head, with the understanding that all cattle that returned to their home range were not to be reclaimed. He sold these cattle over and over, for they would break away in the timber and drift back.

"Uncle Dave Evans and I went over to the Frenchman's and bought 200 head, agreeing to his proposition that those that worked back were to be his. We corralled the bunch and wired boards across the horns of the ones we spotted for the leaders. When we got out some distance these leaders tried to run back through the timber, but the boards on their horns caught and stopped them so we could catch up with them and head them back into the trail. In this way we got our cattle out and made good money on them.

"On September 8, 1867, I married Missouri Ann Wright, who was around 15, on the high seas, off the mouth of Yaquina Bay. Last September we celebrated our 58th wedding anniversary. So, you see, elopements sometimes turn out all right, and the captain of a boat can tie as tight a knot as a preacher can."

Oregon Journal
December 12, 1925

# Uncle John Bentley
# Pendleton, Oregon

"I had relatives, friends, and neighbors on both sides in the Civil War, and I didn't feel called upon to kill them, as I would have been apt to do whichever side I joined, so I came west. I joined my older brother, Jefferson D., who had gone to California in 1850. I mined for a year or so, then I ran a dairy for five years. In 1868 I was married to Mary Yoakum, whose father was killed by Indians in 1854 while they were crossing the plains.

"In 1871 I moved to Yoakum, between Echo and Pendleton, in Umatilla County. In 1872 I moved to Pendleton. That's a little more than 50 years ago. At that time there were only 13 families and some unmarried young fellows living there. Among the people living at Pendleton when I moved there were O. F. Thompson, Jim Hager, Judge McCarthy,

Jim Moore, R. Baskett, Judge G. W. ('Doc') Bailey, Lot Livermore, George La Dow, W. H. Marshall, the blacksmith; B. B. Bishop, Ed Jacobsen and Bill Switzler. Lot Livermore later married Bill Switzler's widow.

"'Dad' Fraker and I did carpentering. One of the first jobs I landed was building a house for Jerry DeSpain, out on McKay Creek. His widow, Nancy DeSpain, is here in Seaside now. I made all the window frames and doors and all the other finishing work, by hand. The next job I got was building a house for the Reith brothers. In 1876 I started a planing mill at Pendleton. I sold it, but later had to take it back. Then I built a steam sawmill on the rim just below the bridge. When I pulled the whistle cord for the first time every white person in Pendleton, to say nothing of the Indians, ran down to the banks of the Umatilla River to see if a steamboat had made its way up the river. After selling my steam sawmill at Pendleton, I bought one at Willow Springs, on the Pendleton-Camas Prairie road. It burned down. I lost $40,000, as I didn't have a cent of insurance.

"Pretty soon I made another stake. I bought 2000 acres of wheat land and 2200 acres of grazing land. I was one of the best liked men in Pendleton, as I would always sign notes for my friends when they wanted to borrow money at the bank. Along came the panic of 1893, and all the people whose notes I had signed went broke, so I had to pay the notes. I sold 647 acres of wheat land to Tom Hampton for $8000 which later sold for $120,000. When I had cleaned up all my security debts, amounting to over $35,000, I was wiped off the map, financially speaking. I sold my 2200 acres of grazing land to the Cunningham Sheep & Land Company at $3.00 an acre, to get enough money to square the last of these debts. When times got good again I hoped the people whose notes I had signed as an accommocation would pay me, but all I ever got back from my $35,000 loss was $65.00. I still have a pile of notes three inches high, but all they are good for is to paper the wall, as they are outlawed.

"I was one of the first constables in Pendleton. I also served as assessor. I was United States Deputy Marshal, my district extending from The Dalles to the Blue Mountains. I also served as sheriff of Umatilla County.

"J. H. Turner and I owned the **East Oregonian** for a while. We sold it to L. B. Cox. He sold it to C. S. Jackson. In his valedictory Cox said he had bought the paper on jawbone, ran it on credit and was selling it for cash, so nobody could say that he was not a successful newspaper man.

"Some time I will tell you about some of my experiences when I was sheriff. I always wore a gun on the outside of my leg, not really to use, but just so folks would know I was sheriff. One day a man came in and complained to the judge that Hank Vaughn and 'Doc' Whitley had robbed him. I went to Hank's place, four miles from Adams, to arrest him. Did I arrest him? Sure, I did.

"He had made his brag that he would never be arrested. When Hank saw me drive up to his place he came out with a rifle across his arm and his six-shooter in its holster. He said, 'Sheriff, have you come out to get me?'

"I said, 'Well, Hank, that's what I was sort of figuring on doing.'

"He said, 'Have you got a warrant for me?'

"I said, 'Yes. Do you want to see it?'

"He shifted his gun so it lined up in my direction, and said, 'Do you aim to arrest me and take me in with you?'

"I said, 'Hank, there's no call for you and me to be getting unfriendly about this little matter, but I sort of figure you ought to come in to Pendleton and fix it up.'

"He said, 'You go back to Adams and arrest Doc Whitley and wait there for me. Along about an hour from now I'll drift into Adams. You can sort of deputize me to help you bring in Doc Whitley. That will be the best way to fix this thing up without making hard feelings between us.'

"I said, 'That suits me, Hank. I guess you'll make a good deputy.'

"He came into Adams and I turned Doc Whitley over to him. He said, 'You drive on ahead, Sheriff. I don't like to be seen in your company. I'll be in soon.'

"I drove on about my business. Hank brought Doc Whitley in and said, 'What do you need?'

"I told him to bring in $1000 in gold for each of them and I would turn them both loose till the trial. He went out to some of the gamblers and saloon-keepers and got $2000 in gold and brought it to me and I locked it in my safe.

"Then Hank hunted up the complaining witness --the chap that was going to appear against him at the trial. He took him into a saloon, counted out $2000 in bills, and, handing it to the saloon-keeper, said, 'Keep this in your safe till after the trial. If Dick, here, disappears till after the trial, hand it to him. If he appears against me, return it to me.'

"Dick, the chap Hank and Doc Whitley had robbed, said, 'Give me a couple of the 20-dollar gold pieces you got off me and I'll beat it and stay out of sight till the case is dismissed. That's making $2000 pretty easy.'

"When the case came up, the witness could not be found, so the case was dismissed and I returned the bail money to Hank. A few days later the missing witness turned up and went to the saloon to get the $2000 in the safe. The saloon-keeper turned it over to him. When he tried to spend the money he was the maddest man you ever saw. It was counterfeit money.

"Hank was a good-hearted chap, but wasn't a very desirable citizen. One time he and I had a long, friendly talk. He cleared up several murder mysteries for me. He told me he had, for business or social reasons, had to kill 13 men. Some of them may have deserved to be killed, but Hank's method of disposing of them was too irregular.

"You remember how Hank died. He had a friend pull his boots off. Someone had bet him he would die with his boots on, and he didn't want to lose the bet."

Oregon Journal
August 13, 1923

# Henry H. Staub
# Pioneer Realtor
# Sunnyside, Washington

"I was born in Switzerland in 1857. When I was 17 years old I was apprenticed to a baker and confectioner. I worked for three years for nothing, which is the custom in the old country. After three years I went to Germany to learn German methods. I was paid two marks a day for my work in the German bakery.

"In the old country the father is the head of the family. What he says is the law. His children never think of questioning his decisions. My father was a minister and was well-to-do. Whether the children are married or not makes no difference. They consult him about business and other affairs. I never spent $5 prior to my father's death, without asking him his advice.

"Mr. Schindler, who had a furniture store in Portland and who was Swiss consul here, had occasion to come to Zurich, where we lived, to settle the estate of a man from Switzerland who had died in Portland. He met my sister Emma. He told Emma about Portland and of the beauty of Oregon. It is usual there for the children to make a request of their father through the older son, so Emma came to me and asked me to persuade Father to let her go to the United States to see that country. I said, 'Emma, you are crazy. Father would never let you go. Why should I worry him?' But Emma persisted in asking me till finally, in desperation, I said to him, 'Father, Emma wants that I should ask you if she could go to visit the United States.'

"My father was a large man with long hair and a long beard. He was very excitable. He said, 'Henry, my son, are you crazy?'

"I answered, 'No, Father, it is not I that am crazy, but Emma.'

"He said, 'What could she get there that she cannot have here? Why should she want to go out to Oregon, which is a country of barbarians and savages? The natives would kill her. The woods are full of Indians. There are wild animals there. I have read about it. I know! Does she want to bring her father's gray hairs in sorrow to the grave?'

"I went back and reproached Emma, but it did no good. She simply said, 'Keep after Father till you get his consent. I want to go.'

"She made my life a burden. She sent Mr. Schindler to Father. Finally Father threw up his hands and said, 'I will give you 1500 francs. Go and see this barbarous country, and you will be cured of all desire to go there again.' Emma came out to Portland.

"A few months later the postmaster stopped me as I was driving a spirited horse down the street, and said, 'Henry, are you crazy?'

"I was much offended, and said, 'Why should you insult me?'

"He said, 'You must be crazy to let your sister go out to America. I have a government telegram from her, and she wants your father and the rest of you to come there.'

"I went home in great trouble, for I knew how Father would take it. He walked the floor and tore his hair. Finally he said, 'My son, advise me. What shall I do?'

"I said, 'If God wants us to go, we will sell all we have at a big price. If he doesn't, we will not receive good offers for our property.'

"Father agreed to this, and we received offers so good that we were surprised, so we decided that we would have to go. He called my brother John home from college, and once more my father walked the floor, for he said, 'To think that John has a good education, and now he will go out to this savage country, where his education will be of no good.'

"John said, 'Surely, in a savage country an educated man would have a great advantage.' So he, like Emma, did not support my father's position.

"I had a beautiful, spirited horse. This I determined to take with me, but when I asked the agent, he said, 'Yes, if you are going to New York you could take it, but when you get to New York you are not yet half way to Oregon.' This filled us once more with dismay. It did not seem possible there could be so big a country.

"I shall not tell you of our trip to Oregon, but we came to Portland and Father bought, for $20,000 cash, a 220-acre farm at Jennings Lodge. He looked at the mountains to the east of us. He looked at the peaceful river. He looked at the green and fertile hills, and he thought he had found another Switzerland, so he was no longer unhappy."

Oregon Journal
April 11, 1927

# William S. Tull
## Mayor of Barlow
## Barlow, Oregon

"In the spring of 1850 my stepfather, my mother, and their three broods of children started in a prairie schooner for Oregon. I was six years old, so I remember many incidents of our trip. We used to pull into a camp on the Platte and find the sign, 'Don't camp here--cholera', so we would have to pull on and maybe make a dry camp. Our stock began dying on us, till we had only a thin old ox and one milk cow hitched to the wagon. Our progress became slower and slower, till at last we were snowed in in the Blue Mountains. We had no food, no money, good appetites, and no way of going on or of getting anything to satisfy hunger. William Barlow, Sidney Moss, and John P. Brooks came out with a pack train, as they had heard that some immigrants were stalled in the Blue Mountains. They fed us and brought us on to Oregon City."

Oregon Journal
January 22, 1926

# James Frank Tomlinson
# Tillamook, Oregon

"I suppose you wonder how a man who is totally blind can earn his living and get along. For some years I ran a ferry across the Tillamook River. I took passengers in my skiff and teams in my scow. I can travel through the thickest woods or brush, and, in spite of no trail, I can go directly to where I am headed for and return home.

"For many years I ran a 180–acre farm in Tillamook County. I raised beef cattle. I did all my own housework and kept my house as neat as wax.

"I can go anywhere I want, and I never run into anything. I can't explain it to you, and you wouldn't believe it if I did, but when I am passing down a country road, I can tell where a post is, where a fence is, where a lane or a crossroad comes in. It isn't that there is an echo from these things, but I can feel them. For example, in walking down a hall I instinctively make the proper turns. Just as you with your eyes can see the shadow of a thing, I can feel an opening, or the presence of a solid wall or of any other object.

"I used to live in Douglas County and I traveled all over the country on horseback. I also lived in Coos County for a while. I can hear things of which you are absolutely unconscious. For example, in rowing across the river I don't go by the feel of the water on my boat, but I can hear the lap of water on the opposite shore, so naturally I can head straight across the stream. I suppose a person who has lost his sight makes up for it not only in keener hearing but in a more retentive memory. For example, if you take a trip of five miles and want to go back the same way, you would have very little idea of the character of the land over which you had passed, but I would know just about where I was from the feel of the land, whether I was in a footpath that was mossy, whether it was graveled, whether I was on the hard road. I could tell you almost exactly how far I had come to just where I was, which is probably more than you could do."

**Oregon Journal**
June 1, 1927

# George A. Bennett
## Pioneer Publisher
## Coos Bay, Oregon

"You asked me a moment ago about the pronunciation of Coquille. It should be pronounced 'Coquell', to rhyme with 'go-to-hell', instead of 'Cokeel'. When the Spaniards named it they called it 'Coquille', and pronounced it 'Co-kee-a', then the French settlers who came in changed the pronunciation to 'Co-keel', then along came the Americans, mostly Missourians, and they pronounced it 'Co-quill', and some of them called it that, while others called it 'Co-quell', But its real pronunciation, however, is 'Co-quell'.

"You also asked me how Coos Bay got its name... Coos River was originally called Cows River. When the Hudson's Bay Company maintained a trading post at Fort Umpqua some of their cows got away. The trappers later found these cows near the mouth of this river. Thereafter they always spoke of the river where they found the cows as 'Cow's River', and it finally became known as Cow's River.

"When Lewis MacArthur made his reconnaissance of this coast in 1850, he reported the Coos River as the Kows River. The French called it Riviere-des Vaches, which means the river of the cows. Early maps and early documents show that it was spelled Cow's River, also Cowes, Kows, Koos, Coos, and Koose.

"Harry Baldwin, a boyhood friend of my father, who was one of the early settlers of this country, says that when he came here in 1852 the river was known as Cowes River, and the bay as Cowes Bay, so I imagine our river, our bay, and our county took their name from the lost Hudson's Bay Company cows."

Oregon Journal
June 16, 1922

# William P. Berger
# Portland, Oregon

"We organized the Multnomah Rod and Gun Club in Dave Monastes' building at First and Yamhill Streets on January 5, 1883. There were seven of us who were charter members. Eventually we had nearly 40 members. We used to kill geese and ducks in the pond where the Union Station was later built. We shot at clay pigeons where the

Falling School was later built. To be exact, our clay pigeons were glass balls."

Oregon Journal
April 5, 1934

## Captain O. C. Applegate
## In Search of The Blue Bucket Mine
## Klamath County, Oregon

*Many years ago I met Captain O. C. Applegate in the Klamath country. He was a member of a party that went in search of the Blue Bucket Mine. In an article he wrote for the paper at Klamath Falls many years ago, he said:*

"It was 42 years ago that I was one of a party of five men who made a trip across central Oregon in search of the Blue Bucket Mine. Before starting we conferred with Mrs. William G. Parker, who was 16 years old in 1845, when the gold was supposed to be discovered. She was a daughter of Captain Solomon Tetherow, who headed the train of which the discoverer of gold was a member. Mrs. Parker told us that she saw the metal that was picked up, hammered on a wagon tire until it was flattened. Her son, Sam Parker, had taken great pains to get all the details possible from his mother and also from his grandfather, Captain Sol Tetherow, who was still alive when we made our trip in search of the lost mine in 1877.

"Here in brief is the story as given to us by Sam Parker: Captain Stephen Meek, brother of Joe Meek, was in command of a train of emigrants coming down Snake River on the old trail. He had a 'compass in his head', as the old mountain men used to say. Before reaching the Blue Mountains he left the main trail, believing that he could cut across and save many days' travel on the way to the Willamette Valley. Sol Tetherow's wagon train was a few days behind Meek. He decided to follow Meek. He overtook Meek with his party at a spring that had made a marsh at the base of a hill. There was not sufficient water for the use of both wagon trains. Captain Tetherow and Steve Meek had a dispute about which was the way to make the cut-off. Tetherow said they were bearing too far south. Tetherow and his wagon train pulled out that night, heading northward. At 2 o'clock the next day they struck a marsh. A man was sent back on a mule to notify the stragglers.

"The discovery of gold was made by members

71

of the Tetherow wagon train before they had overtaken
Meek. It was found in a range of hills sparsely
covered with stunted juniper. The teams had to
detour around the hills. The gold was found by
the men driving the loose stock. They brought
some of the nuggets in their shot pouches and produced
them when they rejoined the main party that night.
While one of the men was hammering out one of
the pieces of metal on the wagon tire, someone said,
'How much of that stuff did you see?'

"The answer was, 'We could have filled that
thar blue bucket with it,' and he pointed to one
of the blue buckets used for carrying water.

"Many years later Mrs. Parker, whose husband
was a brother-in-law of Jesse Applegate, made a
trip with her son, Sumner, into the Steen Mountain
country to see if she could locate their old camp,
but she was unable to remember just where the
gulch was."

**Oregon Journal**
undated

# William F. Wakefield
# Eddyville, Oregon

"When we came here, if a settler made $100
a year he was a jake. All he needed money for
was overalls and shoes, with calico for his wife
and kids. His wife made his shirts and knitted
his socks. In Corvallis, where we traded, shoes
cost $1.25 to $2.50 a pair. Overalls were 50 cents.
A Sunday suit cost $10 to $12 and they threw in
a pair of two-bit suspenders. When a young blood
wanted to be sporty or was keeping company with
a girl he might get reckless and pay $3.00 to $3.50
for a fine pair of shoes. A well cooked, well served
meal in a hotel or restaurant cost 25 cents and
a room 50 cents.

"In those days Eddyville was called Little
Elk and was in Benton County, for this was before
the creation of Lincoln County.

"The summer I was 16, with some other boys,
I spent in the hills peeling chittam bark. We brought
it out on pack horses and got $25 a ton for it.
Today it sells at 7 to 8 cents a pound, which means
$140 to $160 a ton. We bought eggs all that summer
at 5 to 8 cents a dozen. Sugar was 5 cents a
pound, a 50-pound sack of flour cost 55 cents,
and ham or bacon 10 to 12½ cents a pound retail.

"A man really didn't need much money then,
if he lived in the back country. Unlike the city

72

dweller, we had no bills to pay for wood, water, light, rent, meat, fish, berries, or vegetables. The streams were full of trout. Deer, bear, and grouse were plentiful. We raised all the potatoes and other vegetables we needed, as well as chickens, eggs, and honey. Our cows furnished us veal, milk, and butter. We lived the simple life.

"I always had pocket money, for I got 15 cents a pound for winter deer skins, and 25 cents for summer skins. When I was in my late teens and early 20s, William Toner, express messenger on the Albany & Yaquina train, paid me 5 cents a pound for deer meat. A good buck would bring me $5 to $6. He sold them to the hotels and markets in Portland. I used to kill 50 to 100 deer a year. Pretty soon they began enforcing the law on the open season, so we could only ship deer meat during the open season, but there was no limit to the number you could kill.

"Frank Hyde of Philomath and I killed 26 bears one season, 22 the following year, and 16 the year after that. Tip and Buff, my two bear dogs, were said to be the best bear dogs in the district. We hunted on Big Elk and Little Elk, in the King's Valley country, and along the Yaquina. I took contracts to kill bear. When a bear was killing sheep or calves the farmer who was losing stock would pay me $6 to kill the bear. I picked up a lot of loose change in that way.

"A man living on some stream on the coast certainly had an easy living when we came here. The winter storms threw enough driftwood into his front yard to last him all year. In an hour's walk he could kill and bring in a buck for fresh meat. He could catch a dishpan full of trout in an hour or so. He could dig rock oysters or get clams at low tide. He could catch sea fish whenever he felt so inclined. His garden furnished him carrots, beets, turnips, potatoes, and cabbage for winter use. He could pick and put up all the wild black-berries and strawberries he wanted. He could gather hazelnuts for winter use. He didn't have to worry about the high cost of living.

"I was married 17 years ago to Bell Warnock of Wallowa County. Rex, our boy, is 15 years old. We milk 20 cows and ship the cream three times a week to Corvallis. The milk truck calls for it and returns the cans the same day.

"The old, easy-going days are gone forever, but I don't know where or when the young folks had so much done for them as today. We have banished lonesomeness from the farm, with our paved roads, daily mail delivery, daily papers, the auto-mobile, and the radio. Yes, sir, there is mighty

73

little excuse for a man not making good in this day and age."

Oregon Journal
June 16, 1927

# Carl Helm
# Union County District Attorney
# La Grande, Oregon

"Charley Long? Sure, I knew him. He rode the range for Ben Snipes. He was soft-spoken, quiet-mannered--rather diffident and bashful, but he didn't know what fear was. No two-gun bad man nor outlaw horse could intimidate him.

"You remember when Hank Vaughn of Pendleton came to Prineville and bragged that he could lick anyone that ever wore bootleather? Charley Long said, 'You can't get away with that statement here.' He took off the bandanna handkerchief he wore around his neck, flipped one end of it to Hank, and, holding the other end, said, 'Draw your gun and we'll shoot it out across the table and settle the matter of who is the best man.'

"They emptied their guns into each other, and at that range they couldn't miss. They must have been tough, for both survived the fight. Hank was thrown from a horse in Pendleton later and killed, and Long was also killed, but I don't know the particulars."

Oregon Journal
July 7, 1929

# Dee Wright
# Eugene, Oregon

"The real trouble is that the men who make the laws, though they have the best of intentions, have no real knowledge of what will prove remedial legislation.

"Naturally, I have no use for the man who uses dynamite to catch fish, nor have I much more use for the man who uses salmon eggs for bait. Another fish hog that should be put out of business is the fish duck. A fish duck will kill more young trout than 50 fishermen will catch in a year. The water ousel is another enemy to young trout. Crawfish are death on salmon trout eggs, as they are on the job at the spawning beds at the time the fish is laying her eggs.

"The real sportsman should combine against the human vandals and also against the fish ducks, water ousels, and crawfish, which recognize no game laws and are on the job every day in the year."

Oregon Journal
June 26, 1927

# C. T. Bishop
## Pioneer of 1856
## Salem, Oregon

"My mother's brother, David, who was 14 years old, got a job driving two yoke of oxen, breaking sod on one of the big California ranches. He went barefoot while doing the plowing, as he claimed he would rather go barefooted than wear shoes. As a matter of fact they were so desperately poor they had no money with which to buy shoes, and the money he earned at plowing was spent for wheat, which they ground in a coffee mill to make bread."

Oregon Journal
undated

# J. W. Blakely
## Mosier, Oregon

"My father and mother died within two weeks of each other (in 1854) of winter fever, as they used to call pneumonia. I was seven years old when they died. The authorities bound us out to what they thought were reputable and responsible parties. I was bound out to John Downing. Although I was only seven years old, he expected me to do a man's work. I had to feed the stock, clean the barn, do the chores, and if I did not do everything just as he expected or just as quickly as he thought I should, he would whip me unmercifully. I was so unhappy I would have liked to have killed myself, but I didn't know how.

"When I was eight he lost his temper and whipped me with a stick as large as my thumb. The more he whipped the madder he seemed to get, and when he finally left me, lying on the ground, from my shoulders to the calves of my legs my flesh was torn and bleeding and I could hardly move. I crawled out of his sight, and as soon as I could travel I ran away. I went to an older brother. We went to a wagon train that was taking freight down into Mexico.

"When I was 17 I put an ad in the paper, trying to locate Downing. I had got my growth and I was strong and husky. For more than eight years I had worked toward one end, and that was to go back and beat Downing within an inch of his life. When I advertised for him I got word that he had had a fight with a man and been killed. So that was that."

Oregon Journal
November 19, 1927

# E. E. Tucker
# Native of Aumsville
# Roseburg, Oregon

"On the way across the plains the ox teams stampeded. Isaac Ball, one of the members of the wagon train, was thrown from his wagon and had his leg broken. My father and Dr. Blackerby set his leg and that night the heads of the families in the wagon train met and took a vote to decide what to do with Ball. They decided to leave him with provisions in the care of some friendly Indians, hoping that his leg would heal and that he could join a later wagon train. My father was the only one in the train to vote against leaving him with the Indians. He backed up his vote by deciding to stay with him. The next day Ball thought he would be able to stand the pain of the jolting wagon, so Father tied the leaders of Ball's ox team to the hind axle of his wagon and they traveled on till they overtook the wagon train. When Father arrived at Oregon City he had exactly one dollar in cash and my sister had a silver ten-cent piece."

Oregon Journal
April 30, 1931

# David A. Carter
## Oregon Native of 1842
## Portland, Oregon

"In 1853 they changed the name of the Oregon Institute to Willamette University. When I was going there Squire Purdy's wife boarded the out of town students....I never got into any trouble while I was going there, though I thought once I might be brought up for something I didn't mean to do. I was throwing rocks one afternoon, when suddenly Governor George Abernethy came around one end of the building and the rock I threw hit his hat. I guess he knew it was an accident, for he didn't say anything to anybody about it."

Oregon Journal
July 11, 1923

# Andrew Smith
## Rogue River Indian
## Portland, Oregon

*Major General Andrew J. Smith, after the close of the Civil War, was given command of the Seventh United States Cavalry, which was later commanded by General George A. Custer. Prior to the Civil War, General Smith served as captain in the First Dragoons at Port Orford, in Curry County, and also at Fort Lane, in southern Oregon. He also saw service at The Dalles and in central Oregon.*

*While stationed in southern Oregon in the early '50s, Captain Smith took as his wife a young woman of the Rogue River tribe, later known as Betsy Smith. Recently I interviewed Andrew Smith, the son of Major General A. J. Smith and Betsy, the Rogue River Indian woman. He said:*

"I was born at the time of the falling leaves in 1854, near Table Mountain, in southern Oregon. When the Rogue River Indians surrendered, in the fall of 1855, I was taken with my mother and her tribe to the Grand Ronde Reservation. From there my father had me taken by Captain Miller to the Willamette Valley. I was sent to the home of Mrs. Charlton, on Sauvies Island. In 1861 my father went east to become a major general in the Civil War. I was taken by William Miller to The Dalles.

77

"In the winter of 1862, I took the measles. I was eight years old. While I was sick with the measles a very heavy fall of snow occurred. The sun came out and everything was dazzlingly bright. I did not know that I should not look out at the glare of the sun on the snow. The people with whom I stayed apparently did not know it would be harmful to me. It made me blind.

"One of the things I remember seeing in The Dalles before I lost my eyesight was six Indians taken up on a scaffold. There was some talk, which I did not understand, and one was allowed to come down and the other five were hanged.

"I was of no use to Mr. Miller after I became blind, so he sent me back to Mrs. Charlton, on Sauvies Island. In 1865 or 1866, I went with Mrs. Charlton to visit her sister, Mrs. Nancy Walker, at Hillsboro. Dr. Bailey, who had served in the Civil War, had come to Hillsboro to practice. He saw me and asked about my eyes. They told him I had lost my sight from the measles three or four years before. He began to treat my eyes, and before long he had released the upper lid of each eye and I could see a glimmer of light. He cut some cords and treated my eyes and restored my sight, though I have been short-sighted and have had to wear glasses with thick lenses ever since. But I was some good once more, and you don't know what that means.

"I worked on the ranch on Sauvies Island till I was nearly grown. Then I got a job in a traveling store that traded around Sauvies Island, up the Lewis River, down the Columbia to St. Helens, up Willamette Slough and to all the farms on the waterfront for a score of miles around that country. It was a large flatboat. My job was to row it, or, when we were out where we could use a sail, to sail it. When we pulled up to a landing I would go around to the nearby farms and tell them our boat was at the landing and find out if they wanted any flour, coffee, sugar, calico, nails, tobacco or anything else in the line of general merchandise. I served as crew and solicitor of this trading boat for ten years.

"One time a man fell into talk with me and said, 'Captain, do you know who your father is, or where your mother is?'

"I had never been told about my folks, for my father didn't want me to go back to my mother's people, the Rogue River Indians. He wanted me to be brought up like his people, the whites. I studied quite a while, and finally said, 'No, I can't say I do know who I am. I seem to remember things dimly of the time I was a child, but I am not sure. Who am I?'

"He said, 'You go and see Mr. Miller. He is warden at the penitentiary at Salem. He will tell you all about your people.'

"I went to Salem as soon as I could be spared from the boat, and saw Mr. Miller. He told me about my father, General A. J. Smith, and about my mother. He said, 'I think Betsy, your mother, is still living at the Grand Ronde Reservation. A lot of your people from Grand Ronde have come here at different times inquiring about you, but I have never told where you were. For 20 years your mother has been trying to locate you, but the agent there either does not know, or will not tell her, where you live.'

"I was glad to learn who I was and that I had people of my own flesh and blood. I went to Dallas, where I hired a horse and rode to the Grand Ronde Reservation. I got an old Indian who knew my mother to take me to where she lived.

"My mother was old and bent and wrinkled and poor. She lived in a little shack made of scraps and boards. The agent did not give the Indians the goods issued to them, so Mother had little to eat. Later they turned this agent out for not giving the Indians the rations and blankets and other goods furnished them by the government.

"I could not speak any Indian. My mother could not speak English. I had to find an Indian who understood English to interpret for us. She told me she wove baskets and gathered timothy seed and earned just enough to keep from starving.

"My mother and my Indian relatives could not live like white people. I could not change my whole life and live like an Indian. When Mother and I wanted to talk we had to send for someone to tell us what we were trying to say to each other. I helped my mother, but I decided to go back and work and live in the way my father's people lived.

"My mother was old and lonesome and her heart was heavy and her days were sad, so in 1876 I gave up my work and went back to the reservation and took an allotment of land and farmed and took care of my mother. I soon learned the jargon so I could talk to my people. My mother lived with me 17 years. She had one other child, Valentine. My half-brother was a full-blood.

"I married Jane Bernard, whose people came from French Prairie and who was of French and Indian blood. Of our nine children three are still living. I was appointed farmer at the government school. Though I now live in Portland, I still own my own farm on the reservation. I served 16 years as school director on the reservation.

"Yes, I am 70 years old, and I have seen many changes. I remember, when I was a small boy, seeing Donald McKay march through The Dalles with his Warm Spring Indian scouts. They were carrying the fresh scalps of the Snake Indians on their spears.

"We don't kill and scalp people any more. We kill them with poison gas or drop bombs on them from airships, and kill men and women and children. We are more civilized than in the old days, when men fought hand to hand with guns and knives or bows and arrows. At least, we think we are more civilized."

**Oregon Journal**
undated

# Andrew Wirt
# Pioneer of 1845
# Ilwaco, Washington

"We never officially lost the county seat at Oysterville. One Sunday, when practically everyone was at church, about 20 men came from South Bend, broke into the courthouse, loaded the records in boxes and sacks and took them to South Bend and declared South Bend the county seat."

**Oregon Journal**
May 25, 1926

# J. B. Cartwright
# Portland, Oregon

"Our family lived at Salem till I was 14 years old, when we moved up to eastern Oregon. Forty years ago eastern Oregon was a vast sea of bunchgrass. You could ride all day without seeing a fence."

**Oregon Journal**
June 28, 1921

# The Good Stage Robber

*In the '70s Kelton was the shipping point
where passengers, freight, mail, and express were
transferred from trains to stages and freight wagons.
Bill Winters in the '70s was a well-known employee
of Wells-Fargo. He and his sawed-off shotgun were
known to almost every settler between Kelton and
The Dalles.*

"One man held a gun on Winters,
telling him that if he reached for his
sawed-off shotgun it would be the last
move he ever made..."

*On one occasion Winters was guarding the
Wells-Fargo treasure chest when the stage was held
up in the Blue Mountains. Just about daylight the*

81

driver saw a rope stretched across the road. One man held a gun on Winters, telling him that if he reached for his sawed-off shotgun it would be the last move he ever made. Another man told the stage driver and passengers to line up. The third highwayman took Winters' six-shooter and shotgun and threw out the treasure box. The passengers were relieved of their valuables.

Among the passengers was a young woman, Miss Wilson. After a brief consultation the highwaymen returned her valuables and money. Miss Wilson was billed to Portland, Oregon. Two of the other passengers were cattlemen, going to La Grande. The fourth passenger, Mr. Smithright, was from Iowa and was on his way to the Puget Sound country by way of Portland.

The cattlemen took the holdup as a matter of course. They had lost only a few hundred dollars, and that didn't mean much to them. But Mr. Smithright had lost all the money he had and he felt pretty downhearted. Miss Wilson insisted that Smithright take half of the money she had, as a loan.

When Winters arrived at The Dalles he reported the robbery and asked the Wells-Fargo manager for a lay-off to hunt the highwaymen. It was two years before he finally located them.

They arrived in Portland by boat from San Francisco. They were lodged in the city jail in Portland. All three denied their guilt and offered alibis, but Winters, who had kept in touch with Smithright and Miss Wilson and the cattlemen from La Grande, supbpoenaed them as witnesses. When Miss Wilson went to the jail she said to one of the men, "This is the good stage robber who returned my money to me."

The man addressed said, "I guess you've got the goods on me, all right." All three were convicted.

The sequel of this particular story was that Winters was invited to stay over in Portland and serve as best man at the wedding of Mr. Smithright and Miss Wilson.

*Oregon Journal*
*January 12, 1933*

# Robert G. Smith
# Portland, Oregon

"In the summer of 1881 I returned to Jacksonville, took the teachers' examination, received my certificate, and taught school at Heber's Grove. In the fall of 1882 the school directors of Linkville, now Klamath Falls, wrote a letter to me, offering me the school there. I took the stage from Ashland over the Green Mountain Road to Linkville, which at that time had a population of less than 1000.

"The school directors met and I was summoned before them. The directors were Judge C. C. Moore, Captain D. J. Ferree, and Dr. W. E. Beach. I weighed 95 pounds. The directors looked me over, shook their heads, and Dr. Beach said, 'You have our contract, young man, and you can hold us to it, but we will be glad to pay your expenses back to Ashland if you will surrender the contract. The big boys put the last two teachers through the window, and you wouldn't be a mouthful for them.'

"A young boy named Roberts, the son of a well-to-do man there, insisted on tearing up his books, so, after threatening to punish him a time or two, I finally gave him a good licking. Next day someone came to me and said, 'Old Man Roberts is looking for you with a gun.'"

"I said, 'I refuse to release you from the contract. I have come over here to teach school, and I am going to do so. If, at the end of the first month, my services are not satisfactory I will give you back the contract and make no charge for my services.'

"Captain Ferree said, 'I move that we give the young fellow a chance. I like his nerve.'

"As a matter of fact, I had no trouble whatever with the big boys. A young boy named Roberts, the son of a well-to-do man there, insisted on tearing up his books, so, after threatening to punish him a time or two, I finally gave him a good licking. Next day someone came to me and said, 'Old Man Roberts is looking for you with a gun.'

"I knew that if I didn't find him and settle the matter there and then, everyone would think I was a quitter. I met him on the street. When he saw me coming he pulled out his gun and waited for me. He said, 'Young fellow, you punished my boy. I don't allow anyone to strike my boy.'

"I said, 'Mr. Roberts, your boy tears up his books. This is a bad example for the other children. Your boy is just the same to me as any other boy. If he will mind we will have no trouble.'

"He said, 'Well, I am warning you now not to lay your hand on him again.'

"'I don't intend to, if he behaves himself,' I answered, 'but as long as I am teaching this school your boy and all of the others will have to mind.'

"Evidently he had a talk with his boy, for I had no further trouble.

"I was getting $110 a month, which was top wages. During the spring of 1883 I began having hemorrhages. The doctor told me my lungs were affected and I would have to leave there. Old Man Roberts came up to my room the day I left, thanked me for what I had done for his boy, and asked me to come back and teach the next fall."

Oregon Journal
December 19, 1927

# David Caufield
## Oregon City, Oregon

"At Placerville (in 1862) I landed a job shoveling tailings at $8 a day. Meals were $1.25, a bunk $1.25, the lodger furnishing his own blankets, and pies were $1 each, so a person couldn't save much

84

money, particularly if he were fond of pies."

Oregon Journal
January 22, 1922

# Jim Wallace
## Kelso's Oldest Native
## Kelso, Washington

"I was born right here in Kelso, on August 6, 1851, so I guess I can qualify as Kelso's oldest native son.

"My father, Victor M. Wallace, was born in Vermont in 1807. My mother, whose maiden name was Isabella Ray, was born in Scotland. My father and mother, with their two children, crossed the plains in 1847. Mr. Bewley was captain of their wagon train. Peter W. Crawford, the first settler here, and my father met on the summit of the Rocky Mountains. They were in different wagon trains, but the two trains happened to camp together while crossing the mountains. Later they met at The Dalles. They came down the Columbia River together, and both went to Oregon City.

"The train that Peter Crawford was in, while camped near Pendleton in the fall of 1847, was visited by Dr. Marcus Whitman, who had a mission about two or three days' travel to the northward. The captain of the wagon train asked Dr. Whitman to make a talk to the members of the train. In this fireside talk by Dr. Whitman one of the men asked him what part of the country he liked best. Dr. Whitman said, 'If I was a young man, just coming to the Oregon Country, I would take up a place on the Cowlitz and raise potatoes. The soil is rich, the climate is good, and a man would make no mistake by taking up a place there.'

"As soon as Peter Crawford got to Oregon City he decided to go up to Cowlitz Valley. He liked it and took up a claim that same fall, 1847.

"When the train my folks were in arrived on the Umatilla, where the road turned north to the Whitman Mission, they were out of flour, so they decided to drive up to the Whitman Mission and get flour at the Whitman mill and also get some vegetables. Jacob Hoffman drove one of my father's wagons across the plains.

"The year 1847 was one of the big years in emigration. About 4000 people came across the plains to Oregon that year. Most of them settled in the Willamette Valley.

"When my folks arrived at the Whitman Mission, Dr. Whitman and his wife made things so pleasant and were so cordial to the emigrants that quite a number of the wagon train decided to spend the winter there.

"The Indians had burned down the mill, and as my father was a millwright, Dr. Whitman hired Father to stay there that winter and rebuild the mill. He also gave work to Jacob Hoffman, who was driving one of Father's wagons, and also to quite a number of others of the train, including Peter D. Hall and his family, whose daughter, Mrs. O. N. Denny, now lives in Portland; Lorinda Bewley, the daughter of the captain of our wagon train, who was going to stay and teach in the school; her brother, Crocket Bewley, and Nathan S. Kimball and his family. Father unloaded his wagon and began preparing to spend the winter.

"Joseph Stanfield, a Frenchman, took a liking to my folks. He came to mother and said, 'I have been talking to Joe Lewis, a half-breed Indian, and some of the Indians, and you people had better go on down to the Willamette Valley.' Mother asked him why. He said, 'Don't let your husband stay here. There is going to be trouble. You will be sorry if you stay.'

"Mother became uneasy and said to Father, 'I don't want to spend the winter here at the Mission. Let's go on down to Oregon City.'

"Father had already agreed to build the mill for Dr. Whitman and didn't like to leave, but finally said, 'I'll do what ever you say, Mother.'

"She said, 'Put everything back in the wagon and let's start as soon as we can get away.' So they did.

"A few weeks later Jacob Hoffman, our driver, was killed by the Indians when they killed Dr. and Mrs. Whitman and the others. Lorinda Bewley had a terrible time, for one of the Indians made her come to his lodge, and they killed her brother, Crockett Bewley. They also killed Nathan Kimball and quite a number of the others.

"My father got work at Oregon City, for he was a good blacksmith as well as millwright. In the summer of 1848 the schooner Honolulu came up from San Francisco and bought up all the shovels, picks, milk pans and such plunder and provisions, at Oregon City. After he had cleaned up the stock at Oregon City, Captain Newell, commander of the Honolulu, told of the discovery of gold on the American River. A few days later, when the brig Henry came in from San Francisco, the news was confirmed, so everybody that wasn't crippled started for California.

"My father joined an overland company bound for the California gold mines. Among those in this company were Peter H. Burnett, General Joel Palmer, General M. M. McCarver, A. L. Lovejoy, F. W. Pettygrove, George Gay, Elisha Bird, John M. Shively, Ralph Wilcox, Benjamin Burch, W. H. Rector, Hamilton Campbell, Robert Newell, Columbia Lancaster and a whole lot of others whose names I do not remember.

"I have often heard Father tell about their trip. After they got into California they came onto a wagon road that had just been opened. Pretty soon they overtook Peter Lassen of California, who was taking some settlers in by a new pass that led over the mountains into the Sacramento Valley. Lassen had about ten wagons in his company. He had had to cut down his wagons into carts, and some of the people had abandoned their carts and were using their oxen to pack their goods on. The two parties joined. The party from the Willamette Valley had about 75 men that went ahead with their axes and cut trees out of the way and made the road.

"My father mined in and around Hangtown till the fall of '49, when he came back on board the O. C. Raymond. They ran into heavy gales and the ship sprung a leak, so the captain decided to go to Honolulu instead of to Portland. After sailing for eight days toward Honolulu the storm subsided and they were becalmed for several days. Then a favorable wind sprung up and the captain decided to make another try for the mouth of the Columbia River. They finally reached Astoria after being 27 days at sea.

"Father came back to Oregon City and was employed by a group of men who had started a mint at Oregon City and who planned to issue 5-dollar and 10-dollar gold pieces. Father made the mold for the $10 gold piece. They converted something over $50,000 of gold dust into 5-dollar and 10-dollar 'Beaver' coins. We had some of them for some years, but finally spent them all.

"On October 11, 1850, Father decided to move to the Cowlitz Valley, and he took up a place next to Peter W. Crawford's. The town of Kelso was built on the claim taken by Peter Crawford and on Father's claim. My father's claim is south of Mill Street and Crawford's claim lies north of Mill Street."

**Oregon Journal**
September 5, 1928

# Matthew Small
## Pioneer of 1852
### Silverton, Oregon

"My people went to Tennessee in 1832. They stayed there 20 years and then moved to Missouri to prepare for the trip to Oregon. We started across the plains in the spring of 1852. There were 62 in our party and we had 22 wagons. I was 15 years old then, and I have no more vivid memories than those of some of the scenes and incidents of our trip.

"One thing I remember with a good deal of amusement was of our party being held up by Pawnee Indians. They wanted pay for our traveling through their country and killing their buffalo. Rather than have trouble, McMinn Dodson, my father, and some others concluded they would give them some small present.

"The Indian chief, a wrinkled old man, put down a beautifully tanned buffalo robe and told each family to put something on the robe. My father had more cornmeal than anything else, so he put a pint of cornmeal on the robe. Another man had more salt, so he gave a couple of cups of salt, putting it, of course, in a separate pile. Another man could spare a little sugar, another a handful of pepper, and so on down the line. When all the contributions had been placed on the buffalo robe the old chief spoke to one of the Indians who took the robe by the four corners, so that all the different materials ran to the center, and they went contentedly away. When they went to cook that mess I have often wondered what they could call it. There were sugar, salt, pepper, flour, cornmeal, rice, and coffee. It sure would be a funny mess."

• • • • • • • • • • • • • • • • • • • • • • • • • • • • • • • • • • • • • • • • • • • • • • • • • •

"I am 85 years old and if it hadn't been that I was thrown out of a wagon in a runaway some years ago, I should be able to do as much work as I ever did. In spite of being a little lame at times, I walk from my home to the farm daily to feed the lambs. I also put in a fine garden this spring."

**Oregon Journal**
undated

# William Blakely
# Pendleton, Oregon

"In 1857, when I was 17 years old, I hired out to Jim McHargue. We drove a band of 250 cattle down to the mouth of the Yuba River, where it empties into the Sacramento. In the Siskiyou Mountains we saw where a wagon had been tipped over and the driver killed by Indians. He was taking a load of apples from the Willamette Valley to Yreka. The apples were scattered all over the roadside."

Oregon Journal
August 9, 1926

# Frazier Ward
# Pioneer of 1853
# Roseburg, Oregon

"I was not quite 21 when I came across the plains in 1853. I was born in Warren County, Missouri, in 1832. yes, that makes me 95. Oliver Beagle, also here, is the same age.

"My father, Samuel Ward, was a Kentuckian. My mother's maiden name was Isabella Marshall, a niece of Judge Marshall of Kentucky. Father and Mother had three sons and two daughters.

"I came to Douglas County in 1853. I married Mary Ann Flourney. My wife's father, H. B. Flourney, crossed the plains in 1845. He freighted from Stockton to the mines at the time gold was discovered. He brought back $10,000 in gold dust to Missouri. This started a wave of emigration. He crossed the plains again in 1851, settling in Oregon.

"My wife and I had 10 children, 22 grandchildren and a number of great-grandchildren. My wife died in 1901, and when I lost her I lost everything that made life worthwhile. When a man lives with a woman for 40 or 50 years they become so dependent on each other that when one is taken the one who is left feels lost and life loses its savor.

"My mother died when I was five. I was bound out by the county court to Captain Wyatt. This was in 1837. Captain Wyatt had been an officer in the War of 1812, and was a fine old man. He had a place on the Missouri River about 40 miles above St. Louis. He raised corn and tobacco. I soon became good at plowing corn with a shovel plow. Just before I was 21 I got a chance to drive an ox team to Oregon for Ambrose Newton. He had married a Flourney. He came to southern Oregon, where I met his wife and his wife's sister Mary, who later became my wife.

"When the Indian war broke out I enlisted, but as we couldn't get horses our company was disbanded. We built a stockade near the Sterling Mines and I joined the home guard company there. Thomas J. Gardiner was captain. The miners and settlers around Sterling, Applegate Creek, Jacksonville, Butte Creek, Galice Creek, Vannoys Ferry, Grave Creek and in other neighborhoods enlisted in the volunteers, or home guards.

"A dozen or more Indians took up quarters in two deserted miners' cabins near the forks of the Applegate. The miners, who saw the Indians were fortifying these cabins by piling dirt on the outside, came to Sterling and told us about it. Our home guard company, 60 men, surrounded the cabins to prevent the Indians from escaping. Meanwhile, word was sent to the military authorities and Captain Smith sent Lieutenants Hagen and Underwood, with 25 regulars and a howitzer. The mule carrying the ammunition fell into the creek and was killed and the powder was ruined. Once more help was sent for, and Lieutenant Switzer, with 16 regulars, brought more powder on a pack mule.

"They fired the howitzer. The ball passed through a cabin and killed two Indians. The Indians, however, had been busy. They killed one man at a distance of 500 yards, and wounded several others. Meanwhile, some of Captain Rice's company had come from Bear Creek Valley, some of Captain Alcorn's company, and some from Jacksonville and Applegate. They decided to wait till morning and then rush the cabins and capture the Indians, but next morning they found the Indians had left during the night. We brought an Indian boy who was too small to be carried away back to the mines with us.

"I mined in the Sterling Mine during '58 and '59. In 1859 I bought a place at Melrose, six miles west of Roseburg. I was postmaster at Melrose more than 20 years. I was appointed justice of the peace, but didn't like it, and resigned. It seemed like too quarrelsome a job. Either the people were fussing with one another or at me because I didn't fix up the fusses the way they wanted, so I wouldn't serve any longer.

"Clem Owens, son of old Tom Owens, who used to run a ferry at Roseburg, bought and sold wool and other produce at Roseburg. He got myself, 'General' Holmes, John Dillard, Harry Jones, Mr. Callahan and one or two others to sign a recommendation for him to serve as an introduction to the

90

men he wanted to deal with. We found he had speculated and failed for over $100,000. He killed himself. The bank brought suit against all of us who had signed the recommendation, and it turned out that we had signed his note. They had two trials trying to make us responsible. The jury hung both times. Finally the bank compromised, and I lost my ranch in Cole's Valley. It cost me $4500 to sign his recommendation. It cost some of the others a good deal more.

**"The mule carrying the ammunition fell into the creek and was killed and the powder was ruined."**

"I often wish I could live my life over again, for I would live it very differently. Not that I have purposely done things I shouldn't, but I can see so many places where I could have done so differently and so much better.

"In the long run, life has been good to me. My wife and I lived together more than two score years, we had ten children, I am 95, and I have good health and have many happy memories to look upon."

Oregon Journal
July 7, 1927

# Jesse M. Wise
# Portland, Oregon

"In the spring of 1849 Father went with Jesse Walling to the California gold fields. At first he mined around Sacramento but later moved up near Scott's Bar and Yreka.

"The bear attacked them. Baker threw down his gun and started off at full speed, calling over his shoulder as he went, "Boys, you kill the bear."

"The Indians stole the horses of the party of miners my father was with. They followed the Indians 40 miles and when they caught up with them they found they had killed one of the horses and were eating it. The man whose horse had been killed was so angry that he grabbed a squaw and shot her through the head, killing her. One of the other miners, seeing an Indian crouched behind some sagebrush, shot and killed him. They got all of their horses back except the one that had been killed. Later the Indians attacked them during the night and shot and killed the man who was guarding the horses. While they were camped on the river bottom a cloudburst occurred up in the hills and washed their tents and supplies and sluice boxes away.

"One day Father was out with two members of his company, Baker and Davis, and he saw a grizzly bear. Father shot at it, breaking one of its hind legs. The bear attacked them. Baker threw down his gun and started off at full speed, calling over his shoulder as he went, 'Boys, you kill the bear.' My father and Davis had to put 24 bullets into that grizzly before he was willing to quit fighting. They were offered $1 a pound for the meat, and as the grizzly weighed over 1000 pounds, that meant $1000, but their claim was so rich that the offer didn't mean much to them, for they could wash out $1000 in coarse gold and nuggets in a week or ten days. In fact, the miners thought that gold was so plentiful it would lose its value and probably come down to about the same value as silver. Father brought back with him to the Willamette Valley a jar of gold dust and nuggets which he sold for something over $3000."

Oregon Journal
December 2, 1929

# David Caufield
# Oregon City, Oregon

"Those days are very different from today. For example, at the close of school the teacher gave all of the boys apples and what was called apple toddy, which was made of water, whiskey, and sugar with apples sliced in it. He let them have all they wanted, with the result that there wasn't a single student able to walk home. All of the boys were dead drunk."

Oregon Journal
undated

# John U. Smith
# Newberg, Oregon

*A few days ago I stood on the porch of John U. Smith's farm house four miles northwest of Newberg and looked out over the beautiful rolling hills and prairies of the Chehalem Valley. Pointing to a symmetrical oak about half a mile away, Mr. Smith said:*

"That tree grew from an acorn planted by my mother when she was a girl. She planted it on the grave of Ewing Young. It was the death of Ewing Young that was one of the leading causes for the establishment of civil government in Oregon. He died intestate, and the settlers felt there should be some legal way of disposing of his property.

"My father, Sidney Smith, who came to Oregon in 1839, worked for Ewing Young. Young was an old time mountain man and trapper who finally settled in the Chehalem Valley. He brought a lot of cattle from California. He took up a claim here in the Chehalem Valley. In those days the Willamette Valley was unsettled, so he claimed the valley from Wapato Lake to the river east of Newberg, and from the summit of Chehalem Mountains on the north to the Handley Hills to the south. When Father was working for Ewing Young this whole valley was covered with a luxuriant growth of wild grass so high that a man could ride through it on horseback and be completely hidden from sight. My father was with Ewing Young when he died. Young had suffered from many years of indigestion and the medicine which he took for his indigestion ate through his stomach.

"My father was born at Syracuse, New York, in 1809. He was 30 years old when he came to Oregon. Before working for Ewing Young he worked for a while for the Hudson's Bay Company, but it was used to having employees subservient, and my father was very independent, so that they fell out and he quit its employ.

"My father was a member of the celebrated Peoria Party. Jason Lee gave a lecture at Peoria in the fall of 1838. One of the Chinook Indian boys he took there, Thomas Adams, took sick and was left at Peoria. He told the young men of Peoria what a wonderful place Oregon was, for game and fish. When he told them about the vast number of salmon in the river some of the young men of Peoria decided to go to Oregon and establish a fishery at the mouth of the Columbia. A party of young men consisting of Joseph Holman, whose grandson James Holman Albert, is cashier of the Capital National Bank at Salem; Thomas J. Farnham, Amos Cook, Francis Fletcher, R. L. Kilborne, J. Wood, C. Wood, three men named Oakley, Jourdan and Blair, and my father, banded together and early in May left Peoria for Independence, Missouri.

"The disagreements always incident to traveling across the plains caused dissension and the company broke up at Bent's Port. Members of the company came on to Oregon in smaller groups. Farnham, my father, and one or two others went on to Fort Hall, which they reached early in September. From there they went to Fort Boise, thence through the valley of Burnt River and on to the Grand Ronde Valley and so on to Whitman's Mission. After a brief visit there my father came on down to the Willamette Valley and went to work for Ewing Young. On October 21, 1839, which happened to be his 30th birthday, he helped build the first house at The Dalles.

"I have heard Father tell how he went barefoot for lack of moccasins, and how he worked for six bits a day, living on boiled wheat and deer meat, and how he finally bought a couple of yards of Hudson Bay flannel, cut a hole in the middle through which he put his head, and laced the edges together with buckskin thongs, which made a very durable if not very stylish shirt. He hired an Indian woman to make buckskin breeches.

"Father worked for a little while for the Methodist mission, rafting logs from Mission Bottom to Oregon City. When Ewing Young died my father bought his squatter's right as well as his brand, and the horses and cattle that were out in the hills, agreeing to pay $500 as the purchase price. Father built a log cabin and before long he was well to do in the wealth of the country, which at that time consisted of cattle.

"In 1845 a party of emigrants led by Stephen A. Douglas Meek, a brother of Joe Meek, took what has since been called 'Meek's Cutoff' and came to grief. Among the emigrants who were led astray on this wild goose chase to find a shorter route to the Willamette Valley was Daniel D. Bayley with his wife and seven children. When Mr. Bayley reached Portland he heard that my father was one of the old settlers in the country, so he came with his family to get Father's advice about taking a claim. When the Bayley's reached Father's house they found Father was gone. They had been living on salmon straight, with very little change for a couple of weeks, and when they saw a quarter of beef hung up in the cabin, as well as cream and butter, eggs, and a big pan of fritters, it

95

was more than they could stand. They pitched in and ate to their hearts' content. When my father came home he invited them to come in and help eat his fritters. Mrs. Bayley had to confess that the children had already eaten them all up, so she got a meal for them all.

•••••••••••••••••••••••••••••••••••••••••••••••••••••••

"Before my father had left New York, he had consulted a soothsayer and a crystal-gazer. She told him that in a far distant country he would meet a girl out at elbows, driving a pig, and that this girl would be his wife. When he came home that evening he saw my mother, who was dressed in a very ragged dress, driving a pig away from the house. He decided then and there that this was the girl of whom the crystal-gazer had told him, and he at once decided that she was to be his wife. He said to Mr. Bayley, 'Can I marry one of your girls?'

"Mr. Bayley answered, 'Well, I have five girls. Take your pick. You can have any one of them that will take you.'

"He picked out my mother and they were married."

**Oregon Journal**
undated

# Thomas C. Watts
# St. Helens, Oregon

"No, I wasn't born in Oregon. I was born at St. Louis, November 26, 1846. My father, William Watts, was born at Louisville, Kentucky. My mother was born in Germany. She was adopted by a wealthy couple who were childless. They moved to Kentucky where my mother's foster father bought a large plantation. He was very well off. I don't know what year my parents were married. I was my mother's eighth and last child. She died two hours after I was born. My mother's foster parents took me to raise. They taught me to look upon them as my grandparents.

"My father married again, marrying a young woman named Elizabeth Fuller. In the spring of 1852 my father, my stepmother, and my brothers and sisters started across the plains for Oregon. Father left me with my mother's foster parents.

"After he had traveled about a month, averaging 12 to 15 miles a day with his prairie schooner and ox teams, he got to studying over the matter and decided that my foster grandparents were old, and

96

if they died I might not be well raised, so he put
up the tent and told the folks to camp there till
he drove back to Louisville and got me. He rustled
a light wagon and a span of mules, so it took
him only a month to make the round trip. This
meant that they had lost a month, which threw
them later than most of the other Oregon-bound
emigrants, so we didn't get to Portland till long
after the winter rains had set in.

"He had huge antlers and a very
determined expression. His hair was
standing up on his shoulders as if his
temper had been pretty much upset...I
dropped my Kentucky rifle and beat
it as fast as I could go."

"No, I never saw my foster grandparents again.
They had made my mother heir and they never changed
their will, so when they died Mother's children
inherited the estate. A lawyer came clear out from
Louisville, Kentucky, to see Father about it. He
had Father sign a power of attorney and he took
the will back with him to settle up the estate.
After a year went by and Father didn't hear from
the lawyer he wrote back, but he had given the
lawyer the will and the power of attorney and everything had been converted into cash and the lawyer
had left and no one knew where he had gone.
So, as Kentucky was a long way from Oregon, Father
dropped the matter.
"As my own mother died at my birth, I know
little about her. My first stepmother died not long
after we had come to Oregon. My father married

97

again. This second stepmother left a lasting impression on me. What do I mean by a lasting impression? Just what I say. I will show you. See those scars on my arm? My second stepmother was a woman of sudden and violent temper, and she clubbed me with whatever was handy when she was out of humor, so I have scars all over my body to remind me of her.

"When Father got to Portland he looked around for a claim and finally bought a squatter's right from a settler to a half-section of land on Scappose Plains. My father, coming from Kentucky, was quite a hand to hunt, and most of his six sons took after him.

"I was the youngest boy, so they made me take care of the hounds they ran the deer with, so I didn't get to do much hunting. In those days, where the city of Scappose is now located was a great place for killing elk. Scappose Plains and Scappoose Mountain were alive with elk and deer.

"The first time I ever went out elk hunting my brother posted me by the trail and said he would run an elk past me and for me to shoot it as it came by. Pretty soon I heard the hounds giving tongue, and a little later along came a big elk. He had huge antlers and a very determined expression. His hair was standing up on his shoulders as if his temper was pretty much upset. I had been anxious up to then to see the elk, but when I saw him I was anxious he shouldn't see me, so I dropped my Kentucky rifle and beat it as fast as I could go. I didn't want any elk meat that morning. My brother was plumb disgusted with me.

"I once asked my father where was the best place to shoot a cougar. He told me there was only one place, and that was just back of the ear.

'One day I was going along with the hounds, for I had the entire care of the dogs. That was my job, and I was held responsible for them. I had my father's long-barreled Kentucky squirrel rifle along. Pretty soon the hounds gave tongue and were off. I followed them and when I caught up with them they were leaping up toward the lower limbs of a small tree where they had treed a cougar. I pointed my gun at the cougar, but he kept facing me so I couldn't get a shot at him back of his ear, where my father had told me to shoot. I walked around the tree two or three times, but the cougar kept twisting around and manged to keep facing me. Finally I threw my hat as far as I could throw it, and told the hounds to go fetch it. When they ran for it the cougar turned toward where

98

they had run and turned the side of his head toward me. I aimed for a point directly back of his ear. He gave a terrible squall when I fired, then jumped and fell out of the tree and a second later the hounds were on him. I saw he was dead, and as I didn't want the hounds to tear his skin, I called them off.

"I went home and told Father I had shot a big cougar. That was in 1858, so I was around 12 years old. Father said, 'Don't bother me. I guess what you shot was a chipmnuk.'

"Finally I persuaded him to go with me and see it. When he saw that big cougar lying by the tree he gave me Hail Columbia for shooting it. He said I might have wounded it and it would have torn me into cat meat. However, I think he was rather proud of me, for he bragged about it to some of the neighbors.

"I killed my first deer with a club. I went hunting with the boys and they wouldn't let me carry a gun, so I carried a heavy club. I stood beside a deer trail, and pretty soon along came a deer. I waited till it was directly beside me, and aimed a blow at its head. Either I was excited or the deer was, for it jumped, and I missed its head, but the club came down across its back and crippled it. It tried to run, but it dragged its hindquarters, so I caught it and killed it.

"Where I used to run the hounds after deer and elk is now all farming lands, cities, and paved highways. Where we traveled for hours without seeing a sign of cabins or clearings is now fenced fields, gardens and orchards. I sure have seen great changes since I came to this country, 73 years ago."

Oregon Journal
May 26, 1925

# Jesse M. Wise
# Portland, Oregon

"My father and mother were married in Illinois in the spring of 1859. Whenever there would be a severe thunder and lightning storm in Illinois Father would say, 'They have no severe storms in the Willamette Valley.' When you would have to wrap your muffler around your ears and put on your thickest mittens and tie gunnysacks around your feet and legs to work outdoors, Father would say, 'Right now there is a fine mist falling in western Oregon and you can plow all winter long in the Willamette Valley.' To my childish imagination it seemed that heaven was not located up above the clouds but across the Rocky Mountains on the shores of the Pacific, and that heaven's other name was the Willamette Valley."

**Oregon Journal**
December 7, 1929

# When I was at Pendleton . . .

*When I was at Pendleton I heard many interesting stories from Lot Livermore and the other old-time Pendletonians about Hank Vaughn. One of the most picturesque incidents was Vaughn's duel with Charley Long. Charlie and Hank held the opposite corners of a bandanna handkerchief and, at an agreed signal, began shooting. After they had emptied their guns, every shot taking effect, they fell to the floor and began pounding each other over the head with their empty guns. Finally they fainted from loss of blood. Hank was shot through the lungs, his wrist was broken and he was shot through the arm and leg. Long was also badly wounded. Both lived.*

*Some time after that Hank, who had broken his leg by a fall off a horse, was at the Villard House in Pendleton. Long came up from Long Creek to visit Hank. He asked someone what was the customary thing to do in such cases, and was told he should take Hank some flowers. Not being able to find any fresh flowers for sale, he went into a milliner's shop, purchased $10 worth of artificial flowers, took them up to Hank's room, and put them into a basin of water.*

*Oregon Journal*
*March 13, 1926*

# F. W. Settlemeier
# Woodburn, Oregon

"When Ben Holladay built the railroad Father decided to start a town there. He platted four blocks, A, B, C, and D, paralleling the railroad. In those days there was lots of timber around Woodburn. A lot of timber had been slashed and they were debating whether it would burn or not. They lit it, and it burned, all right. One of the men said, triumphantly, 'What did I tell you? I knew it would burn!'

"My father had been casting about in his mind for a good name for his town. He wanted something out of the ordinary, so he said, 'You said it would burn, and it did burn. I guess I'll call the town that.' So he named it Woodburn."

**Oregon Journal**
October 6, 1926

# Sam Tetherow
# Pioneer of 1845
# Dallas, Oregon

*Sam Tetherow looks and talks as if he had just stepped out of his covered wagon after crossing the plains. When I asked a fellow-townsman of Mr. Tetherow how to find Sam, he said: "Follow the road out toward the fairgrounds till you come to a large house with a big walnut tree in front of it. That's Sam's place. You will know Sam when you see him, for you can tell a Tetherow as far as you can see him."*

*I drove to the house with a wide-spreading black walnut tree in front of it and found Sam piling his winter's wood in the woodshed. "I was just hoping someone would come and drag me away from the woodshed," said Sam. "Piling wood is too much like work on a day as pretty as this." We walked around to the front of his house and sat on the front porch.*

*Sam's most visible and evident trait is good humor. "I have heard a lot from the old pioneers about your father, Sol Tetherow, and what a good man he was. Are you as good a man as your dad?" I asked.*

"That's a pretty hard question to start off with. Can't you lead off with a few easy ones and sort of work up to that one? It won't look well if I brag about what a hell of a good man I am, and, on the other hand, nobody likes to knock himself.

"As a matter of fact, my dad was a pretty good man. He was capable as well as popular. They elected him captain of the wagon train when we came to Oregon in 1845. If you think it's any snap to run a wagon train of 65 wagons with every man in the train having a different idea of what is the best thing to do, all I can say is that some day you ought to try it, and you'll change your opinion.

"My father, Sol Tetherow, was born in Tennessee in 1800, so he was 45 years old when he headed westward with his prairie schooner for the Willamette Valley. My mother's name before she was married was Ibbie Baker. They had 15 children and raised ten of them, five boys and five girls. There are only two of us left now, my sister, Martha Jane Burns, who lives at Portland, and myself.

"Yes, 15 children are quite a few, but in those days big families were the rule, not the exception. Now it's the other way around. A family of 15 children gives you quite a chance to pick out names. Take the ten of us that grew up, for example. My sister Evaline married Paul Hilderbrand, who crossed the plains with us in 1845. Lucindy married Bill Parker. Next came my brother Andrew Jackson Tetherow. I was the next and was born near Platte City, in Platte County, Missouri, March 6, 1836. Next after me came Thomas Benton Tetherow, then Emily, who married Harry Christian; then William Linn Tetherow, who was followed by James K. Polk Tetherow. Martha was next, and after Martha came Cynthia Ann, who married R. M. Johnson.

"I had just passed the age of 9 when we started for Oregon, so I remember the incidents of our trip across the plains very clearly. One of my brothers, David Atchison, who was a twin brother of William Linn, died while we were crossing the plains.

"Nearly 3000 people came across the plains in 1845. Two wagon trains left from Independence. One of them was captained by Presley Welch. Joel Palmer and Sam A. Barlow were his assistants. Another, of about 40 wagons, was in charge of Samuel Hancock. Three good-sized wagon trains left St. Joe. One of them had A. Hackleman as captain. Another, of something over 60 wagons, chose W. G. T'Vault as captain, with John Waymire and James Allen as assistants.

"My father had charge of the other wagon train that left from St. Joe. Nearly 200 families of the emigration of 1845 left the main road at Hot Springs, near Fort Boise, and took what was said to be a cut-off for Oregon. Stephen Meek acted as their guide. They followed an old trail of a fur trapper, but they got off the trail in the Malheur country and had all sorts of grief. It was members of this party, near the head of the Malheur River, who found gold known as the Blue

102

Bucket diggings.

"Three of the 15 children in our family were born after we reached Oregon. We reached what is now Dallas on November 16, 1845. My father bought Sol Shelton's squatter's right to a section of land. He didn't exactly buy him out, but he swapped him a brindle ox named Bright for his square mile of land. The city of Dallas is located on that claim, but it's worth a lot more than a Brindle ox today.

"I crawled on out and scalped him and brought his scalp in to prove to the boys that I had made a good Indian of him. The other Indian I killed was where I couldn't get at him without losing my own scalp, so I let him keep his."

"In 1847 Father found a claim he liked better than the Shelton claim. It was located where the two forks of the Luckiamute come together, so he took up 640 acres there as his donation land claim.

"When I was younger I used to do a good bit of running around. I packed into the Caribou mines from Dallas. We weren't much on speed, but we were strong on distance. I traveled on horseback with a pack horse over 1100 miles before I struck a claim that suited me, and at that I just about broke even on the trip.

"In 1862 I bought up a lot of bacon here in the valley at ten cents a pound and packed it to the mines at Bannock City, where I sold it for 48 cents a pound. I also tried my luck at Canyon City and John Day. Some years later I took up a claim in Harney Valley, about a mile and a half from Burns. I had to leave it for a little while to come back to the valley, and while I was gone someone stole all of my barb wire and tore down my cabin and carted off the lumber. That made me kind of peeved, so I sold my claim and decided to stay here in the valley.

"I ate horsemeat and fought Indians in the Yakima Indian War. I enlisted in Captain A. N. Armstrong's company. There were 104 men in our company and we were enrolled on October 15, 1855. Two weeks later Captain Armstrong was elected major and Ben Hayden became our captain. Our lieutenants were Ira S. Townsend, Francis M. Goff, and David Cosper.

"While I was at The Dalles word came that two companies of volunteers were surrounded by Indians and were nearly out of ammunition. A detail of 11 men was selected to go from The Dalles to the Walla Walla country with 600 pounds of ammunition. Captain Hembree, who was on his way to join his company, joined us, and a French Canadian who was familiar with the country served as guide. We pushed forward as hard as the horses could go. This was in November, 1855.

"Quite a number of men from the companies of Captains Cornelius, Bennett and Hembree had been discharged at The Dalles by Colonel Nesmith, as there were no horses for them and the men couldn't do anything as foot soldiers. Major Chinn, with about 150 volunteers, had been sent to the mouth of the Touchet to protect the baggage and pack trains. Colonel Kelly at the same time with about 250 men marched higher up on the Touchet, where Chief Peu-Peu-Mox-Mox, with several of his tribe, came in under a flag of truce. In the battle that took place a day or two later this chief, with the other prisoners who had come in with a flag of truce, were killed while they were trying to escape.

"In the four days' fight that took place I got two Indians. One of them was hidden in some brush and kept shooting at our men. My gun didn't carry very far, so I had to crawl out quite a distance to get into good range, and when he rose to shoot I got him. I crawled on out and scalped him and brought his scalp in to prove to the boys that I had made a good Indian of him. The other Indian I killed was where I couldn't get at him without losing my own scalp, so I let him keep his.

"In the fight near the farm La Roque a lot of us on the best horses had got ahead of the others. The Indians had barricaded themselves where they could shoot us and where we couldn't get at them. Several of our men had been killed and wounded. Captain Wilson of Company A soon arrived, and a little later Captain Bennett with Company F came up. We drove the Indians away from where they were. The fell back and went into a farmhouse, from which they kept picking away at us.

"Captain Bennett came to the major and asked for permission to charge the farmhouse and dislodge the Indians. The major was against it, and told him it would result only in the needless loss of men, that we could surround the place and capture the Indians. Captain Bennett came back again and asked permission to charge the farmhouse. The major said, 'I am against it, but do as you please about it. If you think best, go ahead.'

"Captain Bennett was a brave officer, but hadn't been trained to fight Indians as the Indians fight, by taking advantage of every bit of cover. The volunteers had enlisted to kill Indians and not to salute officers and to be taught to act pretty with a gun. Captain Bennett was strong for drill in the manual of arms, and so he wasn't very popular with the volunteers.

"When he had obtained permission to charge the farmhouse, instead of scattering his men out he had them charge in company front, as if they were at drill. As they started forward toward the fence around the farmhouse one of the Indians in the farmhouse picked off Captain Bennett, and a private in Company A was also killed. The Indians had all the fighting at the 'Four Day Fight' there, and skedaddled.

"The next spring, while we were out scouting after Indians, we went up into the Yakima Country. On Cannon Creek, early in April, we ran across the Indians. Captain Hembree with several of the volunteers started for the top of the ridge to see if he could locate the Indians and find out how many there were. Not far from the camp they ran across some horses, and as they approached them the Indians, who had seen Captain Hembree and the volunteers coming, attacked them. From camp we could see everything that happened. Captain Hembree fought bravely and killed two of the Indians, but he himself was killed and scalped. Major Cornoyer followed the Indians, overtook them and killed six of them. They took the body of Captain Hembree to The Dalles and from there they shipped it to his home in LaFayette, where they held a big funeral.

"In the spring of 1856 we were mustered out. You can make up your mind we were pretty glad to get home where we could get something fit to eat, for a good deal of the time when we were chasing the Indians we lived on horse meat straight, without salt, coffee or bread."

"After I came back from Walla Walla I went to work on the farm. When I was 22 I married Henrietta Griffith, daughter of John W. Griffith, who came across the plains in 1842. We had four children, all boys. My oldest boy, Columbus M. Tetherow, has a farm on the Luckiamute. My next boy, King Solomon Tetherow, owns a candy store at Spokane. Kane Tetherow lives at Northport, to the northward of Spokane. My youngest boy, Sammy, is a farmer and lives about five miles east of Dallas.

"My first wife died in 1887. After her death I married a widow named Isoline Holman."

Oregon Journal
undated

# Robert Starkey
# Riverboat Pilot
# Marshfield, Oregon

"I became a pilot on the Sacramento River. The present city of Sacramento was known at that time as Embarcadero. There were no frame buildings there--just tents. There were a tent store, a tent restaurant and a tent saloon."

Oregon Journal
June 1, 1922

# E. E. Sharon
# Portland, Oregon

"C. S. Jackson and I were about of an age. He was about 19 or 20 when he landed at Pendleton. He was as green as the grass on the hills of his native Virginia, but was good-hearted and willing to work. He began looking for a job and was referred to J. B. Keeney, who gave him a job as stage agent at Pendleton. The day after he started to work one of the stage drivers came in, sized him up, and after talking to him a few moments said, 'Why in hell are you loafing here? Don't you know the stage agent is required to wash the stage as soon as it comes in from its run?'

"Sam went down to the stage barn and got busy with a sponge and a pail of water. Before long J. B. Keeney dropped in and said, 'What in hell do you mean by doing the hostler's work? I hired you to run the stage office. Get back there right away and don't let any more stage drivers impose on you.'"

Oregon Journal
October 31, 1925

# Haman Shelton
# Pioneer of 1847
# Scio, Oregon

"When there used to be saloons in Scio, in the early days, the city marshal had his hands full, particularly when the Thomas boys came in from their place. They used to be good rough and tumble scrappers, but once I saw Ike Griffon and his gang clean the Thomas boys up. They started the fight in the Saloon and finally ended it in the street and it was certainly some fight. The Thomas boys were quiet, hard-working boys when they were sober, but when they got a few drinks in them they could lick their weight in wildcats."

Oregon Journal
March 31, 1926

# Cash Weir
# Portland, Oregon

"In those days they used to run deer with hounds. We would often see deer or bear swimming across the Columbia or the Willamette. I saw a big buck swimming across the Columbia one day, so I signaled to a man on shore and pointed to where the buck was going to come out. The man ran down the river bank and caught the buck by the horns as it came out of the water. He didn't hold it more than a minute, though, and he was

the maddest man you ever saw. That buck's hoof
were as sharp as a razor. He undressed that man
in less than 60 seconds. He not only cut his clothes
off, but he took off a great deal of the man's hide.

"Along about 1873 we moved to Lewis River.
We lived at Bratton's Bend. I used to be a great
hand to hunt when I was a boy. One night one
of our cows failed to come up. I took my single-

"I jumped a-straddle of him and
pulled his head up by the horns so
I could cut his throat. The minute he
felt the knife up he jumped and away
we went. I guess that deer was scared,
all right, but compared to my feelings
he didn't know what scared meant. I
hung on for dear life."

barrel muzzle-loading shotgun and went out to hunt
up the cow. While walking along the trail I suddenly
ran into a big cougar. We were so close that I
could have put my hand on his head. He jumped
one way and I jumped the other. I pulled up my

gun and let him have a charge of birdshot, and I think he must have jumped 20 feet. Tom Hollingsworth took up his trail and killed him. He was a big one.

"I had a hunting dog, half bull and half black and tan. I used to think that dog would lick anything on four legs. I went out hunting pheasants one day and suddenly heard a lot of squalling in the brush. My dog had bayed a big bear. Every time the bear would get down on all fours to leave, Jack, my dog, would grab him by the hindquarters. I ran toward the bear and shot him. That made the bear mad, and he ran toward me. I fell over backwards into some brush, and if it hadn't been for Jack jumping the bear and keeping him busy that bear would have taken a sample bite or so out of me. No, I didn't follow him. I kind of lost my appetite for bear hunting when the bear turned the tables and started hunting me.

"One time I went out deer hunting with some fellows. I loaded my gun with four fingers of powder and put in a handful of buckshot. The two fellows I was with told me to stand on the trail and they would go and hunt a deer.

"The dog turned a deer and the first thing I knew a big six-point buck was coming down the trail headed for me, and looking as if he meant business. When he saw me his eyes turned green and the hair on his shoulders rose. I let drive and some of the buckshot got him, for he slowed down. I dropped my gun and ran after him to finish him with my 22-calibre pistol. I might as well have tried to slap him on the wrist, as far as hurting him with my little toy pistol. I followed him and presently I saw where he was lying down in a little fir grove.

"I jumped a-straddle of him and pulled his head up by the horns so I could cut his throat. The minute he felt the knife up he jumped and away we went. I guess that deer was scared, all right, but compared to my feelings he didn't know what scared meant. I hung on for dear life. He bucked me off, and as I tried to roll out of the way he jumped at me to strike me with his hoofs. My dog jumped at him, so he turned his attention to the dog. In a moment or so he started to run away, but before he had run very far he dropped, and when I got to him he was dead.

"When I was about 14 years, while we were living at Bratton's Bend, my mother got sick one night. It was a winter night, there was snow on the ground, and it was bright moonlight. It was about four miles to La Center. Father said to me, 'Cash, you strike right out for La Center and tell the doctor to come back with you.'

"I wasn't very anxious to go. As a matter of fact, I was afraid, but I saw that my father meant business, and that I'd have to go, so I got a good heavy club and took a short cut through the timber. I kept feeling that something was back of me. I looked around and, sure enough, there was a cougar following me close enough to sniff my heels. I let out a yell and struck him as hard as I could on the head with my club, and ran all the rest of the way to La Center. When I told the doctor that a cougar had followed me and that I hit him, he didn't believe it.

"He said, 'A cougar wouldn't attack a man.' And I guess he is right, for I never heard of one attacking a man.

" I said, 'Maybe he wasn't going to attack me, but it made me awful nervous to have him follow me along and smell my heels.'

"The doctor and I went by that same short cut to see if we could see the cougar's tracks. I sure hit that cougar a good lick. I guess I must have broken his neck. In any event, we found him lying in the trail. He wasn't very large --about six feet long--and he was thin and gaunt.

"One time when work on the river was slack I got a job as engineer in a sawmill at Gold Creek, Montana. It was summer, so we all slept outdoors under the trees. One morning just before daylight we heard one of the oxen bawling mournfully. The bullwhacker said, 'They've got old Jerry, at last.'

"I said, 'Who's got him?'

"He answered, 'A grizzly bear.'

"We grabbed up some pitch pine kindling and started to rescue Jerry. Pat Meyers and I got within ten feet of Jerry before the grizzly would let go of him. Pat and I were ahead. When the grizzly let go of Jerry he started for us. We hollered, 'Beat it, fellows. The bear is after us!'

"We never stopped for any trail. We ran through the brush for the camp, regardless. We heard the bear breaking through the brush after us, and we put on another burst of speed. When Pat and I got to camp we discovered that it was Jerry, the ox, not the grizzly that had been following us.

"Jerry's hide was ripped from his shoulder to his belly, and the bear had bitten two big chunks of meat out of his back. I never knew before that a bear would eat an ox alive. Poor old Jerry was so badly mangled and lost so much blood that he

passed in his checks. A bear can't catch an ox
or a horse once in a thousand times, for whenever
a bear approaches a band of cattle or horses, some
one of the animals gives the alarm. The way this
bear caught Jerry was by jumping over a small
evergreen back of which Jerry happened to be lying."

Oregon Journal
March 8 & 10, 1928

The bullwhacker said, 'They've got
old Jerry at last.'
    I said, "Who's got him?'
    He answered, "A grizzly bear."

# Uncle Sammy Burch
## Pioneer of 1847
## Rickreall, Oregon

*Uncle Sammy Burch lives at Rickreall, where he has resided for the past 75 years. A day or so ago while in Dallas, I took the motor to Nesmith and walked down the highway to Rickreall and spent the afternoon with Uncle Sammy. He lies in a fine old-time Southern mansion on the banks of the Rickreall. It is like stepping back into the past to visit his home with its big fireplaces and large, comfortable rooms. As we sat in front of the cheerful blaze thrown out by the logs of body fir and applewood, Mr. Burch said, in answer to my questions:*

"I am 91 years old. I was born in Missouri on January 13, 1831. I am named for my father, Samuel Burch. My father was in the war of 1812. He was a midshipman in the United States Navy and was captured by the English. Father lived in Maryland. My mother's maiden name was Eleanor S. Locke and she was born in Virginia. Her people moved to Missouri in 1818, while my father, with his people, went to Missouri in 1820. They met and were married there. My mother was Father's second wife. By his first wife he had three children, all boys. Their names were George Washington, Jonathan Tyrus, and John Wesley. By his second wife, my mother, he had nine children.

"Benjamin Franklin Burch was my brother. He came to Oregon two years before we did, to spy out the land and send back a report. He came in 1845. Ben was born May 2, 1825. He taught the first school in Polk County. Elizabeth, the next child, married James A. Foster. Mary Louise, my next sister, married him after the death of my sister Elizabeth. I was the next child and was christened Samuel Townsend Burch. Mary E. was the next child. She married John Jeffies. Then came the twins, Thomas and Laura. Jacob, the next child, married Angeline Nance. Eleanor was the last child, for Father was killed shortly afterwards.

"I was in my seventeenth year when we crossed the plains. My job was to drive the loose cattle, and if you want to know what dust is just drive a bunch of loose cattle on a windy day. You'll eat your peck of dust, all right. On the banks of the Sweetwater we laid over to bury my brother Wesley's wife. We buried her by the side of the

Old Oregon Trail, drove the oxen over her grave till it was well trodden, and then built a fire over it so the Indians would not discover the grave and dig her up to get the clothes she had on. My brother Ben, who had come here in 1845, started back to meet us. He met us at Bear River.

"We had divided our train into three at Ash Hollow, and after that we didn't have any captain. Captain Levi Scott had come from the Willamette Valley the year before to find an easier way for the emigrants. My brother Ben was one of his party. They surveyed a way by the southern route. Captain Scott met us near Fort Hall. He acted as our guide by the southern route.

"It was on this trip that the emigrants were attacked by Indians and some of their loose cattle were shot. Henry Williamson, one of the men guarding the cattle, was wounded. Garrison, who went with Captain Levi Scott from Polk County to Fort Hall to meet and guide the emigrants, was killed near Granite Ridge by Indians. Captain Levi Scott, though his arm was pinned to his side with an arrow, drew his revolver and killed the Indian. The Indians also attacked the train near Tule Lake, but were driven off. We settled here on the Rickreall.

"In 1849, with nearly everyone else in the Willamette Valley who could possibly get away, I went to the gold mines in California. I came back home late that fall and wintered at the home place. The next spring I went to the Yreka diggings and in 1852 to the newly discovered placer mines in Jackson County, at Jacksonville. I had a pretty fair claim on Jackson Creek. The next year I went to Coos and Curry Counties and mined near the mouth of the Rogue River in the beach diggings. William H. Packwood was also there, mining. He was the last survivor among the signers of the state constitutional convention.

"When I used to go to school, 75 years ago, the geographies called all the country between the Missouri River and the Rocky Mountains the Great American Desert. When I was going to school I never expected to cross the Great American Desert, let alone see it developed into a land of orchards, pastures and grain fields.

"I did my first Indian fighting in 1853. I was with General Joe Lane when he was wounded late that summer. The Indians went on the warpath in August and burned the settlers' cabins from Cow Creek southward almost to Jacksonville. General Lane was in the Rogue River Valley at the time and was asked by the settlers to take charge of the volunteers and punish the Indians. Colonel

John E. Ross of Jacksonville and Captain Alden, a regular army officer, with their men, served under General Lane.

"The Indians, led by Old Joe, Sam, John, and Limpy, were burning cabins and killing settlers wherever they found them. We moved northward in pursuit and came on them in Evans Creek country, toward the latter part of August. The Indians had built a log fort on the hillside. Our men charged. General Lane was shot through the arm. Captain Alden was wounded, and Captain Pleasant Armstrong of Yamhill County was instantly killed by a bullet through the heart. When the Indians recognized General Joe Lane they called out to him to have his men stop firing and they would also stop, as they wanted to have a peace talk. General Lane ordered us to cease firing, and walked, alone, into the Indian camp, where he agreed with the Indians on an armistice for ten days, after which a peace talk should be held at Table Rock.

"General Lane sent for General Joel Palmer of Dayton, who was superintendent of Indian Affairs for Oregon. We camped near Table Rock, waiting for the conference to be held. While we were waiting, George L. Curry, who was acting governor, sent reinforcements. Major Rains of Fort Vancouver furnished guns and ammunition. Captain Nesmith, with his volunteers and with a howitzer and the muskets and ammunition, reached our camp on September 8. Captain A. J. Smith of the regular army, with his soldiers, also joined our force on that day.

••••••••••••••••••••••••••••••••••••••••••••••••••••••

*Right here is a good place to describe briefly the outcome of that conference. General Lane suggested to Captain Nesmith that they go unarmed to the Indian camp and negotiate the treaty. Captain Nesmith, who knew the character of the Rogue River Indians, protested and said that while he was willing to obey as a soldier and lead his company of volunteer cavalrymen into the fight, he did not feel like going unarmed and giving himself into the power of the Indians.*

*General Lane said, "I have given my word to the Indians to go unarmed. If you are afraid to go as an interpreter, I will not insist."*

*Captain Nesmith said, "I haven't any more fear than you have, only I know we shall all be killed. However, if you insist on going, I will go as interpreter."*

*On the morning of September 10, 1853, General Lane, General Palmer, Indian Agent S. P. Culver, Captain A. J. Smith of the First Dragoons, Captain L. F. Mosher, Colonel John E. Ross, Captain J.*

W. Nesmith, Lieutenant A. V. Kautz, R. B. Metcalf, J. D. Mason, and T. T. Tierney mounted their horses and rode across the valley to the foot of Table Rock. Tying their horses there, they went afoot for nearly a mile to where the Indians were camped on the summit of Table Rock. There were about 700 warriors in the camp. Captain Smith's company of dragoons could be plainly seen, drawn up in formation in the valley below. General Lane and Superintendent Palmer made speeches to the Indians, which were translated by Captain Nesmith. When a Rogue River Indian spoke, another Indian would translate his speech into Chinook, so that Captain Nesmith could understand it, and Captain Nesmith would then translate it into English.

In the midst of the conference a naked Indian ran into camp, covered with sweat and dust, and said a company of white men on Applegate Creek had captured an Indian that morning, tied him to a tree, and killed him. Instantly all was commotion. The Indians seized their guns and the interpreter told Captain Nesmith they had decided to tie the white men to trees and kill them to avenge the death of the Indian.

General Lane, whose arm was in a sling, said to Captain Nesmith, "Tell the Indians that I will punish the white men for murdering the Indian. They are not our soldiers. We have come into your camp in good faith, unarmed. You can kill us, but if you do the soldiers will hunt your tribe from the face of the earth and kill you all. What are you going to do about it?"

The Indians decided to put up their guns and to go ahead with the conference. A treaty was arranged and no more trouble occurred until the Yakima Indian War broke out in 1855.

Oregon Journal
March 12 & 13, 1922

# H. C. Todhunter
## Canyon City Undertaker
## Portland, Oregon

"I ran an undertaking parlor in Canyon City some years. I buried a large number of inmates of the poorhouse who at one time had been wealthy. Many of them were old-time California miners, and quite a few had made good stakes at Canyon City, but booze and gambling proved their undoing."

Oregon Journal
February 10, 1928

# Wilson Benefiel
## Lone Fir Cemetery
## Portland, Oregon

"We do not inquire as to the character or lack of it of those who buy lots here. As a consequence I can point out to you the graves of women who were famous in the red light district when Portland was a wide-open town. I can point out the graves of well known gamblers, and of several men who have been hanged. There is no line of social cleavage among the dead. No matter how much better or finer clay a person thinks himself when he is alive, when he dies he finds that if he is a general, he will not outrank the private whose body lies nearby, and the judge and the prisoner he has passed sentence upon find equality and oblivion in the grave."

Oregon Journal
April 23, 1925

# Delazon Smith
## Pioneer of Albany
## Albany, Oregon

*The following is from a letter written by Delazon Smith of Albany, Oregon, to his brother, J. B. Smith, of Freeport, Illinois, in 1854.*

"The Indian war you allude to as having occurred in Oregon was in the Rogue River Valley (now termed Gold River) more than 200 miles south of my residence. There are but very few Indians in this vicinity. Indeed, I don't see one once a month. Twenty-five white men well armed could drive every Indian out of this county. We cannot realize that we are in an Indian country, and do not live in any more fear of them than you do in Illinois. Even in the newer portions of the country, more recently and more sparsely settled, where the white settlers are more exposed to danger, there are idle, roving desperate men and miners who like no better 'fun' or 'pastime' than to shoot Indians. The race of red men upon this coast will soon be extinct. God pity them!"

Oregon Journal
May 31, 1923

# William L. Toney
## Pioneer of 1847
## McMinnville, Oregon

"My father, James Toney, was born in Virginia, and my mother, whose maiden name was Patsy Thornton, in South Carolina. I am their eldest child. I was 20 years old when we came across the plains to Oregon in 1847. I was born in Missouri, January 30, 1827. Yes, I am 95 years old. Did you ever notice that a cracked cup lasts longer than one that isn't? I guess they take better care of it. In spite of lack of health in my early manhood, and many other handicaps, I am still here, after 95 years, hale and hearty.

"I have the uneducated man's reverence and respect for books and education. You see, I could not read when I was married, so I was also handicapped by lack of education. I never spent but 25 cents in my life for a school book, and that was a copy of the old-fashioned Blue Back spelling book. I started to school when I was 17 years old, but the teacher got sick after six weeks, so my education stopped with six weeks' schooling. When the school started again I had to help my father.

"My father had bought the county rights to a shingling machine. He was to pay some cash and to give 40,000 good oak shingles for the county rights. We set up the shingling machine, and I ran it. We hired men at two bits a day to fell the oak trees and to saw them up into blocks. We had to pay an expert machinist $10 a month to run the steam chest and to look after the shingling machine.

"We used to put the oak blocks into the steam box and boil and steam them all night. Next morning he and I would run the shingling machine and make about 3000 good oak shingles a day. When I left St. Joe in the spring of 1847, there were not over ten houses in the entire place that were not shingled with oak shingles that I had helped to make. You see, I ran that shingling machine from the time I was 17 until I was 20.

"I figured on going to school when I got Father's debts cleared up, but I had a spell of sickness that settled in my eyes, and for three years my eyes were very weak.

"We used to make about 3000 shingles a day. We got $2 a thousand for them. That meant we were making $6 a day, but of course we had to pay out of this, $10 a month for the machinist and two bits a day for the men who got out the oak blocks. And then, we had to pay for the timber, so it wasn't all profit by a long shot.

"When we started from St. Joe in 1847, we organized as a military company. We busted up within a week. Pretty nearly everyone in the company had a different notion of what we ought to do and who should be officers.

"For example, Henderson Luelling said he didn't start across the plains to kill Indians or to learn any army tactics. He was a sort of Quaker and believed in doing to others as he would be done by. He believed that if we treated the Indians fairly they wouldn't bother us. You know, I have about come to that conclusion myself. Away back in 1854 I decided that from that time on I was going to treat people the way I wanted them to treat me, and, surprising as it may seem, it works. In any event, that company busted into little groups, and after that we didn't have any captain.

"Before I forget it I want to tell you about Henderson Luelling. Pretty nearly everyone that saw him told him how many kinds of a fool he was for trying to bring his traveling nursery across the plains. He had built two long, narrow boxes that just fitted into the bed of his wagon. He had filled them with charcoal, manure, and earth and planted apples, pears, plums, cherries, quinces, grapes and other fruits in them. He would water his trees, which ranged from three to five feet high, every night and morning. In spite of everybody's advice that he could never get them across the plains, he did get them to The Dalles, where he took them out of their boxes, wrapped them up carefully and took them down the Columbia River by boat and started a nursery not far from Milwaukee. Those fruit trees became the parent stock of most of the orchards in the Willamette Valley.

"There were five wagons in our bunch--our family, my brother-in-law, Owen P. Turner, Henry and Bill Warren, and John Watts. We traveled together clear across the plains. Coming across the plains the Indians stole two of our animals, a mare and a horse. We also lost one at Willow Creek, but Tom McKay sent out word to the Indians they would have to bring it in, so we got it back. When we got to The Dalles there was two feet of snow in the mountains.

"About two weeks before we got into The Dalles three men overtook our wagon train and said they were going to Portland. They told Father that he would have to build boats at The Dalles and if he would board them for the rest of the trip they would stop over and help him build the boats

118

to go down the Columbia River. We boarded the men until we got to The Dalles, when they immediately vamoosed and that was the last we ever saw of them.

"Daniel Barnes, my cousin, who was already in Oregon, came up to The Dalles to take the women folks down the river in his boat. The men cut timber and made a raft. My father and my two brothers drove the cattle overland down to Fort Vancouver, while Collins and I took charge of the raft and brought the wagons down the river.

"We were pretty nearly out of money when we got to Vancouver, so Father and I stopped there and worked for a man named Covington. He had been an employee of the Hudson's Bay Company and he had a big log house out on Fourth Plains, not far from the present town of Orchards. And, by the way, that old log house is still standing there and is one of the oldest in the state of Washington. Mr. Covington was a teacher, a very aristocratic man and rather good looking. He hired us to cut rails for him to build a fence around his place. He paid us one dollar per 100. In those days the Hudson's Bay Company's cattle ranged all over the country. He didn't want them to get into his wheat, so he had us make a stake-and-rider fence nine rails high. We didn't care how high it was, so long as we got our dollar a hundred for cutting the rails. We made a good, substantial fence and locked it so the cattle couldn't knock it down. After we got the place fenced, he had us plow and seed 15 acres. We worked for him until the middle of February, 1848.

"My brother-in-law came and got the stock and took them into Yamhill to Uncle Jesse Henderson's place. We left our wagons at Portland. We went over the Indian trail past Wapato Lake and on to where the town of Sheridan is now located.

"My father took up a donation land claim near Sheridan. He didn't exactly take it up. He bought the squatter's right from Zed Martin. The way it came about was like this: A young fellow had taken it up, but had enlisted to fight the Cayuse War. This young chap died of the measles in Portland. Zed Martin claimed the young fellow owed him about $50, so he took the claim in settlement of the debt. Father gave Martin a yoke of oxen for it. My brother-in-law, Owen P. Turner, traded a pony for a fine half section of land. Later we bought Zed Martin's place for $800. He had a good cabin put up and 30 acres under fence. I took up a claim in the fall of 1848.

"In the spring of 1848 they decided to raise

more troops to serve in the Cayuse War. They raised three additional companies. One company was enlisted in Polk and Clackamas Counties under J. W. Nesmith. Captain William P. Pugh raised a company in Linn County, and William J. Martin raised a company in Yamhill and Tualatin. I enlisted in Bill Martin's company. We were mustered in about the middle of April.

"The different men that knew each other chipped in and formed different messes. G. W. Burnett, father of George H. Burnett, now supreme judge, with the three Martin boys and Riley Bean and I made up the mess. Bean furnished an extra horse for us to use for our pack horse. Grandmother Cooper had just brought in some groceries from the Sandwich Islands to Portland, so we bought from her some sugar, tea and coffee. We also bought 100 pounds of flour. We then started for The Dalles.

"When we got to the lower rapids Martin thought the road was too rough for our pack horse to carry our load. He found that a boat with rations for the soldiers was about to start up the river to The Dalles, so he asked the man in charge if they would take our provisions. They said if he would furnish a hand they would carry our supplies. Martin asked me if I would help row the boat from the Cascades to The Dalles. I had had considerable experience boating when I lived on the river near St. Joe, Missouri, from the time I was 17 until I was 20, so I told him I would do it.

"We portaged the goods around the Cascades. Then the man in charge of the boats tried to cordelle the boat around the falls. One man was put into the boat with a pike pole to keep the boat from hitting the rocks. The boat got caught in the current and came back like chain lightning.

"I was a modest Missouri boy and kind of bashful, but I saw right away that if they did not change their tactics they were going to wreck that boat and lose our provisions as well as their own. An officer named Coffin was in charge of the boat. They stood around talking quite a while about how they were going to get the boat through the rapids and up over the falls. Finally I mustered up courage and, stepping up to him, said, 'Sir, if you want me to, I can rig up a tackle on that boat so she will go up the river.'

"He turned and saw how young and inexperienced-looking I was and, turning on his heel, said, 'What in hell do you know about it? When I want your advice I'll ask for it.'

"Well, sir, I didn't like that very much, but he was an officer and I was a private, so

I kept out of their way and let them go on with their powwow. Finally, when they had all concluded they couldn't get the boat up on account of the rocks, he came to me and said, 'If I should decide to ask your advice, what would be your plan?'

"I knew by the way they had handled it that there wasn't a boatman in the crowd. I showed him how I would rig up ropes from bow to stern. He said, 'I don't understand your scheme, but it looks reasonable. I will put you in charge and hold you responsible for getting the boat through the rapids. I directed the men on shore how to manipulate the ropes and I took charge of the boat and in 30 minutes we were up and beyond the falls and above the rough water.

"We went up ten miles and camped. We were afraid of being surprised by the Indians, so they put out sentries. There were 16 of us with the boat. Jess George of Polk County and Jim Robbins from Salt Creek were selected to stand the first watch. It happened that I was the only man in the party with a gun. The others were to get their guns at The Dalles. They borrowed my gun so as to take a shot at any prowling Indians who should come around.

"I had shared my blankets with one of the other men and was sleeping, with my boots for a pillow. We were all sound asleep when suddenly we heard a gun discharged and our two guards called, 'The Indians are on us! Run for your lives!'

"The fellow that was sleeping with me grabbed the blankets and started for the boat. I didn't want to lose those blankets, so I hung onto them. He ran as fast as he could and made a jump for the boat, missed it, and went head first into the river. I was glad I had held onto the blankets.

"Waking men up at the dead of night in Indian country makes them kind of panicky. I figured that if the Indians were coming there would be more than one shot, and there would be some Indians yelling, so I decided to watch developments. But the rest of the men beat it for the boat, except for George, Robbins, and myself. George and Robbins couldn't go, they were laughing so, but finally they went down to the boat and told the rest of the bunch that it was just a joke and they had been having a little sport with them.

"When I got to The Dalles I found my company was camped on Three Mile Creek. When I joined them I found the whole company swarming like bees. You never heard so much talk. We found out that Colonel Cornelius Gilliam had been accidentally killed and that H. A. G. Lee had been appointed colonel. Some of the men wanted to do one thing and some another. Some were for going home and some were for sticking it out. Captain Martin decided to resign, and his lieutenants resigned with him; so that left our company without any officers.

"Cy Nelson and I talked it over and decided we would try to get into some other company, since our company was going to be disbanded and the men sent back home. We went to The Dalles and asked Uncle Billy Shaw if we could fight with his company. He said, 'Boys, I would be glad to have you, but I can draw rations for only the regular number of men, so you fellows will have to furnish your own grub.'

"We went back to Three Mile Creek to get my share of the grub, but when we got there we found the head officers had said that if 60 of our men would stay and fight, we could elect new officers, so Cy Nelson decided to stay with our bunch, and we voted for G. W. Burnett to act as our captain. Burnett had been in my mess. Riley Bean, another of my mess, was put in for lieutenant, and they elected me to lead the packhorse with our grub. Cy Nelson stuck with us until he ran across a company that was in command of his brother-in-law, Clark Rogers, when he joined his company.

"It was a mighty unlucky thing for me that they found out I knew how to handle a boat on the river, for whenever we came to a river, I was elected to rustle the logs to make a raft and then ferry the men over. We crossed the Snake River just below the mouth of the Palouse during the June freshet. We took the men over in canoes and swam the horses beside the canoes. When we reached the bank of the river, it looked as though we were not going to get across. One of the officers and I rustled some drift logs, made a raft, crossed the river, and located four Indian canoes. I worked from 11 o'clock that morning until two the next morning taking the men over. It was dangerous work, for it was so rough. The men had to bail pretty lively to keep the canoe from being swamped.

"Captain Burnett was still on the wrong side of the river. He was waiting until all of his men got over. He and I lay down on the sand together and rested from two to four o'clock. Then he awoke me and we aroused the other men and began to take them over. I finally got so weak from lack of food—for I had not eaten anything for 24 hours —that I told them unless I could have something to eat, if the canoe should swamp I would be too weak to swim out. They then let me stop an hour or so. I walked to where some of the other men were and they gave me a chunk of beef that had been cooked by putting it on a stick and holding it over the fire. They also gave me bread and coffee. It sure tasted good.

"When we got to Red Wolf Crossing we found the Cayuse Indians had just pulled out. Our company started to scout around and located a big band of horses down near the river. I was riding a Spanish horse that happened to be one of the fastest horses in the company. A man about 35 years old, from Linn County, who belonged to Captain Maxon's company, was also mounted on a fast horse. We rode ahead of the others.

"A young Indian about my age, naked except for his breechclout, rode toward us and told us to stop. We didn't aim to do any stopping, for we wanted to capture those horses. The Indian tried to catch hold of the bridle of the other man's horse. He cracked the Indian over the head with his gun barrel and said, 'I'll teach you how to grab my bridle.'

"The Indian wheeled and started away as fast as his horse could run. My friend from Linn County yelled to him to stop, and when he didn't stop he took aim the best he could with his horse running as fast as it could go, and shot at the Indian. The bullet caught him just between the shoulder blades. He kind of sagged down, and rolled off his horse.

"Just then Dick, our guide, came up as fast as his horse could run, and said, 'What for you kill that Nez Perce boy? He our friend.'

"The Linn County man swung his gun around and was going to shoot Dick. I yelled to him not to shoot, that Dick was one of our scouts. I never saw an Indian more scared. He didn't shoot, and then Dick told us the horses belonged to the Nez Perce Indians, who were fighting with us and not against us.

"When Captain Burnett rode up he gave us Hail Columbia for shooting a friendly Indian, and said we ought to be courtmartialed. But I guess he figured it was all a mistake, so nothing came of it. The Nez Perce Indians were pretty sore about it. Chief Lawyer, one of the Nez Perce warriors, explained to the Indians that it was a mistake, so they let it go at that.

"Some big officer once said, 'You can't make an omelet without breaking some eggs', and it's the same way with fighting. Not all of our boys came back. The worst of it is that most of the wars, whether they are with Indians or with white folks, could be avoided if both sides wanted to do the fair thing and not take advantage of the other fellow.

"After being mustered out of the service in the Cayuse Indian War, I went back to our donation land claim. The next spring my father and I went to California on a Spanish boat. We worked in San Francisco, sawing redwood logs into lumber. We sawed about 400 feet of redwood flooring every day and were paid five dollars a day. After that job played out we got a job helping Sam Brannon load an old boat that he was going to take to Sacramento. While we worked in San Francisco we camped out near a spring on the beach. There was a big mud flat there, so the ships couldn't come in close. There was a sand beach, and back of that the land rose in benches and hills. Tents were pitched helter-skelter all along the beach and on the benches.

"We acted as deckhands on this boat going to Sacramento, and got our trip for nothing. When we got into the mines I cut down a couple of good-sized trees and hollowed them out and used them for rockers. On our way into the mines there was nothing at Sutter's but some tents and shacks, but when we came back they had started a city there, which they called Sacramento.

"We decided to come back to the Willamette Valley overland, so we bought a horse and saddle from a miner at Mormon Island and a couple more at Sacramento, and, with eight other Oregon men, we started for the Willamette Valley. I would not have gone back to the Willamette Valley but for the fact that I had sown 40 acres of wheat in the spring and there was no one at home to harvest it. When I got home I cut the 40 acres of wheat with a cradle, hauled it on a mud sled to the corral, and tramped it out with horses. It didn't turn out very well, though, because I got only 400 bushels on the whole 40 acres.

"After I had harvested my wheat I went with my cousin Dan Barnes back to California. We went to the Shasta diggings. Tom Ramie went with us down to Sacramento to get grub for the winter. You remember about the big flood they had that year. We got waterbound and for two or three months you couldn't get a horse out of the country. They would bog down. Ramie took sick. Dan Barnes was a good nurse. He told me to go on back and hold down our claim and he would nurse Ramie. It was six weeks before Ramie could get out of his bunk.

"When I got back I found some other fellows had taken our claim. They took $5000 out of it, and we could not find another good claim, so in midsummer of 1850, I again struck back for the Willamette Valley. I needed to make some money that winter, so I went in with Reuben Gant. He had a turning lathe and we spent the winter making chairs of maple wood with split bottoms made of ash.

"On March 4, 1851, I married Elsie Carlisle. She was a Canadian. We had 11 children—eight boys and three girls. Most of our children died of diphtheria or scarlet fever. Only two of the boys and three of the girls grew up. Our twin boys died of diphtheria.

"In 1863 we went to California, where we bought a ranch. My crop burned out that summer and fall, so I traded my ranch for 30 pack horses and came back to Oregon with the intention of running a pack train into the Idaho mines. I put my Spanish horses into a pasture in Polk County until I could get the rest of my outfit together. A cold storm came up, with driving sleet and rain, and when I went out to get my horses the next day a lot of them had pneumonia and 12 of them died. That ruined my pack train.

"I had to sell a band of sheep I had, to get money to buy some more horses. I had a band of mutton sheep, some yearlings, but mostly 2-year-olds. with a few 3-year-old wethers. I decided to drive them up to Canyon City, where rich diggings had just been struck and where money was plentiful. When I got to Portland with my sheep I got word that there were 16 cases of smallpox at The Dalles. I figured that I was not particularly anxious to die of smallpox, so I decided to sell my sheep in Portland. I put my sheep into Johnson's corral, at Second and Yamhill Streets. There used to be a butcher named Joe Bergman. I asked him if he would buy the sheep. I told him I had to sell them and I would take a profit of two-bits apiece off them. He thought he had me where he could get them still lower, so he told me he would think it over.

"Meanwhile, I ran across a man named Johnson, who said, 'I am going up to Victoria. I will give you $3.50 apiece for your yearlings and $4 for the rest of your sheep. They are in prime condition, and I can make enough profit on them in the Victoria market to pay my expenses for the trip.'

"Shortly after he had bought and paid for my sheep I ran across Bergman, who said, 'Well, have you decided to sell me your sheep?'

"I told him I had sold them and what I had got for them. He was greatly upset by it and said he would have paid me four bits a head more than that. He asked me if I could get him 75 yearlings, as he had an order for some sheep and needed them badly. I knew where I could pick up 75 yearlings, so I went out to Reuben Gant's place, bought them, and brought them in. Then Bergman asked me to go out and buy him some cattle. The upshot of the matter was that he hired me as a stockbuyer, and for the next nine months I rode all over the valley buying stock for him.

"My wife thought the children should be in school, so in the fall of 1863 we moved from our ranch near Sheridan to McMinnville. We didn't have the money to keep the children in school and pay our expenses at McMinnville unless we could scheme some way to make money as we went along, so we rented Uncle Tommy Shaddon's hotel and the whole family pitched in and worked. The next year I built a house. Our old boarders liked my wife's cooking, so a good many of them followed us to board with us. I finally had to build an addition on the house to accommodate the transients.

"I decided it would be cheaper to own a butcher shop so I could get meat at wholesale cost, so I ran a butcher shop in connection with the hotel and soon was making good money selling meat. So many travelers wanted to put their horses up that I bought out a livery stable and ran it in connection with my hotel. I ran the hotel, butcher shop, and livery stable for eight years, until all my children had a good education. Then I sold out and went back to farming. I saw to it that my children got what I had always wanted, and that was a good education. I figured that if I could get along without education, they could get along a heap better if they had it, and I didn't want them to have any more handicaps in life than I could help."

Oregon Journal
April 18-21, 1922

# William Blakely
# Pendleton, Oregon

"During the more than 50 years I have lived at or near Pendleton, I have seen remarkable changes occur. The old days—the frontier days—are gone. The Round-Up is about the only reminder of what was a part of our daily life when I went up there. In those days all the young chaps knew how to break a broncho. Now they learn to break a Tin Lizzie instead."

Oregon Journal
February 21, 1921

# George C. Compton
## Government Scout, Deputy Sheriff
### Florence, Oregon

*...I went to a small cabin almost hidden by high rhododendrens, knocked on the door and responded to the summons, "Come in." I went into the front room, where an old man wearing a black felt hat was sitting by the table reading. His face was completely covered almost up to his eyes with a heavy gray beard.*

"Have I got time to talk for awhile? Time is about all I have got. What do you want of me? What are you selling? How's that? You're not selling anything? All you want is to know about early days here? I've only been here about 43 year, so I can't tell you much about early days on the Siuslaw. But I can tell you about early days back in Kansas.

"My name is George C. Compton, and I was born in Pennsylvania on June 8, 88 years ago. I enlisted with the government as a government scout in Kansas. The Cheyennes, Arapahoes, Comanches and Kiowas were pretty restless in those days. I used to often see General Custer at Fort Riley and Fort Hays.

"The first time I ever met Bill Hickok, or 'Wild Bill' as they call him, was at Springfield, Missouri. He had just come from St. Louis. Someone at Springfield got into a dispute with him, so Wild Bill killed him. Later I saw him at Fort Hays and still later at Dodge City.

"Yes, I used to know Buffalo Bill, but in those days nobody thought anything of him, for he was just a buffalo hunter and scout and there were hundreds of other men doing the same kind of work. Once I ran across and counted 118 dead buffalo on the Smoky Hill River. Some hunting party had killed them for sport and never put a knife on them, not even to get their hides. I used to kill buffalo, but I only killed them for meat. Lots of people shot them just to be shooting.

"Did I ever kill any Indians? Let's talk about buffalo hunting. Naturally, when a man is a government scout and fighting Indians it's often a case of killing or being killed, and I'm still alive. Sometime I'll tell you about an Indian fight on the Smoky Hill River about 75 miles above Fort Riley, where I saw 23 white men killed.

"I took up a homestead in Cowley County. That's on the southern border of Kansas, joining

No-Man's-Land, as they used to call the Cherokee Strip. At that time Arkansas City, on the Walnut River, didn't have over a dozen houses. Wichita was the county seat. I took up a homestead at about where Maple City is now. That's due east of Arkansas City. In those days that country was fairly alive with wild turkeys and prairie chickens as well as quail. We never wasted our ammunition, though, on quail. I used to shoot prairie chickens and take a wagonload to Winfield or nearby places to sell.

"Having been a government scout, I had met quite a number of army officers and officials, so I was recommended for a deputy United States Marshal. I served for five years. Yes, I had some more or less interesting experiences while a deputy marshal. I was on the go most of the time, running down horsethieves and murderers.

"One time they arrested a mixed-blood for stealing a horse in Indian territory. His father was a white man and his mother was half Indian and half Negro. He was known as a bad man, so a posse of four men went out to arrest him. They got the drop on him and arrested him. He didn't put up any scrap at all, so they got a little careless, and as they were bringing him in he watched his chance, got a .45 from one of the members of the posse and in the resulting fight he killed all four of the posse. I was sent out to bring him in. I trailed him down into Mexico. I couldn't arrest him there, so I stuck around until he went up to Denison, Texas. I followed him, arrested him, and took him to Fort Smith, where he was tried by Judge Parker and convicted and hanged.

"I hate to arrest a young fellow. You take a young chap in his late teens or early twenties, and he has no judgment. Look at the number of men that Billy the Kid killed. I always aimed when I arrested a man to keep cool, take it easy, to talk slow and low, so the man I was arresting wouldn't get excited. You get a man excited and he's apt to start shooting. No, I never killed a man that I was sent out to arrest. Once in a while I've had to shoot him in the hand as he pulled his gun but I never aimed to more than cripple him temporarily.

"In 1867, in Wichita, with two other deputies, I arrested two noted horsethieves. We recovered the horses they had stolen and the two horsethieves were sent up to Leavenworth.

"I served as constable in Missouri for a while and also served as constable in Kansas. I was marshal here for a while and I was city marshal

128

for some years here in Florence.

"My grandson, who is 27 years old, lives with me. I was married young, just a month before my 18th birthday. All seven of my children are still living."

Oregon Journal
December 15, 1932

# Frank B. Tichenor
# Port Orford, Oregon

"My grandfather, Captain Tichenor, spent his boyhood at sea. Later he moved to Illinois. For some time he was a roommate of Abraham Lincoln, and, like most Lincoln's acquaintances, was a great admirer of Lincoln. My grandfather was elected a state senator in Illinois in 1848. He was the worshipful master of the local Masonic Lodge. Lincoln presented a petition to my grandfather, as worshipful master of the lodge, to become a member of the lodge. This was late in 1848. News of the discovery of gold in California became known, and my grandfather decided to try his luck in the gold diggings. He told Lincoln that he would see that his petition to join the lodge was taken care of by some other member of the lodge, but Lincoln said, 'There is no hurry about it. Let the matter stand until you return.' My grandfather never returned, and I think Lincoln took no further steps to become a Mason.

"My grandfather went to Marysville and located what is still known as Tichenor Gulch. He took in with him a young man as partner, and, unlike many of the gold miners, they had unusually good luck, striking rich ground. When they pulled out for San Francisco my grandfather's partner, who had quite a bit of gold dust before they became partners, had 125 pounds of gold dust. My grandfather had 75 pounds. Figuring the gold at $16 an ounce, he had cleaned up over $18,000. They paid an ounce of gold apiece to spread their blankets in the back room of a San Francisco saloon for one night's lodging.

"The next day my grandfather met Dr. Darcy, an old-time friend from Newark, New Jersey. Dr. Darcy invited him to stay at his cabin. With part of the money he had made in the gold mine, my grandfather purchased the schooner Jacob Riarson. He went down to the Gulf of California and along the shore of northern Mexico, buying turtles. He took these turtles back to San Francisco. He found the price of any kind of meat exceedingly high, so he cleaned up a lot of money on his cargo of turtles. My grandfather then chartered his boat to take a party to Humboldt Bay. The old Spanish chart showed that the Eel River was the mouth of the Trinity, but they found the chart was wrong. They found no gold, so my grandfather and 17 others of the party took up, in 1850, what is now Eureka. They got scurvy and some of the men died. My grandfather and some of the others went back to the vessel, where they recovered from the scurvy.

"In March, 1851, my grandfather took command of the Sea Gull, a vessel of 400 tons burden. She was put on the Columbia River route. Passengers paid $80 a ticket from San Francisco to Portland, and freight was $60 to $80 a ton. Governor Gaines of Oregon gave my grandfather an appointment as a pilot for the Columbia River bar. This was the second license issued up to that time. Captain White was issued the first license.

"My grandfather was looking for a place to settle. He believed there would be a large city somewhere between Astoria and San Francisco. After sizing up the coast and finding vessels could anchor in deep water at Port Orford, he decided to found a settlement there. At Portland he enlisted nine men to start a settlement at Port Orford. They went south on the Sea Gull, landing at Port Orford on June 9, 1851. He landed the men on what is now known as Battle Rock and furnished them, in addition to their supplies, the ship's cannon, with powder and sheet lead. He then told the men he would return in 12 days.

"At San Francisco it was found necessary to make some repairs on the Sea Gull, so Captain Knight offered to take up more recruits for the settlement and also the promised supplies. My grandfather was to go on the Pacific Mail Company's ship, the Columbia, to pilot her into Humboldt Bay, with which he was already familiar. When they reached Battle Rock they found the nine men were gone, and they also found a diary that told of the attack of the Indians on the men and of their leaving for the mouth of the Umpqua River.

"The men who were camped on Battle Rock were J. H. Eagan, John P. Slater, T. D. Palmer, Joseph Hussey, James Carrigan, Erastus Summers, J. M. Kirkpatrick, George Ridoubt and Cyrus W. Hedden. They loaded the ship's cannon that my grandfather let them have, with two pounds of powder and a lot of bar lead. A canoe with a number of Indian warriors came up the coast from toward the mouth of the Rogue River. One of the men in the canoe, apparently their leader, was a tall man wearing a red shirt.

"The Indians in the canoe joined the other Indians on shore and, led by the man with the red shirt, they charged the nine men on Battle Rock. There were about 100 Indians who made the charge. Carrigan held a board about 8 feet long, 15 inches wide and about an inch and a half thick, in front of Kirkpatrick, who had a tarred rope with a lighted end ready to fire the cannon when the Indians came up on the rock. Thirty-seven arrows buried their heads in that board. Palmer was shot through the neck with an arrow and Ridoubt was shot in the breast.

"When the Indians who had climbed the rock were about eight feet from the mouth of the cannon, Kirkpatrick touched the lighted tar rope to the priming. About 12 or 15 Indians were killed outright and a large number wounded. Later the men on the rock picked up 17 dead Indians. The other Indians jumped into the ocean and about an hour later one of the chiefs came and made signs that he wanted to gather up their dead. They took away all of their dead except the man in the red shirt. They refused to take him. The chief tore off his shirt and kicked him in the ribs. The nine men on the rock later buried him in the sand. They found he was a white man and it later developed that he was a Russian whose vessel had been wrecked on the coast. He had joined this tribe and become a chief.

"This battle occurred on June 10, the day after the men were landed on the rock. Kirkpatrick told the chief when he came to carry away the dead Indians that the Sea Gull would return in 14 days. On account of the Sea Gull being delayed by being repaired in San Francisco it was not able to come back as soon as expected, so, on the morning of the 15th day, several hundred Indians in war paint came back to kill the men camped on the rock. The chief with whom Kirkpatrick had talked led the Indians in this attack. When the chief was about 100 yards from the rock, James Carrigan and J. M. Kirkpatrick both fired at him, both their bullets hitting him in the chest and one of their bullets going through his heart and killing him instantly. This stopped the charge. The Indians picked him up and carried him back up the beach.

"Once more the Indians gathered, and another chief, brandishing a long knife and yelling ferocious-ly, attacked the men on the rock. He also was killed when he approached the rock, and once more the Indians stopped and carried him away.

"The Indians, supposing they had the men

131

surrounded, withdrew and had a war dance. While
this was going on the nine men, leaving their tents
and all supplies on the rock, quietly withdrew
and started for the settlements, which they eventually
reached. Two or three days after the men had
escaped from the rock the Columbia anchored off
Port Orford. They fired a gun on board the ship
to attract the attention of the men on the rock.
No answer coming from Battle Rock, a small boat
was sent ashore and it was discovered that the
men were gone, and it was supposed that they were
killed by Indians.

"My grandfather returned to San Francisco
on the Columbia, reaching there on July 10. The
Sea Gull was ready for sea, so he recruited 67
men and landed them at Port Orford on July 14,
1851. They built two blockhouses of heavy logs,
as a protection from the Indians. My grandfather
went on to Portland, where he purchased some horses,
some hogs and other supplies and engaged W. G.
T'Vault, who had been the first editor of the **Oregon
Spectator** when it was started in Oregon City in
1846.

"My grandfather and Phil Kearney had been
schoolmates at Newark, New Jersey, and Colonel
Kearney recommended T'Vault as a good man to
find a practicable road between Port Orford and
the Oregon Trail, leading from Portland to San
Francisco. My grandfather filed his donation land
claim at the land office at Oregon City. At that
time General Preston was surveyor general for Oregon.

"My grandfather returned to Port Orford on
July 26, 1851. He found that some of the men he
had recruited at San Francisco were worthless as
settlers. They were turbulent, lazy and unwilling
to take orders, so he shipped 14 of them back to
San Francisco.

"A few weeks later, Dr. Anson Dart, Superintendent of Indian Affairs, with Reverend H. H. Spalding,
came to Port Orford. H. H. Spalding had been an
associate of Dr. Whitman, having crossed the plains
with him in 1836. On September 3, Lieutenant Whyman,
with a mountain howitzer and some soldiers, arrived
at Port Orford. My grandfather sent out Colonel
T'Vault with a party of men to cut a trail between
Port Orford and the Oregon Trail. He sent another
party out under M. Nolan.

"Not far distant was a high peak, known
as Sugar Loaf Peak. The men thought this was
the hogback of the range, so they tried to cross
it, thinking they were crossing the range of mountains.
As a matter of fact, it is an isolated peak, one

of the highest on the Oregon coast, bordering the sea. After climbing through ravines and brush for a week, all they had done was to climb around the mountain, so they returned to Port Orford and named this mountain Tichenor's Humbug, which name it still bears.

"Colonel T'Vault's party had a still more disastrous time. They had to abandon their horses and the men became so disgusted with Colonel T'Vault that they were going to leave him, but Cyrus Hedden, who later settled at Scottsburg, persuaded them not to leave T'Vault.

"About two miles above the mouth of the Coquille River they had a fight with the Indians, on September 14, 1851. Five of the party--Patrick Murphy of New York, A. S. Dougherty of Texas, Jeremiah Ryland of Maryland, J. P. Pepper of New York, and John P. Holland of New Hampshire--were killed. Those who survived were Colonel T'Vault, Gilbert Brush, T. J. Davenport, L. L. Williams and Cyrus Hedden. Williams was badly wounded by an arrow, and Brush also was wounded."

Oregon Journal
May 24-26, 1929

# George Turner
# Albany, Oregon

"My folks were Scotch. Like most of the Scotch, they were Presbyterians. My mother made me go to church and Sunday school. I was fed on the shorter catechism when I was a boy. We had a Scotch preacher whose usual theme was the worm that dieth not and the fire that is not quenched.

"He certainly was an artist at describing hell. I used to wake up at night covered with gooseflesh, I was so sure I was going to hell. I thought I could stand it to be burned up, but what got me was to think of burning in hell for ever and ever.

"This preacher was one of the most obstinate men I ever saw. He also had a violent temper, and he utterly lacked all sense of humor. I was very tenderhearted when I was a boy and I loved horses and dogs devotedly. This preacher had a gentle little white pony that he drove hitched to a cart on his visits about the country.

"One day when on my way to school I came across this hell-fire and damnation preacher beating his pony unmercifully with a stay chain. The pony was frantic with pain and fear. The preacher would say as he hit the pony, 'I'll teach you not to resist the hand of constituted authority. I'll put the fear of God into you. I'll show you the evil of your ways.'

"I looked on in horror, expecting to see God strike him dead for his cruelty. After waiting several moments for God to attend to his case, without result, I decided to act for Him, so, picking up a nice round rock about the size of a walnut, I threw it with all my might at the preacher. It caught him in front of the ear. He dropped like a struck bullock.

"I waited for him to get up, but he lay where he fell. I struck off down the road like a deer pursued by a pack of hounds. All day I literally felt my flesh singe from the unquenchable fires of hell prepared from the beginning of eternity for murderers. It takes a whole lot to make a boy miss a meal, but I had no appetite for lunch that day.

"After school I sneaked home past the preacher's house expecting to see crape on his door. Instead, I saw him walking back and forth on the path in front of his house, with his hands behind him as though in deep thought. I was so relieved and delighted that I turned a handspring, for which I got a disapproving look from him for my levity.

"He never beat that horse again. He explained that while punishing his horse for its contumacy he lost his temper and that God punished him by sending a stroke of some kind, through which he had fallen unconscious by the roadside. He took it as a mark of divine displeasure at his belaboring his faithful animal.

"While I was handling threshing machines in Wyoming near Laramie a bunch of us decided to have a stag dinner Thanksgiving Day. Some of us went out into the wheat fields and killed some wild geese, and we chipped in a dollar or so apiece for whiskey. By the middle of the afternoon we were pretty mellow. Some of the crowd were making speeches and others were singing.

"In the midst of our festivities we heard a knock at the door. One of the most sober of the gang opened the door. There stood a Jewish peddler smiling ingratiatingly as he slipped the pack from his back and asked if we wanted to buy suspenders, socks, or jewelry.

"'Bring him in,' sang out a young attorney who later made his mark in the political history of Montana during the days when Clark and Daly were fighting for political supremacy in the Treasure State. The Jew was brought in.

"'It was some relatives of yours that put Joseph down in the well and sold him to the camel drivers bound for Egypt,' said the lawyer. 'Take him out, boys, and put him down the well till we can decide on adequate and appropriate punishment for that ancient and unpunished crime.' They took him out and dropped him down the well, which was about 25 feet deep.

"We went on with our revelry for several hours. Everyone had forgotten all about the Jewish peddler down the well. I had a cloudy recollection about it. Finally it came to me and I said, 'Boys, what are we going to do with the Jew down the well?'

"There were several lawyers in the crowd. They decided to have a mock trial. 'Bring him in,' said a lawyer who hailed from the Emerald Isle. 'We will try him on the charge of being accessory to the crucifixion of Christ.' We hauled him out of the well. He located his pack and slipped the straps over his shoulders.

"You never heard such oratory. The trial lasted for two hours and the lawyers fairly outdid themselves. The Irish lawyer acted as prosecuting attorney. A man who had studied for the ministry, a sort of reformed preacher, defended him. The Irish lawyer wound up his speech with an impassioned plea that the Jew be hanged at once. The chap that defended him asked that the sentence be commuted and that his client be shot instead of being hanged.

"You could have knocked that peddler's eyes off with a stick. He kept licking his lips, and his forehead was covered with cold sweat. While the impromptu jury was wrangling over the form of their verdict, the vender of shoestrings and suspenders took to his heels. The last we saw of him he was still running.

"I remember weeping on someone's neck, who mingled his tears of laughter with mine. The rest of that stag dinner is a blank in my memory, but there is one thing I am willing to make a solemn affadavit to, and that is that it was a real Thanksgiving Day for the peddler, he was so thankful to get away.

"After the trial we were going to give him a good dinner and send him on his way rejoicing, but he was no mind reader and took the whole thing seriously."

●●●●●●●●●●●●●●●●●●●●●●●●●●●●●●●●●●●●●●●●●●●●●●●●●●●●

"Yes, we are a mixed race, but our predominating strain is from Great Britain. There's a good bit of Scotch in me. You needn't smile. There isn't so much Scotch in me as there used to be before the country went dry. Scotch or anything else in the form of liquid refreshment is too hard to

135

get these days to have much Scotch in anyone."

**Oregon Journal**
undated

# Richard Watson Helm
# Pioneer of 1845
# Salem, Oregon

*An octogenarian, a pioneer of 1845, tells Mr. Lockley of his family's trip across the plains and mountains to Oregon, of his father's personal prowess in managing hostile red men, of the journey by way of the Meek cut-off, and of the processes of establishing a home on the soil of Oregon.*

*Richard Watson Helm lives at 777 Cottage Street in Oregon's capital city. He has been a resident of Oregon since 1845, almost 80 years. When I visited him recently at his home, he said:*

"I am a Kentuckian. My father, the Reverend William Helm, was a Virginian. I was born May 29, 1839, and when I was two and a half years old I went with my parents to Missouri. My father was born in 1800. My mother, whose maiden name was Martha Scroggins, was born in 1805. She, like my father, was a native of Virginia. They had six children, five boys and one girl. In 1842 they moved from Kentucky to the Platte Purchase in Missouri. In the spring of 1845 they started from St. Joe for the trip across the plains by ox team to Oregon.

"While my father had gone to school but three months in his life, he was a well educated man, deeply versed in the **Bible**, and a man of strong and deep religious convictions. My father would not join a train whose members planned to travel on Sunday. He circulated around among the emigrants and quietly organized a group of men who were willing to lay over on Sundays. There were 70 wagons in the train. The members of this train passed a subscription paper around and raised sufficient money to purchase a large tent in which to hold Sunday services. Each Saturday night this tent was put up, and on Sunday my father preached both morning and evening. The wagon train had an uneventful and on the whole a pleasant trip all the way across the plains to Fort Hall. They overtook many of the other emigrants who had nearly run the legs off their oxen by travelling hard and fast and not giving their oxen a chance to rest up on Sundays.

"My father, like most Kentuckians, either did not know what fear was, or, if he did know, he disregarded it. While camped on a stream somewhere near the western border of Idaho, some young Indians came to our camp. They tried by signs and motions to talk to us, but our people could not tell what they meant, and they could not tell what we meant. As they were endeavoring to make themselves understood, an old white cow, belonging to Mr. Ridgeway, came out of the brush with two arrows sticking in its side. When the Indians saw the cow come up they set up a war whoop, charged our riding horses, which they stampeded, and rode away in a cloud of alkali dust.

"My father asked for 40 volunteers. In a few moments there were 40 men, well armed, who were ready to go with him and recover the horses. There was an Indian camp up the stream a short distance. They walked up to this camp, and Father stopped in front of the best-looking teepee and called to have the chief come out. The chief called a half-breed interpreter, who said to Father, 'What you want?'

"My father said, 'We want you to round up and bring in the 40 horses you have stolen at once. And we want you to give us one of your best horses in exchange for Ridgeway's white cow that your young men have wounded.'

"The chief listened, looked around at the armed men and said, 'My young men will bring back your horses as soon as possible, and we will also send you a good horse for the cow they shot.'

"Within an hour all of our stolen horses and an extra horse were staked out near the wagons.

"We met in that part of the country Stephen Meek, who said he could take us into the Willamette Valley by crossing the mountains near the head of the valley and we could save six weeks time by doing so. A vote was then taken. Father opposed the plan, but as the others were for it and he believed in majority rule, he went with them. Others joined our train, till there were nearly 200 wagons that followed Meek on what he claimed was a short cut to Oregon. Meek started out on an old Hudson's Bay or fur trapper's trail. We soon got into rough country in the Malheur Mountains. The grass was short and the cattle became hungry and gaunt. The water was alkali. The cattle wandered away.

"Up near the head of the Malheur River, near the brakes, one of our party, while looking for cattle, found in the stream what was afterwards said to be a gold nugget, though no attention was

137

paid to it at that time, but later several expeditions were outfitted to find what they termed the Blue Bucket Mine, discovered by members of our party. Many of the children became sick with mountain fever. We were more interested in finding grass for the cattle, good water for the families, and a way out of the stony and desolate desert than in discovering gold. Finally, Meek confessed that he was not sure of the road.

"Among the emigrants who had joined our wagon train were some rather rough characters, and they decided to kill Meek. That night my father told Meek he had better go at once, as the men meant harm, and might kill him. Meek didn't want to leave, because he believed he could guide them out, but when he learned they were actually making preparations to hang him, he stole out of the camp and got away. The morning after he left, three men were sent out to try to locate water, among them my brother, who found a small stream which ran into the Deschutes River. Meek reached The Dalles and sent Black Harris, who knew the country, to guide our party to The Dalles. He brought some food on pack horses and met us not far from where Tygh Creek enters the Deschutes.

"At The Dalles Father met the Reverend Alvin F. Waller who was there with his family, as well as Mr. Brewer, the mission farmer. They persuaded my father to stay with his family at the mission at The Dalles till the next spring.

"At that time the only two buildings at The Dalles were two large log buildings. Mr. Waller lived in one, Mr. Brewer in the other. We moved into the Brewer house and spent the winter with them. Mr. Brewer was a good farmer, kind-hearted and easy to get along with. During the winter Father helped him with the work about the place and also assisted Mr. Waller in his work with the Indians.

"One day about 150 Indians--Cayuse Indians and others--rode up to our place and surrounded Mr. Brewer's house. They were dressed in war paint and armed with a few flintlocks and with bows and arrows. They held a war dance. Father asked Mr. Brewer what it meant. He said the Indians had come from the upper country and he was afraid it meant trouble. Father said, "We can't remain in uncertainty. I'll go out and see what they mean.'

"The Indians were dancing, not exactly in a circle, but in the form of an ellipse. Each warrior had a knife in his hand with which, as he danced, he would lunge savagely at a supposed enemy. Some of the Indians were beating a drum, and the

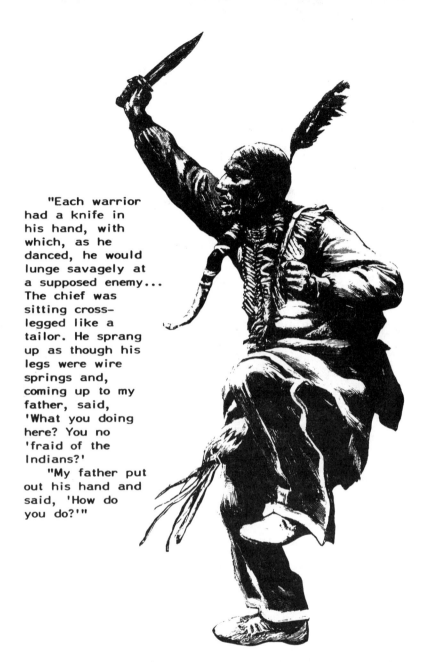

"Each warrior
had a knife in
his hand, with
which, as he
danced, he would
lunge savagely at
a supposed enemy...
The chief was
sitting cross-
legged like a
tailor. He sprang
up as though his
legs were wire
springs and,
coming up to my
father, said,
'What you doing
here? You no
'fraid of the
Indians?'

"My father put
out his hand and
said, 'How do
you do?'"

Indians who were dancing sang a queer, monotonous
chant. As they sang they would leap high into
the air, their arms and hands flailing around like
the sails of a windmill.

"Father opened the door and stepped out.
Mr. Brewer shut the door and put the bar up.
As Father stepped out the chief of the war party

gave a command, and all but about a dozen Indians squatted down, while the others surrounded Father and continued their war dance around him.

"I was just a little chap, but I can remember as though it were yesterday seeing my father surrounded by those half-naked, savage, leaping, yelling Indians. The chief was sitting cross-legged like a tailor. He sprang up as though his legs were wire springs and, coming up to my father, said, 'What you doing here? You no 'fraid of the Indians?'

"My father put out his hand and said, 'How do you do?'

"The chief was a fine-looking Indian. He held out his hand and said, 'What you come here for?'

"My father said, 'I came to find out what you are here for. Have you come to kill the men who came across the plains to tell you of the white man's God and to bring you his book? I can talk to you better in the house. Come on in with me --if you are not afraid.'

"The Indian said something to the other Indians and came with Father into the house.

"Dinner was just about to be served, so Father invited the Indian to sit down with us at the table. Before eating we followed our usual custom, which was to kneel around the table while Father or one of the others asked a blessing. The Indian kneeled and never moved a muscle till the prayer was over. He ate dinner, after which Father told him why the missionaries had come to Oregon. Finally, he said, 'You good man,' and, going to the door, he called to the Indians and made a short talk to them. A moment later he mounted his horse and all of the Indians rode off at full speed. I have always thought the Indians intended to kill us, for they were in a surly mood when they came, and it was only two years later that they rose and killed Dr. Marcus Whitman, his wife, and many others at the Whitman Mission.

"The next April we put our two wagons and the family on a flatboat made of logs and started down the Columbia River. We landed above the Cascades, where they made a portage of the goods and turned the raft loose. The Indians caught it below the Cascades, and, after making some minor repairs in it, the goods were reloaded, the family got aboard, and we floated down the Columbia to the mouth of the Sandy, where the goods were landed, the wagons set up, and the oxen brought up and yoked and we drove to Oregon City. From there we drove up the valley where Father gave a settler a pony for his squatter's right to 640 acres of land and his cabin.

"There were five boys in our family--Walter, Wesley, William Benjamin, myself, and Asbury Coke, and my sister Mary. My father rode all over the country, preaching wherever a group of settlers got together, while we boys cut fence rails, fenced the place, cleared the brush and plowed the land. After we had the place fairly well fixed up, Father sold it to Mr. Shannon. This was shortly after the discovery of gold in California.

"Father then took up a donation land claim 12 miles south of Salem. My father and Hamilton Campbell, together, built a schoolhouse. Professor Hosford was our first teacher. He had crossed the plains with us in 1845. Later, Hamilton Campbell served as teacher. Among the students were the Looney children, the Campbell children, and the children of our family. Maria Campbell Smith, daughter of Hamilton Campbell, now lives in Portland. We boys worked on this farm, near Parrish's Gap, till it was said to be one of the finest farms in the entire neighborhood. My father felt that the Lord had called him to preach, so he stayed on the job, regardless of other distractions or attractions. My father sold his donation land claim to Mr. Looney for $8000, which in those days was a big price.

"We moved to Lebanon, where we children attended Santiam Academy, of which the Reverend L. R. Woodward was the principal. In those days there were a number of smaller academies, such as Dallas Academy, Santiam Academy, Wilbur Academy, and Sheridan Academy. Santiam Academy suspended in 1870, but for many years prior to that it was one of the influential colleges of the Valley. Such men as Delazon Smith, Alvin S. Waller, W. C. Gallagher, Reverend Thomas H. Parne, Luther R. Woodward, and others of that type were its trustees.

"Among my schoolmates at Santiam Academy were Owen N. Denny, Melvin C. George and his brother, Tom H. Crawford, and other well-known pioneers who have made their mark in Oregon. My father bought a farm a mile and a half southeast of Lebanon, so that his sons should be able to keep busy. He also bought a half section of good land for my brother Will near Washington Butte. Will had married Elizabeth Sager, one of the survivors of the Whitman Massacre. She now lives in Portland.

"In 1858 T. H. Crawford, O. N. Denny, myself, and three other students of Santiam Academy came to Salem to enter Willamette University. After attending the University three years my father told me to take up Hebrew, as he wanted me to be able to read the Bible in the original. He planned for me to be a preacher. This scared me out. I didn't want to preach, so I stopped school and, loading some grub and tools on a pack horse, I mounted my riding horse and started for the newly discovered diggings at Florence. I was at Boise when the first tents were put up there. I landed a job at $5 a day and worked there all summer, returning to the Willamette Valley late that fall.

"In the spring of 1863 I drove a band of cattle to Fort Simcoe. The following year, 1864, I drove 450 head of cattle to the Klickitat Valley. I kept them there till the spring of 1865. We sold them for $22,000.

"On December 4, 1864, the Reverend William Roberts performed the ceremony in the Methodist Church at Salem, Oregon, that united Eliza Barger and myself in a marriage that continued for 66 years. C. D. Parrish and Laura Bell were the witnesses. My brother-in-law, Willard Barger, is an old-time stage driver. He lives in Portland and is employed by the **Oregon Journal.**

"For 37 years I bought and sold cattle. For much of that time my saddle was my pillow and the sky was my cover. In 1880 I drove a band of 1847 cattle to Cheyenne, Wyoming, for shipment to eastern markets. I was like the nomads of old. I had no settled habitation. For nearly two-score years I lived in Washington Territory and the upper country. I will tell you a rather remarkable thing about outdoor life. I have gone for days when trailing cattle with my clothes wringing wet, have slept in wet blankets, have forded swollen streams, and, though I am 85 years of age, I have never yet had a doctor. My wife and I lived together 66 years till her death through a stroke of paralysis, and the only time we ever had a doctor was when children were born, and sometimes on these occasions we were so remote from doctors that we had to get along without one.

"I have never touched a drop of intoxicating liquor in my life. I have never tasted tobacco in any form. Up to 60 years ago I used to drink coffee, but when I was in my middle 20s I decided to get along without coffee and have never tasted it since.

"My brother Walter built a church at Goldendale, Washington, in which he preached for 25 years. In 1905 I came to Salem from Coquille, and I have been here ever since, and here I propose to remain till the summons comes for me to take the long trail."

**Oregon Journal**
February 11-13, 1924

# Speaking of living on horse meat . . .

Speaking of living on horse meat reminds me of what happened to Colonel Johnson, who was in command of the 108th regiment, Illinois Volunteer Infantry.

Colonel Johnson was a very strict disciplinarian. The two military offenses upon which he frowned most severely were straggling and foraging. No matter how lucky a man was to be able to get a sheep, a pig, or a chicken, Colonel Johnson always seemed to get wise to it and confiscate the foraged rations. Rather than have the stolen delicacy go to waste, he would have it served on his own table.

One of the privates in the 108th regiment had gained the reputation of being the best forager in the whole regiment, and, as a consequence, Colonel Johnson had him watched more closely than any of the other men. Several times he had made him disgorge a choice young pullet, some spareribs, or a leg of mutton, till the disgruntled private vowed he would get even.

Just about dusk one evening he stole in past the colonel's tent and the sharp eyes of Colonel Johnson detected that he had a full haversack. The colonel halted him and made him open his haversack. The private was sent to the guardhouse and Colonel Johnson and his staff had fresh meat for their supper and breakfast.

As Colonel Johnson and his fellow officers were finishing the fried mutton they had had for breakfast, his orderly came in with the information that the private from whom they had taken the confiscated meat had confessed that it was not a leg of mutton, but a dog's leg.

The colonel and the other officers ran out of the tent sick at the stomach. Instantly all over the camp the men began yelping and barking like a pack of dogs. Colonel Johnson's temper was short. He drew his sword and rushed at the nearest group of men who were barking, but they made a hasty getaway, while from behind trees and back of the tents the other men continued to howl and bark. Thereafter Colonel Johnson refrained from consuming any foraged meat captured from his men, and the rule against foraging was greatly relaxed.

**Oregon Journal**
undated

# J. T. Simpson
# Pioneer of 1846
# Sheridan, Oregon

"One of the officers at Fort Yamhill of whom I was very fond in the late '50's was Lieutenant P. H. Sheridan. Phil Sheridan had a remarkable carrying voice. The drill ground was at least 250 yards from the porch of our store. He did not seem to raise his voice, and yet I could hear every command he gave, distinctly. The Indians stood very much in awe of him. They referred to him as the 'Tyee', though, of course, he was only a second lieutenant under Captain Russell.

"Sheridan was a very strict disciplinarian. The soldiers jumped to attention and saluted him much more quickly than they did when Captain Russell came around, who was more indifferent to matters of this kind. In the store or in our home Lieutenant Sheridan was very boyish and jovial. He had a charming and magnetic personality. You couldn't help like him.

"While Sheridan was at Fort Yamhill a squaw, an Indian doctor among the Rogue River Indians, was called in to cure one of the sub-chiefs of the Rogue River tribe. He died and in accordance with the Indian custom his friends and relatives decided to kill her for not curing him. When they came on their errand of vengeance she escaped and ran for the cabin in which Sheridan lived, to take refuge. Just as she got inside of the garrison gate the Indians overtook her and killed her. The post surgeon conducted a post mortem on her and found 16 bullet wounds in her body.

"Captain Russell ordered Lieutenant Sheridan to prevent any further outrages of this kind. Sheridan, who understood the Chinook jargon, called a council of the Rogue River Indians and told them that the 16 men who had killed the Indian medicine woman must be given up. Lieutenant Sheridan had taken Sergeant Miller with him. The Indians became very much incensed at Sheridan's insistence and began closing in on Sheridan. He reached back for his pistol, but found that one of the Indians had taken it. He made the best of a bad bargain, and mounted his horse and rode back to the post to secure help.

"Mary, one of the chief women of the tribe, came to the fort and told Sheridan that the Rogue River Indians had donned their war paint, were armed, and were camped on the Yamhill River, waiting to be attacked. At midnight that night Sheridan, with 50 men, made a roundabout march and came up in the rear of the village, taking the Indians by surprise and capturing Sam, their war chief, and told them that if they fired a shot he would instantly kill Sam.

"Sam's brother, Joe, who was with the hostiles, asked for a parley and finally agreed to return the sixshooter and give up 15 of the men. On the hills surrounding the opposing forces several thousand Indians were gathered to see the fight. The 16th Indian refused to surrender, and was shot. The 15 men came in and surrendered, and for some time thereafter worked around the post with a ball and chain fastened to their ankles. The man who was wounded eventually recovered.

"When the troops were ordered east at the breaking out of the Civil War Lieutenant Sheridan was left in charge of the post. He was to care for the government property until he was relieved by Captain J. J. Archer of the Ninth Infantry. He was to be stationed there with his company. Lieutenant Sheridan refused to turn over the fort to him, for Captain Archer had openly boasted he would sieze the fort and the supplies there for the Confederates. Captain Archer threatened to have Sheridan arrested, but did not make good his threat, and shortly thereafter left for the south and became an officer in the Confederate service. Captain Philip Owen was sent in his place and Sheridan rejoined his regiment and served throughout the Civil War."

**Oregon Journal**
undated

# Captain O. C. Applegate
# Klamath Falls, Oregon

*Captain O. C. Applegate lives at Klamath Falls. He is a son of Lindsay Applegate, who, with his brother Jesse, came across the plains in 1843. Major Lindsay Applegate was the first agent appointed for the Modoc Indians. He was one of the men represent-ing the government when the treaty was made with the Indians in 1864. In a recent letter to me, Captain O. C. Applegate gives much interesting history of the early days. In speaking of the causes leading up to the Modoc War, he writes:*

"My father, Captain Lindsay Applegate, the first agent to take charge of the Indians of this region after the treaty of 1864, assisted in making the treaty. He was well known to many of the

Indians, and it was at their request, made at the time the treaty was signed, that he was appointed. He took charge of the Indians in 1865. I was his clerk and assistant. In the summer of 1869, having served four years, he was succeeded by Captain O. C. Knapp of the United States Army, supernumerary army officers having been placed in charge of nearly all the Indian agencies.

"Captain Jack, a sub-chief of the Modoc tribe, had signed the treaty as Keintpoos, but was never on the reservation with his band during the incumbency of Agent Applegate. Old Sconchin, head chief of the Modocs, voluntarily came onto the reservation with more than half of his people soon after the treaty was made, although it was not ratified until some years after, and loyally remained thereafter. In the fall of 1869, Superintendent A. B. Meacham, of the Oregon superintendency, removed Captain Jack and his band to the Klamath Reservation and established them at Modoc Point, where they remained during the succeeding winter, but in the spring of 1870 they folded their tents like the Arabs and quietly stole away to their old country about Tule Lake. They claimed that the Klamaths mistreated them and that Captain Knapp, the agent, did not treat them as well as he did the Klamaths.

"During the succeeding years several councils were held with Keintpoos, and repeated efforts were made by the authorities, and by the old loyal chief, Sconchin, to induce him to come onto the reservation in accordance with the treaty, but without avail. Finally, in the fall of 1872, Superintendent T. H. B. Odeneal, whose office was at Salem, was instructed by the authorities at Washington to bring Captain Jack's band onto the reservation, 'peaceably if possible, but by force if necessary', they having become a menace to the settlements in the region occupied by them.

"Now we come to the actual cause of the war. On the arrival of Superintendent Odeneal at Linkville (now Klamath Falls) he sent a Modoc Indian woman to Captain Jack, asking for a conference with him, but Jack abruptly refused, and Mr. Odeneal immediately placed the matter in the hands of Colonel John Green, commander of Fort Klamath, and asked that Jack and his band be removed to the reservation without delay. It had been supposed that Colonel Green could detach the 50 troopers for this purpose on short notice, but the sequel proved that only 35 men were available, and these, under Captain James Jackson of B Troop of the First United States Cavalry, left Fort Klamath at noon on November 18, 1872, and after riding 65 miles arrived at Captain Jack's winter camp on Lost River at daylight on the morning

146

of November 29.

"Preliminary efforts for a peaceful settlement failed and the fight was on. The force proved insufficient. Though Jack's men were driven out of this encampment, about a fourth of Captain Jackson's men were killed or wounded and the Indians escaped to the lava beds and there occupied one of the strongest natural fortifications in the world, and 18 settlers in the settlement at the head of Tule Lake were killed by a band of Modocs who were enroute to the lava beds.

"Had General Frank Wheaton, who was in command of the District of the Lakes, his garrisons being Camp Harney, Bidwell, and Warner and Fort Klamath, been called upon, he could have put into the field 150 troopers without depleting his garrison too much, and this force in all reason could have protected the menaced settlers and made the efforts to bring in the insurgent band a success. It was my belief then, as it is now, that had that been done there would have been no Modoc War. This was the advice of the man who had charge of the loyal Modocs, the Piutes, and the Upper Klamaths at Yainax Sub-agency, a man well informed on the situation and who was in correspondence with General Wheaton and knew how promptly that fine officer would have complied had he been called upon.

"When Superintendent Odeneal received the rebuff from Captain Jack he failed to heed the counsel of the man at Yainax, and the result was a failure. Doubtless no living man knows the truth of this statement better than I do myself, for I represented the Indian Department as United States Commissary at Yainax, and had made a trip to Klamath Agency on purpose to advise calling on General Wheaton for 150 men, in case force should be required to compel Jack's return to the reservation and make the settlements safe."

Oregon Journal
October 23, 1921

# Matthew P. Deady
# On White Man's Justice

*Did you ever stop to wonder what an Indian thinks of the white man's justice? When a white man gets into trouble he hires a shrewd lawyer and gets cleared on a technicality. When an Indian does the identical same thing as did the white man, he is tried, convicted, and either sent to prison or hanged. It must puzzle an Indian to figure out where the justice comes in in his particular case.*

*Chief Joseph could never quite figure out why the whites could break every treaty they had solemnly signed, violate every pledge, take the Indians' land and kill the Indians for trespassing on their own land, and have all this considered right, when he and his people were held to strict accountability for promises they had never made but which had been made for them by a minority of the tribe.*

*This same question as to what is justice creeps up constantly in the writings of our former fellow-townsman, Judge Matthew P. Deady. Here is a letter of his that is worth reading, for it throws a clear light on some of our early-day relations with the Indians. He says:*

"On September 1, 1853, I left my farm on the Umpqua and started for Jacksonville on horseback to hold the United States District Court there. At the Umpqua Canyon I overtook Lieutenant L. F. Grover with the advance company of Colonel Nesmith's company, hastening to the scene of war. He shared his blankets with me that night on the bank of the South Umpqua. The next night we slept at Levens, on Cow Creek, after a day of drenching rain. Late on the morning of Saturday, September 3, I left Levens. Grover remained behind to await a portion of his command. At Grave Creek I stopped to feed my horse and get something to eat.

"There was a house there called the Bates House after the man who kept it. It was a rough wooden structure without a floor and had an immence clapboard funnel at one end which served as a chimney. There was no house or settlement within 10 or 12 miles or more of it.

"There I found Captain J. K. Lamerick in command of a company of volunteers. It seems he had been sent there by General Lane after the fight at Battle Creek on account of the murder of some Indians there. Bates and some others had induced a small party of peaceable Indians who belonged in that vicinity to enter into an engagement to remain at peace with the whites during the war, which was going on at some distance from them. By way of ratification of this treaty they invited them to partake of a feast in an unoccupied log house just across the road from the Bates House. While the unarmed Indians were partaking of the proffered hospitality, the door was suddenly fastened and they were shot down by their treacherous white hosts. Nearby I was shown a large hole into which the bodies of these murdered Indians had been unceremoniously tumbled. They were covered with fresh earth.

About this same time these same parties captured

148

an Indian chief and his boy. They agreed with the boy that if he would go into the mountains and hunt down an Indian chief who had refused to come in and treat with them and bring in his head, they would liberate his father. If he failed to bring in the Indian chief's head they would kill his father. The filial young savage, for the sake of his father, undertook the task. Taking his gun he went along upon the trail of the Indian chief. In due time he returned with the head, which Bates hung by the hair to the rooftree of his house, as an Indian trophy, where, with my own eyes, I saw it.

"Instead of liberating the captive, they killed both him and his son.

"After Bates left the country the place passed into the hands of James Twogood, who, in partnership with Mr. Harkness, made it a famous resting place for man and beast."

**Oregon Journal**
February 13, 1925

# Bill Vandervert
# Bear Hunter
# Bend, Oregon

*People up Bend way say that Bill Vandervert knows every bear within 100 miles of Bend by its first name and that he also knows its home address. He is a native son of Oregon, having been born in Lane County, not far from Cottage Grove, April 22, 1854. His father, Jackson J. Vandervert, was born in Ohio, of Hollandish ancestry, and came to Oregon in 1848.*

"My father was born in 1822--just 100 years ago. He was 25 years old when he started for Oregon, in the spring of 1848. He was in the wagon train with Boliver Walker, W. H. Walker, John Purvine, Thomas Clark, and other equally well known Oregon pioneers.

"During the winter of 1848 he worked for Dr. John McLoughlin in his mill at Oregon City. The next spring, with Thomas Clark and John Magison, he went to the California gold mines. They went on horseback, leading packhorses laden with their grub and outfit. They had good luck in the mines. Thomas Clark and my father decided to invest the money they had made from their claim in buying blooded stock. At that time most of the cattle in the Willamette Valley were half-wild, long-horned Spanish cattle. They figured that by bringing out some blooded bulls they could soon breed up a better strain of beef and work cattle.

"In the spring of 1850 Thomas Clark, father's partner, went east with all the money they had made, while Father stayed on the mining claim to rock out more gold. Father returned to Oregon in 1851, settling among old friends on the Santiam River. Clark traveled throughout the East, buying up good stock to bring to the Willamette Valley. He bought a number of Morgan mares in Kentucky, and also some blooded mares in Ohio. By the spring of 1851 he had 65 horses and 63 Durham cattle ready to drive across the plains. He started for Oregon with his blooded stock and was accompanied by a number of his relatives.

"Thomas Clark was an Englishman and had the Englishman's love of sport. He was a great hunter, both of large game and of small, and also a lover of hunting dogs. He wanted to bring his blooded stock to Oregon in good condition, so he drove them only about 12 miles a day. Usually, Mrs. Clark with her daughter, Grace, who was 19 years old, and her son, Hutchinson, 17 years old, would drive ahead to select a good camping place and prepare dinner for the rest of the party.

"One day Clark, while riding ahead of the cattle, said to Mrs. Clark, 'There is a good camping place just ahead. I have just looked it over. There is good water and plenty of wood. While you are getting dinner I will go up Raft River and shoot a few ducks. He took his shotgun and his dogs and rode on. The others drove up to the trees on the bank of the river and started to prepare the meal. Soon Sperry and Hoffman came up with the horses. This camp was on Raft River, about 40 miles west of Fort Hall.

"They had heard that the Shoshone and Bannock Indians were stealing stock from the emigrants, so when Mrs. Clark looked up and saw a party of Indians coming toward them she suspected trouble. She told her son and the others to drive the loose horses back to the main wagon train. Hutchinson Clark was 17 years old. He saw the Indians taking their guns out of their leather scabbards, so he said, 'Now, Mother, I am not going to leave you and Grace. These Indians means mischief. I am going to stay and protect you.'

"He climbed upon a wagon wheel to get his gun, which was in the wagon. Mrs. Clark and Grace were in the wagon. Sperry and Huffman ran and took shelter in the rocks by the river bank. The Indians fired and Hutchison Clark fell with a bullet through his heart. Mrs. Clark screamed and the Indians fired at her. Grace threw her arms around her mother to protect her. The bullet went through her wrist and went on through her mother's heart, killing her instantly. Grace started to get out of the wagon, when one of the Indians fired at her, the bullet entering just below the armpit and passing entirely through her body. She fell beside her brother. The Indians tore off her clothes and threw her down over the bluff. She fell on the sand beside the river. The Indians rolled stones down on her, some of which struck her, leaving scars on her forehead that remained the rest of her life.

"Thomas Clark, hearing the shooting, rode at full speed toward the wagon with his hounds, which were baying loudly. The Indians, seeing him coming, thought he was leading a large number of whites, so they mounted their horses and fled, driving the blooded Kentucky horses with them. When the main wagon train came up a party was organized to pursue and punish the Indians. Charles Clark led the party. They overtook the Indians, who attacked them, killing one of the white men and wounding another. The Indians fled, taking the stolen horses with them.

"The wagon train waited there a day or so for the wounded girl to die, but as she did not die, they started forward slowly. The train bore southward toward the Three Sisters. They were the first party to pass over the site of what is now Bend. Thomas Clark named Pilot Butte. They came pretty well to the foothills of the Cascades and then swung north, crossing the mountains by the Barlow Trail and coming on down into the Willamette Valley.

"Clark and my father, of course, lost all the money they had made in the mines when the Indians drove off their stock. Father, however, found that his partner had brought to Oregon something infinitely better, for Grace Clark had recovered from her wounds, though it was not until the spring of 1853 that the patch from the bullet that had gone through her body worked out, after which the wound in her side healed completely.

"In 1853 Father took up 320 acres of land near Cottage Grove. He rode on the foothills trail up the valley, as the Willamette Valley was under water in places, to get Reverend Robert Robe, a Presbyterian minister who had come to Oregon in 1846. Father loved hunting and loved dogs. While going to summon the minister to marry him he ran across two fine hound puppies, so he slipped one into each coat pocket and brought them along. I still hunt bears with the descendants of those puppies.

"Father married Grace Clark in 1853. I was their first child, born in the spring of 1854. Four of their seven children lived to maturity. The other three died of diphtheria. Walter, who was born in 1855, lives at Redmond. Charley was killed in a runaway. Dick lives at Oakland, in southern Oregon. Mother died in 1875.

"Clark, after losing his blooded stock at what is now called Clark's Grade, went back east the next year to get more. He came back to Oregon in 1853. While passing through Salt Lake City he met Brigham Young and purchased from him for $1600 three blooded mares of trotting strain. If you will look up the records of the early state fairs in Oregon you will find Thomas Clark won many a blue ribbon for his blooded horses and cattle.

"I took to hunting like a duck takes to water. When I was a youngster deer and elk and beer were plenty. Two of my mother's brothers—the Clark boys—were bachelors. They were great hunters. When I was a boy ammunition was expensive and hard to come by, but they always saw to it that I was never out of powder or lead. I went to California with them in 1869. I was only 15. We sure had a wonderful trip. I'll tell you about it some day. I will carry the scars I got on that trip to my grave.

"When I was about 19 I carried mail from Fort Bidwell in California to Camp Warner, in the Klamath country. I was there while the Modoc War was going on. In 1875, when I was 21, I went to Humboldt County, California, and the following spring I went to Texas, where I stayed some years. I lived about midway between Dallas and Fort Worth. On November 11, 1879, I married a Kentucky girl, Sadie Vinceheller. She was a teacher.

"A good many years ago, when I was living near Silver Lake, a fellow rode up to my ranch on a bicycle. Bicycles in those days were about as plenty as airplanes are now. Everybody would turn out to see one. This chap asked me if he could put up at my place. I made him welcome. He noticed some hounds lying in the yard and said, 'You sure are long on dogs. What do you do with so many?'

"I said, 'Those are bear dogs. I killed a silver tip a few days ago.' He didn't think there were any grizzly bears in Oregon, so I showed him the hide and told him how I ran across the bear and killed it. First thing I knew he had published two or three columns in a paper about it. It turned out that the fellow on the bicycle was a newspaper writer. Some city fellows, seeing the article, wrote to ask me if I would take them on a bear hunt. So I did, and from that day to this I have been acting as guide and bear locator for city hunters.

"Come up to Bend some day and I will take you out with my dogs and we will get a bear, and then you can see how it comes. I have killed hundreds of bears. There is quite a knack in it."

"I took out E. H. Harriman's two sons on a bear hunt. I also went out on a bear hunt with Anna Crocker of San Francisco. She would take out her cigarette case, hand me a smoke and take one herself, just as sociable and free and easy as you please.

"I have eight children and I sure am proud of them. Mittie, my oldest girl, lives in Portland. Bill, my oldest boy, is running the ranch near Bend. Maud, now Mrs. Catlow, lives in Portland. She has three children. J. C. and George are doctors, with offices in Bend. Claud, who served overseas, is on the ranch with Bill. Arthur, my youngest, is at Louisville, Kentucky, studying to be a doctor. All the rest of our children graduated at the University of Oregon, so my wife said she wanted one of our children to get his education in her native state, and that is how it comes that Arthur is in the Louisville college.

"Come up to Bend some day and I will take you out with my dogs and we will get a bear, and then you can see how it comes. I have killed hundreds of bears. There is quite a knack in it.

"No, sir, I am no spring chicken any more. I am a five-times grandfather, but I can still tire out most young fellows who go out in the hills with me. I have done a lot of roaming in my time, but when a man marries his roaming days are pretty well over. He exchanges the joys of the long trail for the comfort of the home fireside."

Oregon Journal
November 22-23, 1922

# William P. Berger
# Mule-back Soldier
# Portland, Oregon

"I crossed the plains on mule-back. When the Civil War broke out (Captain Medorum Crawford) was appointed captain of a company to guard emigrants crossing the plains. I enlisted in the company. We went to Omaha, where we were furnished mules on which to ride across the plains. There were 85 of us in the company, and the mules, which were unbroken, had halters put on them and a tag with a number was tied to each halter. The members of the company drew numbers to correspond with the numbers on the mules. I hunted up the mule with my number on and, with help, got him saddled, but he was too bucky. Every time I got on I got off a good deal quicker than I got on. I finally concluded I would have to walk across the plains and leave my mule, but one of the other soldiers didn't like his mule, because it wasn't spirited enough, so we traded, both being well pleased with the trade.

"It took us over two weeks before we could

get those mules saddled and get them to go forward instead of up and down. I was on the road from Waterloo, New York, to Fort Walla Walla five months and 17 days. We were paid $13 a month and keep. As soon as I was discharged at Walla Walla I came down to Portland, arriving here in December, 1862."

Oregon Journal
March 24, 1934

# Colonel J. C. Cooper
# McMinnville, Oregon

*Colonel J. C. Cooper, pioneer resident of McMinnville, is an old-time newspaperman. In 1877 he became editor of the Valley Fountain, a temperance paper, at McMinnville, and ran it for the next ten years. He is the author of The Military History of Yamhill County, The Yamhills, The Cooper Family, and Red Pioneers. When I visited him his wife was binding his latest book, Red Pioneers. "We had it printed in Carlton," said Mrs. Cooper. "I have bound about 600 of them. We had 1000 printed."*

"My father and my folks pulled out from Missouri for Oregon in the spring of '63. I was discharged from the army in April, 1865. I went to stay with my brother Henry's family at Fort Scott. He was in the 9th Kansas Cavalry and didn't get his discharge till the fall of '65. While I was at Fort Scott, I worked at the wagon-making trade. I got kind of homesick to see my girl, Melzena Paralee Spillman, who lived on the farm next to our old farm in Missouri, so I left Fort Scott and went to visit my sweetheart. I worked around there all winter, and early next spring I landed a job driving a six-mule team to Helena, Montana. I drove with a jerk line. We had 5200 pounds of bacon and sugar. We forded Tongue River, the Big Horn, the Little Big Horn, Sun River, Powder River, the Cheyenne and a number of other streams.

"At Bridger's Ferry, the captain of the wagon train learned that the Indians were killing off every party of whites they could run across, so he hired Jim Bridger, who had a place on the North Platte, as guide. Bridger rode a flea-bitten gray mare. He wore a blue army overcoat and a felt hat and he had a long gun that he carried just back of his saddle horn. Some of the wagons in our train were loaded with whiskey. Maybe Jim Bridger drank, but if he did, I never saw him. He always seemed mighty busy watching out for Indians, finding camps and seeing that things were

155

going all right. We had three or four skirmishes with the Indians. Bridger stayed with us till we came to the crossing of the Yellowstone. From there on he said we would have no trouble in making our way to Helena.

"When I got to Helena one of the men there pointed to a tree with a heavy limb, and said, 'That's Judge Lynch of Montana. We hung several men on that limb not long ago.'

"I had no money. I went to a butcher shop and said to the butcher, 'I have no money. I haven't been paid off, but I want some meat.' He cut me off a good-sized piece of beef, wrapped it up for me, and handed it to me and said, 'Come in and pay when you get your money.' He didn't ask my name or anything else. Later I went back and paid him for it.

"Along about the middle of September I started for Oregon. When I got to Walla Walla I was broke. I sold my cayuse and the pack saddle for eight dollars. The buyer wanted to pay me in gold dust, but I didn't know anything about gold dust and wouldn't take it. Pretty soon another man came along and bought my outfit for $12 in cash.

"I had hoofed it all the way from Helena to Walla Walla. I found that the price of a ticket on the boat from Wallula to Portland was $18. I was shy six dollars. I went down to the corral where the freighters put up their outfits and heard a man say, 'Can any of you fellows drive a six-horse outfit with a jerk-line?'

"I pricked up my ears at that and said, 'I drove a six-mule team from Fort Leavenworth to Helena with a jerk line. I guess maybe your horses can understand mule language. I'll take the job.'

The owner of the outfit had been drawn on the jury at two dollars a day. He agreed to give me his pay as a juror. I went up into the Blue Mountains and bought out a load of timber to be used on the Walla Walla aqueduct. This was the first timber brought out on that job. The trip took me three days and I earned six dollars.

"I walked to Wallula. After paying $18 for a ticket to Portland I only had 25 cents left. The boat laid over on Sunday at The Dalles. It got there Saturday night. My clothes were pretty well shot to pieces, and one of my boots had worn out so I was wearing one boot and one rubber.

"I decided to sit up by the fire all night in the Umatilla House. Nick Sinnott, the proprietor, came over to me and said, 'Young fella, how much money you got?'

"I said, 'Twenty-five cents.' I told him I had put in three years in the Union Army and

156

was on my way to the Willamette Valley.

"He said, 'You go into that room and go to bed, instead of sitting up all night. Be sure to turn up for all three meals tomorrow, just as if you were a paying guest. You can pay me some other time. Keep your quarter for seed.'

"It was 25 years before I got back to The Dalles to pay that bill.

"When I got to Portland I invested my two-bits in a bed. Next day I walked up as far as Ramp's, near the present town of Brooks. The 42-mile walk about wore me out. I asked Mr. Ramp to direct me to Spong's Ferry and then I asked him if I could sleep in his barn. He said, 'I don't want people sleeping in my barn—too much danger of fire—but you can stay in my house, if you haven't got any graybacks.

"I said, 'I'm sorry to say I have had lice pretty steady for the past five years. They're pretty hard to get rid of when you haven't any change of clothes.' I told him I had boiled all my clothes in Walla Walla and taken a bath, but I couldn't guarantee that I hadn't picked up a few graybacks since.

"He said, 'Well, you're honest about it, anyway. I'll take a chance.' I can still remember how good the ham and eggs tasted that his wife gave me.

"Next morning I struck out and as I got to Kaiser Bottom, I recognized the team of horses that was coming toward me as the ones we had owned in Missouri. It was my brother. He recognized me, pulled up the team and said, 'Get in, Cal. I'm going to the state fair.'

"I said, 'Not much. Everybody would stop looking at the animals to look at me. I'm a sight. I'll go on to the place.'

"He said, 'All the folks are camped out in the grove at the state fair for the week. If you go on to the farm they'll feel that they have to come back to see you.' So I climbed up on the seat with my brother and we drove on to the fair-grounds at Salem. My father took me to Werner Breyman's store, and he furnished me with an outfit on credit. As soon as we got back from the fair I went to cutting cordwood and splitting rails till I got money to pay Breyman for my clothes.

"One day an old-time neighbor of ours, William Ernest from Missouri, came over, watched me splitting rails awhile, and said, 'Cal, you're good and husky. I want you to come to our neighborhood and teach school.'

"I said, 'A cow is big enough to catch a mouse, but I never saw them catching any. I may

157

be big and husky, but I never had much education, so I don't see how I could be a school teacher.'

"He said, 'You don't have to know much to be a school teacher. The principal thing you have to be is strong enough to lick the big boys. I'll give you $100 to teach a three months' term of school, providing you help us build the school house.' I accepted his proposition, and he said, 'You go to the county school superintendent and get him to give you a certificate to teach.'

"I said, 'I knew there was a catch in it. If it was cutting wood or driving mules I could pass the examination, but I don't know anything about book learning.'

"Mr. Ernest said, 'That don't cut any figure. Tom Butler, the county superintendent, is a Democrat, and so am I. He'll give you an examination you can pass.'

"Mr. Butler only asked me one question. He asked me what was the capital of Mexico, and I told him I didn't know, so he gave me a third grade certificate to teach.

"I had 12 pupils. Some of them were pretty husky guys. Most of 'em knew a whole lot more than I did, so I asked them questions. Of course, they didn't know that they were teaching me. If they asked me any questions I said they'd remember it better if they looked it up for themselves. I studied till 2 o'clock every morning.

"I got through that term and they never discovered I didn't know anything.

"At the end of the term my brother Dan and I started the store at Lincoln. In those days there were lots of boats running up and down the Willamette River. We bought wheat. Sometimes we made good money on it, and sometimes we had to sell it for less than we paid. Most of the time, though, we made a little margin on it. What broke us was, we gave credit to anybody and everybody that asked for it, for we figured they'd pay us if and when they could, but a lot of them never seemed to come to the 'if and when' time. We sold our store at Lincoln to Mr. Abrams.

"Later we built a store at Zena and one at Perrydale. My wife's name is Melzena. Her sister, Arbozena, married my brother Dan. Being as they both had 'zena' for the latter part of their names, we named the post office "Zena Post Office'. I was the first postmaster at Perrydale. Later I served as postmaster at McMinnville under President Harrison. I was postmaster there for five years.

"In 1875 the town of Amity wanted a school house. I secured the contract at $2500. Old Man W. T. Newby, who, with S. C. Adams, founded the

town of McMinnville, came through the country selling
stock for a proposed steamboat line. When he asked
me to buy some stock I said, 'I'll buy two shares
at $25 each if you'll make me secretary of the com-
pany.'

"He said, 'All right. You can be secretary.'
I accepted the job and moved to McMinnville in
the summer of 1876. They called this company the
People's Protective Transportation Company. Henry
Warren was president, I was secretary, and the
directors were W. T. Newby, J. K. Sampson, W.
Warren, W. McChristman, and W. Savage. If I
remember correctly, Newby raised $12,000. We built
the steamer McMinnville at Canemah, launched her
in November, 1876, and she made her trial trip
on the Yamhill River in February, 1877. Captain
I. B. Sanborn, now a resident of Portland, was
master of the McMinnville till 1879, when we turned
her over to the Oregon Steam Navigation Company.
In 1891 she was taken to Salem and used as a wharf
boat and was later burned for the iron in her.
Our company bought the steamer S. T. Church and
we put Captain L. E. Pratt of Salem in charge
of her. The S. T. Church was an old tub. We
paid $8000 for her and I think we were stung.

"I was elected county surveyor, and later
I secured a government survey for work in the
Blue Mountains. I figured that I would clean up
about $400 in this contract, so when David P. Thompson
offered me $1500 to turn the contract over to him
I didn't hesitate about letting him have it. With
that $1500 I built a fine house in McMinnville.
Building was cheaper in those days than now.

"When was I married? I could tell you quite
a story about that, but I'll make it short. It
began to snow on New Year's Day in 1868. I was
living at Zena, in Spring Valley, about nine miles
from Salem. The Willamette and the Columbia froze
over. The steamers were frozen in, and they stayed
frozen in till late in February. I bought a ticket
on the Ajax, which broke the ice in the Columbia
River and went out over the bar on February 19.
It took us five days to get to San Francisco. On
account of a rate war, I got a ticket from San
Francisco to New York, by way of the Isthmus,
for $40. When I got to New York I went to see
a play called 'The Black Crook'. It was kind
of scandalous, for those days, for the girls' skirts
only came down to their knees, and the preachers
and the papers roasted it so they had big crowds
all the time.

"I went to Missouri and married my sweetheart,
Melzena Spillman, on April 26, 1868. We went to
New York to catch the steamer, so I took her to

see 'The Black Crook', but she was so scandalized at those girls' wearing their dresses up to their knees that she wanted to leave, and when I told her it would make her conspicuous she kept her eyes shut and wouldn't look.

"We have had eight children, six of whom are now living. Our son Louis died when he was 17, Nora married Professor R. W. Doane. He was a classmate of President Hoover and teaches at Stanford. Our son Dr. Arthur Spillman Cooper practiced his profession in South America for 14 years but now lives at San Francisco. Wells died six years ago. Nelly, who married M. P. McCroskey, lives in Portland. Dr. Paul B. Cooper is in Portland. Fred, our youngest boy, has been an artist and cartoonist for **Life** for the past 24 years. Both Wells and Paul served in the Spanish-American War in the McMinnville Company."

Oregon Journal
March 22 & 23, 1929

# Judge William M. Colvig
# Medford, Oregon

"Jesse James and I were born in the same town and in the same year. We were both born at Richmond, Missouri, in 1845.

"I spell my name Colvig, though my father's grandfather signed his name Jean Baptiste Colvigne. He was a sea captain and merchant-trader. He became a partner of Mr. Lyngae, a wealthy Greek merchant. He married his partner's daughter, Zelesta Lyngae. She was born in Athens. My great grandfather had charge of the Paris branch of the firm. Their son, Jacob Lyngae Colvigne, my grandfather, was born in Paris in 1776. When he was 18 he enlisted under Napoleon. He was wounded at the Battle of Lodi, in 1795, when he was 19. With Napoleon in Egypt, he took part in the Battle of Marengo. In 1801 he was part of a detachment of French troops sent to put down a slave insurrection in the West Indies, led by Toussaint L'Ouverture. L'Ouverture proclaimed himself governor, promulgated a new constitution, abolished slavery, adopted free trade, and confiscated the estates of the absentee French landlords. Napoleon sent a naval force to put down the insurrection. France and England at this time were at war and Napoleon was threatening to invade England. Jerome Bonaparte, in charge of the expedition, to escape a battle with a superior English fleet, put in at Baltimore, a neutral port. Here Jerome met, wooed, and won a Baltimore belle,

Miss Elizabeth Patterson.

"Meanwhile, my grandfather's enlistment had expired, so he took French leave and settled at Leasburg, Virginia. As a young man he had been apprenticed to a cabinetmaker, so he took up his old trade, and soon his cherry and walnut furniture

"On the Sweetwater the men killed a number of buffalo and jerked the meat. After that, whenever we boys begged for something to eat, Mother would give us a hunk of buffalo jerky to chew on."

was in demand and he had all he could do to supply his hand-made chairs, highboys, bedsteads, and tables to the wealthy planters.

"In 1809 he married Winifred Hoffman, a cousin of Robert E. Lee's father. She was only 15, and her relatives bitterly opposed the match. They promised to forgive her if she would leave her husband, but she was a high-spirited southern girl and refused. Her relatives bought up a note of my grandfather's, and when it fell due refused to renew it. They had him imprisoned for debt, thinking his wife would leave him. Instead of this she sold her jewelry, paid the note, and, with her husband, moved to Ohio.

"My father, Dr. William L. Colvig, was born at Leesburg, Virginia, in 1814. When he was 23 he was married at Marietta, Ohio, to Helen Woodford. My mother, Helen Woodford Colvig, was born at Hartford, Connecticut, in 1816. The Woodfords and the Woodruffs came from England to Connecticut in 1640 and the two families have intermarried till I have a host of relatives in both families.

"On May 4, 1861, when I was six years old, we held an auction in our home at Parksville, Platte County, Missouri, and sold everything that Mother did not want to take to Oregon. Our home was six miles from Westport, now Kansas City. Though I was only six years old, I still remember hearing the neighbors bid us goodbye and godspeed.

"We camped at Platte City. Father and four other men who were on their way to Oregon decided to organize a wagon train. They constituted themselves a committee to pass on all applications of those wanting to join. Many applicants were rejected either because they did not have the required amount of bacon, cornmeal, brown sugar, and other supplies, because their firearms and ammunition were not up to the standard required, because their wagons and oxen were not considered heavy enough to make the trip across the plains, or because their moral character was not up to requirement. Some others who were acceptable, refused to subscribe to the regulations drawn up by my father and the other four charter members of the company, so that when they were ready to go there were but 23 families who had signed, agreeing to obey the captain and stand by and assist the other members through thick and thin till their destination was reached. James Dunn, who located in Benton County, was elected captain. My father was elected assistant.

"I can still visualize our family wagon. In it were my father and mother, we four boys, and my baby sister, Wilda, nine months old. On a rack, fastened to the hickory wagon bows, was father's Kentucky rifle, and beside it his powder horn and bullet pouch. On the side of the wagon bed the coffee mill was fastened. Mother had reduced the library to just a few books--the **Bible**, a hymn book, **Pilgrim's Progress, Frost's Pictorial History of the United States, Webster's Elementary Spelling Book**, and **Mcguffey's** First and **Second Readers**. During the six months or more we were on the plains Mother had me recite to her, so that by the end of the trip I was reading in the Second Reader.

"On the Sweetwater the men killed a number of buffalo and jerked the meat. After that, whenever we boys begged for something to eat, Mother would give us a hunk of buffalo jerky to chew on.

"To every member of the train certain duties were assigned. My job was to gather buffalo chips for Mother to cook supper over at night. The Indians had burned the grass, so our fresh cows soon went dry and we had to do without the fresh milk. One day we had a heavy thunderstorm, and one of the wagons was struck by lightning. The lightning exploded a can of gunpowder in the wagon bed and wrecked the wagon and scattered its contents over the prairie.

"On one occasion the Indians gathered to attack the train. An old trapper and mountain man in our train had one of the wagons pull out to one side of the road, and told the woman to cry out loud. The Indian chief, dressed in his war paint, rode forward and asked why the women were wailing. The trapper said, 'They are crying for their dead who have died of the cholera.' The chief rode back to his braves and a moment or so later all we saw was a cloud of dust. They were deathly afraid of the cholera. They passed the word to the other tribes, who gave us a wide berth.

"Four of our oxen died, so we had to abandon our largest wagon at Fort Hall. Near Salt Lake City our train divided, some going to California, and others decided to lay over for a while. With six other families we pressed on to the Willamette Valley, where we arrived on October 5. We went to the home of Tom Carter, at the head of Clay Street, in Portland, where we spent the winter of 1851 and '52.

"It takes all kinds of people to make the world. Take the matter of crossing the plains, for example. Some were natural leaders. Others had no initiative and were natural leaners. Some were helpful, others helpless.

"In our wagon train, in 1851, there was a fat, bald-headed little old man who had started out with two yoke of oxen. Two of these oxen played out in Utah, so Captain Dunn of our wagon train went over his load to see what best he could abandon. Among the things Captain Dunn threw out first were some flatirons, a heavy grindstone, and some bricks. The owner of the wagon was greatly distressed and said, "I swow, Captain, I can't allow you to throw them bricks away. I've hauled them upwards of a thousand miles and I might need them in Oregon.' The captain proving adamant, the old gentleman turned to the other members of the wagon train and said, 'By zounds, gentlemen, I don't want

163

to leave them bricks.    They might come in mighty handy out in Oregon.'

"Just east of Grand Ronde Valley two disreputable looking Indians rode up to our camp and unsaddled their horses.    Captain Dunn said to Father,  'If you have anything left from supper, scraps of any kind, we'd better give it to these two Indians, and then I'll make them move on.    I don't like their looks.'

"Mother had a few bones left from our supper. She put these on a piece of canvas with some scraps of bread and Father motioned for the Indians to sit down and eat.    The two Indians sat down, took off their hats, bowed their heads, and the older of the two said, in excellent English,  'Father we thank Thee for this food.    Bless it to our use and us to Thy service.    Bless our white friends.    Guide them on their journey safely and at last take them to be with Thee.    Amen.'

"Captain Dunn gave my father a peculiar look and motioned him to one side and said,  'I guess, Doc, I won't make 'em move on after all.'

"The Indians told us they were members of Doctor Whitman's church at Waiilatpu and though Dr. Whitman had been dead four years, they still gave thanks at their meals and tried to practice what Dr. and Mrs. Whitman had taught them.

At The Dalles Father hired a couple of Indians to take Mother and the children by canoe to the head of the Cascades, while he took the wagon on to the Willamette Valley over the Barlow Trail. My father and Tom Carter of Portland were old-time friends and neighbors at Athens, Ohio.    Carter had crossed the plains to the Willamette Valley in 1847.    He and Father had both planned to go that year, but Father was delayed and didn't get started till 1851.    Father sent word to Carter by some emigrants that we were on our way.    When we got to the foot of the Cascade Rapids it was dusk.    The steamer Lot Whitcomb was just pulling in.    Carter stepped off the gangplank, recognized Mother and took us all aboard the Lot Whitcomb, and we went with him to his newly-finished, large and comfortable house at the head of Clay Street in Portland.    When we got to his home, Mr. Carter gave my brothers--Volney, Mark, and George--and myself new hats and shoes, for we were barefooted and bareheaded from our long trip.

"Mr. Carter's daughter married Lafayette Grover, a rising young attorney who later became governor of Oregon and United States Senator.    We spent the winter of 1851 and 1852 at the Carter home. Mr. Carter wanted Father to take 640 acres at Mount Tabor.    Father said,  'Tom, I haven't crossed the continent and come clear out to the Willamette Valley to settle in a dense fir forest way out in the country.'

"In the spring of 1852 Father hitched John and Charlie, our faithful oxen, to our prairie schooner and we went down the valley to Winchester, in southern Oregon. Colonel William Martin told Father we could move into his cabin and have all his garden truck we needed. We stayed on the Martin place till the following October, when Father took up 640 acres near Canyonville. The following year, 1853, Father was appointed postmaster at Canyonville.

"B. F. Dowell, whose widow now lives in Portland, and whose son, Biddy Dowell, was chief of the Portland Fire Department some years ago, carried the mail from Jacksonville to Oakland. I used to watch eagerly to see him coming on his mule, leading another mule with the mail on it.

"Father started a drug store at Canyonville in the winter of 1852. The winter of 1852 was severe. At one time we had over 20 travelers staying in our house who were trail-bound, not being able to go through the 12-mile Canyon. Mother kept two kettles over the fireplace all the time, one filled with boiled wheat, the other with venison, so our guests had plenty to eat, even if there wasn't much variety. Among these storm-bound travelers was Judge Orange Jacobs, then a resident of Jacksonville, but later a supreme judge of the Washington Territory.

"The settlers near Canyonville decided to have a school, so they employed Samuel Strang as teacher. They made him sign an agreement not to get drunk for three months, the penalty being forfeiture of salary. He was a well-educated man and a good teacher. He died a few years later at Jacksonville, of delirium tremens.

"Later, the directors employed I. M. Choynski. He taught one term and was employed to teach a second term, but the big boys put him out of the schoolhouse through the window and ran him off. His son, Joe Choynski, later won a national reputation as a prize fighter. Binger Hermann, later Congressman from Oregon and Commissioner of the General Land Office, taught several terms. Later a young man from Iowa, Rufus Mallory, who had come out to Oregon to die of consumption, served as teacher. He recovered from his lung trouble, represented Oregon in Congress, and became an able and honored judge.

"My brother Andrew was buried in Ohio. My brother Volney was county judge of Josephine County. He died two years ago.

"It must have been about January, 1852, or

possibly a little earlier, when Tom Dryer, editor of the **Oregonian,** who lived next door to us in Portland, gave Volney a job running the press once a week to get off the **Weekly Oregonian.** Mark was a miner, prospector, and telegraph operator. He died at Canyonville. My brother Manson died in Missouri. I was the next child. My brother George is an attorney and lives at Grants Pass. My sister Wilda, who was a baby when we crossed the plains, married H. S. Emery of Ashland. John was chief of scouts under General McKenzie. He was killed by the Indians in Arizona. Oren and Aphia are dead.

"Shortly after the Civil War I was working at Burning Springs, West Virginia. Before going to Burning Springs I had met, in Ohio, Lizzie Keller, the daughter of a preacher. I finally got so homesick to see her that I quit my job at Burning Springs and started on foot for Ohio. The country in West Virginia and thereabouts, immediately after the Civil War, was full of desperate characters, so holdups and murders were numerous. I put a $50-bill in my boot, so that if I were held up it would not be found. In wading a stream it suddenly occurred to me that my $50-bill had probably got pretty wet and I had better take my boots and socks off and dry the bill before it was ruined. I put it on a stump beside the trail to dry, and while I was wringing out my socks and pouring the water out of my boots, three men came along the trail, saw me, pointed their guns at me and told me to throw up my hands, saying, 'If you move, you're a dead man.'

"They took my purse and valise and told me to put my boots on and come with them. I said, 'Hold on a moment.'

"They pointed their guns at me and told me to come without any further conversation. I pointed to the stump and one of the men went over and found the $50-bill and brought it along. We went down the trail and presently joined some other men, one of whom, apparently the leader, said, 'Did you get him boys? Who does he say he is?' These men were Southerners.

"The leader searched me and found my honorable discharge from the army. He turned to me and said, 'So you're a Yankee, are you?'

"I said, 'Yes, I'm a Yankee, but during the war I was fighting Indians out in Oregon.' I showed him some letters from my folks at Canyonville, Oregon, and told him I was on my way to see my sweetheart, Lizzie Keller, in Ohio.

"One of the men said, 'Did you say Lizzie Keller? What's her father's name?' He asked me a few more questions and then, turning to the leader, said, 'You might as well turn this young fellow loose. I know Keller, and he's all right, and probably this young fellow is, too. He don't look like a murderer.' They gave back my purse, my $50-bill, and my valise, and told me to start out and keep going in the direction of Ohio.

"I asked them why they had held me up. One of the men said, 'We've got sick of so many murders going on here, and we're sort of a vigilance committee. We found a man's body this morning near the mouth of the railroad tunnel and we're out after his murderer.'

"I went to Tremont, Tazewell County, Illinois, and entered Tremont Collegiate Institute. Tremont had formerly been the county seat and the old courthouse was used as the college. Abraham Lincoln had frequently tried cases at Tremont before the county seat was moved to Pekin. The janitor hunted me up a table to use and pointed to the initials 'A. L.' cut into the table, saying, as he did so, "The man that cut those initials used to be a country lawyer and became president of the United States.' I used Abraham Lincoln's old table for the 18 months that I was at school there. I took the examination for teacher and secured a second grade certificate and secured a position as a teacher. Later I secured a first grade certificate. During the summers I sold nursery stock. Later I studied law in the office of Judge Rodecker at Pekin, the county seat.

"I was married to Addie Birdseye, June 8, 1879. This was four years after I came back to Oregon. I served as district attorney in 1886. For some years I was attorney for the Southern Pacific, with headquarters in Portland. Some of these days I am going to write a book of reminiscences. I have seen enough curious and humorous things in my experience to make a book.

"In the fall of 1852 we moved to Canyonville. A man named White ran a saloon there. One day he said, before a bunch of us boys, that he was fond of crow's gizzards. He said, 'I would be willing to pay $2 for a mess of crows' gizzards, say a dozen of them.'

"I had visions of quick and easy riches, for there were hundreds of crows on Gazley's Bottom, on the South Umpqua. Jasper Roberts and New Yocum beat me to it. They hurried home, got their shotguns, and went to Gazley's Bottom. Soon they were back, and putting a dozen dead crows on the bar, they said, 'There are your crows, Mr. White. You said you would give us $2 for a dozen.'

"Mr. White said, 'What I said was, I will pay you $2 for a dozen crows' gizzards. Take them out in the back yard, bring me their gizzards, and I will pay you $2.'

"They cut the crows open to get their gizzards. They came back and said, 'We can't find their gizzards.'

"I would be willing to pay $2.00 for a mess of crow's gizzards, say a dozen of them."

"Mr. White shook his head sympathetically and said, 'Maybe those crows haven't got any gizzards.'

"That was the first time I knew crows didn't have gizzards.

"Many years later I walked into a hotel at St. Charles, Missouri, and wrote my name on the register. I noticed a fine looking man with a silky black beard and a Prince Albert coat sizing me up. He walked over to the counter and looked at my name in the register. Presently he took a chair next to mine and said, 'Have you any relatives in Oregon, Mr. Colvig?'

"I said, 'Yes, my father, Dr. Colvig, lives at Canyonville.'

"He said, 'Do you remember me? I used to live at Canyonville. My name is White.'

"I told him I only remembered one man named White at Canyonville, a saloonkeeper, who was fond of crows' gizzards.

"He said, 'I am pastor of the Methodist Church here. I have got over my liking for crows' gizzards. I would rather you didn't tell the people here about my liking crows' gizzards. They might not understand.'

Oregon Journal
May 11-13, 1927

# J. B. Wright
# Portland, Oregon

*Though J. B. Wright has celebrated 96 anniversaries of his birth, the incidents of his trip across the plains are etched in his memory so indelibly that he can tell even the minor incidents of his trip with fidelity and vividness. In telling me of this trip, he said:*

"In March, 1863, I bought a wagon in which I put an extra decking about 15 inches above the wagon bed. Between this decking and the wagon bed I placed my stores and my supplies. We slept on the decking in the wagon. At the back of the wagon I had a grub box made with a double lid. When opened this extra lid made a table. When the lid was folded up I roped three chairs above the grub box, so that we could always eat in comfort.

"A neighbor of mine volunteered to drive my two yoke of oxen in exchange for his board. I also brought with us some milch cows, so that we had fresh milk, buttermilk, and butter all the way across the plains. We left Dorris County, Iowa, in April, and crossed the Missouri River at Nebraska City. We camped there till the grass grew stronger.

"We started on May 10. The Platte was high, on account of melting snow. The Old Oregon Trail, which had been traveled for 20 years, was deeply rutted. Near Fort Kearney there was an occasional sod house, where settlers had homesteaded. Beyond this for 400 miles there was no settlement and at that time this rich and fertile district was known at the Great American Desert.

"Most of the emigrants we overtook or came across were from Missouri. They were leaving that state because of the troubled condition caused by the Civil War.

"Just beyond Fort Kearney we forded the Platte River, as we were told that the grass was better on the north side of the river. The river was about a mile wide and in most places was about knee-deep for the oxen, though in places it came up to the wagon bed. The bottom of the Platte was sandy and the current of the stream washed the sand out from beneath the wagon wheels.

"After crossing the Platte we found a wide and beautiful prairie of emerald-green, rolling land waves. We camped near the foothills, built a campfire of buffalo chips, and dug a well through the sod about two feet deep and struck clear, good water. The year before had been a drouth year and thousands of buffalo had perished for want of water, for the Platte in the late summer of '62 had gone dry. All along the road could be seen the bleached and whitened bones of the buffalo. The shoulder blades and broader bones had been used as calling cards by the emigrants who had preceded us. We constantly ran across the names of Davis, Hill and Hauser, who had autographed buffalo bones with the information that they were bound for East Banock, Montana.

"The wagon trains were constantly shifting. Some members of a train would drop back and others would drive ahead and join the trains in advance. At Grand Island there were six wagons and 13 men in our train.

"We noticed that the grass on the island was better than along the river, so we drove our cattle through the river so they could graze overnight on the island. One of the members of our party --an old man named Gad--and his son swam the river next morning to bring them back. His son swam back without difficulty, but the old man became frightened and midway of the stream turned round and swam back to the island. Once more he tried it, and once more lost his courage and turned back. One of the number, a young man named Charles Conover, from Illinois, taking a small rope betwen his teeth, swam over to the island. One of our men on the shore paid out the rope and when Conover had fastened the rope around the old man's body under his arms we pulled him into the river and across to our camp.

"When we reached Fort Laramie in June, we camped in a grove, and that night a dead Sioux Indian and one mortally wounded were brought in. The soldiers had been out rounding up hostile Indians. The Indian squaws gave the death wail and tied the dead Indian in one of the trees in the grove. Many of the trees had dead Indians tied in their upper branches.

"On the North Platte some of the members of our wagon train headed northward for Montana, but three of the outfits stayed with us on our westward way to Idaho. We found gooseberries in the mountains, so we had gooseberry pie. My neighbor, who was driving my ox team, killed an antelope on Sweetwater Creek.

"We reached South Pass on July 8. The grade is so gradual that it was hard to realize that we had been climbing. In fact, I could hardly tell which way the water ran. We camped at the head of Sweetwater Creek, which flowed into the North Platte, thence into the Missouri and Mississippi and so on to the Gulf of Mexico.

"Just beyond this I found water running west —a tributary of the Colorado River. At South Pass one fork of the road turns southwest toward Salt Lake and California, while the other fork--called Lander's Cutoff--goes to Idaho and thence to Oregon.

"While going down the slope toward Green River Valley we met over 400 Indians in war paint who were out on the war path to fight the Utes. The wagon train just next to us, consisting of 80 wagons from Missouri, was attacked while camped on Green River and the Indians captured some mules and a few oxen. The next day DeKalb Musgrove of Alexandria, Missouri, formerly a newspaper editor, in trying to recover his stock was killed by the Indians.

"Our narrowest escape from death occurred one day when we had camped for our noon rest near the Snake River. We had camped on a knoll, where there was a little spring of water. A rain came up, so we took shelter in our wagon. A few moments later I looked out and saw a column of water five feet high rolling down the gulch. A cloudburst had occurred, which swept all before it. Fortunately, we had camped where we were not in its path."

Oregon Journal
June 22, 1931

# Frank M. Collins
# Pioneer of 1846
# Dallas, Oregon

"When I was 12 years old we started with our ox teams and prairie schooners for Oregon. I was born in Warren County, Missouri, November 19, 1834, so I was coming 13 when we started across the plains.

"My father's name was Smith Collins. He was born in Orange County, Virginia, December 25, 1804. In 1827 he went to Warren County, Missouri. Two years later he married Eliza Emily Wyatt, who was born in Kentucky. My father's people came from England to Virginia in the colonial days. My mother's people, the Wyatts and the Campbells, came from England and Scotland. There were 12 of us children. My oldest sister, Jane Eliza, married Matthew Nealy. The next child was a boy. They christened him James Layton Collins. He was born May 9, 1833. My brother Jim had the choice of the whole Willamette Valley, but he never took up a donation land claim. He was a bookworm and became a lawyer.

"I was the third child in our family and was christened Francis Marion Collins. The next child, Eliza Melvina Collins, was born October 22, 1836. After Eliza came Douglas Wyatt Collins. My brother, George Smith Collins, was killed while we were crossing the plains, three miles from Soda Springs. He fell out of the wagon and the wheel ran over him, killing him instantly. William Wallace, the next boy, was born March 2, 1843. He married Letitia Fuqua. The next child was named David Crockett Collins. He was born February 17, 1845. He was killed by his horse in his early 20's while fording a stream. The first of the children born in Oregon was Alexander, October 25, 1847. The next child to arrive was Emily Arathusa. Amory Samuel Collins was born on January 27, 1853. The youngest child in our family was Mary Isadora Collins.

"Now that I have called the roll of the family, I want to tell you something of my boyhood back in Missouri. A boy's recollections are very vivid, and I can remember very distinctly how good the papaws, the persimmons, the fox grapes, the wild blackberries, and the wild strawberries tasted back in Missouri. A small stream called the Sharat River ran through my father's place. There was timber all along this stream. All through that country there were black walnut and hickory trees. My hands used to be as brown as a gypsy's from gathering the black walnuts and hulling them. In the woods along the river were quail and wild turkeys and any quantity of gray and red squirrels. Out in the prairies were plenty of prairie chickens. All a person needed was a stout pole, a few yards of fish line, a hook--or, in the absence of a hook, a bent pin--and a can of angleworms, to get all the catfish he wanted. I remember yet how good the squirrel pies tasted that Mother used to bake.

"Orrus Brown had crossed the plains to Oregon in 1844. He came back the following year to get his family, his mother, and other relatives. He told my father about Oregon. Father got the Oregon fever. That's how we happened to come to Oregon in 1846. Orrus Brown's brother-in-law, Virgil Pringle, also decided to come. In fact, they made up a good-sized party of emigrants in our neighborhood. My father rented his farm and bought three new wagons with two yoke of oxen for each wagon. We left home about the middle of April. We had been out only a few days when we were joined by a number of wagons from Georgia. These people had started from their home early in March. We passed Grand Prairie and Boon's Lake over pretty good roads. We passed through Huntersville, county seat of Randolph County, also through Keytesville, and came to Brunswick, on the Missouri River, near the junction of the Grand River.

"Toward the latter part of April we had frequent thunderstorms and heavy showers, which made muddy roads and heavy pulling. Many of the emigrants stocked up with bacon in Jackson County, paying $3\frac{1}{2}$ cents a pound for it. They put in enough to last them for the trip across the plains. We stopped to purchase flour at Blue Mills, famous in those days for a high grade of flour. Blue Mills was not far from Independence, where we arrived May 7, 1846. After passing Independence it was decided that there were too many wagons in our train, so they were divided into two trains. William Keithly was elected captain of our train, with Orrus Brown as guide for both trains. Captain Robinson was chosen captain of the other wagon train.

"On May 23 our party crossed the Blue River. The wagon beds were raised with blocks put between the bolsters and the beds. Next morning we added an additional member to our party, a baby having been born to Mrs. Aaron Richardson during the night. In the timber along the Blue Earth River, toward the latter part of May, we ran across some elk and a few days later we saw plenty of antelope. We stopped for half a day under the head of Grand Island to bury a daughter of Mr. Shelton. In the early part of June we began coming in sight of huge herds of buffalo. In fact, during the entire month of June we were rarely out of sight of buffalo, antelope, or prairie dogs. On Ash Creek we children found plenty of chokecherries and wild currants.

"We passed through Ash Hollow about the middle of June and two days later passed Parker's Castle. The next point of interest that we passed was Scott's Bluffs. Occasionally we would see hunting parties of Pawnees and just beyond Scott's Bluffs we came to a Sioux camp with about 20 lodges. We passed Fort Laramie June 22 and soon entered the Black Hills. Lost cattle, broken axle-trees, and an occasional stampede of oxen helped to vary the monotony of the trip. The thing the emigrants were always vitally interested in was the finding of a camp with good wood and water, with plenty of grass nearby for the cattle. Occasionally parties of trappers would be met coming in toward Fort Laramie with loads of beaver pelts.

"We reached Independence Rock on July 4. A few days later we were on the Sweetwater, where we saw mountain sheep on the high bluffs. We stopped over on Sunday, July 12, and during the

173

day Mrs. Townsend gave birth to a daughter.

"The road wound up and across the Wind River Mountains, beyond which we came to the Big Sandy River. The next stream we reached was Green river. Then we crossed the Black Fork of the Green and later struck Ham's Fork. A few days after that we followed up the course of the Muddy, where there was plenty of water and good grass. Crossing the divide between Green River and Bear River, we struck good water and grass and plenty of willow for fire. We met here about 600 Shoshone Indians. Early in August we reached Soda Springs. About an hour after leaving Soda Springs, on our way to the Portneuf, my brother George fell from a wagon and was killed. We camped there and buried him by the side of the road.

"Just beyond American Falls we met Jesse Applegate, who had come to tell us about the new route to the Willamette Valley by way of Southern Oregon. On Raft River the road forked, one branch leading westward to Oregon and the other to California. We took the California road, intending to follow it for 300 miles and then turn westward by way of Klamath Lake into Oregon. We turned south on August 10 and traveled southward until September 5, when we left the California road and struck westward for Oregon. We had to cross a 55-mile desert with only two springs to water our stock in the entire stretch. Our oxen were so weak that we had to leave two of them while crossing the desert. As we entered the timbered foothills on September 19, one of Virgil Pringle's oxen was shot by an Indian with an arrow and two of the loose cattle were shot.

"Some of our party had kept tally on the mileage, and this day saw the passing of the 2000 mile mark. During the latter days of September we were passing through a country of lakes--Klamath Lake and others. Some of our party lost some cattle on Klamath Lake, which were driven off by Indians. On October 15, we camped on Rogue River. Four days later we stopped to bury Mr. Crowley's daughter, who was 14 years old. The going was very slow and difficult along the Umpqua, as the roads had to be made, and the rains had started. We did not get to our destination until early in December, the last month's travel being very difficult and unpleasant.

"We left our cattle on Eugene Skinner's donation land claim, where the city of Eugene is now located. Our oxen were so weak we had to leave them there, packing what goods we could carry, as well as the women and children, on our mules and going on to Luckiamute and stopping at what is now called Parker's Station. A couple of bachelors had a log cabin there. They offered to share it with us for the rest of the winter. One of these bachelors, Mr. Nealy, married my sister.

"My brother Jim, better known in later days as Judge Collins, with a man named Turnidge, stayed that winter in Eugene Skinner's unfinished cabin to look after their cattle. The cattle just about held their own during the winter. As soon as the cattle were strong enough to travel and the roads had dried up a little, early in the next spring, they drove the wagons to where we were staying on the Luckiamute.

"In the spring of 1847 my father took up a donation land claim near where the town of Suver was later built. When I was old enough I took up a claim near Airlie.

"In 1854 I went to the mines on Scott River, near Yreka, California. I stayed there until the spring of 1855, when I moved to my claim and put in the summer getting out fence rails, fencing my place and improving it. I sold it shortly after that for $1000 and bought the place owned by Mrs. Mary Gilliam on the Peedee Creek. That creek was named by Marcus Gilliam. He used always to be humming a tune, one line of which was 'On the banks of Sweet Peedee', and so the creek took its name from that.

"I met my wife at a campmeeting held on the Luckiamute and conducted by the Reverend Sweeney. We were married the year Oregon was admitted to the Union, 1859."

Oregon Journal
March 17-19, 1922

# Dunham Wright
# Medical Springs, Oregon

"I was born at Burlington, Vermont, March 13, 1842. My father, John D. Wright, was born in Virginia in 1807 and moved to Illinois just before I came of age. It was just about this time that the Hanks and Lincoln families also moved to Illinois. My father married Celia Hanks. She was a cousin of Abraham Lincoln, and, like him, was born in Kentucky. My father was a teacher as well as a civil engineer. He brought with him to Illinois a small library of good books. If you will look up the history of Abraham Lincoln's life you will find that my father taught him grammar and surveying, and that Abraham Lincoln served as deputy surveyor under my father, and also served as deputy clerk when my father was sheriff. Later, when Abraham Lincoln was elected captain of a company in the Black Hawk War he appointed my father orderly sergeant in his company.

"My mother died when I was six years old, and I went to live with her mother and father, William and Elizabeth Hanks. My grandfather, William Hanks, was a Virginian by birth and had fought in the Revolutionary War. When I was about seven years old my father married again, marrying Evaline Simmons. My father had four children by his first wife, Celia Hanks Wright. He had six children by his second wife, my stepmother.

"'Abe', as they called Lincoln in those days, would bring in a great armload of hickory bark and throw it into the fireplace so there would be plenty of light to read by. One morning he was visiting my aunt, Nancy Hanks Miller. It was a cold morning and my aunt noticed that Abe was shivering. She said, 'Why, Abe, you are nearly frozen.'

"'Yes, it is pretty cold,' said Abe.

"'No wonder you are cold. Your breeches are nearly worn out,' said my aunt.

"Abe gave her a rather rueful smile and said, 'I know it, but I haven't any money to buy more.'

"'I have enough jeans left to make a pair of pants,' said my aunt, 'and you can cut wood to pay for them.'

"'That's a bargain,' Abe said. 'I will cut seven cords of wood if you will make me a pair of trousers.'

"He started out the next morning with a lunch my aunt put up for him and walked six miles to the timber to cut wood. By the time he had felled and cut seven cords of wood my aunt had made his jeans trousers, and he was very happy and proud of them.

"My uncle, John Hanks, and Abraham Lincoln used to split rails. They also worked together making a flatboat on which they traveled down the Mississippi to New Orleans with bacon and other produce raised by the neighbors. At New Orleans they sold the boat and the produce, receiving Mexican silver dollars in exchange, and walked back to Illinois. The making of a flatboat in those days was quite an accomplishment. It usually took two men all winter to make one of these large wooden scows. The timbers were hewed together with a broadaxe and pinned together with strong wooden pins.

"One of the loads that my uncle John Hanks and Abraham Lincoln took down the river consisted of a number of live fat hogs. The hogs refused to be driven on the boat, so Lincoln solved the question by saying, 'If they won't go on under their own power, I will carry them aboard.' And he proceeded to do so. As some of these hogs weighed over 250 pounds and kicked and squealed and struggled, you may know Lincoln had great muscular strength.

"Years afterwards it was some of these moss-covered rails split by Uncle John Hanks and Abraham Lincoln that were carried into the Republican convention and caused Abraham Lincoln to receive the name 'Railsplitter'. It was these same old moss-covered rails split by Abraham Lincoln and my uncle that caused such a demonstration for Lincoln that he was made Republican candidate for president, thus resulting in his election.

"When I was 21 years of age I went in with a man named Peter Pence and dug a ditch three miles long to our placer claim in the Boise Basin. We couldn't make the water run up hill in our ditch, so we had to abandon it. I soon landed a job at six dollars a day. In those days a shift was 12 hours, and by putting in a shift and a half, or 18 hours, I made nine dollars a day.

"I decided I could make more money working for myself, so I bought a pack train and went to Umatilla Landing, where I secured a load of flour and supplies, for which I was paid 30 cents a pound freight. The supplies were billed to Idaho City. I made a winter trip, through deep snow all the way, my pack horses living on dry bunch grass and having to scrape down through the snow to get at it.

"J. M. Shepard was running an express from Walla Walla to Placerville. He brought in the **Sacramento Union** and the **San Francisco Bulletin**, and sold them at a dollar apiece, but he could never bring in enough to supply the demand. The papers were passed from hand to hand till they were completely worn out. This was in 1863, when the war was at its height and the papers were full of news of the great conflict. He carried letters for a dollar apiece. He was never able to travel the same trail twice, on account of road agents and hostile Indians. A man named M. H. Abbott started a paper, which he called **The Sagebrush**. This was at Baker City. **The Sagebrush** became **Bedrock Democrat**, and J. M. Shepard became its editor and proprietor.

"Thomas and Ruckel, who ran a stage from Walla Walla to Salt Lake City, shipped a Buckeye mowing machine into the Grand Ronde Valley to cut hay for the stage horses. I bought it from them and took a contract to furnish them hay.

This was the first mowing machine brought into the Grand Ronde Valley. I charged $2.50 an acre to cut hay, and I ran three shifts of men, keeping the mowing machine going 24 hours a day. The valley was full of picket pins, which jerked the teeth out of the sickle of the mower. A blacksmith made teeth for me out of wornout shovels, charging me $5 apiece for the teeth and $10 to put on a sicklehead. I found there was such a demand for hay that I rented a hotel at Hendershott Point, now known as the Cove. I charged two-bits a night to furnish hay for pack horses, and often I would have from two to four pack trains staying overnight at my place. This meant 75 to 125 horses at two-bits each. I ran this hotel during the winter of 1865-66. I ran across three men who had teams who were willing to work all winter for their board and for hay for their horses. I kept them busy hauling wood and hay to my hotel. In the spring of 1866 I moved to a place called Sanger, northeast of Baker City. This was a placer and quartz district.

"On July 4, 1867, I married Miss Artemesia Duncan. Fifty-five years ago I took up as my claim my present home at Medical Springs. It had a number of fine hot springs on it, and for untold generations the Indians had used it to cure their ailments. At that time the Indians were our only neighbors.

"One day in 1872, when I was 30 years old, I received notice from the Democratic county convention held in Union County that I had been nominated as joint candidate for Union and Baker Counties for member of the lower house of the Oregon Legislature. My district was bounded by the states of Washington, Idaho, and Nevada on the north, east, and south, and by the summit of the Blue Mountains on the west.

"I certainly was surprised to think that anybody but the Indians knew where I lived, and I was still more surprised to think I should be chosen as a candidate. M. H. Abbott was told to notify me of my nomination. He told me that S. S. White would run against me.

"I had homesteaded Medical Springs a few years before and I was poor as a snake. I couldn't raise enough cash to buy a 3-cent postage stamp. S. S. White had known my father at Burlington, Iowa. Instead of going out campaigning for himself, he campaigned for me, and I was elected by a big majority. My wife and I made and sold all the butter we could, and sold a lot of our ducks, chickens, and pigs to some Chinamen at Auburn so I could buy a suit of clothes to go to Salem. I invested $13 in a suit of store clothes. The stage fare to Umatilla Landing amounted to $15, the fare on the boat from Umatilla Landing to Portland was $10, and from Portland to Salem on Ben Holladay's railroad it was $2.50 more, and this did not include the eats or sleeps.

"Fortunately I ran across a friend named Williamson at La Grande who had come into town with a load of produce. He invited me to stay all night with him. He said, 'How much money have you got?'

"I said, 'Uncle Tom, I haven't got very much —just about enough to take me to Salem.'

"He said, 'Hold out your hand.' I did so and he dropped three $20 gold pieces into my hand.

"It made me seasick riding on the stage, so I rode on the boot with the driver. It was raining hard, so he loaned me a gunnysack to serve as an overcoat. There was no Pendleton in those days. We changed horses at Swift Station, not far from the present town of Pendleton. The first boat ride I ever took was the ride from Umatilla to Celilo. The first time I ever rode on a railroad train was the ride on the portage road from Celilo to The Dalles.

"How did it come that I got seasick riding in the state? Well, in those days the road over the mountains from La Grande to Swift Station didn't much resemble the highways we have today. Barger and some of those old stage drivers would send the stage through at breakneck speed, so their old rockaway stage was like a boat pitching and bounding on a choppy sea in a storm. It made me so deathly seasick I thought I was going to die, and was glad of it, but the driver, not wanting to have a corpse on his hands, had me ride with him on the boot.

"From Swift Station we took the long hill for the Twelve Mile House. The heavy rain had made the road a sea of mud and the teams couldn't pull the old boat more than twenty or thirty feet through the sand and mud without having to stop. The brakes wouldn't hold, so I rustled a rail to chock the wheels with and walked back of the stage in the rain all the way up the hill, chocking the wheels whenever the team stopped to rest.

"The legislature paid me mileage of ten cents a mile. I imagine if some of the other legislators had followed an old stage coach afoot with a rail on their shoulder, through the mud and rain, they would have thought they earned their ten cents a mile.

"Union County was cut off from Baker County in the fall of 1864, and the following March was the time set to take a vote to locate the county seat. La Grande and Union were the candidates. Excitement was rampant. Each candidate retained teamsters and packers weeks and months in advance to vote favorably. Every person was allowed to vote at least once, irrespective of race, color or nationality. On election day on all prominent corners near the polls ten-gallon kegs were there with their heads knocked in and loose handled cups hanging on the chimes as thick as beads on an Indian papoose's neck. This is the way the county seat question was settled some three score years ago on the viva voce of voting. La Grande was elected by a small majority.

"I took a pack train load of flour from the Umatilla landing to Boise Basin in the winter of 1863-4 at 30 cents a pound freight. I loaded the train with baled hay on the river below La Grande to carry over the mountain. I started out one windy morning, and had got to where the town of La Grande now stands, when a pack came loose on a rear animal. It started to run and stampeded the whole train of 40 animals running to all points of the compass, spilling hay all over the present townsite of La Grande.

"On my return trip I stopped over one day in La Grande. In Judge Alberson's store I met an emigrant. He had with him his two little children who were thinly clad and shivering with cold. He wanted to make them comfortable with something to eat and wear, but had no money and was among strangers. He had with him a little pony that was the pet of the family and which he wanted to sell. This made me know he was in dire need of help. I paid his price for the pony with a promise to him and the children to take good care of it. The price of the pony was $50. He immediately went to buying food to make his family comfortable, and I went to looking for something to load this little pony with that would be profitable.

"Judge Alberson said he had 300 pounds of oats that a farmer had pounded out with a club and was lucky enough to find wind enough in the valley to blow the chaff out of them. I loaded the pony with 200 pounds of these oats, for which I paid the old judge $26 or 13 cents a pound. I sold them to Nims Brothers, on Horseshoe Bend, on the Payette, at their first offer of $60. I have wondered many a time if this good fortune was not due in part for helping those that needed help in a strange land. These two sacks of oats were the means of furnishing the seed oats for Boise, Payette, and Weiser Valleys.

"It was a perilous undertaking at that early date to attempt to make a trip from Umatilla to Boise Basin with the pack train in the dead of winter. The animals had to gather their living from the bunch grass on the bleak, high points where the snow had been blown away. Men had often to build their beds down on from 12 to 15 inches of snow with a few branches of sagebrush thrown down for feathers. We used our riding saddles for pillows. We had the broad canopy of heaven for a cover, while snow drifted over our beds for warmth and the yelling of hungry coyotes in the distance lulled us to sleep.

"We camped one night at Express Ranch, near Durkee. We heard some disturbance at the station in the night. The next morning, when driving in our pack train, there was a man hanging on a juniper tree with a rope around his neck. This man was a rough character. He left the mines pretty well ginned up and every station he passed he pricked his mustang with his great spurs and pushed him through the door, asking the barkeeper to set 'em up at the point of a gun, riding away afterwards at full speed. A small party followed him and left him hanging on this juniper tree.

"A few evenings later we camped near Olds Ferry where a friend of mine and his partner had camped a few evenings before, taking his winter supplies into the mines. His name was Sam Hogan. He thought he heard a noise about the camp in the early morning. He sat up in his bed and a shot rang out. A bullet pierced Hogan's back. He fell back on his blankets and died.

"A search was made for the party doing the shooting. Fresh tracks were found in the light snow, and down on the banks of the Snake River, nearly in the willows. These tracks were made by old Big Foot, who terrorized southern Idaho in its early settlement. He was finally killed on Reynolds Creek, near Silver City, by a man named Wheeler. Big Foot was a desperate Indian and a giant, making a track 17 inches long. He carried a double-barreled rifle and could swim the Snake River whenever he came to it, and carry his gun. He could talk fair English and acknowledged to Wheeler while his life blood ebbed away, the massacres he had been in. He claimed to be of Cherokee and Negro blood.

"The first American flag unfurled to the breeze in Union County was on the Fourth of July, 1863, at the little town of Union, which was then a part of Baker County. Who conceived the idea of doing this, as well as furnishing the cloth and making the flag, I feel should be made a matter of history. Mrs. Harriet Hendershott of Hendershott Point and Mrs. Harriet Lewis of Union were the promoters. The Civil War was at high tide. Those ladies were loyal, patriotic women, and they wanted to appropriately celebrate our national day.

"They couldn't do so without Old Glory, and there was no place in the whole country to obtain cloth to make a flag. Mrs. Hendershott took a red worsted dress she had laid away as a keepsake, belonging to one of her daughters who had died. She cut it into strips and pieced it, for the red stripes. Mrs. Lewis furnished a white sheet for the white stripes. But where the blue field was to come from was the puzzle.

"Mrs. Hendershott remembered seeing Miss Martha Kroger, a young lady of Cove, riding horseback, having on a long, blue riding habit. This was the only chance for an American flag. Miss Kroger was interviewed and consented to allow the skirt of her riding habit to become a part of the first American flag made in the county.

"Soon needles, thimbles, and fingers got busy, and 13 stripes and 13 stars on the blue field were put together by the two Harriets. All the contributors to this flag have answered the final summons.

"The first settlement in what is now Baker County was made in 1861. The first settlements were made at Auburn and Griffin Gulch, by Dave Littlefield and by Griffin and Party, who were miners. At the same time, Ben Brown and party settled in Grand Ronde Valley. They were homeseekers and farmers.

"I was a member of the first wagon train to go through Pine and Eagle Valleys. This was in August, 1862. Tim Goodell was the leader of the train. There was no road through the Pine and Eagle Valleys. In fact, Indian trails and game trails were the only roads in the country at that time.

"There were 60 wagons in our train. Tim Goodell and several others went ahead to size up the country and select the best road, while all the men we could spare from driving the ox teams followed them, cutting trees and rolling rocks out of the way to make a passable road. When we reached the middle valley of the Weiser our road searchers spent two weeks looking for a pass through the Seven Devils Mountains. We were trying to make our way to the newly-discovered gold diggings in northern Idaho. We were headed for Florence. Our grub gave out and we had to eat serviceberries.

"The men who were scouting to find the pass through the Seven Devils finally came to Brownlee

Ferry. They told the proprietor about the 60 wagons on the Weiser. He came to where we were camped and offered to ferry us over the Snake River without charge if we would make a road from where we were to the ferry. We accepted this proposition, crossed the river, passed through Pine and Eagle Valleys, and went over the rough hills to the upper Powder River Valley.

"Some members of our wagon train found work in the newly-discovered placer fields of Auburn, now Baker City. Others took up claims at what now are known as Pocahontas and Wingville. Still others landed jobs digging a ditch to bring water to Auburn. There were so many men out of work that the wages for digging were low. A few members of our party retraced their way and took up claims in Pine and Eagle Valleys. Among those who settled in Eagle Valley were J. O. Wood, Uncle John Daley, for whom Daley Creek is named, and Mr. Mead. Those who settled in Pine Valley were Steve and Reese Pindle, Tom Corsen, and Mrs. R. A. Pearce.

"At that time there was only one white man living in this district--an old trapper named Charlie Fee. The homesteaders in these valleys put out vegetable gardens. Next spring and summer they sold all they could raise, in the mining camps at Lookout Mountain, Rye Valley, Mormon Basin and a small camp on the west side of Pine Valley. The produce was taken to the camps on packhorses.

"Chief Egan, with his Piutes, frequently passed through Mormon Basin and the Lookout Mountain country. Mr. Scott and his wife, who owned the Weatherby Ranch on Burnt River, were killed by the Indians while returning from taking produce to Mormon Basin. The Sheepeater Indians of the Snake River country used to keep the people of Pine and Eagle Valleys restless and uneasy. Occasionally the settlers would raid an Indian village to keep the Indians afraid of the white men. James Summers was one of the most public spirited of the early settlers there. He and Rattlesnake Jack often stood guard to warn the settlers of the coming of the Indians.

"One spring morning Summers came to my place in Pine Valley and said he was tired, hungry, and about worn out from traveling all night from Snake River. He said, 'Dunham, I wish you would see what's the matter with my shoulder.'

"'What kind of a scrape have you been into?' I inquired.

"He said, 'I shot an Indian on Snake River. I know I killed him, for I never saw anyone jump higher at the crack of my gun. I thought there might be other Indians nearby, so I started for a high, shelving rock that would give me protection in case they attacked me. Just as I got near the rock I heard a rifle crack and, looking up, I saw an Indian standing on the rock where I was going to take protection. I laid under that rock till nightfall. My shoulder seems awfully stiff.'

"I took Jim's shirt off, which was matted with blood, and found he had a bullet wound an inch deep and five inches long. I washed his shoulder, tied it up and it soon healed.

"Summers told me he was born in 1838 near Crabtree, Kentucky. He died alone in his cabin near the Galena Mine on October 1, 1893. He was buried there. Myself and some other friends subscribed enough money to erect a monument to his memory in the cemetery at Halfway.

"Much of the emigration of 1862 stopped at Auburn, while some located ranches west of Baker, at Wingville and Pocahontas. Auburn in its palmiest days had a population of 8000. It was discovered by prospectors looking for the much sought Blue Bucket Mine.

"The first settlement of Grand Ronde Valley was made around the margin of the valley. The upper part of the valley was a lake and tule swamp, and was so reported to the government by Dave Thompson, who sectionized the valley in 1861. The lower part of the valley, or sand ridge, was considered a desert waste and often the expression was heard, 'What a pity that so much of a beautiful valley is nothing but swamp and desert.' This land was donated by Congress to the state and sold by the state for $1.25 an acre. Now the million-dollar wheat and grass fields of the valley are in evidence, dotted with comfortable farm homes.

"Auburn was the original county seat of Baker County. Joe Wilson was our district judge, and a very capable jurist. It was not an unusual thing for an officer to have to ride 100 miles to subpoena a witness or a juror. B. F. Bonham, L. O. Stearns, Cage Baker and Royal A. Pierce were the first disciples of Blackstone.

"Now about the Old Oregon Trail. I am going to describe the route taken by the first wagon train to cross the country from old Fort Hall to Fort Dalles under guidance of Dr. Marcus Whitman in 1843 and used as a trail by the Hunt party as early as 1811. There were other routes branching off, one to California and one to Oregon on the south side of the Snake River by the Owyhee and Malheur Rivers. This was a desert and circuitous route. It was from this route that Stephen Meek led an emigrant train in 1845 into the John Day country and there left them, lost and wandering. It was in the wanderings of this train that the gold of the much talked of Blue Bucket Mine was found.

"Another route was crossing Snake River near Fort Hall by the way of Lost River, Wood River, Big and Little Camas Prairie to the intersection of the original Old Oregon Trail, or Whitman Route, at a point where a great emigrant train had been massacred in 1852. There had been no travel on this route, or north of Snake River, since the massacre, as the Indians had said no train should ever pass down the north side of Snake River. The old road had grown up in weeds. I was in the train that made the road by Lost River in 1862. We had 300 wagons. The Indians put on their war paint. So did we. We expected to have a scrap with them. Great numbers of Indians were constantly in sight on the hills in the daytime. We were heeled for them.

"We had to make a road. We had a working crew and a guard on either side and behind the train, leaving on the roadside some one of our number at almsot each camp we made. Our guard on the lava land side of the train found a trunk in a cave. It was brought into camp and opened. It contained a small amount of wearing apparel for small children and two letters that had been written to a friend in Ohio. The letters were opened and read by the captain of our train. They were dated 1852 and were to be mailed at Fort Hall. The name of the woman writing the letters has faded from my memory. By whom that trunk was left in the cave of the lava beds remains an unsolved mystery of the plains.

"Another route intercepted the Old Oregon Trail, where the great massacre was perpetrated in 1852. Our train stopped there for some time to view the ground where the human butchery had taken place ten years before. There lay in the tall rye grass the wagons in corral form and strewn about many heaps of human and animal bones and human skulls. What a sad feeling crept over this 20-year-old boy when I viewed the scene.

"This first old trail led in a northwesterly direction to the Boise River and down that stream to old Fort Boise, crossing Snake River and on to Burnt River, where Huntington is now located, then up Burnt River to the Weatherly Ranch, then a detour up Grave or Chicken Creek and on to Burnt River at the Swagey Ranch, leaving Burnt River at Durkee for Straw Ranch on Alder Creek and from there over low hills to Mud Springs east of Rockefellow or Virtue Mine to Powder River Slough, where Uncle Billy Baldock and Chris Hinkle kept a station, crossing South Powder River at the Quigley Ranch and North

Powder at Monehan Springs; thence west of North Powder to Ladd Hill and the old town of La Grande, over the Blue Mountains eight miles to Rock Creek, crossing Grand Ronde River and on to Lee's Encampment, or Meacham, thence down Crawford Hill to near Umatilla River or Cayuse Station. Here a span of the old trail branched off for Whitman Mission. The main trail passed on to Butter Creek, John Day, Deschutes, ending at The Dalles, which was the end of wagon transportation and further travel had to be made on boats or log rafts on the Columbia River, until the Barlow Road was made around Mount Hood.

"I feel the engineers were fortunate in finding ground for the new Old Oregon Trail on which to build the boulevard that has been constructed. Old La Grande and Pendleton are directly on the Old Oregon Trail. Summerville is 20 miles north and Heppner is that far south. The Daly Route was never any part of the Old Oregon Trail—no more than was Pyle Canyon.

"It is gratifying to know that today it is only a matter of days to travel over the trail as compared to months over the route from the Missouri River to Portland. It is still further gratifying to realize that the anxiety, privations, and suffering of the original pathfinders are eliminated and a trip over the Old Oregon Trail is a joyride, with its scenic grandeur everywhere greeting the eye."

**Oregon Journal**
February 10 & 11, 1924
February 24, 1928
September 18, 1931
January 4 & 5, (year illegible)

# Jesse Applegate
## St. Clair County, Missouri

*When I interviewed Mrs. M. L. Alford at her home at 517 West 10th Street, Medford, recently, she told me many interesting incidents about her father, Lindsay Applegate; her uncle, Jesse Applegate, and the other members of the Applegate clan who crossed the plains to Oregon in 1843.*

*On April 11, 1843, Jesse Applegate, who at that time lived in St. Clair County, Missouri, wrote to his brother Lisbon the following letter:*

"I will start with my family to the Oregon Territory this spring. Lindsay and perhaps Charles go with me. This resolution has been conceived and matured in a very short time, but it is probably destiny, to which account I place it, having neither time nor good reasons to offer in defense of so wild an undertaking. We are all well, and I only snatch this opportunity to write to you for this purpose of ascertaining if the same species of madness exists on your side of the Missouri."

**Oregon Journal**
October 12, 1933

# One day in Athena

*One day when I happened to be at Athena one of the pioneer residents took me to a store and showed me where Hank had once hidden, behind the spool case. The man who took me to the store had happened to be present at the time. Hank, when he was drinking, had a pleasant habit of making any stranger who came into the saloon dance and, if the stranger refused, Hank pulled out his six-shooter and shot at his toes, which usually resulted in the stranger's dancing. One day a man named Caldwell came into one of the saloons at Athena where Hank was, and refused Hank's invitation. Hank pulled out his six-shooter and made Caldwell dance till he was tired, punctuating his dancing with shots from his six-shooter around his feet. Hank then made Caldwell order drinks for the crowd and said he would forgive him for not dancing at his first invitation.*

*A day or two later Caldwell ran across Hank in Hollis & Cleve's store and shot Hank through the lung. His second shot shattered Hank's right arm. Hank jumped behind a stand containing spools of cotton thread. Caldwell continued to shoot through the case, making the spools of thread jump in all directions, till his gun was empty.*

*A week or two later a visitor found Hank sitting up in bed with his shattered right arm in a sling, shooting at a playing card on the wall with his left hand, so as to become an expert shot left-handed.*

●●●●●●●●●●●●●●●●●●●●●●●●●●●●●●●●●●●●●●●●●●●●●●●●●●●●●●

*One time two bandits held up a train near Pasco on which Hank was a passenger. He was asleep at the time. He woke up and asked what the trouble was. One of the passengers told him to be still or he would be shot, and pointed at the two robbers relieving the passengers of their money. Hank said, "This proposition don't ¿o with me," and, pulling out his gun, he shot one of the bandits. Both bandits jumped off the train before Hank could get another shot.*

Oregon Journal
March 13, 1926

# J. A. Wisdom
# Freed Slave
# Portland, Oregon

"My half-sister is all white. I'm half-white and half-black, but I'm more proud of my black blood than of my white blood.

"Maybe you've heard of Dr. Cook, who lived down in Virginia. He came up into Kentucky before the Civil War and bought a lot of land at 20 cents an acre and brought over 100 slaves there from Virginia. Mary, one of Dr. Cook's daughters, married Elijah Wisdom. He was an Abolitionist. Dr. Cook said if Mary married him she could consider herself dead, so far as he was concerned. He gave her $500 in cash, and one slave, to be her maid. Mary Cook married Elijah Wisdom, and they had 12 children. Wisdom had two children by my mother, who was Mrs. Wisdom's slave. My sister has been dead many years. My mother died when I was seven years old.

"I was born on April 8, 1848. Wisdom had a double relation to me—he was my father and my owner, and I was his son and his slave. In 1861, when I was 13 years old, the Civil War was brewing. Most folks in the South thought the Yankees were 'storekeepers' and wouldn't fight, so they expected to win if there was a war. My father, though, came from the North, and he knew the folks up North would fight. He figured that if there was a war the North would win and the slaves would be freed, so, on January 4, 1861, he sold me for $400. Pretty soon the war was in full blast.

"When President Lincoln wrote his proclamation saying slaves were free, a lot of slave owners paid no attention to it, for they thought the South was going to win. Even after General Lee surrendered, many planters still made their former slaves work. The man I was working for wouldn't turn me loose. If you tried to get away they set the dogs on you, and if they caught you they clubbed you, so I didn't want to try it. They passed a law saying any former slave owner who was still holding his slaves, and it was proved in court, would be fined and sent to jail.

"Say, I never will forget the procession the colored folks had on New Years' Day, 1866. Every

"Wisdom had a double relation to
me—he was my father and my owner,
and I was his son and his slave..."

colored person that had any money at all, or any credit, hired a buggy. There was snow on the ground, but it seems to me that procession was finer than the Rose Festival parades we have here in Portland.

"Right after the war I worked as a field hand, hoeing cotton, digging basements, carrying brick, or driving a buggy, then for 12 years I worked as porter for the Pullman Company. I quit the Pullman Company in 1897, and the next year I had charge of the chair car for the Columbia River Railroad, between Portland and Astoria. I worked for this road three years. I worked one summer at the Flavel Hotel at the time they were trying to make Flavel a summer resort. Then I got a job in Portland as assistant janitor in the old post office. I worked there two years and four months. At the time they were going to remodel the post office I got a job as assistant janitor at the custom house and worked there 25 years. John Logan, a colored man who had been a waiter in the Hotel Portland, was head janitor 23 years. I worked under him.

"I had two children by my first wife. I married my second wife, Sarah Frances Johnston, here in Portland, on September 23, 1895. She had worked for a rich woman in Louisville 25 years. This woman left her $500 when she died. My wife had worked for Mr. Bourne, who owned a mill back East. She took care of Jonathon Bourne when he was a baby. Here is his picture, which he gave her.

"After the death of my second wife, I married Cinderella Gray. We were married on June 14, 1911. She had worked ten years for Mr. Wright, who had a jewelry store on Morrison Street between 4th and 5th. My present wife has been a maid in Meier & Frank's store 16 years."

Oregon Journal
November 2, 1934

# W. P. West
## Danish Pioneer
## Arlington, Oregon

"I came to Rock Creek in the fall of 1863. I was born in Denmark, on the Isle of Bonholm, on February 2, 1841, so you see I have passed my 88th milestone.

"No, my father's name was not West. His name was Nelson Pederson. He was a farmer. Our farm was known as West Goard. One time my father signed an official paper, signing it Nelson Pederson, West Goard, Isle of Bonholm. The officials thought his name was West instead of Pederson, so our family name was listed down as West and we were never able to change it.

"A Dane who had been in the United States came back to visit his people. He told us that in this country you could pick pieces of gold out of the ground. He told us that at a place called Pike's Peak you could go down with a pan and wash the dirt at the edge of the stream and make more money in a day than we could make in Denmark in a month. I talked it over with some other young men and finally 12 of us pooled our resources and decided to come to America. I was 18. Most of this party ranged in age from 17 to 20. This Dane who had told us of the riches of America agreed to act as our interpreter if we would pay his passage from Denmark to Fort Leavenworth. We bought a ticket for him and tickets for ourselves on a sailing ship that was going to New York. From there we bought emigrant tickets· to St. Louis, and from St. Louis we went up the river to Fort Leavenworth. There we bought a wagon and four mules and provisions and started for Pike's Peak.

"When we had nearly got there—this was in 1859—we met a lot of men returning, who said all the claims had been taken and all the gold washed out, which made us feel very sad, for we had come clear from Denmark to wash out some of that gold for ourselves. While we were camped a man named Montgomery drove up to our camp. He had about 250 very fine large American horses that he was taking to California to be used as stage horses. In those days you went from Sacramento to Portland by stage. Our interpreter told him that we wanted to go to California, since the gold was all gone at Pike's Peak. He also told him that we were nearly out of food.

"Mr. Montgomery said, 'You can go along with me and help drive the horses and I will board you till you get to California. In exchange for the food you can give me your four-mule team and your wagon.'

"We talked this over and agreed to do it, for none of us were familiar with mules and we were glad to find a way to get rid of them when we got to our journey's end.

"It was all very strange and new to us on the plains. It was not at all like our home in Denmark. When we got to Honey Lake Valley Mr. Montgomery advised us to scatter out and get work in the mines. It is curious, but from that day to this I have never met nor heard from any of my fellow countrymen with whom I came from Denmark to make our fortunes in America.

"I knew no English, but I got a job cutting wood at a stage station called the Mountain House. Later I got a job on Goodyear Creek, wheeling ore from a tunnel. The tunnel ran several hundred feet into the hillside. It was my job to wheel out this ore and dump it in the sluice box and each night shut off the water and gather the gold from the riffles. Sometimes I would find nuggets of gold that would weigh four or five ounces. I worked there from the fall of 1859 to 1861.

"I went to San Francisco, where I took a steamer for Portland. I arrived at Portland in July, 1861. From Portland I went up the Columbia River and then up the Snake River to Lewiston, arriving in the late summer of 1861. Captain E. D. Pierce, who had been mining in California and later in British Columbia, discovered rich gold on Orofino Creek in the summer of 1860. Orofino Creek flows into the Clearwater. Captain Pierce went to Walla Walla and came back with some miners who spent the winter of 1860-61 in whipsawing lumber for sluice boxes and rockers. They staked claims and in the spring, when they went back to Walla Walla, one of the men had $800 in gold dust to buy supplies.

"The word went out that rich gold had been found on the Clearwater and it traveled all over the West. It reached me where I was wheeling dirt in the tunnel in California, so I and thousands of others quit whatever we were doing and hurried to Idaho. By the spring of 1861 there were 300 miners in the Orofino diggings. Soon there were thousands of men prospecting the streams and gulches in the Clearwater country. A camp was started named Pierce City, and another camp sprang up called Orofino. Where the Snake and the Clearwater River joined, a little town of tents sprang up. They called it Lewiston.

"When I reached Lewiston, late in July, 1861, there were no houses there--nothing but tents. Even the stores were in tents. Prospectors soon found other creeks and gulches that had rich pay dirt, particularly on the south fork of the Clearwater, in what was called the Elk City District. North of the Salmon River District, a few weeks after I reached Lewiston, rich pay dirt was found and a camp was founded that was called Florence. This was in the autumn of 1861. Peter Bablaine washed out 75 pounds of gold dust from his claim in Bablaine Gulch. His name was corrupted to

Baboon, and this rich gulch is known as Baboon Gulch.

"There was gold all over that country, but I always dug where it wasn't. I prospected and mined in the Clearwater and Salmon River Country from the fall of '61 to the fall of '63.

"In Denmark people usually acted in a very law-abiding way, but in Idaho there were many quarrels and fights. Men stole the gold from the sluice boxes. Others became road agents. I passed one place at Lewiston where three men had been hung, or lynched, as they called it in those days.

"I decided to quit the gold-mining business, where, no matter how hard I worked, I only made enough to pay expenses. I came on down to The Dalles, went out on Rock Creek and worked on a ranch. Later I took up a homestead on Rock Creek, 16 miles from Arlington. My post office was John Day. I was here 17 years before the town of Arlington was started. It was not started till after the O. R. & N. company began building its road between Portland and Huntington, in 1880, and the next year a town was started called Alkali, at the mouth of Alkali Canyon. Later, they changed its name to Arlington."

Oregon Journal
June 20, 1929

# The Lure of the Placer Mine

*It is easy to understand the lure of placer mining, when at any time a person is liable to find a rich pocket or to run across a nugget worth hundreds of dollars.*

*W. L. Wade, who for many years ran a store in North Salem, had a claim on Scott's Bar. He took out one nugget which he sold for $1260. In 1854, Samuel N. West, from his placer claim in Nevada County, California, washed out a lump of quartz mixed with gold which he sold for $6675. Another nugget, from a near-by claim, was sold for $8500. Near Yreka a Chinaman washed out a nugget worth $225. On the American River a miner found in his sluice box a roughly shaped piece of gold weighing 16 pounds, four ounces.*

*A prospector picked up in the tailings which had been thrown away in the Hope and Despair claim in Sierra County a nugget weighing $1770. David Robinson washed out a nugget worth over $900 and, strange as it may seem, the following year, while working on his place nearby, he picked up a buckskin poke of gold dust and nuggets in which was more than $900.*

*What was said at the time to be the largest nugget found in northern California was a mass of gold and quartz weighing 240 pounds, picked up on Remington Hills, in Nevada County, and from which more than $20,000 worth of gold was taken. On the Monumental Claim, 13 miles from Downieville, in Sierra County, a lump of gold quartz was found from which 97 pounds, troy weight, of gold was taken. Two nuggets were taken from a claim at Shingle Springs, one of which weighed 64 ounces*

"...two prospectors...came upon a layer of decomposed quartz which looked like red and white castile soap. This slab of quartz was three feet wide by eight feet long, and, when crushed up, it yielded over $5000 in coarse gold."

*and the other 136 ounces. At Little Grizzly a nugget which was sold for $2000 was picked up. At Baltimore Ravine two Australian prospectors found a nugget, mixed with quartz, weighing 106 pounds, which yielded $19,000 in gold.*

*Some Chinese miners dug out a nugget, weight 40 pounds, on the middle fork of Feather River.*

They cut it up into small chunks, bringing the chunks in from time to time and turning them in with the rest of their dust. At Placerville a Chinaman found two nuggets, one of which brought $170, the other more than $700.

At Mormon Bar a Frenchman who had been annoyed by a rough rock in the trail kicked it out, and when about to throw it to one side discovered it was a gold nugget weighing 68 ounces. One of the most valuable finds was made on Moore's Flat by some Chinamen who were working abandoned claims. They found a discolored quartz boulder weighing 240 pounds, from which they took over $50,000 of virgin gold.

On Randolph Flat two prospectors named Reese and Depew came upon a layer of decomposed quartz which looked like red and white castile soap. This slab of quartz was three feet wide by eight feet long, and, when crushed up, it yielded over $5000 in coarse gold.

*Oregon Journal*
*March 5, 1927*

# C. B. Wiley
# Pioneer of 1860
# Tillamook, Oregon

"Wisconsin is my native state. I was born on a Wisconsin farm, June 27, 1846. My father, Joseph L. Wiley, hailed from New York state, and was a farmer. My mother, whose maiden name was Matilda Batcheldor, was a native of Ohio. I was the fifth of their seven children. Up to my fourteenth year I had attended two or three terms of school, taught in a log schoolhouse three months each winter.

"In the spring of 1860 Father yoked up our work cattle to a prairie schooner and we struck out for the Willamette Valley. We crossed the Missouri River at Council Bluffs and kept on the north side of the Platte. I was 14, so the trip made a deep impression on my mind. I can in memory still see the shaggy-shouldered buffalo galloping away across the prairie as our white-topped wagons topped the rise of the ever-recurring land billows. I can still smell the smoke of our campfire made of buffalo chips or sagebrush, and I can still remember the delicious odor of frying antelope steak mingled with the fragrant aroma of coffee and sizzling bacon. We passed through vast cities of prairie dogs, the residents of the cities sitting bolt upright in the mouth of their underground homes as straight as picket pins.

"Do you happen to know Walter Norton of Portland? He was a boy at that time. His people
were neighbors of ours in Wisconsin. One night
his father was on night guard. We were camped
on the banks of the Snake River. It was a starless,
moonless night. He had a fine riding mare, and
a 3-year-old from the mare. An Indian crept up
through the darkness, caught and mounted the mare

"The Indian with
the deep scar across
his face had been
killed in the first
attack on the Vanorman
train. They examined
him and to their sur-
prise found he was a
white man dressed like
an Indian and having
his face and arms
stained and painted."

and made off. Norton jumped on the three-year-
old and took after him. Strain his ears as he would,
Mr. Norton could not hear the hoofbeats of the stolen
mare. He rode on. The colt nickered and the
mare answered. He gave the colt its head and
it joined its mother. The mare had a halter on.
Just as he grabbed the halter the Indian let fly
an arrow. The steel arrow lodged in Norton's arm.
He broke the shaft of the arrow off close to his
arm. The Indian slipped off the mare and got
away in the darkness.

"The next day as we were eating lunch seven
Indians came into camp, begging for food. Our
men folks paid no attention to them. All but one
of them left, and a moment or so later the dry

grass on all sides of us was ablaze. The Indian who had stayed in camp jumped up and, waving his blanket, dashed at our stock to stampede them. The other six charged into camp, waving blankets and shouting to stampede our cattle. Some of the men ran to where the frightened cattle were about to break away, while others ran for their guns. The Indians vamoosed and our men quieted the cattle.

"Next day at noon seven other Indians came into our camp to sell buckskin. One of their number, their leader, had a cut across his face that extended from his eyebrow to his chin. We yoked up and started on. As we started down a draw my father saw an Indian peering over the brow of a nearby hill. We had with us a French Canadian, a former trapper and mountain man. He told us to corral in a hurry. More than 100 Indians poured over the brow of the hill, but we were ready for them so they gave us up as a bad job.

"Major Grier, who had been escorting emigrants through the Indian country, had taken his troopers for the winter to Walla Walla.

"Just back of us there was another wagon train, the Vanorman party, consisting of eight wagons with over 50 people. An escort of dragoons had brought them for six days westward from Fort Hall and returned, thinking there was no further need of protection from hostile Indians.

"The Indians that had unsuccessfully attacked our train met this train and attacked them. The leader of the wagon train corralled and gave the Indians more than they bargained for, so the bulk of the Indians rode away. A few of them made signs of peace and were allowed to come into camp. They begged for food and soon withdrew and the oxen were yoked and the train started on. They had not gone far when the Indians swooped down on them, shooting three men. The train was once more corralled, and the Indians kept up a more or less ineffective fire all day and for most of the night. They kept up the fight all of the following day.

"By this time the children and cattle were suffering for water, for they had made a dry camp. That evening at sunset the emigrants, leaving half of their wagons, started onward, the Indians keeping up a running fight. Four soldiers, deserters from Fort Hall, who had joined the wagon train, were furnished riding horses and guns and were sent ahead to keep the road open. These four men-- Snyder, Chambourg, Murdoch and Chaffey--rode on at full speed, leaving the emigrants to their fate. The emigrants decided to leave the wagons and cattle, hoping this would satisfy the Indians. John Myers and a man named Utter were killed as the party started on afoot. Mrs. Utter would not leave her husband, and, with her boy and two little girls, stayed to protect her husband's body. The Indians killed her and her three children.

"It was dark by now and, having 11 of their number at the hands of the Indians, the others hurried on afoot. They reached the river and, hiding by day and traveling by night, they finally reached the Owyhee River. They stayed here till they were starved out. Vanorman, with his wife and five children and two men of the party, struck out to secure relief. They got as far as Burnt River, where all of the party were killed except the four younger children. Captain Dent and a party of soldiers finally rescued the few survivors. Of the 54 in the party, 39 had been killed. A brother of Vanorman came up from California and finally located two of the Vanorman children. The Indians had sold them to the Mormons.

"The Indian with the deep scar across his face had been killed in the first attack on the Vanorman train. They examined him and to their surprise found he was a white man dressed like an Indian and having his face and arms stained and painted.

"One of the survivors of the Vanorman party, now Mrs. W. W. Martin, lives at Salem. Her husband was a leading jeweler of the Capital city for many years.

"It took us six months to a day to make the trip from our home in Wisconsin to Portland. My father, Joseph L. Wiley, moved to a farm two miles from Dallas. A year later we moved to Uncle Jimmy Riggs' place on Salt Creek. Uncle Jimmy settled there in 1844. Five years later Father bought the place at Chehalem Gap on which Rexburg is now located. My half-brother, Mate L. Wiley, still lives on the place.

"In 1864 I went to Tygh Valley, where I put in the summer working on a ranch. That winter I came back to the Willamette Valley and attended school at Salt Creek. R. H. Tyson was the teacher that winter.

"I was 20 the next spring, so I decided to strike out for myself. I saddled my riding horse and struck out for Walla Walla. I took the first job I could land, which was breaking wild horses to the saddle. After I had broken a string of horses to ride I struck out for the Grand Ronde Valley. While I was in the livery stable where I had put up my horse, General W. H. Odell came in and said to the proprietor, 'Do you know where

I can get a good reliable man?'

"There were nine of us sitting around talking, and every one of us was looking for a job. Work was slack right then. Before the liveryman could answer General Odell's question, I stepped up and asked, 'What do you want me to do, and what are the wages?'

"General Odell said, 'I want a packer for my surveying crew, and the wages are $60 a month.'

"I said, 'All right. I'll take the job,' and we walked out together.

"I had just been telling the men that I'd be glad to land a job at $25 a month. I guess they liked my nerve, for they didn't give me away.

"We went up into the Wallowa country. I was surprised to learn that the base line that goes through Bay City, in Tillamook County, and which is known as Stark Street in Portland, goes through the heart of the Wallowa Valley.

"I thought I had never seen a more beautiful lake than Wallowa Lake, and I still think so. Large, red-meated fish, like salmon trout, were running out of the lake into the small streams to spawn. We killed them on the riffles with clubs. Deer and elk were plentiful. The only thing to worry us was Chief Joseph's band of Nez Perces. That country had been theirs from time immemorial, and they had been promised that they could keep it 'as long as grass grows and water runs', so they resented our being there running section lines and they pulled up the stakes we set.

When we had finished our summer's work there General Odell asked me to go with him on a survey on the Oregon-California border line. He was a fine man, square and just and reasonable. I wanted to try my luck in the Idaho mines, so I turned down his offer and took a job driving a bunch of beef cattle up to the Silver City Mines. Mr. Cottle hired me. He sold the cattle to a man named Osborn, who told me to stay on the job at the same wages. I herded them all winter. Every week he would come and get a few of them to kill for meat and sell to the miners. I bached all winter. I had to corral the cattle every night. The Indians were bad. I always carried a Henry rifle and two six-shooters. The Indians killed the settlers on both sides of me, but I was lucky and kept my scalp on.

"A soldier who had served with Crook said he had found good placer ground near Goose Lake, so that spring 30 of us started out, traveling by the lay of the country, and prospecting. We spent three months and most of our savings and came back with a lot of experience but no gold dust.

"While at Silver City I found that wood was selling for $18 a cord, so I put in the winter cutting cordwood. I couldn't get it out that winter, on account of deep snow. When I sold it next spring the price had gone down to seven dollars a cord, so I didn't make much.

"I put in the summer and fall herding sheep near Camp Lyons, and also sheared the band I was herding. After shearing them I drove them to Elko, Nevada, where I sold them to a butcher. I sold my saddle horse and outfit at Elko and went by way of Winnemucca to San Francisco on the train.

"At San Francisco I boarded the steamer Oriflamme and came to Portland. This was in the fall of 1868. I wanted a job for the winter, so I went out to Sheridan and landed a job as farm hand for Tom Fristoe. I thought I was just getting a job for the winter, but you can never tell, for I also got a wife. I married Emma T. Fristoe, my employer's daughter. We rented a farm for two years and then I bought a place three miles north of Sheridan.

"In 1890 we moved to Tillamook County. I took up a homestead on the sandspit at Netarts Bay. There were no roads in those days. It took us three days to go from Sheridan by way of Dolph to my homestead. There was no road and not much of a trail beyond Tillamook. In fact, I had to swim my horses across the bay to get to my land. I bought 160 acres adjoining my homestead. My wife and I milked 30 cows and sold butter. Later I built a cheese factory on my place. I also built and operated a clam canning factory. Clams were so abundant that one man could dig from three to four bushels of razor clams on one tide. After a few years a big winter storm carried the sand out to sea and left a rocky beach, so of course that put my clam canning factory out of business.

"Maxwell owned a place up the beach from me, at Maxwell Point. It is now a fine up-to-date summer resort. I rented the Maxwell place and pastured my cattle on it and also rented pasture to campers for their teams. I sold my place at Netarts to a party of Portland capitalists who were going to make it into a summer resort, but they have done nothing with it but rent it to Tom, Dick, and Harry, so, while it is a beautiful site, its future is all before it.

"I served as clerk of the school board in my district for more than 20 years. I also served as clerk of the election board for about the same length of time. I live now just at the edge of town in Tillamook. My son-in-law, W. S. Buell, is a teacher in the public schools at Tillamook, and he and my daughter keep house for me. My wife died five years ago.

"I have seen Tillamook County brought within three hours of Portland by autos and good roads. That's a big improvement over mountain trails knee deep with mud and a three days' trip to get from Tillamook to Portland."

Oregon Journal
April 7 & 8, 1924

# Joseph C. Wooley
# Justice of the Peace
# Harrisburg, Oregon

"I was born in Missouri, October 22, 1855. I have been justice of the peace near Harrisburg for more than eight years. My father, William H. Wooley, was born in Kentucky. My mother, whose maiden name was Grizzela Mitchell, was also born in Kentucky. Father and Mother were married in 1837. Of their nine children I am the only one now living.

"We started across the plains in the spring of 1863, when I was about $7\frac{1}{2}$ years old. There were 270 wagons in our train. Not far from Laramie we were attacked by the Indians. We made two circles of the wagons, one within the other. The women and children were placed inside the inner circle and the horses and cattle were corralled between the two circles of the wagons. The men were posted in the outer circle of wagons to shoot at the Indians. The Indians would ride around our wagon train, shooting bullets and arrows at the wagons. The Indians could hang on the opposite side of their horses as they circled the train, so they didn't make much of a mark to shoot at.

"The first night we were corralled and surrounded by the Indians four men slipped out and went to Laramie to summon help. A troop of soldiers hurried to our assistance, and when the Indian scouts saw the soldiers approaching they gave warning to the Indians and they all skipped out. I remember distinctly how thirsty I was the second day, for we had used up all the water in the train and the children were, so thirsty they were crying for water.

"The Indians in 1863 were very troublesome. Travel was heavy, and, of course, the men in the wagon trains were killing antelope and buffalo for food. The Indians were afraid that the white

men would kill all of their buffalo, so they were
in an ugly mood. One day the Indians stampeded
our wagon train just as we were about to cross
a river. The oxen ran with the wagons into the
river. Our wagon tipped over, drowning my mother's
mother. Several others were hurt, but my grandmother's was the only death.

"The wagon train was divided into two parties,
or factions. One lot would fiddle and dance at
night and the other party of the wagon train would
hold campmeetings and prayer services. My folks
were strict Presbyterians. Father and Mother believed
that the fiddle was an invention of the devil to
lure people to hell. They also believed that cards
were an invention of the devil. Most of the members
of our wagon train were from the South.

"Near Salt Lake the emigrants held a meeting
as to their future course. Some wanted to take
the southern route to California while the others
believed the wagon train should stick together until
they reached Oregon. The wagon train split up
after the meeting, about half of them going on to
Oregon and half of us taking the southern road
to California.

"Our cattle were pretty badly fagged and
we had a hard time crossing the Sierras. We wintered
at Stockton. A man named Campbell unloaded a
big tract of land on my father and some of our
relatives. My father, my brother-in-law, and four
of my uncles bought a big tract of land at a dollar
an acre. They paid 25 cents an acre down and
had a long time to pay the balance. Father plowed
his land and put in barley, wheat and corn. For
the next four weeks there was a steady north wind
that dried out the wool and in places uncovered
the seed. They decided they had bought a white
elephant, so they forfeited their payment of 25 cents
an acre and pulled out for Oregon.

"We reached Eugene on July 16, 1864. Last
spring I went down to Stockton and just for curiousity
I went out to visit the tract of land my father
and his relatives had bought at a dollar an acre.
It was selling for $1500 an acre and was considered
fine land.

"Father bought a donation land claim about
five miles northeast of Eugene. He wanted to make
some extra money, so he took a job at building
a grist mill for P. J. Pengra. Mr. Pengra and
Father were getting out boom logs for the mill.
A snag on a log caught Father's clothing, dragged
him into the river and drowned him. Mother was
unable to complete the payments on the place Father
had bought, so she had to give it up. We went
to live on my uncle John Bailey's place.

"I went to school for two three-months' terms near Trenton, Missouri. The next school I attended was in Oregon, at Wallace Butte, about three miles west of Eugene. Later I went to school for three months at the Brown schoolhouse near Monroe in Benton County. That was all the schooling I ever had.

"When I think back to my boyhood I think of the red-letter days when I went to barnraisings, taffy pulls, spelling matches, singing school, barn dances and campmeetings.

"When I was 20 years old I went to Granite and prospected for a few years. When I was 28 I came back to the Willamette Valley and married Minnie Hembree of Eugene. Our son, Aleck, is in California. Shortly after I was married I went to Harney County and in 1883 took up a homestead three miles from Burns. Egan was our post office and trading point. I came here to Harrisburg in 1916."

Oregon Journal
October 23, 1930

# Ned Wicks
## '49er
## The Dalles, Oregon

"I was born in New York City, October 23, 1829. If I live two years more I will come to par at 100. My father, like myself, was born in New York City. Our family name used to be Van Wyck. My mother's maiden name was Harriet Van Scudder. You can see, from the names, that my people on both sides of the family hailed from Holland. They came to Manhattan Island when New York was called New Amsterdam. Father and Mother had ten children —seven daughters and three sons.

"When I was a boy I took to the sea. I was about 14 when I shipped on board a clipper ship for my first trip to China. We carried American manufacturers' goods to China and brought back sandalwood, sugar, spices, tea, rice and silks. The goods were brought out to Wampoo in lighters. The China sugar came in woven straw bags or mats. We were in Chinese waters when word came of the discovery of gold in California. I was aboard the famous old clipper ship Horatio. We made a quick trip to New York. There I reshipped as an able seaman aboard the clipper ship St. Lawrence, sailing around the Horn and arriving in San Francisco in December, 1849.

"I doubt if you run across many genuine California '49'ers any more. They have pretty nearly all taken the one-way trail. I love the sea and have always regretted that I left the sea to become a prospector, miner, packer, freighter, and Indian fighter.

"When I arrived in the tent city of San Francisco I ran across an old-time acquaintance of mine who had been foreman of the **New York Sun**. He had brought with him on the Apollo a small cylinder press, some cases, type, paper, and other materials and was going to start a paper in San Francisco. He knew I had some mechanical knowledge, so he hired me to set up his cylinder press. I ran the press for him for the first few days, till it got tuned up. I saved the first copy run off, for years. It was marked 'Volume 1, No. 1'. When I stampeded to the Klondike in 1897 I left my early-day California treasures and other possessions in charge of a friend, who died while I was in Alaska, and his goods and mine were scattered and I never saw my things again.

"When we arrived at San Francisco, in December, 1849, we anchored the St. Lawrence in the bay, and the sailors, as well as the passengers, struck out for the mines. In the latter part of 1849 and in 1850 the bay was full of sailing vessels whose crews had abandoned the sea to try their luck in the placer diggings.

"Hudson Bay trappers had explored northern California. A man named Reading claimed to have found rich diggings on the headwaters of Trinity River late in '49. One party struck out from San Francisco on a sailing vessel, while another party struck out by land. Two Hudson Bay trappers came in to San Francisco and reported rich strikes on the Klamath River. Captain Bob Parker of Boston was running the 'Dobe Hotel in San Francisco. He organized a party to go up the coast early in April, 1850, on the schooner James R. Whiting. We went too far up the coast and headed into the mouth of the Umpqua River, thinking we were at the mouth of the Trinidad. When we found our mistake we turned south and landed in the little horseshoe of water at Trinidad Bay.

"We soon laid out a city, surveying the town into lots and electing an alcalde. Sam Brannan and his brother fitted out the General Morgan and came north to see if they could strike rich diggings. They sent in a boat crew, and Sam Brannan wanted to name the river Brannan River, but the name didn't stick.

"Brannan wanted to buy our townsite. We held a drawing, and each member of our company drew a slip from a hat entitling him to a designated

lot. Captain Parker and our party couldn't agree
with Sam Brannan about the sale of our townsite,
so he went on to Humboldt Bay, where he planned
to locate a town. He was going to connect his
town with the river by digging a canal.

"Captain Warner, in command of the Isabel,
laid out a town near ours, called Warnersville.
Towns were started all over that district by the
different parties of miners who came in on the Sierra
Nevada, the Hector, the Laura Virginia, the Malleroy
and other schooners. Our town, Trinidad, was
the first one to be located. We had ambitious plans
for our newly organized city of Trinidad. Before
long we had 30 buildings up, and things were booming.
The Trinity Mines were near by. In 1850 Trinity
County was created and our town was made the
county seat.

"That winter—1850-51—a big crowd of people
came up from San Francisco to mine on the beach.
This was called the 'Gold Bluff Excitement'. We
cut a blazed trail from Trinidad to the Klamath
River, a distance of about 30 miles. We didn't use
particularly good judgement in this, because,
instead of cutting the trail by the lay of the land,
we took the most direct route, traveling by compass,
which took us over the tops of hills where we could
easily have skirted the hills if we had had a good
surveyor. We used this trail for shipping stuff
into the Klamath by pack train from Trinidad.
We found good gold prospects on a bar in the Klamath
River, which we named American Bar. Further
up we found a still better bar, which we named
Orleans Bar.

"Different members of our party prospected
not only the Klamath River but also the Salmon
River. Our party of prospectors varied from seven
to 12. At the mouth of the Salmon River we struck
coarse gold. We could easily rock out an ounce
of coarse dust a day. The price of gold then was
$16 an ounce.

"An ounce of gold a day didn't seem like
very big pay, so, with eight other men, I started
to explore the Klamath River. In our party was
a Shaker preacher from Oregon City. He had crossed
the plains in 1846 to California, and later had
gone on to Oregon. He said that in 1846, while
going to Oregon, he had struck gold in a small
stream near where they camped one night. He thought
he could find this stream again. However, we struck
no worthwhile prospects till we got to what we called
Happy Camp, 40 miles from Scott's River. When
we struck Scott's River, we struck rich ground.
The gold we rocked out was coarse and we found

lots of nuggets. Whiting rocked out over $6000 of coarse gold and nuggets in a sort of pocket.

"We camped six miles above Scott's River, as there was good grass for the horses there. The Indians ran our horses off and we never found hide nor hair of 'em.

"We were getting short of grub, and couldn't seem to find any deer, so we tightened our belts, broke camp and started for Shasta Valley. We struck the old emigrant trail that ran from Sutter's Fort to the Willamette Valley, near what is now Yreka. We ate our last bread just as we hit the old trail. We followed the trail, hoping to meet some emigrants who would furnish us food, for we were about starved out. For the next few days we ate grass roots and rosebuds, and once in a while got a digger squirrel. While camped near the foot of Mount Shasta we killed two deer and, believe me, we filled up on deer meat. From there we crossed the McCloud River, went on to the Pitt River, which we followed down to the Sacramento River.

"We went down the Sacramento, and in taking a cut-off we found a sack of flour on the trail. It had evidently been lost from a pack horse taking supplies into the mines. Our party of eight or nine prospectors was about evenly divided as to whether we should eat it or leave it alone. Some claimed it was probably poisoned. 'Dad' Wilson, who had been one of Fremont's Guides, settled the matter by saying, 'We'll eat it. If that flour was poisoned there'd be a lot of dead mice and squirrels lying around. You can see they have been eating at it and there isn't a dead squirrel in sight.'

"We were pretty hungry, and we figured that if the flour didn't kill the squirrels it wouldn't kill us, so we all got busy, rolled balls of dough and whittled long sticks, and, building a campfire, we held those dough balls over the fire till they were cooked. Some of them were as black as a cinder on the outside and dough inside, but neverthe-less, they tasted mighty good. I ate so much of that half-cooked dough it gave me cramps. This flour lasted us clear to the Shasta, where we stopped a few days and washed out a grubstake, and then we started over the mountains for Trinity River.

"We followed the Trinity for 50 or 60 miles. We met an Old Hudson Bay trapper who knew that country, who told us of a cut-off through a low pass in the mountains which would save us 50 miles of hard travel. At the foot of the mountains we struck off for the headwaters of Scott's River.

After traveling down Scott's Valley for 25 miles or so, we crossed the low divide and went back to Scott's Bar, which we had originally discovered but had left because we could only pan out an ounce a day to the man. While we had been wandering all over the face of the landscape, eating squirrels and crickets, grass roots and rosebuds, a lot of newcomers had come in and taken all the good claims on Scott's Bar.

"Our party broke up at Scott's Bar. Some of them went back to Trinity City and others went to Klamath, while I stayed at Scott's Bar.

"One day, while at the Deadwood Mine on McAdams Creek in Scott's Valley, a young chap came in who looked like a Mexican half-breed. His hair was long, he was dressed in buckskin like an Indian, and also, part of his outfit was a Mexican rig. He wouldn't pass the time of day with the rest of us so we were kind of suspicious of him.

"A man named Bill Hearst had a deep mining claim there. He took his ore out in a tub by means of a swinging derrick. He raised the tub of ore on a rope which ran over a pulley and was operated by a horse. He hired this young fellow, who said his name was Miller and who claimed to come from Oregon, to lead the horse to pull up the tubs of ore. One morning young Miller failed to turn up, and Hearst's calico horse was gone, too. Miller had left during the night, with the horse.

"Hearst was certainly hostile. He swore that if he ever laid eyes on that young horsethief he would fill his carcass with lead. He traced him to Captain Jack's band of Modoc Indians. There he lost all trace. Later, he heard he was with the Shasta Indians and had an Indian wife.

"Some months later, when I was in Shasta, I saw a big, spotted California horse that looked like Hearst's horse that Miller had stolen. I went over, sized him up, and recognized him. The new owner told me he had bought him of a young fellow rigged up in a Mexican and Indian outfit, and he described him so I recognized him as Miller.

"Miller lived with the Indians for the next year or two. Bill Hearst and Captain Martin later headed north and struck rich ground at Canyon City, in eastern Oregon. Miller came back to Deadwood, on Scott's Bar, when he heard that Hearst had gone. However, there was a reward out for Miller, as he had been posted as a horsethief. Badley, the constable, tried to arrest Miller, but Miller shot him through the thigh and got away.

"Along about 1862 or thereabouts I was in Canyon City. One of the first men I ran across was Bill Hearst. A few days later I met Miller and recognized him as the horsethief who had stolen Hearst's horse. Miller recognized me. He told me he was running an express train, and was anxious to pay Hearst the value of the spotted horse he had taken. He said that taking that horse was a boyish indescretion he had often regretted. He got Dr. Horsley and myself to go to Bill Hearst, pay for the horse, and square the matter up. Miller had studied law, so he was elected county judge. Later he took the name of 'Joaquin' Miller, and made quite a hit writing poetry.

"Two Hudson Bay men and a squaw, all of whom had scurvy badly, came to the camp where I was, in the spring of 1850. We doctored them up the best we could and sent them to San Francisco, but they all died.

"General Joe Lane met some Indians who told him that white men were washing out gold dust on Scott's River. He built a cabin next to mine. I told him all the rich claims were gone, but I thought we could get a fair claim on Poor Man's Bar. There were lots of big boulders on Poor Man's Bar, and it was hard to work. I secured a rocker and we worked together till the water froze up.

"We had no wild hay and when winter set in our pack horses and pack mules were up against it for feed. We called a miners' meeting to see who would go into Scott's Valley, where the animals could find dried grass. A man named Lewis, a college graduate, and myself told the miners if they would build us a good cabin and corral in Scott's Valley we would take care of the stock. Lewis was a good man when he wasn't drunk but he was drunk most of the time. We had pretty good luck with our stock. We only lost one mule, with its saddle and bridle. Lewis was riding it and left it tied to a tree while he went to look for some of the other animals and the Indians stole it. It was General Joe Lane's riding mule.

"We needed supplies, so Lewis volunteered to go to Scott's Bar and buy them. He solemnly promised he would not take a single drink. I ought to have known he couldn't keep his promise, for after he got one drink it was all off with him.

"He tried to pick a fight with a Cherokee half-breed. The Cherokee half-breed didn't want any trouble, and refused to fight. When Lewis insisted on fighting, the Cherokee half-breed threw Lewis down and held him down without hurting him. A medium-sized Irishman who had had trouble with Lewis stabbed Lewis as he lay on the floor, dropped the knife, and disappeared. The miners wanted to discourage murders and make an example, so they looked for the Irishman, but, not being able to find him and wanting to punish someone for the death of Lewis, they hung the Cherokee half-breed.

"A few months later the Irishman got in a drunken row in San Francisco, killed a man, and was sentenced to be hung. Before being hung he confessed he had killed Lewis and that the Cherokee half-breed had nothing to do with it.

"In the spring of 1852 I was at Yreka Diggings. We ran out of grub, so Billy Mosier, Henry McCleaver and myself took some pack horses and crossed the divide to Trinidad Bay, where we loaded our eight pack horses and started back. There was lots of travel in those days. Two and a half miles from Blackburn's Ferry we came to a man who had a tent with a sign on it, 'Pioneer Camp'. He wanted to pull out, so we bought his tent and, unloading part of the supplies, I stayed to run the tent store while my two partners went on with the rest of the supplies to Yreka Diggings. While I was there an old man, who told me his name was Blackburn and who said he lived at Salt Lake City, stopped at my tent. He had walked 25 miles that day and was about all in. I said to him, 'It's pretty near dusk. You better stay here tonight, and I will go with you to the ferry tomorrow morning.'

"He said, 'No, my son is at the ferry. I haven't seen him for 12 years. I will stay here a little while and rest, and then I will go on to the ferry, for you say it's only 2½ miles.'

"I got him a cup of coffee, fried some bacon for him, and after supper he started down to Blackburn's Ferry.

"I had noticed a few days before that tnere were quite a number of Indians camped on the flat above the sandbar where young Blackburn had his ferry. Next morning I started out early to go down to the ferry. I hadn't gone more than a mile when I found Old Man Blackburn lying dead in the trail. I suspected the Indians had killed him, though, of course, I didn't know. I continued on toward the ferry, keeping my eyes peeled for Indians. Presently I came in sight of the ferry and saw some Indians trying to roll a big rock from the hillside above the Blackburn shack down the hill so it would smash the shack. The Indians were armed with bows and arrows. Three of them were near the ferry. I didn't see any of the people around, so I concluded the Indians had killed them.

"I shot at the Indians. All three of them ran and jumped in the river to swim across. Evidently I hit one of them, for only two of the Indians emerged on the other side. The one I had shot must have been badly wounded, for he sank.

"I saw a party of men coming down the river trail. They were surveying, to establish a better trail. We found at the ferry that the Indians had killed three men and a 14-year-old boy. Blackburn himself and his wife were in their cabin and were uninjured.

"No, none of the men were scalped. I have seen a lot of men killed by Indians, but I never yet saw one that was scalped. The Indians for some reason had cut the flesh away on each of the ankles of the boy.

"I told you I saw a party of men coming down the trail. There were 15 miners in this party. Shortly thereafter Alonzo Raines and three miners from the Klamath District who were going down to the bay to arrange to get their mail came along. Captain McMahon, who had been a Texas Ranger, was with the larger party. He and I asked for volunteers and, taking what grub we needed, we started out on the trail of the Indians. We trailed them to the forks of the Trinity River. We killed most of the Indians and destroyed their village.

"When we got back I learned that my two partners, who had gone on to Yreka Diggings, had been killed near Happy Camp, on the Klamath. We went there and found their bodies. Mosier, one of my partners, had a sister in New York City. He had taken out insurance on his life before he came out to California. She wanted me to send her an affadavit about his death. All I could tell her was that he was killed by the Indians and that we had buried him, but the insurance company required her to say by whom he was killed, and also to prove that he had not committed suicide, and a lot of other red-tape regulations, so that she was never able to collect his insurance.

"I came to Portland in 1861, going from Portland in 1862 to the mines in Canyon City. From Canyon City I went to Camp Harney, which at that time was a four-company post. General Crook appointed me sutler. He supposed I would take the matter up at Washington, to get his appointment confirmed, but I knew nothing about this, so the first thing I knew some politician got a senator to endorse him and secured the appointment. This meant I was out and injured and had to sell my goods for whatever I could get to the new sutler. I lost quite a bit of money.

"Canyon City was founded in 1862, though it wasn't incorporated till 1864. It is located on the headwaters of the John Day River. In 1865 it had a population of nearly 3000. I worked a claim in Canyon City in 1862, but I found that selling liquor at two bits a glass brought in a much more certain and larger income, so I ran a saloon there for some time.

"If you are at all familiar with the early history of Canyon City you will remember hearing of Mike Gallagher, who came up from San Francisco and ran a pack train between The Dalles and Canyon City. Gallagher was a good-hearted chap. Berry Way struck him for a lift, so he let him ride one of his extra saddle horses in going from Canyon City to The Dalles. Way murdered Gallagher, robbed him of $900 in gold dust, and took his horses. Some miners who saw Way driving Gallagher's horses recognized Gallagher's pack outfit and reported the matter to Tom Howland at Canyon City. Howland swore in five or six men to go with him, of whom I was one, and we overtook Berry Way between Juniper Flat and Canyon City. Canyon City didn't have any good facilities for taking care of murderers and horsethieves, so, for fear Berry Way might escape, we hung him.

"I was married in 1864 to Isabel DeLashmutt. Her brother, Van B. DeLashmutt, was mayor of Portland in 1890. The DeLashmutts came across the plains in 1852 and settled on a farm in Polk County. My brother-in-law, Van DeLashmutt, learned his trade as a printer on the **Salem Statesman**. He went to work there in 1857 as a printer's devil and worked for three years.

"While Van was serving in the Third Infantry of California Volunteers, they guarded the emigrant route from Julesburg to the Nevada line. While they were stationed at Salt Lake City, Van started a newspaper called the **Union Vidette**, which was the first daily paper ever issued in Salt Lake City. After the war he went to Nevada and published the **Times** in Washoe City. This was in the winter of 1865 and 1866. Two or three years later he came back to Portland and worked at the case. He and Judge Thayer and Harvey Scott started the Metropolitan Savings Bank in the fall of 1882. He made a lot of money in the Coeur d'Alene mines. He was elected mayor of Portland and was reelected after the first term expired.

"My wife died on the 4th of July some years ago.

"After I lost out at Camp Harney and disposed of my sutler's stock, I moved to Portland and opened a saloon at the foot of Washington Street. Old-timers will remember the American Exchange, which is what I called my saloon. It was in the Estes building. I rented the rooms where Mr. Walling used to have his printing office, over the saloon, for a billiard parlor.    I ran the saloon and billiard parlor for some years.

"When Ben Holladay came to Portland he wanted to secure control of the political situation of the state.    When he couldn't buy a man's vote in the legislature he generally fixed it up for the man to get some office or did him some other favor, to get his vote.    He was anxious to send J. H. Mitchell back to Washington, as a senator.    One day he sent word that he wanted to see me.    When I went to his office he had his feet on the table and was tipped back in a big office chair.    Pointing to a box of cigars, he said, 'Help yourself.'

"After our cigars got to going well, he said, 'They tell me the old 'Modoc ward' is pretty strongly Democratic.'

"I said, 'They tell you the truth, all right, for it never yet has gone Republican.'

"He said, 'It's going to go Republican this year, and you are going to help me make it roll up a Republican majority.'

"I said, 'That will cost you a whole lot of money, Mr. Holladay.'

"He said, 'Don't worry about the money. The money will be forthcoming, and you will get your share.    I'll pay you well for your work, no matter how it comes out, but I'll give you a big bonus if it goes Republican.'    He said, 'Size it up and see what you can do.'

"I went down near the steamboat landing and talked with the proprietors of the different hotels. I found that the proprietor of the Grove Hotel could swing about 40 votes and that they were all Democratic.    The proprietor of the New York House told me there were from 40 to 50 Democratic voters in his place.    I told them that I could make it well worth their while if they could get rid of their lodgers and colonize the ward with Republican voters. I went to Ben Holladay, who furnished me with a sack of $2.50 gold pieces.    I kept pretty busy till election day, and on election day I served as paymaster.    I would go to the different hotels and lodging houses, furnish the men with a Mitchell ticket, go with them to the polls and see that they voted it, and as they came out I would hand each one a $2.50 gold piece.    We carried the old Modoc ward--the Democratic stronghold--and for the first time in its history it went Republican.    We rolled up 120 majority.    At one saloon I got 30 votes at $2.50 each.    This election was really the cause of Harvey Scott's falling out with Ben Holladay and Senator Mitchell, particularly the latter.

"For the past 40 years or more I have lived

212

here at The Dalles."

Oregon Journal
February 28–March 4, 1927

# Uncle Billy Wiley
# Driver for Lincoln and Douglas
# The Dalles, Oregon

"For 80 years I celebrated May 10 as my birth-day. I had always supposed I was born on May 10, 1839, at Cleveland, Ohio, but in 1920 one of the members of my family located our old family Bible, which shows I was born on May 9, 1839, so I have had to change my birthday celebration to that date.

"I was 19 years old in the fall of 1858, when I went to work for Blodgett, who owned a livery stable and hotel at Stevens Point, Wisconsin.

"Stephen A. Douglas had an almost national reputation in those days. Abraham Lincoln was considered a long-legged, awkward, uncouth country lawyer, and while Douglas was looked upon as a statesman, people thought Lincoln was an ambitious politician who would never get very far. They liked him, because he was a good story-teller and a natural mixer, but he was no orator, and he wasn't considered in the same class with 'The Little Giant', as Douglas was called. Douglas was United States Senator and was running for reelection. He was looked upon as a future presidential candidate.

"On June 16, 1858, the Republican State Convention met at Springfield and passed a resolution endorsing Abraham Lincoln as the first and only choice of the Republicans of Illinois for the United States Senate, to succeed Stephen A. Douglas. Greeley opposed Lincoln.

"Wherever Douglas spoke he created great enthusiasm. In July he spoke in Springfield and elsewhere in Illinois.

"Late in July, Abraham Lincoln sent a challenge to Douglas to hold a series of joint debates. These were to be held at Ottawa, Freeport, Jonesboro, Charleston, Galesburg, Quincy, and Alton. The one who opened the debate spoke an hour. The other would speak an hour and a half, and then the first speaker would have half an hour to demolish the other man's argument.

"Mr. Blodgett was asked to furnish a good team and a rig to take Lincoln and Douglas to the various places where they spoke. I had worked in a livery stable and was a good driver, so Blodgett assigned me the job of driving them around the

213

country. I met them at Warren, Illinois, on the Illinois Central Railroad. They put in 100 days on that campaign. I only drove them about three or four weeks. Douglas made 130 speeches between the beginning of July and the beginning of November, and I guess Lincoln made about the same number. Douglas was always trying to get Lincoln in a corner and make him ridiculous, but he couldn't do it.

"There were three seats in my rig. Lincoln and Douglas sat on the back seat. As we drove through the country I would often pick someone up who was walking to town to hear the debate, and Lincoln or Douglas would ask them questions about their political views and the questions of the day. Once in a while some man I picked up would know either Lincoln or Douglas, but usually they didn't. Sometimes they would roast the tar out of Lincoln and sometimes they would jump on Douglas with both feet.

"Douglas was a polished man. Lincoln was homely and kind of awkward, and while Douglas had a deep, booming voice, Lincoln's voice was higher, and while you could hear him plainly, people seemed to take to Douglas better than Lincoln. I suppose one reason was that Douglas was United States Senator and had the giving out of jobs and offices, while nobody supposed Lincoln would be elected, so they paid more attention to the well dressed, polished candidate, Douglas, than to the one who was trying to get his job in the United States Senate. I certainly used to enjoy hearing Lincoln tell stories.

"You can't understand how strong the feeling was before the Civil War. Nowadays every schoolboy looks up to Lincoln, but in those days they abused him like a pickpocket. My! How the Southerners hated him! As a matter of fact, if the Democratic Party hadn't split, Lincoln would never have been elected.

"Whom did I vote for for president? Why, for Douglas, of course.

•••••••••••••••••••••••••••••••••••••••••••••••••••••

"I celebrated my 21st birthday on the plains. That was in 1860. I had three yoke of cattle on my wagon--two yoke of oxen and one of cows. I milked those cows all the way across the plains, and there was never a day that we didn't have fresh milk and butter. I put the churn over the hind axle of the prairie schooner, and by evening the jolting through the chuckholes of the Old Oregon Trail churned the milk into butter.

"I landed at The Dalles on September 5, 1860, in the forenoon. I went at once to Wells, Fargo

& Co.'s office and struck them for a job. They gave me a job as driver and told me to report immediately after lunch, so, within two hours of my arrival I had landed a job. I drove from The Dalles to Miller's Bridge, on the Deschutes. That winter I was stationed for three months at Miller's Bridge as tolltaker.

"In 1862 I went to Florence. That was a rich camp. I took a claim there and made good money. I heard about the strike on the John Day at Canyon City, so I went there. I took up a claim in the city limits. The gold at Canyon City was mostly in the form of nuggets or coarse dust. There is a thrill about placer mining hard to describe. You never know when you are going to strike a rich pocket. One day while I was digging on the point of a ridge about 12 feet above the stream, I dug up a wedge-shaped piece of quartz, about one-third gold. I got more than $500 in gold out of this one chunk of quartz.

"For a while I ran a pack train from The Dalles to Canyon City. I took out letters and gold dust. I made big money at Canyon City. I remember, when I first went there, I asked the blacksmith if I could leave my roll of blankets in his shop. The blacksmith shop was made of poles, the roof of brush. Not long after that I paid the blacksmith $75 to make a wagon bed for me. I bought the running gear of an old wagon and had the blacksmith fix it up. I hauled charcoal from the charcoal pits and sold it at $50 a ton. I could haul two loads a day. Many's the day I cleared $50 on my charcoal.

"In the fall of 1862 I built a log house and put up a shed made out of poles, with a shake roof, and ran a livery stable. That turned out to be a good money-maker, too.

"One night my tooth began aching, and I walked the floor all night. Next morning I went to a doctor in Canyon City and asked him to look at my tooth. He didn't have any tools for plugging it, so he pulled it out and charged me five dollars for the job. I thought this was pretty steep but didn't say anything.

"He told me he would like me to haul some cordwood he had cut on his claim and bring it to his house. There were three loads of it. When I went to collect the money I told him it would be $10 a load, or $30 for the three loads. He said, 'Isn't that pretty steep? It took you less than a day to haul it.'

"I said, 'Yes, and it didn't take you more than a minute to pull my tooth, yet you charged me five dollars for it.'

"He gave me a funny look and said, 'Well, maybe when we get better acquainted we won't charge so much for our services.'

"He was worshipful master of the Masonic Lodge there, and in spite of my having charged him $10 a load to haul his wood he gave me the job of hauling all the squared timbers from where they had been cut to Canyon City to build a Masonic Lodge. Not only that, but he officiated when I was made a Mason. I was the first one to be raised in that lodge.

"In 1866 I started freighting between The Dalles and Canyon City. I got 20 cents a pound, so I made good money. When I was running the toll bridge across the Deschutes, in 1861, it was a regular mint. I charged $1.50 for a team and 25 cents for a man on horseback.

"In 1866 I took a contract from Orlando Humason and his father-in-law, Jonathan Jackson, to freight a ten-stamp mill into Idaho. I used one large freight wagon with five yoke of cattle and one with six yoke, and I myself drove a four-horse team. I hired a couple of men to drive the bull teams. I took it to their property, 30 miles north of Boise City. I started from The Dalles on April 6, and didn't get to where I was to deliver the stamp mill till well into July. They furnished me 40 men to go along and make the roads. We had to plow roads on the sidehills, scrape the dirt off and fasten ropes to the wagons and have a gang of men on the upper side to keep the wagons from tipping over on the sidehills.

"Two men I got well acquainted with in Canyon City were Judge C. H. Miller, or 'Joaquin' Miller, as he called himself later, and Tom Brentz. Later Tom served as congressman from Walla Walla.

"I ran a butcher shop at Dixie for a while, and butchered and sold over 150 cattle. For a while I carried the mail for the government. I also worked for Humason & Jackson on their farm for a while. Later I bought this place. I built a hotel at Cold Spring Camp, about 60 miles from The Dalles, near Antelope. I ran a stage station and put up travelers. The freighters used to stop and feed their teams. I used to charge from four bits to six bits for meals.

"I got my start in the stock business in an odd way. A young fellow and myself came to The Dalles to attend a fair. They were auctioning some cows. Neither of us had any money. I bought three of them and gave a note, with this young chap as security on the note. Then he bought three and I went security on his note. In 30 days I paid for these three cows from the money I realized on the sale of butter which I sold to the miners.

"I was married two weeks after I reached The Dalles. I married Mary McEwen. We were married by a justice of the peace on Five-Mile Creek. We had eight children. My daughter, Mrs. High McCauley lives in Portland. Mary married Tom Condon, formerly of The Dalles. She is a widow and also lives in Portland. Mrs. George Thompson lives at The Dalles, and my son Rowland Wiley lives at Hood River. Ellsworth is dead. Will lives in North Dakota. Cassie married Claude Hill, son of Dr. Hill of Albany. She and Nina are both dead.

"After the death of my first wife I married my present wife, Myrtle Reed of Wisconsin. I have lived in The Dalles since 1879."

Oregon Journal
March 15 & 16, 1927

# "Daddy" Vaughn
# Ilwaco, Washington

*Daddy Vaughn is one of the landmarks of Ilwaco, Washington. He lives by himself in a little cabin at the edge of town.*

*I said he lives by himself. I will have to take that back, for he has half a dozen dogs and twice as many cats that live with him and are pensioners on his bounty.*

*Daddy Vaughn and I sat on one of the benches of Mr. Budd's depot a day or two ago talking about old times, while Badger, his favorite dog, lay in front of us, keeping one eye on his master, as though he thought he would bear watching. Occasionally Badger would dash out and try to catch a passing automobile. I don't know what he would have done with it if he had succeeded in catching one--probably he had never given that phase of the matter any serious thought. Badger is well-named, for he is a dog and a half long, half a dog high, and broad accordingly.*

*As we sat there a little girl came up to get some candy, for Daddy Vaughn always has some candy in his pockets for the little folks. In spite of his war-like record, Daddy Vaughn is in reality the soul of gentleness.*

"I ain't what you would really call old. I will be 84 come the first of next October. My father lived to be 104, and when he died there wasn't anything much the matter with him. He just wore out and ran down.

"Tell you about Ilwaco? Well, I can sure do that very thing. If you want to know all about

Ilwaco you have come to the right person.

"No, sir. I didn't come across the plains by ox team--not by a long shot. I came by water.

"I was born in Harrison County, Indiana. I was not quite 21 years old when the war broke out. What war? Why the only war we ever had that amounts to anything--the Civil War, of course. In those days we didn't have to go rampaging all over Europe to find a war. We believed in patronizing home industry. We made one of our own right here at home, and, believe me, it was some war. I get $50 every month for being in it. Uncle Sam sure does spend money for pensions. I enlisted in the Indiana volunteers, but a regular got hold of me and said, 'What's the use of your frittering away your time with amateurs? Why don't you join an organization of real soldiers? You come with me, and I'll get you with an outfit where you will see real fighting. I belong to the regulars, and fighting's all we do.' As far as that goes, though, before we got through with it the amateurs, as the regular army men call the volunteers, got their share of the fighting, too. I went with him and his officer fixed it up some way so I was transferred from the volunteers to the regular army.

"They sent me to Washington, D. C., to teach me to ride. When the horses would start to jump over the bars a lot of the new recruits would lean backward, instead of forward, so the horse would take the jump alone and the recruit would pick himself up and rub his head and wish he had joined the infantry. The officer watched me a spell and said, 'Thought you were sent here to learn to ride. You don't need any teaching.' So he had me go to one side and he picked out some other chaps who could ride and sent us to Washington, D. C. When we got there an officer lined us up and picked out some of the biggest and best of us to serve in the Second Horse Artillery. We went down to help Sheridan clean up the Johnny Rebs.

"I remember while serving with Sheridan he issued orders for us to burn every barn and every fence and to take every cow and horse and pig and chicken, so the Confederates couldn't secure supplies there. He issued strict orders, though, for us not to go into any of the houses or bother any of the women.

"Well, sir, when Sheridan and we fellows under him had licked the graycoats till they hollered enough, we were frazzled out, so they sent a bunch of us out West. We came across the Isthmus. I was in Captain John I. Rogers' company and we were stationed at Fort Canby. That was in 1866.

"Did I get married after the war quit on us? I should say I didn't, or I would have had a personal war on my own hands. How is that? Why, I was married already. I married when I was 20, before the war ever broke out. I married Mary Knapp.

"I ain't what you would really call old..."

We had four children. She died in Astoria, and I married a widow with two children, and we had one child.

"I served a year and a half at Fort Canby. The whole country was alive with deer and grouse and water birds--ducks and geese and such like

219

—in those days. When I got my discharge from Uncle Sam, 'Daddy' McGowan and I fished. We built tanks, salted the salmon and shipped them to the Sandwich Islands. We didn't have canneries in those days. I helped build the mill at Knapton and then I went to Deep River, where I took up a homestead. I logged off upward 7,000,000 feet of logs. After that I went to Portland and helped build the Hotel Portland. I did carpenter work on it.

"After we got the hotel built I landed a job on the Portland police force. In those days being a policeman wasn't any pink tea affair. You had plenty of practice fighting. I put in four years handling drunks and scrappers in Portland and then went to Astoria and was on the police force there for some time. I was six feet one and a half, weighed around 250 pounds and was all bone and muscle.

"Let me tell you, mister, how to handle a mean man. You take a running jump at him, knock him down before he can get into action, and then choke him until he becomes limber. You can tell by watching his face when he will be peaceable. When his tongue hangs out and he gets black in the face he will soon relax. Then you can handle 'em, for they are discouraged and will go along with you fairly reasonable.

"We used to have a woman in Astoria that would get the goat of the Swedish policeman on the waterfront beat. She would come out in the street and start cursing. She was terrible big and terrible fat and heavy and when he would grab her she would sort of go all to pieces, quiver like a jellyfish and sit down. She was too heavy for him to carry, he couldn't lift her to her feet, and he didn't think it would look ladylike for him to kick her, so he dreaded her sprees something fierce.

"One day he asked me to help him carry her. I said, 'You stand to one side. I will handle her alone and get her to jail.'

"He said, 'I'll bet you five dollars you don't.'

"I went to her and said, 'Lady, get up and come to jail with me.' She got up and we walked down the street toward the jail. I asked, 'Why wouldn't you walk to jail with the other policeman?'

"She said, 'Why, that big Swede never asked me to. He always comes up and grabs me and wrestles with me, so I always lie down until he goes away and quits pestering me.'

"One time when I was a policeman here in Ilwaco a huge logger from Aberdeen, a Finn, came here and got on a drunk. He was mean and vicious and had tremendous strength. He sent word to me that no policeman in a little jay town like Ilwaco could arrest him--that he made all the Aberdeen officers hunt their holes when he went on a rampage. I spotted him and ran at him and lit astride of him. The force of my jump knocked him down. I got my favorite neck hold and hung on. You ought to have seen him flop. I'll say this for him, he lasted quite a long time before he got limp. His eyes and tongue were both hanging out before he quit. I sent a boy for a delivery wagon, for the logger was too heavy to drag. I lifted him in and sat on him while the boy drove us to the jail, and every time he groaned I said, 'Remember, this isn't Aberdeen.' It prejudiced him against Ilwaco. He never came back. He claimed I was too rough in my methods.

"I ain't what I was 50 or 60 years ago. I have gone down until I weigh only 211 pounds.

"All four of my boys are loggers. Two of them are in charge of logging camps. You have to be able to lick the best man in a logging crew before you can hold down a job as foreman. All four of my boys can qualify. My daughter married John Kelly of Portland.

"Ask any of the old policemen on the force in Portland. They will remember me. It used to take a good man to be a policeman in those days. Nowadays about all a policeman has to do is put a little invitation card into an automobile requesting the owner not to park there. That's no way to keep your muscles in good condition.

"Well, so long. Badger and I will have to be moving on."

Oregon Journal
undated

# Hank Was Married . . .

*Hank was married in Nevada, left his wife and went to Pendleton. Hearing his wife was dead, he married a woman named Robie, on the Umatilla Reservation. Hank's first wife later turned up at Pendleton. To prevent any mix-up, Hank secured a divorce from his first wife.*

*Hank was a natural collector. He had a collection of beautifully mounted revolvers. He also had a rather valuable collection of coins, as well as a large number of seal rings and gold nuggets, one of which weighed over $600 in value.*

*He liked to impress strangers with his courage.*

221

One day a stranger at Athena met Hank, and Hank invited him to take a ride behind a spirited team of horses. Hank whipped the horses till they were running frantically, expecting to see the stranger show signs of alarm. When his guest exhibited no symptoms of panic, but instead calmly folded his arms and looked out over the scenery, Hank lost his patience, threw the reins over the horses' backs and folded his own arms. A moment or two later the frightened team crashed through a fence, broke the rig into fragments, and threw Hank and the stranger clear of the wreckage.

*Oregon Journal*
*March 13, 1926*

# Joseph C. Wooley
# Justice of the Peace
# Harrisburg, Oregon

"Shortly after I was married my wife and I went up to Harney County. This was in 1883. There were no fences up there in those days.

"George McGowan had settled at what is now Burns, in May, 1882. McGowan, who was a Scotchman, decided to start a store and post office on his place. The cattlemen signed a petition for a post office and McGowan was appointed postmaster and asked to suggest a name for the post office. Being a Scotchman, he was very fond of Bobby Burns, so he suggested that the post office be called Burns. McGowan, Pete Stinger, and a man named Brown started the town of Burns."

*Oregon Journal*
November 13, 1930

# Dr. M. J. Allen
# Milton, Oregon

"They had a bad scare while they were camped on the Platte River, at noon. The stock were being watered. A body of horsemen were seen in the distance. The warning cry of 'Indians' was heard. Someone called out, 'Hurry up and hitch up and roll out!' Others cried, 'Form a corral; corral, corral.' The captain of the train became rattled and ordered those who were yoked up to form in line. Women began screaming and crying and hunting for their children, and there was a regular panic. In a few moments the horsemen rode up and proved to be Captain Kearney and Lieutenant Fremont with a body of troops. The troops escorted the party for ten days and then rode on to establish Fort Kearney."

Oregon Journal
July 26, 1925

# Judge Charles E. Wolverton
# Portland, Oregon

"My first case was defending John Wesley Fairchild, who had stolen a horse and saddle, and notwithstanding my efforts in his behalf the jury decided he was guilty and the judge decided that three years in the penitentiary would help him in the future to distinguish between his own and some other man's horseflesh. Judge B. F. Bonham had appointed me to defend the prisoner, and he allowed me a fee of $25."

Oregon Journal
undated

# Clinton Wolford
# Portland, Oregon

"In 1866, when I was eight years old, we drove from Silverton to Crescent City, where we waited two months for a boat to take us to Eureka. Father left his stock at Crescent City and returned next spring to get them. In those days there was no road through the redwoods. Father bought a place on what was known as the Bald Hills, on the headwaters of Eel River, about 50 miles by trail eastward from the coast. We went in on horseback and by packhorse. That was a wonderful country. You could see deer in herds like domestic cattle. Of an evening the air was fairly vocal with the hooting of the grouse. From our back door I could look across a canyon when huckleberries were ripe and usually see bears eating the huckleberries. In those days the country was full of grizzly bears.

"A man named Crissy lived with us the first winter we were there. He killed deer for the hides. There was no demand for the meat, so he only used what he needed for himself, leaving the carcasses where he killed them. There was a firm of cattlemen known locally as Catchem and Markem, who hired Crissy to take care of their headquarters at Camp Grant. One afternoon a man named Vaughn came to our place on his way to visit Crissy. Vaughn was a squawman. He had two squaws--an old one to do the work and a younger squaw with whom

223

he lived.  He came back much sooner than we expected, and said that he had found Crissy lying about 50 yards from the house, where the Indians had killed him and scalped him.  The Indians had ransacked the ranch house, carrying away all of Crissy's ammunition and food supplies.  They had also shot Crissy's dogs.

"The Indians only shot what game they needed to eat, and they resented the white hunters killing off the game and taking only the hides."

Oregon Journal
September 20, 1933

# Austin Smith
# Pioneer of 1848
# Silverton, Oregon

"I never had a fight nor was I ever held up.  I think the principal reason why I got along was that I minded my own business, wasn't looking for trouble, and let the other men drink my share of the whiskey.

"Instead of going to the Idaho mines this time (1866), I went up into Montana.  I never will forget my first sight of Helena.  As I entered the town I happened to look up in a tree beside the trail, and I certainly had quite a start, for there was a Frenchman hanging by a rope from a limb of the tree, his face all twisted, his eyes bulged out, and as there was a little breeze, he was swaying and twisting back and forth.

"I asked someone why he had been hung, and they said, 'He joined the vigilantes, and we found he was a spy and was in with a gang that was robbing sluice boxes and holding up miners.'

"Bannock and Virginia City were the two big camps in those days in Montana.  Alder Gulch was a rich district.  I was in Bannock when the vigilance committee decided to hang the sheriff and his principal deputies.  Great Scott! but there was a crowd. Henry Plummer, the sheriff, who was at the head of the cutthroats, sluice box robbers, and road agents, in that district, was taken out and hanged. They found in his pocket a list of 85 names of his gang.  Within a short while they had lynched 21 of his confederates.

"I certainly saw lots of coarse work when I was in the mines, and I saw a number of lynchings and killings."

Oregon Journal
June 23, 1927

## John C. Wood
## Portland, Oregon

"To tell you the truth, I haven't much patience with these chaps who want to hang around town and let their friends or the Community Chest support them. I have run across quite a lot of young fellows who won't take a job out in the hills because it's too far away from the movies and the comforts of the city. If I had my way I would put all of these weak-willed, weak-spined whiners down in a shaft where the water was coming in and I would tell them, 'You can get busy and pump out the shaft or let the water rise and drown you.'

"If there's one person I have no use for it's the individual who will live on somebody else's sweat or community charity when he is able to work. If a person isn't able to work, that's a different matter. If I were a young chap I'd get a slab of bacon and a gold pan and go out into the hills and pan out a living. The young fellows these days seem too soft and lack what the pioneers had—initiative and self-reliance."

Oregon Journal
August 26, 1933

## F. M. Wilkins
## Eugene, Oregon

"Elijah Bristow was the first settler to build a cabin in Lane County. He took up a place at Pleasant Hill in 1846. The first four settlers that took claims in this county were Elijah Bristow, Eugene Skinner, Felix Scott and William Dodson. Dodson built the second cabin in the county. Eugene Skinner, for whom Skinners Butte is name and from whom the city of Eugene takes its name, built his cabin at the foot of Ya-po-ah Butte, now called Skinners Butte, in the spring of 1847. In the summer of that year Mrs. Skinner with her little girl moved into the log cabin near the foot of the butte and thus became the first white woman to make a permanent home in Lane County."

Oregon Journal
November 19, 1921

# James Davis Slater
## La Grande, Oregon

"By the by, ours was the first wagon to cross the Blue Mountains by what was known as the Daly Road. This was in July, 1864. Frank Ensign, for whom Ensign Station was named, drove us in a four-horse wagon. I remember him very distinctly, because he had the end of his nose shot off by an Indian in the Indian war of 1856."

Oregon Journal
July 16, 1929

# J. T. Simpson
## Sheridan, Oregon

"I became very fond of Lieutenant Sheridan. My father, like most army sutlers, carried a large stock of liquor. In fact, the bar was more profitable than any other department of the store. Sheridan and the other officers usually bought the highest-priced bottle goods we carried.

"Sheridan, being the post quartermaster, made frequent trips to Salem, and he would often invite me to go with him. He had a team of small roan mules that could eat up the miles. He usually took two bottles of good liquor along with him, and about every mile or so he would take a drink. Sheridan was big-hearted and very generous and there was never any question as to his courage or bravery. When I went on trips to Salem with him he would never let me pay for a thing.

"I never saw a man who could drink as much liquor as Sheridan without being affected in any way by it. I spoke of it to him once, and he said: 'Liquor has been the ruination of many a good man. I hope you will leave it severely alone. It can do you no good, and is apt to do you a good deal of harm.'"

Oregon Journal
June 1, 1922

# Joseph Yates
## Corvallis, Oregon

"I have never had my name in the paper yet. I am 87 years old. I don't owe a dollar and I still have four bits in my pocket. I have never sued a man in my life nor been sued. I have never been arrested--but that ain't saying

226

I came pretty near it once. A man called me a damn liar, so I knocked him down and when he got up I took after him with a pitchfork--but he outran me. For 50 yards I kept almost near enough to stick the tines into him, but when he looked around and saw how close I was he let out another link and got away. He complained to Judge Boise. I asked for a jury. They cleared me, but one of the jurymen thought I ought to have speeded up a little and stuck him with my hay fork."

Oregon Journal
December 6, 1921

# Professor J. A. Sellwood
# Pioneer Teacher
# Salem, Oregon

*Professor J. A. Sellwood has lived at Salem since the days when Oregon was a territory. He went to Salem 66 years ago and has lived there ever since.*

"I was born February 13, 1843. I was christened Joseph Anthony Sellwood. My father, James Richard William Sellwood, was a shoemaker. His brother was an Episcopalian minister and eventually got my father a job as missionary to poor whites in the South. While doing this work my father studied for the ministry and became an Episcopalian minister and so served for more than 40 years. My mother, whose maiden name was Elizabeth Dow, was born in Penzance, England. My father was also born in England. There were five children of us. My eldest brother, John W., was born in 1839. James R. N., my next brother, was born in 1841. I was born in 1843. My brother, T. A. R. Sellwood, Tom, as we call him, was born in 1844, while my sister, Elizabeth D. H. Sellwood, was born in 1846.

"My uncle John Sellwood moved to South Carolina. After he had been there he asked Father to come there and work with him as missionary to the poor whites. In 1856 Uncle John wrote that Bishop Scott of Portland had issued a call for missionaries to come to Oregon.

"Uncle John and my father noticed that the men of the South were drilling and that there was a very bitter feeling against the North. As they were Northerners things were not altogether pleasant in South Carolina for them, so Uncle John wrote to Bishop Scott asking him if he could use him and my father in Oregon.

"My father's parishioners in South Carolina were very loyal to the church. I know of no better

227

proof of their loyalty than the fact that they took upon themselves the support of my father as a minister to Oregon and agreed to pay him $800 a year for ten years, until he could get established in Oregon. In spite of the fact that the Civil War was soon raging, they kept up the payments promptly and sent the promised $800 each year for ten years.

"We left South Carolina in the spring of 1856, going to Boyd's Landing. From there we went to Charleston and thence to New York City. At New York we took a boat to Aspinwall, on the Isthmus of Panama. The railroad had just been completed across the Isthmus. We reached Panama about supper time on April 15, 1856.

"The Golden Age, the steamer on which we were going to San Francisco, was not to leave until about ten o'clock that night, when the tide was at the full. Most of the passengers decided to put in the four hours before the steamer's sailing taking in the scenes of Panama. About 50 or 60 of us stayed at the depot.

"One of the passengers at the depot had a dispute with a native about the price of a melon. A quarrel ensued and blows were exchanged. A few moments later the natives came up, looking for trouble. I was only 13 years old, but the events of that night are just as plain as if they had happened last week. I heard a pistol shot and then I heard someone cry, 'The natives are attacking us.' One of the passengers shut the big door of the depot and barred it. A few moments later the native troops were called to quell the riot. They shot over the heads of the crowd outside, the bullets splintering the boards all around us. One of the passengers called out 'Lie on the floor or we shall all be killed!' We heard the bugle sound, and several more volleys crashed into the building just above our heads. The natives rushed around to the other side of the depot, where the tickets were sold, and came in from that end.

"Uncle John opened the big door and told Tom and me to come with him so we could escape. A native hit Tom on the head and knocked him unconscious, then attacked my uncle. They broke his nose, wounded him in both hands, and shot him through the body, the bullet going within half an inch of his heart. I decided that this was no place for a minister's son, so I hurried back into the building. The natives were still shooting the passengers in the building. I was frantic. I had lost my people, and I saw the natives killing the passengers up near the ticket office. They killed 17 of our party.

"One of the Spaniards said, 'Follow me.'

I went with him to where some other passengers were. They made us kneel in a circle while the soldiers came up and pointed their guns at us and were going to shoot us. One of the men, who seemed to have authority, finally persuaded them not to shoot us, and we were taken to the governor's house. While we were there they brought in a passenger all covered with blood. He looked as if he had been killed. As a matter of fact, he had been rolled around where the others had been killed and wounded and did not have a scratch on him. However, he was nearly scared to death.

"A Spaniard saw my brother Tom lying in the street after the crowd had moved on. He took him to his house. The Spaniard's wife washed the blood off Tom and gave him a good supper and put him to bed. The next morning his host took him to the American Hotel.

"Meanwhile I had rejoined the family. My father and mother were feeling very unhappy. They were told that Uncle John and Thomas were both killed. Father went to where the 17 dead passengers were lying in the depot to see if he could identify Uncle John. He couldn't find him. Someone told Father there were some wounded passengers lying in another part of the depot. He went there to look them over but could not find them there. Finally Uncle John, who was lying desperately wounded, called to him and Father had him taken to a hotel. Meanwhile a passenger said there was a lost boy at the American Hotel who might be his son, so Father went there, and sure enough it was Tom.

"We waited there five weeks and caught another steamer for San Francisco. Uncle John was not yet able to travel, so he waited for a few weeks more before coming. The Panama government paid my uncle $10,000 as damages. He invested the money in 320 acres near Portland, for which he paid $12 an acre. This farm is now called Sellwood. He also bought another farm on which Oak Grove is now located. He also bought some land in Yamhill County and several city blocks in Portland. So, while being shot was rather unpleasant at the time, it proved the nucleus of his fortune.

"We came from San Francisco on the steamer Columbia. From Portland we came up to Salem, arriving here June 17, 1856. My father became the first rector of St. Paul's Church. I remember very distinctly our trip from Oregon City to Salem. We were aboard the steamer Onward. Our boat pulled two flatboats up to the mouth of the Yamhill River. Lieutenant Sheridan was in charge of a large number of Indians on the flatboats who were being taken to the Grand Ronde Reservation. This was just after the Rogue River War in 1855.

"Father rented a little cabin near Lincoln Wade's brick store in North Salem. The night we moved in we suddenly heard a terrific racket just outside. We were terrorized. We thought the Indians had come to kill us. We had seen the Indians on the flatboats the preceding day and we had seen the massacre at Panama, but it turned out that this was only a party of young men and boys giving a charivari to a newly married couple, so we decided our scalps were safe for awhile."

Oregon Journal
May 29, 1922

**•••••••••••••••••••••••••••••••••••••••••••••••••••••••••**

"...I was offered a school at Devil's Half Acre, three miles from Independence. That was considered a very tough district, and when the directors sized me up they thought I was not smart enough or big enough to teach the school. I asked them to give me a chance at it. One of the directors said, 'Wright Tatum, one of the big boys, has made his brag that he will run out any teacher we hire, and I am afraid you are rather light for the job.' However, they told me they would give me a trial, but they didn't expect me to last long.

"The first thing I did was to hunt up Wright Tatum. I said to him, 'I understand you have more influence than any other boy in school. I don't think I shall be able to teach the school without your help. I am going to ask you to help me enforce discipline.' He was pleased at my consulting him and promised to help me. Not only was he a model student, but he certainly helped to keep the rest of the boys in line. By the by, Ike Patterson, who is running for governor, was one of my pupils."

Oregon Journal
May 31, 1922

# Joe Simon
# Portland, Oregon

"I lost the first case I had, to my great surprise, for my client was entitled to the decision by every right of law. I took the case of a merchant and after looking into the case thoroughly I didn't see how I could lose it. The defendant was represented by Judge E. C. Bronaugh, father of Judge Earl C. Bronaugh of Portland, and, by the way, the opposing counsel later became my law partner.

The case was tried before Barney Trainer, an east side justice of the peace. He ran a hotel and saloon in addition to administering justice to the residents of the city of East Portland. After hearing the case he said, 'After listening to all the evidence produced I am in some doubt as to the merits of the case, but inasmuch as the defendant is a widow woman, and moreover as she lives here in East Portland, I'll decide the case in her favor."

Oregon Journal
September 18, 1922

## John G. Wright
## Pioneer of 1853
## Salem, Oregon

"Uncle Huston's wife died on the Green River Desert and was buried at the side of the road. I shall never forget how desolate we felt as we hitched up the oxen and pulled out, leaving the freshly broken earth by the side of the Old Oregon Trail as the only visible sign that one of our number had finished the journey, while we must still travel on."

Oregon Journal
undated

## Nathan H. Bird
## Pioneer of 1849
## Portland, Oregon

"Father took cholera while crossing the plains. The other members of the wagon train hurried on so they would not catch it. We layed over a week or ten days and joined another train."

Oregon Journal
October 11, 1927

## Lloyd Scott
## Deputy Sheriff and Sourdough
## Salem, Oregon

"In 1898, when I was 22 years old, I went to Fort Wrangell. I landed there with 25 cents in my pocket. I went to work in a store on the Wrangell dock at $35 a month and board. Some of 'Soapy' Smith's gang from Skagway made their headquarters at Wrangell. They put up a tent, on which they put a sign, 'Chamber of Commerce and Information Bureau.' They would steer strangers to the Chamber of Commerce and, by hook or by crook, get what money they had.

"One old man of about 60, with his 16-year-old son, got off the boat and was taken in tow by one of 'Soapy' Smith's lieutenants. They found the old man had $600 and, to pass the time away, they started the three-shell game, with the result that in about an hour the old man came out with tears streaming down his face. Shaking his head, he said, 'I have been cleaned out, and haven't a cent left.'

"His 16-year-old son, when he learned what had happened, borrowed a revolver, went to the Chamber of Commerce tent and said, 'Unless I get my father's $600 back I am going to start shooting. I don't care if I am hung for it, I am going to kill a few of you crooks.' He meant just what he said, and the man who had the $600 saw how nervous the boy was on the trigger, so he handed the money back, explaining he had just done it as a joke.

"Captain Ellsworth, with a company of the 14th Infantry, was stationed at Fort Wrangell. He used to come into the store and his one subject of conversation was that he couldn't understand why his company was being kept at Wrangell when there was a war going on in the Philippine Islands. He suggested that we organize a militia company, thinking that if this was done his company would be relieved from duty there and sent to the islands. We organized a militia company and his first sergeant served as our drillmaster.

"The merchants of the town had contributed generously, so that we had a pretty good sum in our treasury. We elected one of the members of our company treasurer and the next thing we knew the treasurer and the company funds were both gone. We elected another treasurer and raised additional money, and once more the treasurer and the company funds disappeared. I was elected to serve as the third treasurer, but, as a burned child dreads the fire, the members of the company decided not to raise any money except when it was needed, so there was no temptation for me to beat it. Captain Ellsworth finally got his orders with his company to the Philippines and immediately after arriving there our troops had a skirmish in which Captain Ellsworth was killed.

"A barkeeper from San Francisco came to Wrangell, bringing with him a bulldog that cleaned up every dog in Wrangell. One day a soft-voiced, undersized stranger came down the Stikeen, bringing with him a malamute dog. He was warned not to take his dog past the saloon, as the bulldog would kill it. He said, 'Thanks ever so much, but I guess my dog can take care of itself.'

"When the malamute got opposite the saloon the bulldog jumped at it, but the malamute crouched and caught the bulldog by the throat. The barkeeper rushed out and pulled his gun to shoot the malamute. The undersized stranger pulled his gun and said to the barkeeper, 'Let the dogs settle their own fight. If you mix in, you'll never mix in another fight.' What that malamute did to the bulldog was plenty.

"After that the owner of the malamute couldn't spend any money in Wrangell. We gave him free meals, free drinks and free cigars, we were so delighted to see that big bully of a barkeeper and his big bully of a bulldog cleaned up.

"It used to be quite a problem for the butcher shop to get fresh meat. One of the West boys—I think it was Ossie West's brother—was running the shop there. For several days he was out of meat, and then we were delighted to see meat on his block once more. He said he had killed a yearling. The meat tasted rather sweet and peculiar, but we were not critical.

"One day I went out to feed a lump of sugar to his horse, and couldn't find him. West laughed, and said, 'I couldn't afford to feed him any longer, so I fed him to you and the others here. How do you like horse meat?'

"Another time, one of the boats brought a bull up to Wrangell. It got loose when they were unloading it, and it chased everyone on the wharf to the top of the coal pile. Every time we would try to get down, the bull would charge us. He nearly ran us to death. Finally someone shot him, so we ate bull meat for the next week or two.

"One time there was a fire at Fort Wrangell, and I was sent up on the roof to chop a hole in the roof so they could get a hose through. While I was chopping through the roof another bright genius chopped the rafter in two, letting me fall to the ground.

"When the boom quit at Fort Wrangell, the population drifted away. I landed a job as dishwasher on the Steamer City of Seattle, and worked my way to Seattle. The only money I got on this trip was a 25 cent tip given me by a passenger, which I still have as a souvenir of the trip."

Oregon Journal
April 5, 1927

233

# Robert M. Wood
# Harrisburg, Oregon

"I will never forget the first steamer I ever saw and heard. I was less than eight years old when we moved to Harrisburg in the spring of 1854. One day I was out in the timber beside the Willamette and I heard a queer sound like some huge animal breathing loud. It puffed louder and louder, so I ran down to the edge of the river to see if I could see it. It was the steamer Elk, and it looked like a house coming right upstream. As I looked at it, wide-eyed with curiousity, what looked like smoke came out of a pipe, and at the same time the boat gave a terrible screech, like a wounded animal. At the sound of its whistle I beat it while the going was good. I hid behind a big tree where it couldn't see me, and watched it puffing and splashing its way up the river."

Oregon Journal
July 24, 1933

# Dr. Franklin M. Carter
# Siletz Indian Agency

"Where we settled in Coburg there used to be lots of rattlesnakes. On sunny days Diamond Butte would be fairly alive with snakes. Finally the farmers around there organized a party to clean out the snakes. I remember, in addition to the members of our family, there were Ben and Sam and Jim Holt, some of the Miller boys--I don't remember whether Joaquin was along or not--some of the Wilkens family, and others. In any event, we spent three days killing rattlesnakes, and we rounded up and killed over 1500 snakes. That's some snake story, but, nevertheless, it's absolutely true."

●●●●●●●●●●●●●●●●●●●●●●●●●●●●●●●●●●●●●●●●●●●●●●●●●●●●●

"Tyee John (a Shasta chief) and his son, Alum, were rather turbulent, so they decided to take them to Fort Alcatraz. Tyee John thought they were taking him down there to kill him, but they told him he would have to stay there for the rest of his life, so he and his son captured the ship when they were off the southern Oregon coast, but they were finally overpowered and beaten up so thoroughly that both he and his son died shortly thereafter."

Oregon Journal
September 10, 1930

# Troy Shelley
## Pioneer of 1848
## Hood River, Oregon

"I was born in Iowa on January 6, 1845. My father, Michael Shelley, was born in Kentucky, while my mother, whose maiden name was Sena Mays, was born in North Carolina. They were married in Illinois in 1835. There were ten children of us. We started across the plains on April 10, 1848, starting from St. Joe, Missouri.

"Bolivar Walker, who settled in Spring Valley, Polk County, was captain of our wagon train. Dr. W. L. Adams was a member of our wagon train, as were the Purvines, Blackerbys, Coffees, Bowmans, Bristows, and others. About the only things I remember of our trip across the plains was the fact that the oxen stampeded several times and also that my mother carried me down Laurel Hill.

"My father, unlike many of the emigrants, was well-to-do. He started out with two wagons, seven yoke of oxen, four cows, a riding mare, and arrived in Oregon without the loss of a single animal. Father also had $200 in money when he reached Oregon.

"The children of today have no conception of the life of the children of that day. I didn't see an oil lamp till I was 12 years old. We used candles, which my mother dipped, or we managed to get along by the light from the fireplace. My mother made all the soap we used. She also knitted the socks and stockings and made our clothes. I wore buckskin breeches till I was in my teens. My father made shoes for Mother and himself and all the children.

"Father's report of the Willamette Valley was so favorable that his father, George Shelley, started across the plains in 1852. That, as you well know, was the cholera year. Grandfather Shelley died of cholera and was buried on the plains.

"Father took up a donation land claim at Pleasant Hill, ten miles southeast of Eugene. This was the first part of Lane County to be settled. When we settled there there were only four families there--Elijah Bristow, who was a relative of ours, having married the sister of my father's mother; Eugene Skinner, who had taken up a place near what is now known as Skinner's Butte--Eugene is named for him, and occupies the site of his claim --and a man named Briggs, who had a grist mill about where Springfield is now.

"My father's uncle, Elijah Bristow, was a

man of great force of character and resolution. He was born in Tazewell County, Virginia, in 1788. As a young man he had the reputation of being the best woodsman and the best shot in that part of the country. He moved to Kentucky, where he took up the trade of gunsmith and blacksmith. He served in the War of 1812 and also in the Creek Indian War. He served under General Jackson against the Creek Indians. On account of his ability as a sharpshooter General Jackson detailed him as a scout. Mr. Bristow moved from Kentucky to Illinois and in 1845 crossed the plains to California and in the following year came to Oregon Territory and settled in Lane County.

"In these days you can go to the corner grocery to get whatever supplies you need, or you can telephone and have them brought to your door. When we settled at Pleasant Hill our trading place was at Oregon City, and it took two weeks to make the trip there to get supplies.

"I used to drive four yoke of oxen when I was a young man. I have just returned from a trip to the coast resorts of Tillamook County, and during the three weeks my wife and I were gone I did the driving. I think one thing that helps me drive an automobile is that my eyesight is unimpaired. I read the newspapers, and, in fact, small print, without the use of glasses.

"We lived in Pleasant Hill till 1857. School advantages there were not of the best, so my father decided to move to Monmouth, where we children could get better schooling. I went to school at Monmouth for seven years. J. B. Stump was my first teacher, and he was not only an excellent teacher, but a fine man. Professor John T. Outhouse was also one of my teachers. He hailed from New Brunswick and taught the first public school in Portland. This was in the late fall of 1851. He taught in Portland till the spring of 1853. After teaching at Monmouth for some time he moved to eastern Oregon and taught school at Union.

"I decided to be a teacher, so I went to the normal school at San Francisco. H. P. Carlton was the principal of the school. I graduated in the class of 1868. Among my classmates was Annie H. Lewis. We decided to be life-mates as well as classmates. We were married June 20, 1871, at Rickreall, Oregon, by Dr. L. L. Rowland, formerly a professor in the Bethel Institute, in Polk County. He was also a minister and a physician. Elder Glen Burnett assisted in performing the marriage ceremony.

"In 1869 I was ordained a minister. After

236

our marriage I taught on Fifteen-Mile Creek, south of The Dalles. I taught the first school ever taught in Tygh Valley. This was in the winter of '63 and '64. I taught for three years at Mayfield, California. I was principal of the school there in 1869. Mayfield is now called Palo Alto. I taught between Independence and Dallas in Polk County, also at Three-Mile and Fifteen-Mile in Wasco County, and I was principal of the school at Prineville in the winter of 1878 and '79. I was teaching on the Malheur Reservation when the Bannock-Piute War broke out, so my wife and I forted up at a grist mill near Canyon City. When the war excitement was over we went to Prineville, where my wife's sister and her husband, Mr. and Mrs. Ed Sommerville, lived, and where I taught school that winter. Because of my knowledge of the schools in Wasco County I was appointed county superintendent of schools for Wasco County and served from 1890 to 1896. This was before Sherman County or Hood River County was cut off from Wasco, so I had a pretty good-sized field to cover."

Oregon Journal
September 30, 1926

# C. J. Carlson
# Hood River, Oregon

"C. S. Miller of the Monitor Mine had told me I could go to work for them if I would make my way to where they were installing their machinery. I walked from Pendleton to Pilot Rock. The McKay was high, so I undressed and swam across. When I got to Pilot Rock I found C. S. Miller, Sam Burnham, and Big Steve, the butcher, at the hotel there. Mr. Miller said to me, 'Well, I see you got this far. How are you figuring to cover the rest of the distance?'

"I said, 'I guess I'll have to hoof it.'

"Big Steve said, 'I've been buying cattle around Pilot Rock and I've an extra mule along. You can ride the mule if you want.'

"I didn't confess that riding horseback was one of the things I knew but little about. We rode to the Daily Ranch, where we put up for the night. I was so sore and stiff I could hardly crawl off that mule. Next day we reached the north fork of the John Day. By this time my mule had discovered I wasn't much of a horseman, so he decided to haze me a little. While fording the stream the mule lay down. Naturally I got good and wet. When we got to Crane Flat, which was run by Joe

Tryon, the rest of the party went in to eat supper. I was nearly frozen, so I went out to the barn and burrowed deep into the hay to get warm."

Oregon Journal
undated

## Thomas Harrison Cooper
## Pioneer of 1852
## Corvallis, Oregon

"I guess when I was a young fellow I was what you call a 'country jake'. Corvallis seemed like a pretty good-sized city to me, and I felt awkward and ill at ease. One day I had come in from the farm and was standing on the street when one of the town boys, named Nat Steward, began calling me a country jake and making fun of me. I resented what he said, so he thought he would come out and lick me. I knocked him down, sat on him, and hammered him good and plenty. When he got up he ran into the hardware store, near where we had our fight, grabbed a pitchfork and tried to run it through me. I dodged, grabbed the pitchfork, got it away from him, and was going to spear him with it, but a lot of the town folks took it away from me. The next time we met I thought maybe he would want to fight again, but he was friendly, and we never had any more trouble. Later he went down to Los Angeles and was elected Sheriff of Los Angeles County."

Oregon Journal
June 14, 1926

## Frank Bulger
## Portland, Oregon

"I worked as conductor on the Metropolitan Railway Company. In an accident my right foot was badly mangled. I was taken to a drug store and a doctor was called. The doctor was sort of a bully. He said, 'I'll have to take your foot off at the ankle.'

"I said, 'Don't take my foot off. Just trim my toes off, and try to save my foot.'

"He said, 'I know my business. I'm going to take your foot off,' and he tried to give me an anaesthetic.

"I kept pushing his hand away, which made him angry. He slapped my face. That was too much. I slid off the counter, braced myself, and hit him a good jolt on the jaw, which floored him. He threw up the case then and there.

"There were no ambulances in those days, so the druggist tied something around my ankle very tight to stop the blood and sent me to the hospital. They cut off my toes, and my foot is practically as good as ever."

Oregon Journal
April 7, 1933

# Lemuel C. Skellenger
## 1st Regiment, Michigan Volunteer Cavalry
## Portland, Oregon

"I was 31 years old when I enlisted in the First Regiment, Michigan Volunteer Cavalry. Most of the young chaps who enlisted were younger than I, so I fudged on my age and took off a few years. Some of the other chaps had to fudge and swear they were older than they really were, for in the beginning of the war they wouldn't take you if you were less than 18, and in the company I enlisted in they wanted young chaps from 18 to 25. Later they weren't so particular.

"They began recruiting for the First Cavalry on August 21, and we gathered at Camp Lyon, near Detroit. Thornton F. Brodhead was appointed colonel of the regiment. We were mustered into the service on September 13, 1861. We had 1144 officers and men on the roll. Colonel Brodhead came from Grosse Isle. Lieutenant Colonel Joseph P. Copland was from Pontiac. All three of our majors, William S. Atwood, Angelo Paldi and Charles H. Town, were from Detroit. I was assigned to Company L. Melvin Brewer was our captain. He had some Indian blood in him. I think it was Sioux. He was certainly a good officer. He was one of the bravest men in the regiment. He was killed at the Battle of Winchester.

"At Gettysburg we charged the Confederate cavalry. A confederate trooper of the First Virginia Cavalry told me to surrender, and when he saw I had no intention of surrendering he raised his sabre to split my head open. I raised my right arm and the next thing I knew I was in a dressing station. Just as he brought his sabre down my horse was shot, and fell. I lay under my horse, unconscious, for five hours. If you will feel my head you will see I have a deep ridge across my skull made by his sabre, and this broad white mark on my wrist is the scar from the sabre.

"Our second lieutenant secured his appointment through pull. He was related to an influential man. None of us liked him very much. We were serving as body guard of General Banks. The Confederates were shelling us. They were getting our range, too. A shell struck in our ranks, killing Joel Frost, Darius Dibble, Richard Olcott, and two men of the Fifth Cavalry who were with us on detached service. A fragment of the same shell nearly cut off my horse's head, and a smaller fragment buried itself in my shoulder. This rattled our second lieutenant. He turned his horse, ran away at full speed, and they didn't see him again for four days.

"I had all sorts of curious adventures while serving with the First Michigan Cavalry. One time General Dadwalader, who was our brigade quartermaster, gave me an order for six bottles of whiskey. We were on the march and he told me to deliver them to him at Fredericksburg. It didn't look right to me that the officers should have all the whiskey, so I changed his order from six bottles to 12 bottles, and delivered six bottles to him and kept six bottles for myself.

"Our first lieutenant, Hasbruck Reeve, learned that I had some whiskey. He gave me $20 for a bottle. I figured on selling the other five bottles at $20 each, but some low-down skunk that had no idea of honesty went to my saddlebags and took every bottle I had, so I was out and injured. It's a curious thing that I never drank or smoked, but I was always willing to help other folks out along that line.

"It is curious the effect that war has on some men. Most of the men were as law-abiding as if they had been at home, but some of them were needlessly destructive. While we were marching from Staunton, Virginia, one of our men, at every opportunity, would go into the beautiful homes and shoot at the pier glasses and break up the fine old furniture. In one house he stole a whole drawerful of women's underwear. Our captain made him wear some of it and carry the rest on his head for the rest of the day. He went along looking like a fright for 14 miles. Everybody that saw him would nearly laugh their heads off. That night, when the captain let him take off the women's underwear he had been wearing, he made a solemn vow that he would never steal another thing while in the army.

"For a while we were with Blinker's brigade. They were Germans. They had a lot of women among their camp followers, and when they first joined us they had a lot of feather beds. They had fought under Sigel for a while. Later they were with

Blinker, and still later they fought under Howard. They used to have a song--I've forgotten just how it goes--but it was to the effect, 'We fought mit Sigel, we drank mit Blinker, and we run mit Howard.'

"I saw one of the men of Blinker's brigade do something that made me want to shoot him. I love animals, particularly horses, and I hate to see them abused. We camped near a farm where there were a lot of milk cows. This soldier caught a number of these cows, pulled their tongues out as far as he could pull them, and cut them off, then turned them loose.

"Three Virginia women are responsible for my being alive. I got sick with typhoid fever. They carried me into their home and took care of me. The only ones at home were the mother and the two grown daughters. This woman's husband was a captain in the Confederate Army and her son was a major. One day the son came to their home to visit. I asked one of the girls if he would come in and see me, but he sent word that he couldn't come in, because, if he saw me, he would be compelled to take me prisoner.

"A week or ten days after that one of the girls came in and said, 'We have just had word that the Confederates are coming, and if they find you here they will capture you.'

"I told her I was too weak to saddle my horse. She saddled my horse, brought it down to the door and helped me into the saddle and I got away. As I was hurrying away I came upon some Zouaves. They were called 'Ellsworth's Avengers'. I told them that the Confederate cavalry would be there shortly, so we rode at full speed. A detachment of rebel cavalry saw us and chased us. Four of the Zouaves took refuge in a church and hid under the pulpit. The rest of us managed to get away.

"Ed Clark was a clerk in Hank Cassell's store at Armada, Michigan, where I lived. Ed had the consumption. The doctors told him he couldn't live long. They didn't want to let him enlist in our company. Finally they let him in, figuring he might as well be killed in the war as to die of consumption.

"He was thin as a rail when he joined us but he soon fattened up and became strong and husky. I saw Clark do a curious thing one day. Deardorf, our color-bearer, while carrying the colors, had both arms taken off by a solid shot. The solid shot also cut the flagstaff in two, so the colors fell to the ground. A Confederate reached down to get the colors. He said, 'Hold on, Johnny Reb. Those are our colors you're trying to take,' and he thrust him through the groin with his sabre, picked up the colors and rode off. Clark was made color-bearer. After the war Ed had his mother and sister to support, and instead of doing outdoor work he took an indoor job and died of quick consumption.

"I was part of a detachment of the First Michigan Cavalry serving as the body guard to General N. P. Banks. One day while we were riding along we saw a span of fine white-faced horses. General Banks said to me, 'I think those horses are from General Pope's headquarters. Catch them and take them there.'

"Just after General Banks and the other had ridden on, General Fremont and his staff came along. Fremont stopped, saw me leading the horses, and said, 'You stole those horses.' A soldier can't talk back to a general. He said, 'Where did you get them?'

"I said, 'General Banks told me to catch them and take them to General Pope's headquarters.'

"As I approached Pope's headquarters, General Pope and his staff were riding along. He recognized the horses, and said, 'Those horses belong to my headquarters. What do you mean by stealing them?'

"I said, 'General, I didn't steal them.'

"He turned to a sergeant and said, 'Arrest that man.'

"The sergeant made me dismount and was going to take me to General Pope's headquarters. I pulled out my Colt's 44 and said. 'Throw me your gun, or I'll drill a hole through you.' I was mad and I meant it.

"I picked up his gun, threw it as far as I could in the brush, jumped on my horse, and at full speed lit out to rejoin General Banks. When I told General Banks what General Fremont and General Pope had done, he just laughed and said, 'You're here, all right, aren't you? Forget it.'

"I have always been a good hand with horses. While our regiment was campaigning in Virginia a nigger who saw me handling my horse and saw that I understood and liked horses, said, 'I know where one of the finest horses in Virginia is hid.'

"I told him I would give him $20 if he would show me where it was. This was near Little York, Virginia, and the animal was within enemy lines. As we were going along through the timber we heard some horsemen, and we were just in time to duck out of sight when a detachment of rebel cavalry came by. The nigger showed me where the horse was. It was a black stallion, one of the most beautiful pieces of horseflesh I ever saw. I gave the nigger $20, eluded the Confederate patrols, and got back to our lines.

"Major Perkins, who was on Banks' staff, went crazy about my black stallion. He kept raising his offer till he offered me $1000, which I accepted. Some Zouaves a few months later came to Banks' headquarters, which at that time was a farmhouse, and broke open a hive to get the honey. The bees attacked the black stallion. I don't know whether he choked himself to death trying to break loose or whether the bees stung him to death, but I saw him lying there near the broken hive, dead, with his tongue out.

"A good cavalryman won't keep a poor horse. At different times I was issued poor horses, but I always managed to swap them--usually without the consent of the owner--for a better horse. General Pope had accused me of stealing horses, which made me mad, so I watched my chance, stole a good horse at his headquarters, rode it hard for a few hours and traded it for a horse I liked equally well.

"While we were in Pleasant Valley, Maryland, someone told me that a rebel named Wolf had a fine cavalry horse with the U. S. brand on it. I went to Captain Melvin Brewer, who was in command of Company L, my company, and asked him if he would give me a pass. I told him I was going to do a little scouting around and might not be back for a few days. He gave me the pass and said, 'See that you get back, and don't get into any more trouble than you have to.'

"I went to the farm and I saw that the rebel was driving a team of horses in the field, and, looking closely, I saw that one of them had the U. S. brand on it. I went to the house, knocked at the back door, and asked the lady who came to the door if I could see Mr. Wolf. She was very much younger than her husband and she turned out to be a Union sympathizer. I told her I was going to try to get the horse. She said, 'I hope you get it.'

"I went to Wolf and said, I know where you stole that cavalry horse. I have come here to get it.' I told him I was willing to get it by peaceable means, but I would use force if necessary.

"Finally he said, 'If you'll help me put in my crop of wheat and if you'll give me $5 so I can get some whiskey, I'll let you have the horse.

"I was a good hand at sowing wheat with both hands. I could sow it evenly. I helped him get in his wheat, gave him $5, and rode off on the horse. I traded that horse to an officer for a fine gold watch.

"In the summer of 1863 I was shot through my right shoulder, and when the wound healed

243

it left my arm crooked, so I couldn't swing a sabre. My enlistment had expired while I was convalescing from the wound. I wanted to reenlist, but they wouldn't let me. I went back to Michigan and I put in that winter catching 'coons. I caught 140 that winter. A relative of mine, Jesse Adams, was going to Detroit, so he told me he would take the 140 coon skins I had and sell them there for me. He figured that he could get more than 50 cents apiece for them.

"I never learned what he got. When he returned he was very hazy about the whole transaction. He said he had sold the 'coon skins for a good price, stopped in a saloon to take a few drinks, and he had stayed drunk till the money was all gone, so I never got anything for all my work.

"Not long after that Jesse, who had a team of fine heavy horses for which he had paid $500, hitched his team in front of Hank Cassell's store in Armada and went in to play cards. Hank rolled a barrel of salt out on the porch, which scared the team, causing them to break loose and run away. They were fixing a bridge near there. They had taken all the planks off. The team ran onto this bridge, knocked over the barricade, fell through and were both killed.

"I married Sarah Dibble in 1866. We had four children, all of whom live in Michigan. One of my boys has worked for a firm in Grand Rapids for 23 years and has never lost a day. He has the first dollar he ever earned and most of the others he ever got. His wife is a dressmaker. They are both wonderful managers and they own land all over that part of the country."

Oregon Journal
October 1-3, 1928

# Frank Blakely
## Silverton, Oregon

"The Silverton of my boyhood was a friendly little village nestled in hills, whose valleys were filled with deer and elk and on whose wooded crests plenty of bears and cougars could be found. It is rather strange that the first recollection I have of Silverton was of a Fourth of July celebration in 1858. As we drove in I saw a flagstaff near the end of the bridge that crossed Silver Creek. From the flagstaff a large new flag was flying. Somehow the beauty of that rippling flag floating in the breeze has always dwelt in my memory, possibly because there was a great deal of excitement in those days about the issue which a year or two later involved our country in the Civil War."

Oregon Journal
undated

# Robert Booth
# Eugene, Oregon

"Once they were completely out of food, but my father said that God had promised he would not forsake the righteous, nor should their seed beg bread. It looked, though, as though God had forgotten his promise this time, but as Father was talking about it three men rode up and asked Mother if she would make some bread for them, and they brought in part of a sack of flour. They paid her 50 cents and gave her half the bread she baked. No, Father wasn't at all surprised. He said all you needed was sufficient faith."

Oregon Journal
May 4, 1920

# The bones of my father's arm

*A day or two ago I received a letter from my nephew, J. L. Sherburne, vice president and cashier of the First National Bank of Browning, Montana. Joe has spent a good part of his life on various Indian agencies. Browning itself is the trading point for the Blackfoot Indians. Joe's father, my brother-in-law, J. H. Sherburne, is president and manager of the Sherburne Mercantile Company of Browning, Montana, and is also the president of the First National Bank. In Joe's letter he told me of a rather peculiar thing that had occurred in their store recently. The development agent of the Great Northern Railway came to Browning to secure some articles for a Blackfoot Indian exhibit. Among the things he purchased were some small bones used in the Indian gambling game known as the hand game. The Indian who sold these gambling bones took the bones in his hand and after singing the gambling song and going through the motions of the hand game, he said:*

"When my father was a young man he was shot in the forearm with an arrow. It poisoned his arm so he had his arm cut off at the elbow. He saved the bones of his arm as a reminder of his young days when he was a warrior. When he danced, he hung the bones of his arm from his shoulder and as he danced you could hear them rattle.

"After his death I kept the bones of his arm for a long time, but when I thought of it, it seemed they should not be hid away, like his body, which is buried and hid away. I remembered how he used to play the hand game, so I cut the bones of his arm into gambling bones, so they could be used in the hand game and be merry with us when we had our dances and good times. For years I took my father's bones to all of our social gatherings.

"This winter I brought them to the big fair at Browning. When Mr. O'Donnell, the Great Northern Man, wanted to buy them, the thought hurt me, for it seems that these little bones were like a part of myself. The thought of parting with them made me feel very sad. How could I ask for money for something that was a part of my father. If I asked a big price it would be like making a profit on what is sacred, yet if I kept the bones till I died they would have no value to others and they would be lost or scattered.

"Then I thought, if I let them go to the museum they would be taken care of long after I am gone. When I am dead and forgotten, others will still be interested in looking at them in the museum. Long after the Indians are gone, and when the gambling game is played no more, my father's bones will be there, and when they point to them, they will tell the story of how the Blackfoot Indians played the gambling game with my father's bones. So I gave them to Mr. O'Donnell, so he can take them to the place of my dreams."

Oregon Journal
May 11, 1928

# John Lyman Slater
# Portland, Oregon

"I was born in La Grande on July 8, 1867. La Grande at that time was a village. The La Grande I knew as a boy is now known as Old Town. When the stage was succeeded by the railroad the new town grew up on both sides of the railroad track.

"My first teacher was Professor J. T. Outhouse, who, by the way, taught the first public school in Portland. This school was taught in the City Hotel at the northwest corner of 1st and Oak Streets and began on December 15, 1851.

"I'll say this for Professor Outhouse: he not only was a well-qualified teacher, but he certainly was some disciplinarian! There was always a bundle of switches on his desk and some of them were as thick as your finger. The switches were not there for ornament, either. He not only knew how to use them, but did use them, frequently and effectively.

"My mother, whose maiden name was Edna Gray, was about 19 years old when she crossed the plains with her parents to Oregon. With them came her two married sisters with their husbands and families--the Garrets and Taylors. My uncle, Mr. Taylor, had made two round trips across the plains prior to 1852, so he was elected captain of the wagon train. He saw to it that all of his relatives and friends started out properly provided with plenty of provisions to last until they reached the Willamette Valley. Some of the others in the wagon train were unwilling to take advice, so they ran out of food before they reached Oregon and my people had to share with them.

"They crossed the Snake River in an improvised ferryboat made of a wagon box. Just after crossing the Snake the wagon train divided, some going by way of the Barlow Trail, while others decided to go with my uncle, Captain Taylor, who believed he could find a shorter route to the valley by following the base of the Cascades southward to about where the Three Sisters were. He followed the Malheur River to the lakes and was told to strike due west from the Malheur lakes to a low pass just south of the Middle Sister.

"While the wagon train was going around the Malheur Lakes, Captain Taylor, with another man, dropped behind. The Indians decided to cut them off. Taylor and his companion decided to go between the lakes, thinking they could turn northward and rejoin the wagon train. To their consternation they found that the lakes were connected by a deep neck of water. Most of the Indians were armed with bows, though one had a gun. My uncle and the other man, when they came to this deep neck of water, turned around and charged the Indians. The Indian with the gun fired at my uncle, the bullet passing close to his head. After escaping from the Indians they rejoined the wagon train and struck westward.

"There was a dense pall of smoke over the country, which obscured the mountains. They were short of water and grass. They traveled for three days and struck fresh wagon tracks. They found they had made a wide circle and come upon their own tracks. My uncle, realizing that the oxen were almost famished for water as well as food, decided to trust to their instinct. He let them take their own course. The oxen turned north and presently struck Crooked River. They followed Crooked

River to its junction with the Deschutes, which they followed to what was later known as Farewell Bend, where the city of Bend is now located. Here they camped to rest their oxen before attempting the trip across the Cascades.

"While they were camped here Charles McClure and three other men from Corvallis came into the camp and served as guides across the mountains by what is now known as McKenzie Pass. They had to cut the trees and build a road across the pass. Some of my mother's relatives camped for awhile on the McKenzie River.

"My mother's family pressed on to Corvallis. My uncle, Captain Taylor, moved up to Walla Walla, later taking up a place near Elgin, Oregon. He was elected to the legislature and died some years ago at Baker, Oregon, at the age of 95."

Oregon Journal<br>
December 29, 1931

# Clarence L. Andrews
# Plowing the Old Oregon Trail
# Seattle, Washington

"The Old Oregon Trail forked near Echo, one branch coming westward and the other southwestward. One went across the Stanfield Ranch, the other forked through Henry Thompson's place, thence down Rock Creek to the John Day country. The Old Oregon Trail crossed my quarter section. I plowed it up. Thousands of ox teams and prairie schooners had passed over this old trail and it was some job to plow it up."

Oregon Journal<br>
April 14, 1928

# Jesus K. Urquides
# Freighter
# Boise, Idaho

*Recent press dispatches have commented on the successful launching of an air freight line. Stimulated by the success of the passenger and mail carrying airships, a company has inaugurated an air freight line.*

*I wonder what "Kasuk" Urquides of Boise, Idaho, thinks of carrying freight by airplane. He freighted continuously for 62 years and has operated pack trains or freight wagons to most of the newly-discovered mining camps of the old days. Shortly after his 91st birthday, last spring, a reporter* of the **Idaho Statesman** *interviewed him. In speaking of his work as a packer and freighter, he said:*

"My name is Jesus K. Urquides. For more than 60 years I averaged less than six nights in a real bed a year. I went from Sonora, Mexico, to California in 1849. I kept up freighting till 1912, when my eyes went back on me, though in every other way I was fit as a fiddle."

*Urquides used to pack around Pendleton and Walla Walla in the early '60s. He had not been in California long when he decided that there was more money in packing than in mining, so he secured 35 mules and started a pack train to take supplies into the mines. The highest price he ever received was 25 cents a pound, packing from Marysville, California, to Virginia City, in 1859. He reached Walla Walla in 1863 and in 1864 he packed a 65-mule train from The Dalles to Boise Basin. From that time, until he quit work in 1912, his packing was done principally with the Basin and Boise as his objective points.*

"I used to pack all of Cy Jacobs' whiskey from the railroad point to Boise and received 18 cents a pound."

*The most strenuous trip he ever made was when he got lost for three days on his way to Fresno, California, having nothing to eat during the time. For several years he packed ammunition and supplies for the government. In 1877 he packed ammunition for Colonel Bernard and Colonel Green.*

"I had 100 mules loaded heavily when I took supplies for General Howard from Boise to Canyon City, Oregon. The fight occurred near where Pendleton now is, and we followed the Indians over the Blue Mountains."

*Mr. Urquides claims the distinction of packing the first mill into Thunder Mountain, later doing all of Colonel Dewey's packing. It was on one of these trips that he packed the biggest load on one mule, 600 pounds, up and down the steep mountain sides. He also packed all the rails for the railroad to the Yellow Jacket Mine. It was in this region that Mr. Urquides accomplished what he considers the greatest feat of packing in any freighter's history, that of packing a coil of copper wire that weighed 10,000 pounds for the tramway of the Yellow Jacket Mine, out of Challis.*

"It was necessary to get this wire to the mine without any break, for a splice would have been too dangerous for tramway work. I loaded it on 35 mules, spreading it out with the mules in three rows. We had to pack between 60 and 70 miles up and down the steepest of mountain sides.

249

Several times some of my mules would roll down the side of the mountain, taking the rest with them. Then it was necessary to get them all up, repack again, and start out. I never coveted another job like that.

"I have packed in snow from one to 20 feet deep, but the nearest I ever came to freezing to death was on one trip to Atlanta, Idaho. It grew dark before we got to Dixie. The snow was deep and the weather exceedingly cold. There was no shelter for my 45 mules, and no wood in sight. I gathered them in a circle and took the boxes in which some canned goods were packed, made a tiny fire and cooked some coffee over this, and the hot drink sustained me so that I could resist the cold until morning when we could see to move.

"I was completely lost when I first gave up my freighting and felt obliged to remain at home on account of my failing eyesight."

**Oregon Journal**
undated

# David Arba Carter
# Native son of 1842
# Portland, Oregon

"I have seen a lot of ups and downs in my life, but it is a long lane that has no turning. My youngest son is a miner. I am going to try to get him to give up that line of work and go with me to Idaho and start raising sheep. People will always need mutton and wool, and I have seen old-time friends of mine who stayed with the sheep business through thick and thin come out ahead of the game and become wealthy. I guess the reason why I have never accumulated any great amount of money is that I have moved around a good deal, often leaving good opportunities to look for better ones."

**Oregon Journal**
undated

# George Harkleroad
# Agate Beach, Oregon

"My father came to California with his brother, Eugene, in 1849. They went back to Iowa in 1853. They just about broke even on their trip. In 1859 they went to the Pike's Peak excitement, near Denver, and stayed there two years. About all they got for their time and work was the experience.

"In 1863 Father came to Auburn, in eastern Oregon. He got there the night they lynched Spanish Tom. This was on November 22, 1863. Spanish Tom and two other men had been gambling in one of the saloons at Auburn. A quarrel arose over the card game and the two men went out on the street. Spanish Tom left the saloon, and, seeing the two men standing out in the street by the saloon door, stabbed them both. A few days later Spanish Tom was arrested at Mormon Basin. Two or three months before this Baker County had been organized and John Q. Wilson of Salem had been appointed county judge and S. A. Clark, also of Salem, county clerk, and George Hall, sheriff.

"Hall put Spanish Tom in a log cabin and placed guards over him. Captain Johnson, at the head of a crowd of miners, demanded that the trial of Spanish Tom should be held in the open, where all could see that justice was done. Sheriff Hall, believing that the men were going to try to lynch Spanish Tom, appointed 40 deputies. Justice of the Peace Able held the trial on the hillside, the prisoner and the lawyers being furnished chairs in an open shed.

"Captain Johnson gave a signal and his men closed in around the sheriff and Spanish Tom. A man named Kirkpatrick climbed on a stump and made a talk, asking the miners to allow the law to take its course. Captain Johnson mounted another stump and urged the miners to hang the murderer. The mob grabbed the chain around Spanish Tom's ankle, and the sheriff and some of his deputies tried to hold Spanish Tom, but the mob was too many for the sheriff and his deputies, so the mob dragged Spanish Tom to the street and fastened a rope around his neck. Tom called out to some of his Mexican friends to shoot him so he would not be hanged. Dozens of men grabbed the rope and started running down the street, Spanish Tom bumping along in the street at the end of the rope. As they crossed Freezeout Gulch his head struck a log, breaking his neck. At the lower end of town the mob threw the rope over the limb of a tree, pulled Tom up and left him hanging there.

"Father was in Auburn during the second election of Lincoln. A large number of miners from what they called at that time 'the left wing of Price's army' had settled in eastern Oregon. Some of the men, like Matt Bledsoe and his gang, who were Southern sympathizers, passed the word around that any man voting for Lincoln was courting trouble. The Union men were in the minority, so a lot of them decided not to vote. My father was told that if he voted for Lincoln it would mean a fight, and so a lot of Union men asked him to stay away from the polls. There was no secret ballot in those days. The judge of election, with his clerks, sat in the store beside an open window, the voters filed past this window and announced whom they were voting for. My father was 5 feet 10½ inches high, weighed 187 pounds, and felt perfectly able to take care of himself in a fair fight. Father went to the store where the election was being held, took off his belt, to which was fastened his holster with his gun, and laid it on the counter.

"Quite a crowd had gathered to see what would happen when my father announced he was going to vote for Lincoln. Father walked up to the window and said, 'I cast my vote for Abraham Lincoln.' Then he turned around quickly and was ready for any trouble. The crowd stood tense and silent, and after a few seconds Father walked away. Immediately thereafter a whole group of Union men walked past the window and voted for Lincoln. They saw that all the talk had been mere bluff.

"In the spring of 1871 we moved to the Turnbull place, on French Prairie. In 1871 we moved to Waconda, near the present town of Woodburn. I went to school at Gervais. There were five of us children in the family—my sisters, Mrs. Allie Bradly and Kate George; myself, the third child, then my brother Eugene and my sister Maud.

"In 1882 I went up to Prineville. In the spring of that year A. H. Crooks and his son-in-law, S. J. Jory, were killed in a dispute over a line fence. Garrett Maupin, who was passing the place and heard the shots, saw Lucius Langdon leaving. The jury returned a verdict that A. H. Crooks and Stephen Jory came to their death from gunshot wounds inflicted by Lucius Langdon. J. M. Blakeley, with a party of men, started out to capture Langdon. They overtook him and locked him in a livery stable till they could turn him over to Sheriff Storrs at The Dalles, for at this time Crook County was a part of Wasco County. A man named W. H. Harrison, who had been with Langdon, was captured also, the supposition being he might serve as a witness.

"Sheriff Storrs, when Harrison and Langdon were turned over to him, took his prisoners to the hotel and, with another guard, sat up all night with them. Just before daylight, the hotel door was thrown open violently. Sheriff Storrs was caught and blindfolded, and a moment later there were several shots and the men left the room. When Storrs took the blindfold off he found Langdon lying on the floor dead. The other man, Harrison, who was being held for a witness, had been taken away. They found him next day, hanging from the iron bridge over Crooked River.

"Barnes said to Mogan, 'You owe me six dollars. You're mighty slow pay. If you don't give me the six dollars at once, I'm going to kill you.' Mogan didn't have the six dollars, so Barnes shot him through the lungs, and Mogan bled to death in a few minutes."

"I was working in Prineville when Sidney Huston and Charles Luster were killed. I went up to Prineville just after Crook County was organized. Crook County was cut off from Wasco County by the legislature in the fall of 1882.

"The killing of A. H. Crooks and Stephen Jory by Lucius Langdon in March, 1882, resulted in the formation of a vigilance committee. The vigilance committee was organized to suppress the activities of horsethieves. Some people claimed that its members were no better than those they were trying to rid the country of, but that's a mooted question.

"A rival organization, called the Moonshiners, was formed to suppress the activities of the vigilance committee. The vigilantes secured political control of the newly organized county government. When one of their members was accused of crime, no matter how strong was the evidence against him, the members of the vigilance committee were selected as jurymen and the man was cleared.

"After the killing of Langdon and the hanging of Harrison a man named Al Swartz openly defied them, saying the vigilantes were a bunch of criminals and crooks. On Christmas Eve, 1882, Swartz went into Burmeister's Saloon to play cards. He sat at the card table facing the door, for he knew that he was apt to be assassinated for taking a stand against the vigilantes. A few minutes after he had sat in the game the shadow of a man's form appeared for an instant in the window. There was a tinkle of glass, the sound of a shot, and Swartz dropped his cards and lay across the table with a bullet through his head. He had been shot through the back of the head and killed instantly.

"This same night a party of vigilantes went to the home of J. M. Barnes, routed Sidney Huston and Charlie Luster out of bed and, after shooting them both, took them out, declared them guilty, and hanged them. The charge against Huston was that someone had said he was planning to steal some horses. The reason they killed Luster was that he had promised to throw a race. A number of the vigilantes had bet on the other horse, but Luster, instead of throwing the race, had bet $60 on his own horse and had crossed the line a winner.

"The following spring J. M. Barnes killed Mike Mogan in Burmeister's Saloon. Barnes said to Mogan, 'You owe me six dollars. You're mighty slow pay. If you don't give me the six dollars at once, I'm going to kill you.' Mogan didn't have the six dollars, so Barnes shot him through the lungs, and Mogan bled to death in a few minutes.

"On December 18 of that same year, Mike Mogan's brother Frank was killed by Bud Thompson. Bud Thompson, or, to give him his more formal title, Colonel William Thompson, met Mogan in Kelly's Saloon. Mogan had worked for Thompson and there was a dispute about the payment of money due. Thompson in the course of the quarrel walked back of Mogan and shot him through the back of the head, killing him instantly.

"The grand jury, as was its usual custom,

brought in a 'Not a true bill.' Mogan's widow sued Thompson and received a judgment of $3600, but never got the money.

"Colonel Thompson, prior to taking up ranching, had been a newspaper man. He had been a member of the editorial staff of the **Oregonian** and had also worked on various other Oregon papers. He had served in the Modoc War and, as a consequence, was called Colonel.

"The Moonshiners were organized to couteract the vigilantes. Probably the Moonshiners were more interested in wresting political control of the county from the vigilantes than in bringing some of their members to justice. At that time the voters in Crook County were not Republicans or Democrats--they were Vigilantes or Moonshiners. The next time you are up in Crook County hunt up some of the old-timers and you'll get a mighty interesting story about the activities of these two organizations.

"While I was up there I drove a freight outfit between The Dalles and Prineville, cut cordwood and worked at anything I could get to do. In 1883 I went to Oak Point, on the Columbia River, and ran the first shingle jointer in that part of the country. In 1885 I went to the Couer d'Alene District, where I spent eight years as a packer, freighter, prospector, miner, and hammer-and-saw carpenter. My father and I bached. I was there during the Bunker Hill & Sullivan strike. I was in Wardner and was about to be put in the bullpen, but I met a provost marshal who knew me and let me out.

"I went to Elk City, in the Clearwater country, and during the next few years I had all the deer, elk, and bear meat and trout I could eat, but I didn't strike any rich placer ground, so I went back to the Coeur d'Alene country and then to the Colville Reservation when they threw open the north half of the reservation for mineral entry. From there I went up to British Columbia, where I worked in the mines till 1901 when I went to Sumpter, in eastern Oregon, where I did teaming, mining, and prospecting. I was up in that country till 1904, when I went to California.

"I was married in 1909 at Colville, Washington, to Mrs. Bertie M. Hall Sloan. She had one child, a son. He lives in Wenatchee. We had four children, all of whom are living. Three of our children are in California and one of my daughters works at Lipman & Wolfe's in Portland.

"When I was in the Coeur d'Alene country they elected an Irishman, Terrence B. Guthrie, sheriff. He was elected by the saloonmen and gamblers. Shortly after his election, Walt Smith, one of the principal gamblers, and one who had much to do in electing Guthrie, got on a spree. Guthrie was summoned, and said to Smith, 'Walt, I don't want to make any trouble for you, but if you don't go to your cabin quietly and sleep off your drunk, I'll have to arrest you. You are being too quarrelsome.'

"Walt said, 'You can't arrest me. I made you sheriff, and if you get gay with me I'll throw you out.'

"Guthrie was quick as a cat. He just hit Smith once, and Smith fell like a log. He turned to two of the loungers in the saloon and said, 'Carry that man to the jail. If anybody else wants to know who's sheriff here, now is the time to find out.'

"Nobody wanted to know, and as long as Guthrie was sheriff he kept order in that camp, regardless of whether the lawbreakers were friends or foes. He was the best sheriff Shoshone County ever had."

**Oregon Journal**
June 4 & 5, 1929

# A few firsts

The Oregon Spectator, whose first issue appeared at Oregon City on February 5, 1846, was the first paper to be published west of the Rocky Mountains. Its first editor, Colonel W. G. T'Vault, was paid $25 a month for his services.

The first Protestant church to be built on the Pacific Coast was the Methodist Church that was begun in 1842 at Oregon City and dedicated in 1844.

The Beaver, built on the Thames in 1835 for the Hudson's Bay Company, was the first steamer to ply the waters of the Columbia River. She arrived off the mouth of the Columbia on March 18, 1836, having made the trip by steam and sail from England in six months and 22 days.

The first marriage of white people in Oregon took place on July 16, 1837, near Salem, when the Reverend Jason Lee was married to Anna Maria Pittman. The Reverend Daniel Lee performed the marriage ceremony. Immediately after his marriage Jason Lee performed the marriage ceremony for Cyrus Shepard and Miss Susan Downing.

*Oregon Journal*
December 12, 1933

# W. M. Turner
# Southern Oregon

*In yesterday's article I spoke of picking up an old-time legal brief and in glancing through it I ran across an account by W. M. Turner of southern Oregon of the killing of George W. Harris by Indians and the heroic and successful defense made by his girl wife of her family. The Harris family had recently moved from the Willamette Valley to southern Oregon, where they had taken up a place. Harris was killed by the Rogue River Indians on October 9, 1855. His little girl was wounded by the same volley that killed him, but she crept upstairs and lay on her bed, not telling her mother about it. After standing the Indians off for five hours Mrs. Harris saw them give up the attack and retire. Her husband lay dead near the doorway, where he had fallen. She saw blood on the floor in another part of the room and, looking up, saw drops of blood falling from the ceiling. She hurried upstairs and found her little girl had fainted from loss of blood. In describing what then took place, Mr. Turner says:*

"Carefully bandaging the wound and applying restoratives, her next thought was for little David. Just before the attack the little fellow had accompanied Samuel Bowden, who lived about a quarter of a mile north, to his home, and as neither made his appearance, the mother feared they, too, had fallen victims. Anxiously she waited. Patiently she listened, till evening fell, and still the child came not, and as she watched and listened in vain the mocking wind among the pines seemed to say to the poor throbbing heart, 'No more--forever!' Evening came and a new danger threatened. Should the savages return they could steal to the house under cover of darkness and fire with perfect safety, and Mrs. Harris determined on flight. Taking Sophie in her arms, and with a sad, parting look at the white face of him who had given his life for theirs, she stole from the house and hid in the chaparral.

"Who can write the memory of that dreadful October night? Who can tell the anguish that wrung the heart of that heroic woman? As the night wore on and the sky grew higher and the stars grew colder, still they looked coldly down on her as she kept sleepless watch, holding in her arms the faint and bleeding child--the only treasure left her on earth.

"Now and then the stealthy footsteps of a coyote were heard close to the hiding place of the fugitives. Approaching within a few feet, one of them had smelled the blood with which little Sophie's garments were saturated, and it set up that peculiarly dismal howl that only a coyote can make. From point to point it was answered by others. From hill to hill the howl gathered and rose and swelled in melancholy cadences on the cold night air, till the bereaved and stricken woman feared they would gather and tear her darling to pieces.

"Hour after hour passed, but the stars seemed motionless. How that woman prayed for daylight, unmindful of the damages it might bring! Her thoughts now were wholly absorbed by the probable fate of the handsome, blue-eyed child, who had been so suddenly separated from them, and her anxiety was torture. Could she have known that he had been killed outright, it would have relieved the pressure on a mind already overburdened with horrors. He might have escaped to hide and perish from cold and hunger, or be torn to pieces by the wolves. He might have been captured to undergo tortures indescribable, and when at last daylight broke it was only a wonder that agonizing doubt had not driven the mother mad.

"Again the morning dawned beautifully. Again the shadows of the tall pines crept down the hills. Again the songbirds filled the little valley with melody, and still the anxious mother watched. Peering out carefully she saw an Indian in the brush who himself seemed to be watching, and she shrank back again under cover. Commanding a view of the house, she soon observed three persons boldly approach it and break down the door. Supposing the savages had returned in force, Mrs. Harris now gave herself up as lost, and to add to her terror it was scarcely a moment till a band of mounted warriors poured down the valley. But a second glance disclosed the fact that they were in flight, and she knew that help was at hand. Scarcely were the Indians out of sight when her quick ear discovered the sound of heavier hoofs thundering down the road from the south, and in a few moments a detachment of dragoons and a few volunteers, under command of Major Fitzgerald, were sweeping gallantly across the valley. On came the brave boys, filled with vengeance, fresh from a battle at the ruins of the Wagner place where they had surprised and killed five of the Indians. On they dashed, still nearer and nearer, and Mrs. Harris recognized their uniforms and ran with Sophie in her arms to meet them.

"Drawing rein suddenly, the troopers gathered around the fugitives. Covered with blood and blackened with powder, worn and haggard with exhaustion, they were hardly recognizable, and the major exclaimed, 'Good God! Are you a white woman?' Closer the gallant fellows gathered to hear her simple story, quickly told, and more than one bronzed cheek was wet with tears.

"The pursuit of the Indians was at once discontinued. After attending to the immediate needs of the survivors and burying the dead, Major Fitzgerald ordered a diligent search for the little boy, but not a trace of him could be found. Subsequently the major furnished Mr. Harkness with an escort of eight men for the same purpose. Every ravine, every hollow, every thicket for miles around the Harris place was carefully searched, but not even the child's wagon, which he had taken with him, could be found.

"Mr. Bowden, who fled toward Grave Creek on the first fire, stated that the little fellow had started home before the attack and the most careful examination revealed no trace of his remains in the Bowden house, which had been burned. There was but one hypothesis--the child had been captured and carried away, but this was abandoned. During the war that ensued, and long after hostilities had ceased, captive squaws and strolling bands of Indians were closely questioned, but they persistently denied all knowledge of the child.

"A year went by, and the remains of a man named Reed were found on the Harris ranch, and search was renewed for Davy, but without result, and still the pines whispered to the sad and sorrowing woman, 'Never and nevermore!'

"Little Sophie, afterwards the wife of John S. Love, one of the honored citizens of Jacksonville, was carried away by the fearful epidemic that scourged that town in 1869, joining her husband, who had preceded her only a few months. The intrepid mother, who did a deed as brave as any ever recorded in ancient song or story, became the wife of Aaron Chambers, and, widowed a second time, lives among us, honored and beloved."

Oregon Journal
February 3, 1925

# R. A. Booth
# Eugene, Oregon

"The salary of a circuit riding Methodist minister, when I was a boy, was not large enough to raise a family of 12 children, so we all did what we could to help out the family revenue.

"In addition to caring for her 12 children, Mother kept seven boarders. She did the cooking and washed the clothes, while the girls washed the dishes and did the other housework. Mother made all the clothes for our family.

"In addition to doing janitor work and cutting wood, I used to trap beaver on Camas Swale, near Wilbur. Beaver were legal tender then, and Mother used to take them to the store and trade them in for groceries.

"I shall never forget how proud I was of the first suit of store clothes I ever owned. I was nearly 17. I was herding sheep in eastern Oregon. I always carried a gunnysack with me. I would gather wool caught on the branches when the sheep worked through the brush. I also pulled the wool from any dead sheep I found. At the end of the season I hauled this wool to Max Vogt at The Dalles. He paid me enough to buy a suit and a hat, which together cost $17.

"I used to know every trail in that part of the country between the Cascades and the Blue Mountains. Oftentimes now, as I go out inspecting the highways, I will come across some place that brings back a flood of memories. For example, I will see a ledge of rock that I took refuge under as a boy during a heavy snow storm, or I will see some rugged old juniper that my dog and I stood under while we were out with the sheep, back in the '70s."

Oregon Journal
May 6, 1920

# Judge Cassius Hall Brown
# Forest Grove, Oregon

"One of the vivid recollections of my childhood was the Fourth of July celebration at Turners Grove, Illinois, in 1859. I was about 6½ years old. Philip McChesney, Congressman from that district, was the orator of the day. An Illinois lawyer, Abraham Lincoln, was the guest of honor. McChesney gave a long oration. The Reverend E. J. Thomas, a Baptist minister, who was chairman, asked Lincoln to speak, but I guess he figured the people had heard plenty of talking after listening to McChesney, so he declined.

"That evening a reception was held at the Congregational Church at Atlanta, about a mile from Turners Grove. A baker named Wren baked a cake for Lincoln. He put on it a candle for each letter of Lincoln's name and prepared a long speech of presentation. When it came time for him to make his speech and present his cake he got flustered, so he picked up the cake, handed it to Lincoln, and said, 'Here's the cake.'

"Lincoln was tall, thin, and had a sort of hungry look when his face wasn't lit up. He smiled, thanked the baker, and said, 'I'm not as hungry as I look. I'll give this cake to the Ladies' Aid Society.' The ladies cut the cake up into slices and sold them. I can remember yet that I thought Lincoln was terribly tall, rough featured and rawboned.

"Stephen A. Douglas, who defeated Lincoln for the United States Senate, was a polished orator. A good many of Lincoln's friends felt sorry that he was up against a man so much smarter and better educated. My father was an abolitionist, so he was very strong for Lincoln, and not only voted for him but worked for him. That was the only time I ever saw Lincoln, though in April, 1865, when I was 13 years old, I saw the train with Lincoln's funeral car on its way to Springfield. Our farm was near the railroad. We didn't go to Springfield for the funeral, because the spring work had to be done.

"I guess the people in Illinois were too close to Lincoln to know that he was a great man. They liked and respected him, but he had come up from pretty humble surroundings, so the high-toned folks rather felt above him, though the common folks, of whom he was one, loved him."

Oregon Journal
April 10, 1934

# Captain Patrick Hassan
# Indian Fighter
# Vancouver, Washington

"I will celebrate my 91st birthday on December 23. I was born in Ireland in 1834 and emigrated to America when I was 16. I was 21 years and 20 days old when I enlisted. I was assigned to the 4th Infantry.

"The regiment to which I was assigned was stationed on the Pacific Coast. I was sent with a number of other recruits that had been assigned to the 4th Infantry, to join my regiment. We went from New York City to San Francisco by way of the Isthmus of Panama. I was assigned to Company E and went to northern California, where my company was stationed.

"The regiment was pretty well scattered. For example, Company H was engaged in the fight at the Cascades of the Columbia on March 26, 1856, while we were fighting the Coquille Indians in Coos and Curry Counties. Major John F. Reynolds, with a detachment of the 3rd Artillery, was stationed at Port Orford. General Wool was in charge of the department of the Pacific with headquarters at San Francisco. He made frequent trips to Vancouver. In March, 1856, when he sailed for Vancouver Barracks, he took with him Brevet Lieutenant Colonel Buchanan, in command of the 4th Infantry, with 96 officers and men, and left them at Crescent City, in northern California. When he arrived at Vancouver he issued orders for Captain Edward O. C. Ord, with a detachment of the 4th Infantry, to reinforce Major Reynolds at Port Orford. Captain Floyd Jones, also of the 4th Infantry, was ordered from Fort Humboldt to Crescent City to report to Colonel Buchanan, while Captain Smith, who was stationed at Fort Lane, was ordered to march with a detachment of 80 dragoons across the Coast Range to Port Orford. Colonel Buchanan was ordered to bring all available troops with him to Port Orford, prepared to fight or to hold a council with the Indians."

*It may not be amiss to give a brief statement right here to explain why the troops were being concentrated at Port Orford. This was in March, 1856. A week or so before, or, to be exact, on Washington's birthday, while the settlers and volunteers were having a dance at Whaleshead, as Gold Beach was called, the Indians rose and killed Ben Wright, the Indian agent; Captain John Poland, captain of the company of volunteers; and more than 25 other residents of that section, including a man named Giesel and his two sons, while they took his wife and two daughters prisoners—one of whom, by the way, is now a resident of Portland. The Indians had also burned more than 60 cabins of the settlers along the coast, and the settlers had taken refuge in 'Miners Fort,' where they were besieged for more than a month, until the arrival of the troops from Crescent City.*

"In May Lieutenant Colonel Buchanan, with Company C of the First Dragoons, Company G of the Fourth Infantry, and a detachment of Company E, of which I was a member, went to Oak Flat on the Rogue River near the mouth of the Illinois River to establish our headquarters there.
"On May 21 a council was held with the hostile Indians. Most of the Indians said they were tired of fighting and promised to return on the 26th with their people and deliver up their guns and surrender. Tyee John was the only one to hold out. He said he was willing to live in peace with the whites, but that this was his country long before the whites came there, and he would not leave it and go on a reservation. He said his heart was sick of fighting.

262

and that he was willing to go back to Deer Creek and live peacefully.

"Captain Smith told the Indians that if any of them were found off the reservation with guns in their hands, they would be hanged. We went to the agreed meeting place on May 26 and camped by the side of the river just where the town of Agness is now. It is a beautiful location, one of the prettiest I ever saw. We were there to receive the surrender of the Indians.

"We reached there at about dusk and went into camp. Not long after dark two squaws swam the Rogue River and came to our camp and asked to see Captain Smith. They told him that Tyee John and a band of warriors were going to attack the soldiers at daybreak. We were camped on a grassy plateau beside the river. Captain Smith ordered us to break camp and establish camp on a ridge about a quarter of a mile back from the river. We had two days' rations.

"Captain Tichenor, founder of Port Orford, was the contractor who had charge of the government pack train and was serving as guide. Captain Smith told him to make his way back to Oak Flat, where the rest of the troops were stationed, to secure reinforcements. Lieutenant Sweitzer was detailed by Captain Smith to select a site that could be defended. He selected for our camp a knoll about 800 feet long by 150 feet wide. The approach from the south and the north was quite steep, while on the east the approach was more easily negotiated. We moved camp that night.

"The next morning a number of Indians approached our camp, calling out to Captain Smith that they had come to surrender. They came closer and sized up our six-pounder and looked critically at our arrangements. Captain Smith told them to lay down their arms as agreed, but instead of doing so they went back to discuss the matter with the other Indians. Lieutenant Sweitzer was in command of the detachment of Company E, in which I was serving. We were guarding the western approach to our camp. As the Indians disappeared we saw our sentinel fall, and a second later saw the powder smoke rise and heard the report of the gun that had been used to shoot him. We were ordered to take refuge behind trees, but there were more soldiers than trees. The Indians had climbed to the top of a nearby knoll and were picking us off. They had better guns than we had. We had musketoons while they had rifles. One of our men, without any orders, digging with his bayonet and using his tin plate as a shovel, dug himself in. The other men, seeing what he was doing, followed his example, and we soon had rifle pits that protected us somewhat. The eastern slope was commanded by our howitzer, so the Indians did not attempt to attack us from that side. The Indians would charge up the side of our knoll and we would repulse them, but not without loss. They kept this up all day. We had moved camp the night before and had had little or no sleep, and we got but little sleep this night, either. We had used all the water in our canteens, and the wounded were moaning for water.

"The next morning at daybreak the Indians attacked again. They knew we were thirsty, and they would call out 'Mika hias ticka chuck.' One of the Indians who could speak English would keep calling out, 'One more sun no water, no muck-a-muck, no soldier. All dead.'

"When Captain Smith threatened to hang any Indian found off the reservation they had made a lot of ropes of cedar bark to hang us. Chief John, who was in command of the Indians and who had a strong voice, would call out to Captain Smith, 'O Captain Smith: If you promise to go on the reservation and not travel around the country I will not hang you. See this rope. It is for you, because you do not want to stay on a reservation where you can have plenty of plows and wagons, plenty to eat and white men to teach you.'

"All of the second day, as we fought off their attacks, with our throats parched for water in the hot spring sunshine, they would call out tauntingly, 'Halo chick Boston. Mika hias ticka chuck.' (No water, white man. Wouldn't you like some water?) They would call out that white soldiers were not worth the powder and lead it would take to kill them, so they had plenty of rope to hang us with.

"They did not know that we had sent Captain Tichenor out for help, and of course we did not know whether he had got through to Oak Flat or had been captured, but you can believe we watched with straining eyes all of that second day. Eleven of our men were dead and 16 or 17 wounded, and many of the wounded were delirious and begging for water.

"Late in the afternoon Chief John called out to his warriors to charge and not to stop till they had killed or captured all the soldiers. Just as the Indians were starting up the hill to finish us we saw Captain Augur with 75 men of Company G, Fourtn Infantry, emerging from the ravine. We gave them a cheer as best we could and jumped out of our rifle pits and charged the Indians. We were answered by a ringing cheer from our comrades Company G as they charged the Indians from the rear. Chief John turned to meet the new attack, but it didn't last long, and soon the Indians were streaking away like racehorses.

"Captain Augur was riding a white mule. As they charged he took a gun from one of his men and led his men in the charge. He was said to be the handsomest officer in the entire army, and he certainly looked good to us.

"Captain Augur lost two men in the fight. We dug a pit on the flat where Agness now is and in it we buried our dead. We captured the Indian canoes and some Indians. We placed in each canoe one wounded man, one prisoner, and two soldiers and went down the river to Oak Flat, where Buchanan had established his headquarters. From there the Indians were taken to Port Orford and thence to the Siletz Reservation.

"In May, 1858, Lieutenant Colonel Steptoe, commander of the garrison at Walla Walla, with Companies C, E, and H of the First Dragoons, and a detachment of Company E, 9th Infantry, went out to chastise the hostile Indians. Captain Taylor of Company C and Lieutenant Gaston of Company E were killed, as well as some men, in the fight that took place, and Colonel Steptoe buried his howitzers, left his dead, and escaped during the night. Colonel Wright was sent out that fall to punish the Indians. He did a good job, and gave them a lesson they never forgot.

"Our company and most of the other troops in northern California were ordered north to serve under Colonel Wright. We were stationed at Fort Vancouver. General W. W. Harney was in charge of the Department of Oregon, and when the long-brewing troubles at San Juan Island finally came to a head, General Harney ordered Captain George E. Pickett with his company of 66 men to occupy San Juan Island."

*I am going to interject here a brief explanation of the San Juan dispute.*

*In 1854 Colonel I. N. Ebey, collector of customs for Puget Sound, which at that time was a part of Oregon Territory, visited San Juan Island and found that a flock of sheep had been brought over by the Hudson's Bay Company to pasture on the island. As no duty had been paid upon them he began to investigate the matter. Charles J. Griffin, Canadian justice of the peace for British Columbia, disputed Colonel Ebey's right to interfere with the sheep, claiming that San Juan Island was a part* of British Columbia. The next year some of the sheep were seized and sold to pay the customs duty. Both governments were appealed to for redress.

On June 15, 1859, Lyman A. Cutler, an American settler, killed a pig that had repeatedly broken into his garden. It turned out that the pig was the property of Justice of the Peace Griffin, who refused $10 for it and demanded $100. Threats were made that Cutler would be arrested and taken to Victoria for trial. The American settlers on the island appealed for protection from the Indians and others and asked that soldiers be sent to protect them. General Harney in command of the district of Oregon with headquarters at Vancouver, on July 18, ordered Captain George E. Pickett, in command of Company D, 9th Infantry, stationed at the block-house at Bellingham Bay to go to San Juan Island to protect the settlers from incursions of the northern Indians and "to afford adequate protection to American citizens in their rights as such and to resist all attempts at interference by British authorities residing on Vancouver Island, by intimidation or force."

General Harney sent word to Colonel Casey that Major Hallere had been ordered to go from Port Townsend to San Juan Island. Captain Pickett, with his company, arrived on the island on July 29 and was notified the following day by Justice of the Peace Griffin, acting for Sir James Douglas, that he must not further trespass on land belonging to British Columbia. On August 3 three British warships dropped anchor in front of Captain Pickett's camp. The officers came ashore and proposed to Captain Pickett that he either leave or allow joint occupancy of the island. Captain Pickett informed them that he had no authority to permit British troops to land, and that if they attempted to do so the consequences could not fail to be regrettable in case of a collision, which would be certain to occur. He sent word to General Harney, who wrote to Governor Douglas as follows:

"I placed a military command upon the island of San Juan to protect the American citizens residing on that island from the insults and indignities which the British authorities of Vancouver Island and the establishment of the Hudson's Bay Company, recently offered them by sending a British ship of war from Vancouver Island to convey the chief factor of the Hudson's Bay Company to San Juan for the purpose of seizing an American citizen and forcibly transporting him to Vancouver Island to be tried by British laws. I have the honor to inform your excellency that I shall not permit a repetition of that insult, and shall retain a command on San Juan to protect its citizens, in the name of the

*United States, until I receive further orders from my government."*

On August 8 General Harney ordered Colonel Casey, commander of Fort Steilacoom, to send four companies of the Third artillery to San Juan Island. President Buchanan was not the type of man that Roosevelt and Cleveland were, and he gracefully backed down. He relieved General Harney from duty in Oregon and sent General Scott, who at that time was at the head of the army, to Vancouver Barracks with instructions to accept the British proposal of joint occupancy and that each government should maintain a force of not to exceed 100 men on San Juan Island. This proposition was accepted and each government kept a force of troops there till 1871, when the matter was submitted to arbitration and Emperor William of Germany decided in favor of the claims of the United States government. With this elucidation, Captain Hasson's story may be resumed.

"Captain Pickett was one of the most picturesque men I ever saw. His hair was as black as a crow's wing and as soft and silky as a woman's. It hung to his shoulders. His mustache and beard were also soft and silky and black as night. Colonel Silas Casey, under whom Captain Pickett was serving, reinforced Pickett, so we were sent to San Juan Island, but there was no fighting. The matter was eventually settled by arbitration. A force of 100 men was left on the island and were ordered to report at Fort Steilacoom, where we stayed eight or ten months. I met there Lieutenant Augustus V. Kautz, whose son is now living in Portland.

"From Fort Steilacoom our company was ordered to Fort Yuma, where we fought Indians. My enlistment expired just before the Civil War broke out, and I went back to Philadelphia and secured a commission as captain. I served through the Civil War and at its close was commissioned a lieutenant in the 14th Infantry. For the next few years I had plenty of fighting in Arizona and New Mexico.

"I came to Vancouver in July 1884, and retired in 1892. I bought a 200-acre place near Orchards, which I set out to prunes. I thought all you had to do to make a fortune raising prunes was to set the trees in the ground and let nature take its course. I found I was mistaken, and that raising prunes is a matter of skill, knowledge, and hard work, so I sold my prune orchard and have lived in Vancouver ever since. My son Charles and I live together. My other son, John P., is a lieutenant colonel in the army and is stationed at Baltimore."

**Oregon Journal**
December 2-4, 1925

# Joe Groshong
# Pioneer of 1858
# Albany, Oregon

"My father never lived two years in succession on the same place. As soon as any neighbors came within ten miles of him he was afraid they would spoil the deer hunting, so he moved on to some wilder country. My father made a living for the family, such as it was, by keeping a race horse or two, and a few hounds and building a cabin on some new place and selling out the improvements to some other settler."

**Oregon Journal**
October 4, 1923

## Captain Keys' Journal

*Old-time residents of Vancouver will remember Colonel E. D. Keyes, a brevet brigadier general in the United States Army. Colonel Keyes after graduating from West Point was told to report to Lieutenant General Winfield Scott as acting aide-de-camp. This was in the fall of 1833. Colonel Keyes served with distinction in the Mexican War and in 1848 was ordered to proceed with his company of the 3rd Regiment of Artillery to California. Crossing the Isthmus, he took his men aboard the Oregon, which sailed for San Francisco on March 12, 1849. At San Francisco he joined Lieutenant W. T. Sherman. Captain Keyes, for he was a captain at this time, was employed in making surveys in San Francisco and the line he made is the present western boundary of Montgomery Street. Captain Keyes was assigned to command of the post at San Francisco on May 1, 1849, and continued commander of the post till 1858, when he was promoted to major.*

*General John E. Wool, who was in charge of the Department of the Pacific, sent Captain Keyes with his company—Company M of the 3rd Regiment of Artillery—to the Pacific Northwest in the fall of 1855. They had a rather interesting experience in crossing the bar of the Columbia River. Captain William E. Dall was skipper on board the steamer California. In spite of rough water it was decided to cross the bar and not wait for better weather. About midway of the bar a flue collapsed, driving* the burning coals from under one of the boilers and setting fire to the ship. The California lost headway and refused to obey her rudder. The pilot said, "She's a goner." Captain Dall resumed command, gave orders to feed the fires with lard and an hour later they were anchored at Astoria.

From Vancouver, Captain Keyes was sent to Steilacoom, where he arrived on November 24, 1855. Lieutenant William A. Slaughter with a skeleton company was put in charge of a stockade not far from Puyallup. The water was high, so Captain Keyes sent an Indian on horseback with a message to Lieutenant Slaughter. Lieutenant Slaughter sent back word that he had plenty of supplies and that he and his men were safe in the blockhouse. Four days later, December 4, 1855, Lieutenant Slaughter was killed by the Indians. Lieutenant Slaughter graduated from West Point in 1848 and had been a student under Captain Keyes.

Captain Keyes kept a daily journal and under date of December 7, 1855, he wrote as follows:

"At about 4:30 today news was brought that Lieutenant Slaughter, 4th Infantry, had been shot by Indians. On December 3 he left his camp at Morrison's, near the Puyallup River, with 54 soldiers. He had with him Lieutenant James E. Harrison of the Marine Corps and Dr. Taylor of the Navy. On the afternoon of the 4th they arrived at a deserted farm on Brannan's Prairie, two miles from the fork of the White and Green Rivers, where there is a post commanded by Captain Hewett of the volunteers. Hewett came up to see Slaughter and told him he had been scouting all day and found no signs of Indians. As Slaughter, who had come from another direction, had discovered none, they considered themselves safe and allowed fires to be built and kept burning long after dark. In this they made a fatal mistake, as among hostile savages there is no safety except by keeping dark and well guarded. I had learned that, in a campaign against Indians, the front is all around, and the rear nowhere.

"The men were busy cooking their supper, and the officers--Slaughter, Hewett, Harrison and Taylor--were conversing in a small log hut that stood near the fence at the edge of the prairie. A band of redskins directed by Kanaskat crept up and arranged themselves in a thicket of brush and tall grass 100 yards distant. The sentinel noticed the rustling of the grass and heard what he supposed was the grunting of hogs, so he paid no attention. At a little past seven o'clock the Indians fired a volley, aimed at the hut. One bullet passed between the logs and directly through Slaughter's heart. He fell and expired in a minute. His only words were, 'Take care of yourselves. I am dying.' Two corporals were killed outright and four private soldiers wounded, one of whom died the following day."

Among the Indian chiefs in the Puget Sound district were Patkanim, Kanaskat, Kitsap, Quimelt and Leschi. The first-named chief was friendly but the other four were hostile. In describing Kanaskat, Colonel Keyes says:

"He was a model Indian patriot, hardy and enterprising, perfect in feral stealth, and vengeance was his ruling quality. He hated all the white settlers and rather than they should possess his country he preferred to perish. It chanced that I laid the plan that resulted in the death of Kanaskat."

Colonel Silas Casey of the 9th Infantry left Fort Steilacoom, February 26, 1856, with Captain Keyes second in command. On February 28 they camped on Lemon's Prairie. Captain Keyes was detailed as officer of the day. After a thorough examination of the prairie he posted guards and sentinels. He selected Private Kahl of Company D, 9th Infantry, as a picket. He instructed the pickets to fire at nothing but Indians and if they fired, to be sure they got what they fired at.

Early next morning Private Kahl saw a gleam of light from the fire that the cook had just lit reflected from a rifle barrel up the trail. He saw five Indians. As they came abreast of him he fired, shooting Chief Kanaskat through the spine. The soldiers dragged Kanaskat into camp. His legs were paralyzed but his voice wasn't, and with all the hatred he could muster he called out: "Kanaskat-tyee-mameloose, nica-nica mameloose Bostons," which in English means, "I am Kanaskat, the chief. Kill me. I kill Bostons." And then he added in Chinook, "My heart is wicked toward the whites and always will be. You had better kill me."

Captain Keyes ordered the soldiers to make him stop yelling. Corporal O'Shaughnessy placed the muzzle of his rifle at the chief's temple, pulled the trigger, and blew a hole through the chief's head.

Oregon Journal
March 7, 1932

# R. L. Booth
## Pioneer of 1852
## Newberg, Oregon

"In those days people used to tree grouse and pheasants and shoot them as they sat in the tree. (Lieutenant Philip H.) Sheridan used to shoot them on the wing. The settlers rather shook their heads over this, as they thought he was more fond of the fun of shooting than of getting meat. He used to enjoy catching trout, also, though I never went with him but once or twice on his fishing trips."

Oregon Journal
June 2, 1932

# Robert A. Booth
## Pioneer of 1850

*Robert A. Booth and his brother John Henry are two of Oregon's best-known and most useful citizens. There would have been no Robert A. or John Henry Booth had it not been for a casual call of a physician at the home of John S. and Sarah Scowcraft Booth.*

*Mrs. Booth's health was frail. In the spring of 1817 she gave birth to a son and the doctor told her she would die if she ever had another child. About two years later a physician who happened to be traveling through the city where Mrs. Booth lived called at the home and in the course of his visit told her that it might be beneficial to her health if she had another child. Mrs. Booth promised the Lord that if her health was improved and her life spared if she had another son, she would give him to the Lord to be a minister of the Methodist Church. She had another child, a son, whom she named Robert and dedicated to God. Today a bronze equestrian statue of this same Robert Booth stands in front of the statehouse at Salem. He was the father of Robert A. and John Henry Booth, of Mrs. Sarah Booth Hockett of Portland, and of nine other children.*

*Robert Booth was not converted until he was 23, and he was not told until after his conversion that he had been dedicated to God by his mother. He was married, August 28, 1845, to Miss Mary Miner. Their first child was born September 14, 1846. Robert Booth crossed the plains to the California gold mines in 1850, returned a year later to the East, and in 1852 started by ox team for Oregon.*

*His wife and 4-year-old son nearly died of cholera, and after their recovery Robert Booth took it and was not expected to live.*

*When Mr. Booth was 90 years old he visited his daughter, Mrs. Sarah Booth Hockett, at 5315 Northeast Mallory Avenue. When I interviewed Mrs. Hockett recently, she showed me a journal her father had written on his trip across the plains. Of his sickness he wrote:*

"Although I was brought very low, my life was spared. My wife came to the foot of my bed and said, 'I want you to promise me one thing.'

"I said, 'Tell me what it is. You know I'll do it if it is reasonable.'

"She responded, 'It's reasonable whether you think so or not. I want you to promise that if God will raise you up you will do your duty and preach when you get to Oregon. If you will promise, he will raise you up. If you won't, you are going to die.'

"I said, 'How do you know it?'

"She said, 'I have been praying over it, and I know it.'

"I said, 'If the way opens up so I know it is providential, I will try to walk in it, but I won't do anything to open up the way.'

"She said, 'No, you have always been afraid of doing anything to open up the way, and when the way has opened for you to do the Lord's will you have failed to do it.'"

*Mr. Booth's journal shows something of the hardships of those who came by prairie schooner to Oregon in 1852. Of conditions in the wagon train, he wrote:*

"Some seek every advantage to get gain. Some are generous and kind. Many ran short of provisions and suffered greatly. I sold some beans on Snake River to those who needed them, for less than I had paid at Kanesville. I sold two strangers, traveling on foot, 15 pounds of flour for less than I had paid for it. My wife baked bread, which we gave the needy. By the time we had got to Willow Creek we were out of bacon and flour. I bought flour at 50 cents a pound but by the time we had got to John Day River this was all used. My oxen could go no farther, so I left my wagon there and we went on to The Dalles.

"I hired a man to bring my wagon and goods to The Dalles. With others I built a raft, on which we went to the Cascades. My money was all gone. All I had was two cows and steer, the last of 13 head. I sold them for $87.

"I arrived in Yamhill County late in November with my wife and four children and with $15.40 in money. I took a contract to make shingles and three-foot shaved shakes to cover a barn. In cutting a hanging limb above my head the ax cut my left foot. Later I tore one of the leaders in my leg loose from the knee. I had to cut off my boot-leg and bind it firmly around my knee. Not being able to split rails, on account of my stiff knee, I had to chop off the cuts. While working in the woods I fell and my ax cut the muscles of my left arm, so that I had my foot, my knee, and my arm all on one side disabled. When I was able I put a piece of ground in wheat and it yielded well, but as I had no fence along the river the hogs got in and destroyed it.

"In the summer of 1853 I took a contract to dig a portion of the canal to run water from Baker Creek for Newby's gristmill at McMinnville. I took a yoke of oxen at $165 in payment for my work. While putting up my cabin I cut my left knee badly with a drawing knife, so I had to keep my leg bandaged and straight in front of me till it healed. The fireplace was not completed, and I had not yet put a door in. My wife had to go 22 miles with the two yoke of oxen to buy potatoes and vegetables. The water rose and the streams became dangerous, so our neighbor sent his son on horseback to help my wife ford the streams.

"I am 90 years old, and I am only sorry I have not been able to accomplish more good and to serve my Master better than I have."

Oregon Journal
April 29, 1934

# Reverend T. L. Jones
## Methodist pioneer of 1853
## Portland, Oregon

"My people were Southerners. I was born in Pike County, Illinois, February 4, 1841, so, you see, I am over 80 years old. My father, J. M. Jones, who was born in South Carolina, was a farmer. My mother, whose maiden name was Polly L. Davis, was born in Missouri. Her parents were natives of Kentucky. They were married in 1839. I am the second of their 11 children. Four of my sisters, all widows, are still living and all are here in Oregon.

"I was 12 years old when we started for Oregon,

in the spring of 1853. We came across the plains by ox team and prairie schooner. I walked barefoot from the Missouri River to the Willamette Valley, a 2000-mile walk. My job was to drive the loose cows. Father drove the oxen. Father took up a donation land claim eight miles south of Eugene, not far from the present city of Creswell. At that time there were only four houses in Eugene. Father taught in a log schoolhouse near our claim. The school usually lasted three months in each year.

"In 1861, when I was 20, with four young chaps from our neighborhood I started on horseback for the Idaho gold mines. When we had got to about where La Grande was later located we met some miners coming back from the Idaho mines. They painted such a gloomy picture of the prospects of getting a claim there that my companions decided the Willamette Valley was good enough for them, so they decided to return.

"We camped where we were for three days to thresh the matter out. I could not argue them into going on, nor could they argue me into changing my mind about seeing for myself the mines, so I went on alone, while they took the back track for home. I overtook a party bound for the mines and joined them.

"The horses became frightened a few mornings after and ran away. In trying to stop them I had a leg and an arm badly strained, so I was unable to work when I reached the mines. I traded my saddle horse, my pack horse, what money I had, and my note for $250 for an interest in a claim which, strangely enough, turned out to be rich. We took out a lot of gold from it before winter set in and froze the ground.

"That winter, with two other miners, I struck out across the deep snow for a new strike. We started the day after Christmas. About New Year's Day we ran into a heavy storm and got lost. We soon ate all our grub. The snow continued to fall until it was seven feet deep on the level. We finally came across some other miners who had been snowed in and they shared their food with us. We struck the new diggings broke and without food.

"There was a store there that was selling sugar at five dollars a pound and flour at $50.00 a sack. I secured a sack of flour and a side of bacon for $87.50, on time. My partners and I dug down through the snow to the surface of the ground in a likely looking gulch and then through six feet of clay to the gravel, which we thawed by burning wood on it each night. We soon took out enough nuggets and coarse gold to pay for our provisions. We happened to strike a rich piece of ground and rocked out $100 to $150 a day.

"In March I started back for the claim I had left. I went out with the merchant who had trusted me for our grubstake, and three other men. After traveling a day or so we disagreed as to the lay of the country. A terrific storm came on. Two of the party struck out in the direction they thought right, while the other two men and myself went the way we thought led to our old camp. One of the three men, a Spaniard, finally played out, so we left some grub and blankets with him and hurried on. The storm was so severe and the going so bad that after a while the merchant lay down, unable to go any farther. I finally got him to try it, by carrying his heavy sack of gold dust that had been weighing him down. Finally he was all in and told me to go on, but I knew if I did I would freeze to death, so I lay down with him.

"During the night one of my feet was frozen. We started on at dawn and finally came to an Indian wigwam. They fed us, gave us buffalo hide moccasins, gave us exact directions to our destination, and went back to bring in the Spaniard.

"Another time, when I was lost in the desert and nearly dying of thirst, a Cayuse Indian saved my life by directing me how to get out of a canyon and find a trail.

"I spent the winter of 1865 in the Willamette Valley, and while out here I was converted. I spent two years more in the Idaho mines, and in 1867 I went to the mines in southern Oregon, and there I found a priceless treasure. She had red hair and her name was Mary Baird. Her father, Benjamin Baird, came to Oregon in 1848. My wife was one of 16 children. My wife's father, while hunting, was attacked by a large grizzly within what are now the city limits of Grants Pass. He climbed a tree. The bear attacked his dog. He climbed down to rescue the dog, when the bear attacked him. It bit off one of his arms, clawed off one side of his face and bit a hole in his chest and side. He made his way to a miner's cabin, where he died in a few hours."

*How would you like to work for $180 a year and take your pay in horsefeed and blacksmithing? How would you buy shoes for your wife and babies, or meat? Where would your rent money come from? Wouldn't you begin to look around for a better job? Wouldn't you be likely to seek a new employer? Fifteen dollars a month salary means that your wife and little ones must do without many a thing that the wives and children of your neighbors can have. It means that what are necessaries to others* *are luxuries for your loved ones. Reverend T. L. Jones worked for many years at a salary of $180 a year and didn't always succeed in collecting all his salary, either.*

"How did we get along? Oh, we had occasional windfalls. Once the presiding elder visited us, and when he left he decided that his boots were getting a little disreputable for further use, so he left them. With a little patching they did fine for my wife. The first five years we were married we never spent a cent for meat. I was always a good shot with a rifle, and I saw to it that there was always a deer or bear hanging in our smokehouse. We dried the deer hams and my wife tried out the bear fat for lard. We also made bacon of the bear meat, and it makes surprisingly good bacon if you can't get pork.

"We were married January 13, 1868 by Reverend Samuel Matthews. We joined the Methodist Church ten days after we were married. I had been mining seven years, so I kept on with this work, at which I was fairly successful. But the mere making of money seemed an awful waste of one's life. The more we thought it over the more we were both convinced that real success consisted in sacrifice and service rather than in serving oneself.

"I had been reared in the Disciples Church, but there was no church of that denomination in our neighborhood in southern Oregon, hence we had joined the Methodist Church. We had preaching once a month, and my wife and I walked six miles to prayer meetings. I had never prayed in public, and when Reverend T. F. Royal pointed me out at one of our meetings and said, 'We will be led by Brother Jones in prayer,' I was panic-stricken. I would rather have fought a grizzly barehanded. I prayed possibly a minute and sat down, all in. I determined that if I was ever called upon again I would be able to offer testimony, so I read the Book of Discipline, read the Methodist hymn book through, studied the Bible, and accepted an appointment as class leader. I was instrumental in having revival meetings held in the schoolhouse we used for our meetings, and I was apointed exhorter. I kept on with my placer mining, but I talked in schoolhouses and to miners' meetings whenever and wherever I could.

"We could mine only during the winter, when there was lots of water for our sluice boxes, so in the summer I worked in the harvest fields or freighted. In the summer of 1871 I hauled freight on the railroad that was being built between Albany and Eugene, and made good money. That fall I took a contract to deliver 1000 pounds of mountain balm, which grew on the slopes of the mountains near Grants Pass. It was to be delivered at Albany. While I was in this work a quarterly conference was held, which I attended. The presiding elder decided to send our pastor, Reverend J. W. Kuykendall, elsewhere, so he had to appoint some other minister for that circuit. He said, 'Brother Jones, I am going to appoint you to this circuit.' I told him I had never preached, but he said it was time I did, so, on September 3, 1871, I received my license to preach and was given a circuit 95 miles long and 70 miles wide with 16 preaching places. They turned over to me all the church property in the district--a church record and two class books.

"The first text I preached from was, 'Wherefore, come out from among them, and be ye separate, saith the Lord...and I will receive you and will be a Father unto you, and ye shall be my sons and daughters.' I preached 12 minutes, but during that time I repeated parts of the sermon several times. It was the hardest 12 minutes' work I ever did.

"My first circuit was the Kerbyille circuit. They wanted me to stay two years more, so they changed the name of the circuit to the Grants Pass circuit and appointed me to this newly organized circuit, so I was able to work four years there. From there I was sent to the Clear Creek circuit, near where Estacada now is. Later I had the Sheridan-Willamina-Bellevue circuit. When I preached at Dayton one of my most loyal church members was General Joel Palmer, whose son William still lives there. I preached at Oregon City for a while, and later was assigned to Grants Pass, where we built a fine church. For some years I was in evangelistic work. I served six years as presiding elder, my district being southern and south central Oregon.

"Five years ago I lost my sight.

"We have had four children. Ebbie, our eldest child, is in California. He is married and has two children. Nellie married Reverend F. C. Thompson, a member of the Puget Sound conference. Will is a railroad engineer and lives at Tacoma. Jesse lives near us. He has two daughters. He has worked in the Portland postoffice for the past 16 years.

"Yes, I am 80 years old, but I can look back with pleasure on the work that through the grace of God I have been able to do in the upbuilding of His kingdom here on earth."

**Oregon Journal**
September 24 & 25, 1922

# J. S. Buxton
## Forest Grove, Oregon

"Father used to trade in Portland. One day a smooth real estate agent got hold of him and pretty nearly sold him the block where the old postoffice stands, at Fifth and Morrison. He wanted $250 for that block, but it was a mass of charred stumps with big holes where the trees had been grubbed out, and it was pretty far out of town, so my father turned it down. He didn't think the town would ever build as far west as Fifth Street."

Oregon Journal
February 2, 1922

# Levi Bennett
## Pioneer of 1848
## Midway between Amity and McMinnville

"My son Cyrus, who is 72, is hauling wood today. It makes him pretty mad when people refer to him as an old man. I am 96 and he is my boy, so he don't seem old to me, though I guess when a man is 72 he is considered beginning to get old."

Oregon Journal
October 31, 1929

# Charles F. Hart
## Prospector
## Kerby, Oregon

"Prospecting has a fascination that is hard to explain. You may work for weeks and barely make wages, and then, when you are least expecting it, you will strike a pocket. I remember one day I rocked out $386 from some rich dirt in the seams of bedrock where I was working. One nugget weighed $180, while the rest was coarse gold. A miner in the Althouse district shoveled a 17-pound nugget into his sluice box. He sold it for $4300. Newell DeLamatter bought a claim in the Althouse diggings, 13 miles from here. He paid $250 for it. The claim was supposed to have been worked out, yet in the next two years he took out $37,000 from this claim."

Oregon Journal
May 15, 1927

# C. A. Sweek
# In search of the Blue Bucket Mine
# Corvallis, Oregon

"In 1888 I came out from Canyon City to Forest Grove for the purpose of securing all the data I could obtain from Mrs. Henry Buxton, a member of the wagon train that took Meek's cut-off in 1845. Some of the members of this wagon train, as you know, discovered the gold that gave rise to the story of the Blue Bucket Mine. Forty years or so ago I followed the trail made by the emigrants of 1845 while attempting to reach the Willamette Valley by way of Meek's cut-off. Even then, one could still find the deeply cut wagon tracks where the wheels had been blocked and as a consequence had cut deep into the hillsides. Why the immigrants of this wagon train climbed mountains and traversed box canyons while a perfectly level way was to be had just across the river has always been a mystery to me.

"They came down into the Agency Valley, crossed the valley to the north fork of the Malheur River, and traveled by the north fork for about ten miles. They crossed the shoulder of Castle Rock Mountain, which connects with the main range of the Blue Mountains, and reached the Upper Agency Valley.

"On this bench I found the grave of Mrs. Chambers, who was buried on September 28, 1845. I saw this grave in 1881. It is about 1000 feet or more above the level of the valley. When I was there there was a big juniper tree beside the grave, and at that time the grave was enclosed with a five-foot rail fence, which had been put up by Sam Parrish, Indian agent at the Malheur Agency. When I was there Major Reinhart was the agent. He was the last agent stationed there. After he had gone, sheepherders used the rails around the grave for campfires.

"Mrs. Chambers was a sister of Sol King, who in 1876 was elected sheriff of Benton County, and who held the place so long that the memory of man runneth not to the contrary. Sol King was born in Ohio in 1833. In 1841 his people moved to Missouri and four years later they joined the westbound emigrants to cross the plains to Oregon. Nahum and Serepta King, Sol King's father and mother, with five sons and five daughters, went to St. Joe, Missouri, and joined the wagon train under the command of Captain W. G. T'Vault. In the spring of 1846 Nahum King took up a place in what is now known as King's Valley. He settled

279

there with Roland Chambers and Lucius Norton. From King's Valley Mr. King moved to Portland, where he stopped for a few years, but, liking Benton County best, he came back to Corvallis in the early '50s and purchased a farm of 1200 acres just west or Corvallis.

"If you will read the account of the Blue Bucket Mine you will see that most of the writers speak of the party finding the gold in the stream a few days after the death of Mrs. Chambers. You will also see that many writers think the gold was found on a tributary of the Malheur River. Both of these beliefs are erroneous.

"The gold was not discovered for some time after the death of Mrs. Chambers. The emigrants left visible evidence as to their trail, for, in 1881, when I followed their trail, I would frequently see on the bunch grass hills deep cuts where the wheels were locked going down into Harney Valley —on Cow Creek. They camped on the northwest shore of Harney Lake. In 1907 Dan Harkey of Burns found the axle of a wagon in Spring Creek about 300 yards below where Cricket Creek flows into Spring Creek. Steve Meek left the wagon train on the shores of Malheur Lake. He followed the Big Stick Canyon to Wagon Tire Mountain, where he found an easy pass out. When the emigrants crossed the Malheur River they passed through a canyon now known as Meek Canyon. They later crossed the middle fork of the Malheur and its tributaries near the present town of Post.

"Williams was the man who intercepted Meek and warned him the emigrants were going to kill him. When Meek left, Williams took up the search for water. The fall of 1845 was very dry and there was no water in the lower course of Silver Creek. Williams found water at what is now called Jenkins Springs.

"At Spring Creek they camped and mended the axle of one of the wagons and threw the old axle into Spring Creek, where it was found a few years ago. They went down Spring Creek to Emigrant Creek and turned north toward the top of the mountains, working north to the headwaters of the south fork of the John Day River. Here they followed a ridge to near the head of Murderers Creek, where they met an Indian from Warm Springs Agency, who directed them back toward the headwaters of the John Day, which way led them by the headwaters of the Ochoco and on to the Ochoco.

"In June, 1862, a man named Alread, with a party of miners from Yreka, California, while en route to Auburn, in Baker County, struck the

old wagon tracks of the emigrants of 1845 near
the shore of Harney Lake. They followed it to where
the trail led to Auburn, and when it turned back
they pressed on to Auburn. In 1882 I met Mr. Alread
at Canyon City and he told me about the old trail.
Mr. Herron, whose father found the gold, took up
a donation land claim two miles south of my father's
farm, in the Tualatin Valley. I knew the Herrons
well. My father saw a piece of decomposed quartz,
heavily veined with gold, that Mr. Herron had picked
up while on the Meek Cut-off. Many years later,
when the Ochoco Mines were discovered, it was found
that the gold from the Ochoco Mines was identical
in appearance with the piece of gold that Mr. Herron
had found. As a matter of fact, the only gold that
has ever been discovered between where Mrs. Chambers
was buried and where the emigrants of 1845 left
the mountains to reach The Dalles, was on the Ochoco.

"In the old days the emigrants used to carry
cedar water buckets, painted blue on the outside
and red on the inside. When I was a boy I used
to see these old blue buckets. When one of the emigrants who had been with the Meek Cut-off party
was told of the discovery of gold in California,
he spoke of the gold they had found while on Meek's
cut-off and said, 'I could have filled a blue bucket
with the stuff if I had known it was gold.' So
that was the way in which the Blue Bucket Mine
was named."

Oregon Journal
November 13, 192?
(last digit illegible)

# Albert Harris
# Conser, Oregon

"I was born in Tillamook County nearly 60
years ago. I live at Conser, near Albany. My father,
Truman Harris, was born in New York state in 1824.
He was married when he was 24 years old to Maria
Lewis, who was born in New York state. Mother
was two years younger than Father. They were
married at Kalamazoo, Michigan, in 1848. In the
next four years they had three children, all of
whom died while babies. In 1852 they decided to
go to Oregon. They crossed the plains by ox team
and settled at Salem, where Father worked for a
couple of years.

"Father ran a blacksmith shop. I became his
helper when I was 12 years old. When I was 16
Father turned the shop over to me and took up
logging. I made my own charcoal, made log dogs,

281

set wagon tires, and did the blacksmithing for that part of the country.

"When I was 20 I took up the trade of gunsmith and have followed that off and on for the past 40 years. It doesn't become a man to say he is a good shot, but two weeks ago, on my place near Conser, with my rifle I killed two wild geese, both of which were upward of 100 yards away. The last five deer I killed I brought down with five shots, so you see I didn't waste any ammunition. I would feel ashamed of myself if it took more than one shot to kill a deer.

"In my boyhood I was pals with Claude Thayer, son of Judge W. W. Thayer, who served as governor of Oregon many years ago. One day Claude showed me a new Smith & Wesson revolver his father had bought for him. I too had a Smith & Wesson. Claude put up a stake two inches across and whittled a spot on it as large as a half dollar. We stepped back 40 paces. I fired first and put my bullet into the spot he had made. Claude fired several times, but failed to hit the stake. He wanted me to fire again, but I told him I didn't want to waste my ammunition. As a matter of fact, it was my reputation I was saving, not my ammunition, for if I had shot a dozen times more I doubt if I could have hit the spot again.

"In 1899 I moved from Tillamook to Hubbard, where I ran a blacksmith shop for nine years. I put in the next four years at Monitor. From there I went to Lewis County, Washington, and then moved to Newberg, Oregon. After running a shop there for two years I moved to Alsea, and not long ago I bought ten acres near Conser.

"When I was a boy I made considerable pocket money killing and selling game. I killed a five-point bull elk once near Tillamook City. I sold 500 pounds of meat from that elk, getting five cents a pound for most of it. Governor Thayer bought a good-sized chunk of it at five cents a pound. I killed 21 bears and over 500 deer before I was of age. I could have killed more deer, but I didn't kill them for sport, but only when we needed the meat or when I had an order for deer meat. I served for a while as deputy sheriff and I also served as road supervisor."

Oregon Journal
December 16, 1925

# Ed T. Hatch
# Vancouver, Washington

*"Daddy" Hatch of Vancouver is a candidate for the Republican nomination for county auditor of Clark County. His slogan is to brag little, show well, crow gently if in luck, to pay up, to own up, and to shut up if beaten. I have known "Daddy" Hatch, or, to give him his proper name, E. T. Hatch, for more than 40 years. When he was a representative in the legislature he gave me a scholarship to attend Oregon Agricultural College. When I met him recently, he said:*

"My father, Peter H. Hatch, was a state of Maine man. Father was born at Parsonsfield, Maine, December 26, 1810. His father Ephraim, was also

"One of the saloonkeepers in Oregon City sicked a savage dog upon Father. The dog set his teeth in Father's leg. Father choked the dog till he released his hold and then Father threw the dog with all his force against a stone and killed it."

born in Maine.    My father's mother was a Holt.
She was a descendant of Chief Justice Holt of England.
I was born in Oregon City, March 7, 1852.

"My father was a man of intense convictions.
When he was a boy he was bound out to a blacksmith
to learn the trade. This man drank himself to death
on hard cider, which made Father an ardent prohibition-
ist for the rest of his life. He always carried in
his pocket a number of pledge cards and persuaded
hundreds of young men to sign the pledge. Talking
prohibition in the '40s and '50s at Oregon City
was not very popular, but Father was quick as
a cat and a hard hitter and was willing to back
up his convictions at any time and in any place
with his fists as well as his cash. One of the saloonkeepers in Oregon City sicked a savage dog upon
Father. The dog set his teeth in Father's leg. Father
choked the dog till he released his hold and then
Father threw the dog with all his force against
a stone and killed it.

"Another saloonkeeper threatened Father's
life if he did not quit agitating against saloons.
Father was always a devout Christian, but he was
the kind of Christian that is always willing to
smite the enemy hip and thigh, or any other good
place. This saloonkeeper who had threatened Father
met him on the street in Oregon City and began
abusing him and finally started for Father. There
was only one blow exchanged, the saloonkeeper
being on the receiving end of the blow. His friends
carried him away, for he had lost all interest in
the proceedings.

"To show you how fearless my Father was,
he taught a class of colored people during the Civil
War, and though he was threatened frequently by
Southern sympathizers, he paid no attention to their
threats.

"He organized and conducted a temperance
club for boys in Salem. At the time they moved
the convicts from the penitentiary in Portland to
Salem the prison at Salem was not completed, so
the prisoners were kept in a stockade. My father
at that time was road supervisor. We lived on a
place just south of the penitentiary. Father, with
two or three men, was working on the road. They
heard shouting and shots fired. Father said, 'The
prisoners have broken out of the stockade. They
will probably come here and try to steal this team!'
Father grabbed a pickax and told the other men
to arm themselves with axes and if the prisoners
tried to seize the team to hit to kill. About 100
of the prisoners made the outbreak and 12 of them
escaped. In the mix-up one of the prisoners was

284

killed, and I believe one or two were wounded. I have seen my father under all sorts of conditions, but I never remember seeing him show the least fear.

"When Father was 21 years old he signed on as a blacksmith on a whale ship bound for Arctic waters. His job was to sharpen the harpoons, do cooperage work on the barrels that held the oil, and do other carpenter work on board the ship. He sailed from Nantucket and put in the next seven years sailing on whalers. In 1841 he left his ship at Honolulu. Their custom was to winter at Honolulu. He met a young lady there, Charlotte Sophia Colcord, with whom he fell in love. She was a teacher in the mission school. Father quit his ship and went to work in the mission school, teaching carpentry, blacksmithing work and stonemasonry. Father's sweetheart was born at Parsonville, Maine. They were married at Honolulu in 1841.

"In 1843 Father, his wife, and their baby boy, David Hatch, came to Oregon. They came on board the bark Fama, commanded by Captain Nye. Among their fellow passengers were Francis W. Pettygrove with his wife and child, Nathan P. Mack, and Philip Foster with his wife and four children.

"The first work father did after coming to Oregon was to carry goods in a bateau between Vancouver and Oregon City for Dr. John McLoughlin. That is where Father secured his title as 'Captain' Hatch. At one time my father had a controlling interest in the steamer Multnomah. She was a side-wheeler 100 feet long, was built of Jersey oak and was shipped from the East in sections on the bark Success. She arrived in Oregon City in June, 1851. She plied on the upper Willamette for a while but in the spring of 1852 ran between Oregon City and Portland. In 1853 Captain Richard Hoyt Sr. was in charge of her on the Oregon City run. Later Captain Hoyt put her on the Astoria run.

"William S. Ladd and Captain Ainsworth wanted Father to go in with them when they first went into the steamship business, but Father didn't believe in making money on Sunday, and as the steamers were to run on Sunday, Father wouldn't go in with them. If he had done so he would have been one of the owners of the Oregon Steam Navigation Company, which made a mint of money for its owners. The Multnomah was sold to the Oregon Steam Navigation Company shortly after the death of Captain Richard Hoyt, Sr. The machinery was taken out of her for another ship in 1864.

"My first recollection of Christmas was when we lived a mile above Canemah. My father cut a good-sized Christmas tree and carried it to the Congregational Church for the Christmas exercises.

"For many years Father was a house-mover at Salem. Having been a sailor, he was handy with ropes. The way he happened to get into house-moving was rather curious. A cow fell into a dry well in Salem. They called on Father to get the cow out. He rigged up windlass and tackle and pulled the cow out. Later someone wanted a building moved and Father tackled the job and almost before he knew it he was in the house-moving business.

"When Father was a justice of the peace Dick Williams argued a case before him. Father ruled against Dick Williams, who said, 'Your Honor, your decision is not good law.'

"My father said, 'It may not be good law, but it's common sense.'

"Dick Williams said, 'Just how do you define common sense?'

"Dick's father, Lige Williams, was in the courtroom, and, turning to his son, he said, 'Dick, common sense is what Old Man Hatch has got and what you ain't got.'

"My father used to constantly say to myself and my brothers, 'Whenever you take a job, see to it that you are the best man on the job.' He took great pride in his strength and activity. When he was 65 years old he ran a foot race, and what's more, he won it. At one time he was working on the river. He and the other men were soaked through most of the time, and as it was winter, they were cold. The other men kept drinking to keep warm and urged my father to drink. He said, 'No, I won't drink, and, what's more, I'll work harder and longer and stay on the job longer than those of you who do,' and he made good on his statement."

Oregon Journal
July 10-12, 1930

# W. P. Hawley
# Hawley Pulp & Paper Company

"You will know that we had pretty slim picking during the Civil War when I tell you that my father's wages of $13 a month as a soldier had to support his wife, four small children, and his mother."

Oregon Journal
March 20, 1928

# Miles Cannon
## Boise, Idaho

*Miles Cannon of Boise, formerly a state official of Idaho, is now a federal official. As a by-product of his travels he writes most interesting and readable articles about the early life of Idaho. His book,* **Wa-il-at-pu,** *which describes the rise and fall of the Whitman Mission, is a real contribution to the history of the West. Mr. Cannon was a recent visitor to Portland, being here on official business. In a recent issue of the* **Idaho Statesman** *of Boise he gives some interesting facts about the early life of Joaquin Miller, the Poet of the Sierras. He says:*

On the evening of April 1, 1868, Samuel Lockhart was seated in front of the stage office at Silver City, Idaho, when Marion Moore, accompanied by three others, approached. Within the space of a very few minutes an altercation sprang up between Lockhart and the Moore party, followed by a fusillade of gunshots, which brought to the scene a multitude of excited citizens. Moore received a bullet in the left breast, and, running about 50 yards, fell in a dying condition. Lockhart was wounded in the left arm, but, believing the injury would soon heal, neglected to have it properly treated, until it was found necessary to have the arm amputated. The operation was followed by blood poisoning and death came to his relief on the 13th day of July following.

The trouble seemed to have arisen over a dispute between the Ida Elmore and the Golden Chariot mining companies as to the boundaries of their properties. Finding themselves unable to affect an amicable settlement, all concerned resorted to force. During the month of March, 1868, both properties were strongly fortified and on the morning of March 25 the Golden Chariot force (a San Francisco organization) sallied forth and stormed the works of the Elmore. Desperate fighting continued throughout the day and at intervals during the night, but the following day, owing to the exhausted condition of the combatants, the engagement became less furious. Casualties as reported were, two killed and several wounded and missing. On the 28th Governor Ballard issued a proclamation ordering the belligerents to disperse and a squad of United States Cavalry from Fort Boise was sent along to see that the proclamation was duly respected. On the 29th the troops appeared on the scene and as a result the warring miners were able to compromise their differences without further affusion of blood.

The untimely death of Lockhart, who was one

of the belligerents, entitles him to a more prominent place in the annals of the pioneers than the Silver City affray naturally would accord him. Back in the early '50s, Sam and his twin brother, Harry, were members of a colony of some 10 or 12 families who settled on Pit River, some distance above its junction with McCloud River, Shasta County, California. The town of Shasta, situated about seven miles northwest of the present town of Redding, was then the county seat.

In January, 1857, the Pit River or Digger tribe of Indians fell upon the colony and massacred every member, with the exception of Sam Lockhart, who was temporarily absent down the river at the time. His twin brother, Harry, was among the slain, which so angered Sam that he swore undying vengeance against the whole tribe that had participated in the slaughter. Though often warned and several times arrested by the federal authorities, he persisted, as soon as released, to make Digger hunting his principal occupation.

During the winter of 1859-60, he planned a raid on a small band of these Indians living on McCloud River, and had succeeded in picking off a few warriors, when he disovered a log cabin situated in a recess of a small tributary. Further investigation revealed, to his amazement, the presence of a white man living with a Digger squaw. Lockhart, actuated by the presumption that they had been implicated in the massacre, was in the act of shooting both the white man and his squaw, when the former pleaded his innocence of any connection with the crime and pitifully begged for the life of himself and his consort.

Lockhart, upon reflection, concluded to take his suspect before Judge Rosborough of Yreka for examination and advice. He thereupon tied the captive on the back of an Indian pony and escorted him before the magistrate. The judge at once instituted a searching investigation lasting two nights and a day during which time Lockhart stood guard over the prisoner, and assured him that if he attempted to escape his hide wouldn't hold shucks.

The judge was unable to attach any blame to the man, who it was ascertained, was none other than Hiner Miller, who latterly became more or less distinguished as Joaquin Miller, the 'Poet of the Sierras'. The judge, with much difficulty, persuaded Lockhart not to shoot the captive, who, upon regaining his freedom, made a hurried exit from the country.

Miller, according to the Shasta traditions, lived at that place and vicinity during the years

1856 to 1859, inclusive, and after his precipitous departure his squaw made that her home for many years. He joined the Pit River band in 1856 and for two years lived in the log cabin at the foot of the Shasta Mountains, where, in 1857, his half-breed daughter was born.

It was in the midst of this sort of wild life that Miller first tried his hand at poetry. It was here likewise that he took the name of Joaquin, evidently adopted from Joaquin Murietta, a noted Spanish outlaw who lived in the upper San Joaquin Valley before the American occupation.

After leaving Shasta, Miller read law a few weeks in Oregon and was admitted to the bar by Judge Williams, formerly a member of President Grant's cabinet. He then made his appearance in northern Idaho, where, unable to do anything at the law, he rode the pony express between Walla Walla and Orofino. After the mining excitement abated somewhat he drifted out of the state with the receding tide.

Lockhart followed the Diggers until he had killed every one implicated in the massacre on Pit River--estimated at 25. He then left California and took up his abode at Silver City, only to meet with death under conditions most distressing as well as unfortunate.

Oregon Journal
undated

# Joel Jordon Hembree
# Lafayette, Oregon

"I am a forty-niner. I was born May 6, 1849, on my father's donation land claim. My father, Captain Absolom J. Hembree, came to Oregon with the first wagon train that ever came through. He came with Peter Burnett, Jesse Applegate and other well known pioneers of Oregon. In the spring of 1844 he took up a claim where the town of Carlton is now located. His nearest neighbors were Sydney Smith and Amos Cook.

"My father was a stockman. He also ran a store for some years at Lafayette. Father was an opponent of Joe Meek for marshall, but came out second best.

"I remember very distinctly being out in the field one day helping Father build a fence. George Olds and several other settlers rode up and told him that the company of volunteers had decided to ask him to be their captain. Father was killed

April 10, 1856. With several of his men he rode to the top of a small butte to see if any Indians were in the country. Rising from behind rocks the Indians shot at the reconnoitering party. My father was shot through the body. Wheeling their animals, they started down the hill for the camp. My father was riding B. F. Star's mule. In going down the steep hillside it fell and my father was thrown. Before he could get up the Indians were on him. He killed three of them, but was shot under the eye and killed. They scalped him and rode away. His funeral, held here in Dayton, was one of the largest Masonic funerals ever held in the Willamette Valley up to that time."

Oregon Journal
April 17, 1922

# James E. R. Harrell
## Pioneer of 1847
## Portland, Oregon

"I will be 93 on my next birthday and for the last year or two I have been taking things a little easy, for I have worked pretty hard for 75 years and I feel that I am entitled to ease up a little now."

Oregon Journal
undated

# Orville S. Jones
## Hillsboro, Oregon

"Every boy goes through a treasure hunting stage. Whether they read Stevenson's **Treasure Island,** Poe's **Gold Bug,** or **Robinson Crusoe** or not, they still have in their nature the desire to find buried treasure. When I was in my late teens my stamping ground was around Fort Laramie and Cheyenne. Our farm was on the old California Trail. When I was a little tad my father used to hunt buffalo on the south fork of the Solomon River, in Kansas, but when I had reached my teens buffalo hunting was but a memory, though you could see in all directions the buffalo wallows on the prairie and also see the bleaching bones of the buffalo. The hide hunters were replaced by men who drove over the prairie and gathered buffalo skulls and buffalo bones to be ground up for fertilizer. Our farm was in Scott's Bluff County.

"Now, to come back to my story of buried treasure. I want you to look at a large black silk scarf. When I was a boy cowboys and others wore large bandanna handkerchiefs around their necks, while gamblers and other such gentry usually wore large black silk handkerchiefs, or scarfs. This large black silk handkerchief could tell a most interesting tale if it were able to do so. My chum and I had heard tales of buried gold. The tradition in that part of the country was that a man who had been lynched had buried $20,000 in gold, which had never been discovered. You probably have heard of the Cold Springs Ranch. The money was reported to have been buried on this ranch. My chum and I went over this old ranch rather carefully to see if we could find any indications of buried treasure. The only indication that we could find was a slight depression in the prairie. So we began diggin there. I had dug about two feet when my shovel struck some hard substance. I thought sure I had struck a box or kettle in which the gold might have been buried, but when I dug a little deeper it turned out to be a man's skull. There was a bullet hole through the skull and when I shook the skull the bullet fell out.

"We continued to dig, and the next thing I struck was his arm bones, which were crossed at the wrist and tied together with this black silk handkerchief. We finally dug out the whole skeleton, but even though we dug still deeper, we could find no money. When buried, the man's hat had been put over his face. Some of the remnants of the hat were still there, but silk does not rot, so the silk handkerchief was still in good condition.

"When we showed the skull and the bones to the old-timers around there they told us the body was probably that of Jules Reni, who was a leader among the French-Canadian settlers. He was killed by Joseph A. Slade.

"The tradition in that part of the country was that Jules Reni had sold his place at Julesburg for $20,000 in gold and had buried the money and that it had never been found. In any event, all the treasure we found was this skeleton, with the arm bones tied together at the wrist with this black scarf. I still have the bullet that I shook out of the skull.

"When I was riding the range I was caught in a blizzard. My feet and hands became numb, so I dismounted and, throwing the reins over my horse's head, I held on to them and let my horse lead me to the ranch house, for I had no idea of the direction. In all my life I never wanted to lie down so badly. I had no sensation in my feet, and as I stumped along I thought if I could only burrow into the snow and go to sleep I would be comfortable.

"After what seemed hours to me my horse stopped at the bars of the corral of the home ranch. My hands and feet were frozen. My folks sent for a doctor who said the only thing to do was to amputate my hands and feet. I was 19 years old and couldn't bear the prospect of going through life a cripple, so I told the doctor I preferred to die. My folks sent for another doctor, and he said there was a chance to save my hands and feet. He kept them soaked in bandages on which were poured equal parts of limewater and linseed oil. All I lost was one toe, so I came out of the deal mighty lucky."

Oregon Journal
January 31, 1935

# Captain Ed Carr
# Portland, Oregon

"When I was a boy, doctors did a lot more guessing than they do today. They couldn't take an X-ray picture of you and find out what really ailed you. About all they could do was to stroke their long whiskers, look at you as wise as an owl and twice as serious through their steel-rimmed glasses and give you some medicine that tasted twice as bad as whatever ailed you.

"From the time I was able to toddle around I had something that ailed my stomach and seemed to sap my vitality. I was a regular sack of bones and being so emaciated made me weak. My father was running a hotel on the Perryburg Turnpike in Ohio. He employed one doctor after another and each one thought something different ailed me. One would say I had stomach worms and another would say I had something else. Finally a new doctor came from Boston and he declared that he could cure me. The calomel and quinine and indigo and other drugs that the other doctors had given me had made me weak as a cat--and I mean a sick cat, not one of the husky ones that has nine lives. He tried one drug after another and finally said to my father, 'I'm stumped. I sure thought I could cure your boy. There is only one remedy I haven't tried and I am not sure whether that will work or not.'

"My father said, 'Well, for heaven's sake, try it.'

"The doctor said, 'Well, it will either kill him or cure him, so we'll try it.' He said, 'Your boy is 4 years old. If he has a tapeworm or if he has stomach worms or some other kind of parasites, I think strong tobacco may effect a cure.'

"I am 83 years old now, but if I live to be 100 I will never forget my first experience with the doctor's prescription. My father called me into the barroom of the hotel, filled a pipe with strong tobacco, and told me to smoke it. There were about 20 men in the barroom, drinking, playing cards, or talking. I took a sliver of hickory and lit it in the fireplace, and my father showed me how to draw up the pipe and light it. He set me on the end of the bar, where everybody could see me. I got the pipe going in good shape and though the smoke nearly strangled me I stayed with it.

"Presently I laid the pipe down on the bar, climbed down and staggered over to the fireplace —and when I say staggered, I mean staggered, for everything was whirling around except my stomach, and that felt as if there was a volcanic eruption going on—and lay down in front of the fire. Talk about sick! I never since have felt as sick as I was then. Of course, the men in the barroom thought it was awfully funny, but the deathly pallor of my face and the cold sweat on my forehead alarmed my father. He thought I was going to die. My mother and Judy, my old Negro mammy, came running into the barroom when they heard my father say, 'The boy is dying.' The last thing I remember was being in Mammy Judy's arms and feeling her tears fall on my face. Both Mother and Judy declared that never would they let Father make me smoke again.

"However, several days later Father filled the pipe again and told me I must obey the doctor's orders. It made me shiver and tremble to think of it, but I manfully began puffing away and, strange as it may seem, I felt no ill effects. From that time to this I have smoked and chewed tobacco. If I had stomach worms the strong tobacco must have discouraged them, because within a year I was as husky as other boys of my age.

"Curiously enough my old Negro mammy, Judy, got the habit of smoking from me. I would sit on her lap smoking my pipe and she would smoke a corncob pipe. She got the habit from filling and lighting my pipe for me. When Mother remonstrated with her she said that she had a misery in her stomach and she was smoking to cure it.

"Do I remember the trip to Oregon? Sure. I was nearly ten years old. I was born in the northern part of Ohio on March 20, 1848, and we arrived at Milwaukie, near Oregon City, on March 10, 1858.

"When Father sold his hotel the new owner didn't want the furniture, so Father held an auction. My older brother had bought a bow and a quiver of arrows from the Indians and given them to me. He had also bought me a pair of skates, a single-barrel, muzzle-loading shotgun and some picture books and had given me a sack of marbles and a top. I was ten years old when we left, and I owned a Newfoundland dog and a sleigh with shafts in which I used my dog as motor power. Father said I couldn't take my things to Oregon, so the auctioneer sold my dog and sled and all my other possessions for $3.50. He handed the money to me.

"When we started on our trip we were allowed three trunks to go as baggage, but we could carry as many carpetbags as we wanted. I rustled a carpetbag and, not knowing whether there was any tobacco in Oregon or not, I invested three dollars from the auction money in smoking tobacco and bought five ten-cent plugs of chewing tobacco. I said nothing about it to my folks for fear they would call me down.

"My brother had gone to Oregon in '55 and he wrote such glowing accounts of the rich land that could be had for the taking in the Willamette Valley that Father decided to come here. We left our home in Ohio in November, 1857, and went to Medina County to visit my mother's sister before leaving for the west. We left my aunt's home December 28, 1857, on the New York & Erie Railroad, going from Akron, Ohio, to New York City.

"We certainly had a strenuous trip. There were about 600 passengers aboard and just as we were about to sail we were held up and 600 soldiers marched aboard. The captain of the Moses Taylor made a number of the passengers give up their staterooms to accommodate the officers. He came to my father and said, 'There is an irregularity about your ticket. You are not entitled to the stateroom you have, but rather than make trouble for you or extra expense, you can go second class.'

"The officer who was to have the stateroom my father had been assigned to was standing beside the captain of the Moses Taylor. My father said to the captain, 'I am an old Lake Erie man. If this ticket is not good for what it calls for it is not good for anything. Put the pilot boat overboard and take my family and myself ashore. I will see what the courts have to say about it. I know I can secure damages against your company.'

"The army officer who was in charge of the soldiers said to the captain of the boat, 'This man is absolutely right. You can't make him give up his stateroom.'

"The captain said he would think the matter over, and that was the end of it, as far as we were concerned, but he routed out others and put them in second class accommodations because they did not have the knowledge or nerve to stand up for their rights.

Three days out from New York we developed engine trouble. Having 1200 aboard in place of 600, provisions ran short. After seven days the ship's supplies of food were exhausted. The captain broached the cargo, but all he found in the way of provisions was a ton of split peas, so from then on we had pea soup, boiled peas and fried peas, and they even used peas to make coffee. Fortunately for the captain, we had a stormy trip, so most of the passengers were seasick and ate very little and were too weak to make trouble.

"One day I saw Father searching his pockets, but all he found was a few crumbs of tobacco. He handled them as carefully as if they were diamonds. I slipped down into our stateroom, got one of my plugs of tobacco, and, returning to the deck, I said, 'What's the matter, Pa? Haven't you any chewing tobacco?'

"He shook his head and said, 'No, son, I haven't had a chew for three days.' When I brought my hand from behind my back with a plug of Peach Branch chewing tobacco and handed it to my father, I never in my life saw such a look of relief, anticipation, and joy on a man's face.

"After traveling from New York to the Isthmus of Panama aboard the Moses Taylor, crossing the Isthmus and going to San Francisco aboard the Central America, then taking the Santa Cruz to Portland, we took the little stern-wheel steamer express at Portland to continue to Milwaukie. I was almost ten years old when the mate and the deckhand put our baggage ashore at the beach just south of the old Standard Mill at Milwaukie.

"When we left the Isthmus of Panama for San Francisco on the old steamer Central America in January, 1858, we seemed to be hoodooed. The ship took fire. The fire was conquered and then the ship sprung a leak. A bucket brigade was formed and it looked for awhile as if we were going to sink. I will never forget the moaning and the screaming of some of the women in the steerage, who thought they and their children were going to be drowned. One of the sailors said to me, 'We've got a Jonah aboard. If we could only find him and throw him overboard things would be all right.' I was scared to death for fear they might decide that I was

295

the Jonah, so for the rest of that trip whenever I caught sight of that sailor I made myself scarce.

"My brother had gone out to Oregon in 1855. He had written a letter, which my mother had read aloud. In this he said, 'The Willamette Valley is the Garden of Eden. Adam and Eve left here shortly before my arrival.' I was very fond and proud of my brother and nobody could make me believe that he would tell what wasn't true, so I was all anxiety to reach Portland so I could have my brother point out to me the tree of good and evil.

"I could hardly stand the delay we had in San Francisco. We put up in San Francisco at Hill's Temperance House. It was located over the water on piling near the foot of Sansome Street. Olive Oatman and four half-breed children were staying at the hotel. This itself was very thrilling, for before I left Ohio some boy friends had told me that I would probably either be kidnaped or scalped by the Indians and maybe both. We missed the regular steamer for Portland and were told we would have to await its return to go north on its next trip, but after three days the officials of the steamship company told us they were putting on an extra boat and to get ready at once to leave aboard the Santa Cruz.

"Compared to the steamers we had traveled on the Santa Cruz seemed to me to be a very insignificant little boat. There were about 20 of us passengers and we were crowded into a cabin that should have accommodated not more than ten. It was so small that I asked Father if I would have to sit still to keep it from rolling. The eating accommodations were pretty fierce. At mealtimes the table would be lowered from the ceiling in front of the berths in which we slept. An old woman who occupied the berth next to mine, every time the table was lowered at mealtime, invariably became seasick, with a resulting rush of the rest of us to the deck to feed the fishes. Fortunately this chronically seasick old lady left the boat at Crescent City.

"The captain of the Santa Cruz was new to the route. In those days the ships were not equipped with charts of the Columbia River or the coast. We were too far offshore when we came opposite the mouth of the Columbia, so the captain kept up the coast, finally overtaking a small schooner off the coast of British Columbia. We turned around, hugged the shore on the way back, discovered the mouth of the Columbia and finally reached Astoria. The captain ran across a farmer in Astoria who knew the river and was going up to Kalama, so he hired this farmer to pilot us the rest of the way up. He agreed to stay in the pilot house with the captain and pilot him on up to Portland if the captain would give his Indian family free transportation.

"The farmer brought his squaw on board and a good-sized family of children from a 16-year-old girl down to a baby that was strapped on a board without a stitch of clothing on. My mother made all of the men leave the cabin and she and the other women started in with the baby and scrubbed the girl children clear on up to the 16-year-old and also made the squaw take a bath. The women folks rustled clothing for the Indian children, so when they came out they were fairly presentable. At mealtime the captain gave the old Indian the food, and the squaw and the children sat on the deck, and the way they waded into the rations was a caution. The old farmer proved to be a good pilot. We arrived at the foot of Morrison Street sometime during the night of March 7, 1858.

"When we arrived in Portland we took the stern-wheel steamer Express, which at that time was under the command of Captain James Strang. When I looked at the Express I felt certain that it would turn over before we reached Milwaukie. It was built at Oregon City and was 111 feet long with a 20-foot beam. It is curious that when I was a boy I had a deadly fear of the water. I had no idea that I was going to spend my life on the water. When I learned that it was only six miles to Milwaukie I volunteered to walk.

"(When we arrived at Milwaukee) the rest of the family went uptown, leaving me to guard the baggage. I put in an hour or two skipping rocks on the river. I happened to look back of me and my heart almost stopped beating. Some Indians were coming. I was nearly ten years old--too old to cry and, I thought sadly, too young to die. My legs said, 'Run', but my courage said 'Stay'. One of the Indians had a hatchet hanging from his belt and I could also see a wicked-looking butcher knife , in his scabbard. I knew that my time had come to die. I was almost petrified with fear, but I put my hand on one of the trunks and stuck to my post. I couldn't sell my life bravely, nor dearly, nor any other way, for I knew the minute I stooped down to pick up a rock the Indian would grab me and scalp me. I gave one despairing look toward where my folks had disappeared and to my joy I saw three white boys coming toward me as fast as they could come. Just back of them was a team being driven by my brother. I had always loved my brother devotedly, but I never ealized how much I loved him till I saw him coming and knew that the Indians were not going to lift my scalp.

"We piled our baggage into the rig and I insisted that the three boys who had rescued me climb on the wagon and go with us. We drove to the home of Captain John T. Kerns, who at that time was the leading merchant of Milwaukie. I could hardly believe my eyes, for next to his store was a block of land with a lot of fruit trees in bloom. There was also a garden with some peas three feet high in full blossom. My brother had written to us that the Willamette Valley was the Garden of Eden. When he saw me looking with such fascination at the blooming fruit trees he said, 'What's the matter, Ed?'

"Pointing to the trees, I said, 'Is this the Garden of Eden that you wrote us about?'

"He looked puzzled for a moment, then smiled and said, 'Yes, it's one of them.'

"That puzzled me, for I had often heard Mother read in the Bible and I had never heard her read about any but one Garden of Eden and the Bible didn't say where that one was located.

"Father started a hotel, which he called the Ohio House.

"Before we came to Oregon my father and mother had frequent debates about the matter. My father's parents lived in Vermont and were well-to-do. They wrote Father saying that if he and his family would move to Vermont and take care of them till their death they would leave all their property to Father. My father thought this would be a good thing to do, but Mother said that no house was large enough for two families and she didn't care to move in her mother-in-law's house. It so happened that my mother had a bachelor brother who was wealthy. I don't know whether Mother wrote to him or whether he just happened to make the offer. In any event, he wrote Mother that he was tired of trying out housekeepers and that he had a home that needed someone to care for it, so that if we would come there and live with him he would pay all expenses and leave his property to my mother. My father refused to be a parasite and live off my mother's brother, so coming to Oregon was really a compromise.

"After we reached Oregon both my father and mother were constantly bringing up the matter. My mother would say, 'If we had only gone to my brother's', and that, of course, would make Father mad and he would say, 'What we should have done was to have gone back to Vermont to take care of my father and mother.' The more they talked about it the less they could agree, so finally they agreed to disagree, and the year after we arrived here in Oregon they separated. I was 11 years old at the time.

"In these days when the young folks are constantly running to the divorce court to turn in their life partner on a new model, divorce is not considered a disgrace, but back in 1859, when my father and mother were divorced, not only the divorced couples were looked at askance, but the children of divorced parents were pariahs and were treated as if they themselves were responsible, and were held up as terrible examples. My older brother and my sister were old enough to look out for themselves. The kids I played with told me how terrible it would be if my mother married again and I had a stepfather, so I, though only 11 years old, beat it and struck out for myself. I became the mascot for some gamblers in Portland I stayed at the American Exchange Hotel. I helped around the hotel and I also sold papers, blacked boots, and gathered old iron and bottles and picked up money in any and every way I could.

"My mother's was one of the first divorces secured in Milwaukie. In the latter part of 1859 a divorce had been granted in Multnomah County. The woman claimed that her husband came home in the evening and when she wanted to kiss him he would say 'Klat-a-wa,' which was the Indian term for 'Beat it.' She secured her divorce. My mother divorced Father and was soon married again. I felt humiliated and disgraced. If I saw people I knew, I would walk by on the other side of the street.

"I got a job working for Mr. Meek, who ran a nursery. A man named Ingram was working for him. He had a good-sized family but all of his children were girls. Mr. Ingram asked me how I would like to come and be his boy, as he had no son. I didn't like my stepfather, so I accepted Mr. Ingram's offer gladly. He arranged for me to be bound out to him. He was a good man, all right, but there was divided authority there. I had too many bosses. He was my boss, so was his wife, and so was one of the older girls.

"Mr. Ingram was away from home most of the time. After I had been there about two years things became so strenuous that, with all the money I had in the world, which amounted to 40 cents, and all of my possessions tied up in my handkerchief, I ran away. At East Portland I had to pay my fare over to Portland on the Stark Street Ferry, whose motor power was two husky mules.

"I landed a job working for my board in the American Exchange Hotel. At that time the American Exchange Hotel was the headquarters of the gambling and sporting fraternity of Portland. I became the mascot of the gamblers. One of the leading gamblers became responsible for me. He told me that if he ever caught me gambling he would break every bone in my body, that gambling was a crooked game and a man never got anywhere who lived on the earnings of others. He issued a general order that if he ever caught any man in Portland encouraging me or allowing me to buck any game of chance, that man would have to answer to him.

"The gamblers had a kitty, to which they all contributed, and from which I was outfitted. They dressed me in the height of fashion. They had a plug hat made for me. I had smoked a pipe since I was a small boy, but they said now that I was 13 a pipe was not rich enough for my blood, so they furnished me all the cigars I could use. I wasn't allowed to associate with boys of my own age, nor would they let me have a dog. They told me I was a gentleman and must act like a gentleman. But many a time when they weren't looking I would sneak out into a back alley and would pet and fondle some homeless cur.

"My mother found I was in Portland. Mr. Ingram told my mother that she must hunt me up and that I must either return to his home or the adoption papers must be canceled. Mother sent word to the gamblers that she wanted to have a conference with them. The man who had taken me under his protection met Mother at the American House and told her that I was in much better condition physically and in every other way than when I was doing the work of a scullion at the American Hotel. Mother thanked him for the care he had taken of me and the money he had spent on me but wanted me to come home. I refused to go home and live with my stepfather, so the gambler told Mother that he would arrange to board me in a private home. He took me to Mother Malone, an Irish widow, on the corner of 4th and Morrison Streets. I worked there for my board and when Mother urged me to come home I threatened to run away if I couldn't stay with Mother Malone, so I was allowed to stay there.

"I took a gambler to Mother Malone's for dinner one day and he liked her cooking so much that he brought another gambler, and before long there were 15 or 20 gamblers boarding with her.

"A lot of gamblers had flocked to Portland from Idaho and Montana and their camp followers had come with them. The city papers began an

300

agitation for better conditions in Portland. One day one of the city papers in commenting on the situation said that Mother Malone's boarding house was the hangout for gamblers and thugs and that birds of a feather flocked together. A delegation of gamblers went down to the newspaper office and asked to see the editor, and one of them, pointing a revolver at the editor, said, 'If you do not publicly apologize for what you have said about Mother Malone, your friends will be buying flowers for your funeral within a week!' The next issue of the paper carried a retraction of the article.

"As a matter of fact, it wasn't safe for an honest man to be on the streets after dark if he had money in his pockets. It wasn't the gamblers who took away his money, but it was a gang of bushwhackers who had come to the Coast to live by their wits.

"One day a well-known citizen was shot down in cold blood. Some of the influential citizens of Portland swooped down on Washington Street, threw the paraphernalia of the Dennison Opera House, the den of the tough element, into the street, and gave the idle men in town 24 hours to make themselves scarce. Next morning Mother Malone's tables looked empty, for practically all of her boarders had flitted.

"I was also notified to leave. I went to the head of the committee, laid my cards on the table, and said, 'I have associated with the gamblers socially, but not professionally.' This man told me to go home. I explained to him that my stepfather made home a hell-on-earth, so he told me that if I would go to work I would not have to leave town. I landed a job on the river, running between Portland and the Cascades.

"My stepfather bought a steamer, the Pioneer, from the Columbia River to Yaquina Bay to handle the summer excursionists who went by the hundred to Newport, on Yaquina Bay, which was the leading beach resort on the Oregon coast at that time.

"Yaquina Bay was more than a summer resort. It was the Gretna Green where young folks from Albany and Corvallis or elsewhere in the valley could come down and for a dollar or so be taken out beyond the three-mile limit on the schooner Mist and have Captain Hoxie pronounce the words that made them husband and wife. In those days you didn't have to have any license, and a sea marriage was legal.

"My stepfather, Dr. Kellogg, while coming from Astoria to Yaquina Bay, decided that there should be some lighthouses along the coast, so he invited H. W. Corbett, who was United States Senator from Oregon at that time, to come down in company with W. S. Ladd, Portland banker, and some other influential men to inspect Yaquina Bay with the idea of installing lights there. It was after their visit that my stepfather decided to go back to Corvallis to resume his practice of medicine and put me in as captain of the Pioneer.

"In the '60s Yaquina Bay was a part of the Siletz Reservation. White men were not allowed to cut wood, so we had to depend upon the Indians to supply us with cordwood to operate our boat. The Indian agent was rather touchy and whenever he would get offended he would forbid the Indians to furnish us wood. We would have to tie up the boat until we could bribe some Indian or Indians to supply our needs. In those days a white man marrying a squaw was entitled to all the privileges of an Indian on the reservation. I finally decided that the only way to settle the wood question was to have some member of my crew marry a squaw so we could depend upon a steady supply of cordwood. Personally, I didn't care to offer myself. My brother, who was my chief officer, also refused. My chief engineer had served as a soldier on the Siletz Reservation, but he also refused. Our deckhands and firemen were Indians. This left only one member of the crew as a possible candidate for matrimonial honors. This was our Negro cook, Charley.

"One day I tied up at the wood yard and found that the Indians had been forbidden to furnish us wood. All hands went ashore and gathered chips, driftwood, limbs and trash--enough to complete our journey. I called Charley up to the pilot house and said, 'Charley, I want you to do something for me. We've got to get some wood some way and there is only one way to get it.'

"Charley said, 'All you have to do, Captain, is to call on me. I'll do anything I can.'

"I said, 'Charley, I want you to get married. You're only getting $60 a month as cook on the boat. If I have to tie the boat up for lack of wood you'll be out of a job, and I know that your finances are at dead low water. I am going to make you a proposition that will put you on Easy Street as long as steamboats ply on the waters of Yaquina Bay.'

"Charley said, 'What will my getting married have to do with it, and who would marry me, anyway?'

"I said, 'Don't worry about that end of the proposition. I'll secure a wife for you and I'll give you a contract for 200 cords of wood. You can hire your wife's relatives to do the work and all you'll have to do will be to boss them and collect the money.'

302

"He said, 'You all want me to marry a squaw. Is that it?'

"I said, 'You have hit the nail on the head, Charley. That's just what I want. I have picked out a wife for you and she is no cheap $50 girl. I am going to pay old Coquille Tom $125 for his youngest daughter, Lucy.'

"Charley shook his head and said, 'Captain, I could never learn to talk her language, so how would we ever get along?'

"I said, 'You don't have to learn her language. Teach her to speak English. All you have to do is to pick up a knife and say 'knife' and have her repeat it after you, and then pick up a spoon and say 'spoon', and have her repeat it, and so on till she learns to say all the things in the kitchen.'

"Charley had to go down to the galley to attend to supper, but after supper I had him come up again and said to him, 'If you'll do it I'll give you a new blue suit with brass buttons. You can make an awful splurge with your wife's relatives and I'll have my mother fix Lucy up so she'll be a bride you can be proud of.'

"Charley said, 'All right, Captain. I'll do it. When do you want me to get married?'

"I sent one of my Indian boys up to old Tom's teepee and told him to bring Lucy and her father down to the boat. Lucy had worked for my mother and knew how to use a knife and fork. Charley spread himself and served a fine dinner. Lucy's father ate with his fingers, with the exception of his soup, and he drank that. After I had paid old Coquille Tom $125 for Lucy I said to Charley, 'Do you want to be married to Lucy Indian style or white man's style?'

"Charley said, 'If she's going to be my wife I want to be sure enough married. No Indian style for me!'

"I knew that a Methodist minister was coming in that night, so I got my mother, my youngest sister, and a couple of women campers busy and they cut down two of my mother's dresses for Lucy. My sister gave her a pair of shoes and stockings and Lucy made a very presentable bride. As soon as the minister arrived I had the ceremony performed and then I told Charley that he had better make a wedding trip with his wife and some of his wife's brothers and cousins to the woodyard so he could have wood enough cut to make a round trip.

"The tide served the next day, so I arrived at the woodyard at noon. And glory be! Stacked up on the bank was six cords of wood. Charley came aboard and I paid him for the six cords of

303

wood and he had some of his Indian relatives put it aboard for me.

"I said, 'Charley, is Lucy learning to talk?'

"Charley laughed and said, 'You told Lucy in jargon to listen to what I said and repeat it after me. I pointed to a sack of potatoes, to Lucy, and then pointed to a kettle. When I got back Lucy had the potatoes all peeled and ready and she had put ten pounds of beans in a kettle and put them on to cook. I looked at that big lot of beans, and, pointing to Lucy, I said, 'You are a hell of a cook.' Lucy pointed at me and repeated, 'You are a hell of a cook.' I laughed, so she thought she had pleased me, and kept repeating, 'You are a hell of a cook.''

"Within a few months Lucy was talking a pretty good brand of English, with a strong Negro accent.

"You have seen the miles and miles of whitened tree trunks along the coast. This big fire in the late '60s swept the coast from Coos Bay to Tillamook. The fallen timber completely blocked the Corvallis and Yaquina Bay wagon road. The company that had built this road was paid in land and, as it had already received its payment, it didn't feel called upon to reopen the road. This meant that the summer campers could no longer drive down to the beach, so my stepfather, Dr. Kellogg, not wanting to run the Pioneer at a loss, ordered me to remove the boiler and machinery and moor the boat a short distance up the Yaquina River over a gravel bar so if it sank the hull would be out of the water at low tide.

"Putting the boat out of commission meant that Stormy Jordan and I were out of a job. Someone told us that they were wanting good steamboat men at Coos Bay, so we decided to go over to Coos Bay. We started out June 20 with 45-pound packs on our backs.

"I hated to leave Yaquina Bay, for I knew every man, woman, and Indian in that country. The first night we camped on the Alsea River. The second night we camped at the mouth of the Yachats River. Old Stormy went to the stream, filled the coffee pot with water, came back to the fire and, adding the coffee, put it on to boil.

"Just after starting we had joined two other men, Joe Curliss and Pike Hunsaker. Joe and Pike sat on one side of the blanket and Stormy and I on the other. I took a few slices of bacon on my plate and began peeling a boiled potato. Stormy poured the coffee. Pike said, 'This looks like good coffee,' and he took one swallow, looked sort of

304

dazed, and set his coffee cup down and went on eating.

"What's the matter with the coffee?' asked Stormy.

"Pike said, 'It's pretty hot. I'll wait a while.'

"Joe tried his coffee, strangled a little, and then set it down.

"I knew old Stormy was a bad man to fool with. He had put one notch in his revolver since I knew him. Stormy passed back of me, reached into my bunk, and got my dragoon Colt's revolver. He picked the biscuit from the floor, put it down beside Charley Day's plate and, stepping back, covered us with the revolver, told Charley to eat the biscuit if he knew what was good for him, and said, 'Anyone here who says I don't make good biscuits is a liar.'

"Stormy picked up his cup of coffee and said, 'If there is anything I like, it's a cup of good strong coffee.' He said, 'Here's looking at you,' and he took a good swallow. Stormy jumped up, half strangled, and I thought he would choke to death. I hammered him on the back, while Joe and Pike sat there slapping their legs and laughing like hyenas. Stormy had not realized that the tide was coming in, so he had made the coffee with salt water.

"Joe, Pike and myself took a blanket and, going down to the rocks under the north end of Cape Perpetua, we loaded our blanket with mussels

305

from the rocks. Stormy put on a kettle of water, which was soon boiling, and we spent the next hour or so feasting on mussels.

"Next morning we got an early start. The trail led around the north end of the cape till we struck the cliff. The Indians had cut niches in the rock for footholds. I happened to look down and saw the breakers foaming on the black rocks several hundred feet below. I began to get dizzy. My companions were following me, so I couldn't go back. Joe saw that I was trembling, so he said, 'Shift your blanket to your other shoulder, Ed, so you can't see below you.'

"About the center of the cliff there was a crevice about 18 inches across. I don't know yet how I got across that. It looked wide enough to drive a four-mule team through. You can't imagine how grateful I was when we had worked our way across the face of the cliff and once more struck the trail.

"We camped at the mouth of the Siuslaw River that night, and the next night we camped at the mouth of the Umpqua. A white man and his squaw met us as they came up from the beach carrying a number of large hakes. We stopped at his house that night and had hake for supper and also for breakfast. Next morning as we took our way southward along the beach we found thousands of hakes along the water's edge. The hakes are gluttons. They don't exactly dig their grave with their teeth, like folks do, but they rush into the surf in pursuit of small fish and are washed ashore.

"We hoisted the flag when we came to Winchester Bay and soon the ferryman came across and ferried us over. As we approached the ferryman's house I heard someone singing 'Annie Laurie' and I could smell the delicious odor of bacon frying. We had already had breakfast, but I wanted to see the owner of that voice, so I told the ferryman I was going to stand treat and we would have breakfast with him.

"Joe and Pike had quit us at the mouth of the Umpqua. They stayed there to shoot sea lions for their oil. Stormy was willing to eat another breakfast. I fell for the food, but I fell harder for the young woman who brought in our breakfast. I discovered all sorts of reasons why I should stay over, but the ferryman, when I asked him what the bill was, said, 'You don't owe me anything, but you'd better be on your way, my lad.' So that was that.

"There was no work for steamboatmen at Coos Bay, so I landed a job at $80 a month getting out Port Orford cedar logs for George Sanford, one of the squarest and best men I ever worked for. We were logging on the Warren ranch. He agreed to pay me $80 a month, but when he paid me off after we had finished the work he paid me at the rate of $100 a month.

"When I sized up the men I was going to work with I decided they were a pretty tough bunch. Some of them could hardly navigate when they came into camp. The man that drove the bulls was a sawed-off little Irishman. When he stood beside his ox team his head was just about even with the top of the near ox's back. When he had to goad the off ox he had to jump in the air and reach over the near ox. Our hooktender was a big-footed, big-handed, clumsy Swede. He not only knew his work, but he worked all the time for Sanford's interests. No log was to large for him, and no matter what came up, he always came up smiling.

"When I asked for and landed the job, my companion, Old Stormy, an inveterate gambler, said to the man, 'Don't you want a cook?'

"Mr. Sanford said, 'Yes. I can use a good cook.' So he hired Stormy.

"When Mr. Sanford had left I said to Stormy, 'Why did you take a job as cook? You know mighty well that you can't cook water without burning it.'

"Stormy said, 'Your mother is one of the best cooks I ever ate after, and she taught you to cook, so all I will have to do is to let you coach me a while and I can get by.' I coached him for several days, but I was working hard at my own job so I told him he would have to shift for himself.

"After two or three days I came into the cook shanty and I said, 'For heaven's sake, Stormy, what are you trying to do?'

"Stormy said, 'Sanford bought me some of that damned 'vaporated rice that swells not only once its size but ten times its size. As soon as the beans are done supper will be ready.'

"I said, 'Where are the beans?'

"He pointed to the oven. He had put about a quart or so of dry navy beans in a pan to bake. I took off my coat and went to work. I set Stormy to peeling apples for apple sauce. I found a can of baking powder, mixed dough enough for biscuits, had Stormy put some potatoes on to boil, made some coffee, and put the steak on to fry. I taught Stormy how to set sourdough bread. He fed every logger that come our way and ran out of bread. He decided to make a batch of biscuits. The sourdough had run out, so he put as much soda into the biscuits as he did when the dough was sour. He called out to the crew, 'Come and get it. It's on the table.'

"I have eaten Indian bread, Chinese bread, and pilot bread, but I never tackled anything that could compare with Stormy's biscuits. They were as yellow as gold and as hard as nails. Big Charley Day, one of our crew, soaked one in his coffee for a while and then tried to bite a chunk out of it. It was no go. He threw the biscuit against the wall and it bounced back just as old Stormy came out of the kitchen. Everyone at the table except Sanford and myself were convulsed with laughter. I knew old Stormy was a bad man to fool with. He had put one notch on his revolver since I knew him. My bunk was just back of where I sat. Stormy passed back of me, reached into my bunk and got my dragoon Colt's revolver. He picked the biscuit from the floor, put it down beside Charley Day's plate and, stepping back, covered us with the revolver, told Charley to eat the biscuit if he knew what was good for him, and said, 'Anyone here who says I don't make good biscuits is a liar. What are you going to do about it?' We saw that Stormy meant business, so we all ate his biscuits and assured him he was a good cook.

"The first week I was in camp, George Sanford and I built a shed to store hay and grain for the oxen. When the shed was finished, Sanford said, 'You and I will do some swamping today.'

"I was absolutely green about the logging business. Sanford started up the hill and I noticed that the slough swung around to the right. I was sorry I had no gum boots if we were going to work in the swamp. When we had got pretty well up on the table land, Sanford pulled off his coat and said, 'We might as well start here.' Off to the left some distance was the swamp, and it was so soft that a mosquito would mire in it. The men had been playing all sorts of jokes on me and by this time I was fed up on being made the butt of anybody's jokes. I said to Mr. Sanford, 'If you want to fire me, say so. Don't try to make a fool of me. You said that we were going to do some swamping and here you come up on top of this table land, where it is as dry as a bone, and tell me to commence here.'

"Sanford saw that I was mad. He tried not to laugh, but the more he tried not to, the more he laughed. I became furious and started for him. He said, 'Hold on, Captain. let me explain. Don't think for a moment that if I want to fire you I haven't manhood enough to say so. Swamping is the term loggers use for making roads so logs can be hauled out to the rollway. The next time anyone tells you to do any swamping, he means to build a road.'

"One time I had worked out my brother's poll tax. The road supervisor had been very particular about having no rocks or ruts left, so I decided that Mr. Sanford should have no cause for complaint with my work. I took off my vest and before long I took off my woolen shirt. During the next few hours I cleared 200 feet of road that no one could find any objections to. When Mr. Sanford came back he stopped as if someone had held a gun in his face and he said, 'Why, Captain, you're building a regular wagon road. You have put in enough work here to swamp out half a dozen logs in a row. All you need to do is to cut out the large stuff so the cattle won't have to climb over it. Put on your shirt, wipe the sweat off your face, and we'll go down to camp. You've done a day's work already.

"From then on my job was doing swamping, but I was always anxious to lend a hand at any other work.

"One day Sanford said to me, 'You're a green-horn, and yet you're at work all the time, and work hard. You're setting pace for the other men. I'll remember it when payday comes.'

"One day I heard our Irish bullwhacker cursing and swearing, and our Swede hooktender was also talking pretty loud. I went over there and I found they had been trying to start the butt cut of a cedar log ten feet in diameter and 16 feet long. The Irishman was beating the oxen and the Swede was using the goad as if he was harpooning a school of whales and was afraid one would get away. Our bullwhacker said to me, 'Run down the rollway and bring up a Samson.'

"I went down there and saw a big husky six-footer, strong as a bull moose, so I brought him back with me. The Irishman said, 'What in hell do you mean by bringing this fellow up when I asked you for a Samson?'

"I peeled off my coat and started for the Irishman. He ran around the other side of the oxen and explained to me what a Samson was. It's a slab of wood about eight inches wide, four inches thick, and three feet long. The man I had called went down the rollway and brought up a Samson. The team was backed up and the Samson set on end under the chain, tipped back at an angle of 45 degrees toward the log, so that when the oxen pulled, the Samson would lift the log out of its bed in the mud.

"One day Sanford said to me, 'We've about cleaned up on this work. You had better gather up all the saws, axes, canthooks, chains, mauls and wedges and store them in the feed shed.'

"When I had done so, Sanford said, 'Did you bring in the spudding-tool?'

"'No,' I replied, 'but if you tell me where it is I will go and get it.'

"''I left it where you and I commenced swamping the first day we went to work,' he responded.

"I had no idea what a spudding-tool was, but I thought it was a slang phrase for some kind of shovel used to dig spuds, as we usually called potatoes. When I went to where Sanford directed me all I saw was a handle with a sort of bent chisel on the lower end. I supposed it had been thrown away. I went back to the cook house and told Sanford there was no spudding-tool there. He said, 'I left it standing against a big spruce stump.'

"I brought back the crooked chisel and to my surprise learned that it was used to remove bark and was called a spudding-tool."

Oregon Journal
July 7-14, 1931
January 7, 9, 15, 16, 1932

## William J. Barker
## Portland, Oregon

"No, sir, I didn't get mixed up in any war. I was too young for the Civil War and too old for the World War. I'm not very strong for war. It makes people hate one another and leaves things worse than they were before."

Oregon Journal
April 14, 1934

## John Chapman
## Middleton, Oregon

"When I was in McMinnville running a blacksmith shop I called it a good day if I shod 20 to 25 horses. The largest number I ever shod in one day was 40, and, believe me, you have done a day's work when you have shod 40 horses in a day. I used to build buggies, also. It looked for a while as if horses and buggies had gone into discard, but now you will see lots of farms being plowed with horses in place of tractors, and you can see an occasional team on the road."

Oregon Journal
March 30, 1933

# Oliver H. P. Beagle
## Pioneer of 1843
## Roseburg, Oregon

"You won't find many pioneers who crossed the plains in 1843. I have lived in Oregon 84 years, and I was 11 when I crossed the plains in 1843.

"My father, William Beagle, was born in Kentucky. My mother, whose maiden name was Lucinda Thompson, also was a Kentuckian. I was born in Kentucky on July 6, 1832.

"Peter H. Burnett, the first captain of our wagon train, hailed from the Platte Purchase. We came with the Applegates, from St. Clair County. There were about 300 in our wagon train capable of bearing arms.

"My recollection of Jesse, Charles, and Lindsay Applegate is very clear. I also remember distinctly Peter H. Burnett, Captain William Martin, J. N. Nesmith, and scores of others in the wagon train.

"One time Peter Burnett, Mr. Lennox, his boy, Father and myself went out to get a buffalo. The Lennox boy and I held the horses while Peter Burnett and my father went out to get a big bull they had seen. The bull got away from them. I saw he was coming in our direction, so I tied the horses I was holding to some sagebrush, and as he galloped by I shot at him. I happened to hit him in a vital spot. He ran about 100 yards and fell. When Father and Peter Burnett came up they butchered him and took his rump, loin, and tongue back to the wagon train. We crossed the Platte by stretching fresh hides of buffaloes over our wagon boxes.

"The wagon train usually got under way by seven o'clock. They were divided into platoons of four wagons each. Dr. Marcus Whitman traveled with us, for he and A. L. Lovejoy had made a winter trip back east in the winter of 1842 and he was on his way back to his mission. Peter Burnett served as captain for a short while after starting then resigned and William Martin was elected captain.

"On the Big Blue River our wagon train divided. William Martin and the lighter rigs went forward, while Jesse Applegate took command of the other division,, called the Cow Column. The settlers with stock, who wanted to travel more slowly, went with Jesse Applegate. The two columns traveled more or less together as far as Independence Rock. After passing Fort Hall, where there was no more danger of Indians, the wagon train broke up and it became a 'go as you please'. Captain Martin turned off beyond Fort Hall for California. When we came to the Grand Ronde a Nez Perce Indian met Dr. Whitman and told him that Mr. and Mrs. Spalding, at the Lapwai Mission, were sick, so Dr. Whitman got a Cayuse Indian named Stickas to guide us.

"There were five children in our family when we crossed the plains. Father settled on the Tualatin Plains. They put up a schoolhouse near our place in 1844. William Geiger was hired as teacher. He had come to Oregon in 1839. He died in Forest Grove in 1901. Matilda Jane Sager, who later married Mr. Delaney, and I went to school together at Forest Grove. She and her sisters and brothers had been adopted by Dr. and Mrs. Whitman. Her brothers were killed during the massacre.

"Among the other children who went to school at Forest Grove in '45 and '46 were Joe Meek's and Mr. Ebbert's children and the Pomeroy and Lennox children. I went to school in Forest Grove from 1846 to 1848. Harvey Clark and Grandma Tabitha Brown had a school there.

"In 1855 I enlisted in Captain Joseph Bailey's company for the Rogue River War. From Eugene we went to the Six-Bit House, and from there on south, where we fought the battle of Hungry Hill. The regulars and the volunteers were in the Cow Creek and Grave Creek country and were about to attack the Indians when our company and a company commanded by Samuel Gordon arrived. They assigned our two companies the job of going around the edge of the hill to the north to get the Indians when Captain Rinearson and Captain Welton charged the Indians' position and drove them out. The Indians, however, refused to be driven out. Captain Smith, with his dragoons, charged the Indians, but was unable to dislodge them and some of the regulars were killed. At dark the troops went into camp at Bloody Spring and next morning at sunrise the Indians attacked us. This was called the Battle of Hungry Hill. The volunteers lost 26 men killed, wounded, and missing. John Gillespie of our company was killed and John Walden, John Richardson, Jim Laphar, Tom Aubrey and John Pankey were wounded.

"We followed the Indians to the meadows and our spies reported the Indians on the opposite side of the river. We fixed up a raft to cross, but the Indians, hidden in the brush on the other side, fired at the men launching the raft, so we withdrew. I served 3 months and 14 days.

"In the fall of 1856 I left our place, six miles from Eugene, and went to Jacksonville, and next spring I went to Suisun City. We bought govern-ment land, but it turned out to be land that could be taken up by the railroad, so I lost out.

"I was married on April 27, 1852, to Mary Melvina Crisp, youngest daughter of Major Crisp, who served in the War of 1812. When we lost out on our first place we went to Santa Rosa and I bought on Russian River. Later we moved to Humboldt County, where I ran cattle. In 1862, with my brothers John and Jim, I went up to what is now Idaho, but was then Washington Territory, to prospect.

"Jim and I sunk a hole at what was later known as Florence, and struck rich pay dirt. We had no grub. Jim and John wanted to stake claims, but I told them if we staked claims they would probably be jumped, while if we left the hole we had dug anyone coming that way would conclude we had tried our luck, found nothing, and gone on, so they wouldn't prospect the place. We started for Walla Walla to get grub, intending to come back at once and stake claims. My reasoning was good, but in this case it didn't pan out. A party of prospeting miners ran across the hole and decided to see if there was anything there. They got four ounces of gold out of a few panfuls. One of the party got drunk and told about it. Instantly there was a stampede. We learned of it, so we didn't even go back, for we knew all the claims would be taken. Instead, we went to the newly discovered district at Auburn.

"John and I went up Powder River about 20 miles and I said, 'John, let's unpack. If we sink a hole to bedrock here I know we'll strike colors.'

"We sunk a hole and struck good dirt. I was anxious to get back to Yamhill County to get my wife, so I sold my third interest in this claim for $500 to a settler and started back to The Dalles, where I had left three horses. I brought my wife up from Yamhill County and we wintered in the Grand Ronde Valley. Next spring we went to Idaho City. I bought a quarter interest in a claim there for $140. Water was scarce and we could only have water from the ditch one night a week--Sunday night. Another ditch was brought in, so we arranged to get water every other day. We averaged $100 a day to the man from that claim. That fall I sold my quarter interest for $2500 and located my wife at La Grande while I bought a bunch of mules and started packing supplies into the mines at 25 cents a pound."

"I sold my mule train to my brothers and moved back to the Willamette Valley. I bought a place near McMinnville, where I raised hay and ran cattle. In 1876 I went up to Idaho again and bought acreage that is now a part of Moscow. I freighted from the railroad to town. I was there 15 years.

"After my wife died I went in with my brothers Frank and Ben and for a while we prospected and ran a pack train. Later I got them to go on a ranch with me and we raised cattle and horses. We ran this ranch 11 years, when we sold out and moved to Pendleton. My sister, my two brothers, and I then moved to Virginia. After having lived in Oregon, however, we found we were not happy in Virginia, so we moved back and I bought a place in the Umpqua Valley.

**Oregon Journal**
July 13 & 14, 1927

# Charles Porter Barnard
# Freighter
# Lane County, Oregon

"I have been working for myself since I was 21. I say 'working for myself,' and by that I mean that I have not been punching time clocks and getting a salary from someone else. But no one works for himself alone. They work for their family and for their community and to keep each other employed.

"More than 30 years ago I began taking contracts to carry the mail into Coos Bay. Think back to 30 years ago and you will remember that the roads between the Willamette Valley and the coast were roads in name only. In places in the Coast mountains they were deep with mud and in other places there was corduroy that when in disrepair was as bad or worse than mud. My stages traveled 25,000 miles every 90 days, doubling 64 miles to Myrtle Point and 78 miles to Empire City every 24 hours. I averaged to carry 1500 pounds of mail on the westbound trip on each of these roads every day in the year. In summer we could take it in by stage but in winter we had to take it over the mountains on pack horses. Making 100,000 miles a year over all sorts of roads meant plenty of grief. If it wasn't broken springs or a runaway it was a holdup or something else.

"I remember the stage was held up in Camas Valley about 25 miles out of Roseburg. The driver told me he was going to carry a gun and he hoped that same holdup man would try it again. I said, 'You'd better leave your gun at home. Carrying a gun won't do you any good.'

"The same road agent held him up again a few weeks later and said to the driver in a kindly

314

way, 'I'll just take your navy six-gun away from you. You're nervous. The thing might go off and hurt someone. You shouldn't carry a gun. You might get in trouble some time.'

"The drummer who was a passenger was pretty much scared at the time but he enjoyed telling about it afterwards."

Oregon Journal
January 14, 1932

# Pack Trains, Ferries & Claims:
# Finances & Rules

*Running a packtrain or a ferry was frequently more profitable than prospecting and mining. In 1861 and 1862, D. W. Litchenthaler and John C. Smith operated a ferry across the Snake River near the mouth of Powder River. C. R. Griggs and Green White operated one across the Snake near the mouth of the Grand Ronde. John Messenger and Walter H Manly had a ferry on Salmon River on the Nez Perce trail to Fort Boise. Gilmore Hays ran a ferry across the Snake about a mile from the junction of the Clearwater. E. H. Lewis and Egbert French operated a ferry across the Columbia at The Dalles. W. D. Bigelow had a ferry across the Snake on the old territorial road between Walla Walla and Colville. W. F. Bassett and Lyman Shaffer operated a ferry across the south branch of the Clearwater on the wagon road from Lewiston to Orofino. W. W. DeLacy and Jerad S. Hurd had a ferry on the Snake between Grand Ronde and Powder Rivers. George A. Tykel graded a road over the bluff of Snake River to his ferry near the mouth of Powder River. Dick Holmes and Jim Clinton ran a ferry on the old Indian trail from Lapwai to Grand Ronde Valley across Salmon River. John Drumheller had a ferry on the Clearwater just above Lewiston. Sanford Owens had a toll bridge across the south branch of the Clearwater on the road between Lewiston and that city. The usual rates of toll were 50 cents for a foot passenger, two-horse wagon $2.50, four-horse wagon $3.50, six-horse wagon $4.50, and pack animals 75 cents.*

••••••••••••••••••••••••••••••••••••••••••••••••••••••

*Florence, one of the richest camps in Idaho, was soon worked out. In the winter of '61-62 flour was two dollars a pound and other supplies even higher. Many men without funds lived on one meal a day. The shortage continued from January till May, when men brought goods in over the mountains on their backs, charging 40 cents a pound for freight.*

In the spring of '62 there was a tremendous rush to Florence and the rich ground was worked out that season. Thousands of California miners came north to Portland aboard the Panama, Oregon, Sierra Nevada, Cortez and Brother Jonathan.

The first pack train out of the Florence mines came by way of Walla Walla to The Dalles, bringing 400 pounds of gold dust. The winter of '61-62 was so severe that it was the last of April before the pack trains could get into the Powder River country, and the middle of May before they were able to cross the mountains to the Salmon River district.

On Jacob Weiser's claim at Florence four men with two rockers took out $2688 in one day. On Miller's Creek, Baboon Gulch and Mason Gulches two men to the rocker averaged three to seven pounds a day. John M. Richey and Thomas Jeffrys of Portland happened to be at the Weiser claim when one day's clean-up, the work of five men, was weighed. It weighed $3327.

The Orofino was also a rich claim while it lasted, but by 1863 it had been abandoned by white men and the claims were being worked by Chinamen.

•••••••••••••••••••••••••••••••••••••••••••••••••••••••

At a mass meeting of miners at Orofino on January 5, 1861, a code of rules was adopted providing that each mining claim should consist of 150 feet up or down the gulch or stream and extending from bluff to bluff, but in no case to be more than 500 feet in depth. No claim was to be considered forfeited from December 1 to June 1 on Orofino Creek. Any claim not worked within 15 days from June 1 was considered forfeited. All claims must be worked at least one day in seven. Each miner was to have the privilege of a drain race through his claims and also the privilege of the water to work his claim on any tributary or creek. No person could take water from its natural channel without leaving at least one sluice-head of water running therein. A sluice-head of water was considered 30 square inches of running water. Each miner had the privilege of holding one creek, one hill, and one ravine claim. Any miner disabled by sickness could hold his claim without forfeit. Any person who pulled down or destroyed any notice on a mining claim was to be tried by a miners' court of inquiry. No person who held a mining claim should forfeit such claim by reason of being compelled to leave the district for provisions for himself or company, *provided he was not gone over 25 days.*

*Oregon Journal*
*July 14, 1927*

# Dick Carlson
# Salem, Oregon

"I was born in Sweden on December 6, 1862. My father was well-to-do and sent me to the University of Kalmon, where I put in seven years studying languages, literature, and other cultural subjects. I secured a white collar job, but I tired of its sameness and routine and decided to go to America. My brother Carl had gone to America and had a farm on Salem Prairie, four miles east of Salem, so, in 1887, I left my homeland.

"I bought a ticket for Salem, Oregon, and took along enough money to pay my expenses, but I had figured on the prices of meals in Sweden, not in the United States, and I was down to my last coin in Montana. I there spent my last dime for a cup of coffee, and from there to Salem I tightened my belt three times a day in place of eating.

"I reached Salem and struck out afoot for my brother's farm. It was long after dark when I reached what I thought was Carl's farm, but it wasn't. Two savage dogs came out, as though they would eat me up. I climbed over a fence into a wheat field and sat in a fence corner all night. I would have gone to sleep, but I had read so much about the savagery of the American Indians that I was afraid to go to sleep for fear the Indians might tomahawk me and scalp me while I was asleep. I was so green that it is a wonder the cows didn't eat me.

"In the morning at about daybreak I saw a man going out to feed the stock, and I hailed him to ask if he knew where my brother Carl lived. When he turned around I found it was Carl. I went with him to the house, and maybe I didn't do justice to my breakfast. I had slept in Caplinger's wheat field, and if I had gone to the next farm I would have located my brother. He got me a job on a threshing crew. I had never done hard work in my life and I came to the conclusion that one earned all he was paid for in this country.

"Later I landed a job at $1.50 a day for ten hours' work with the Capital Lumber Company, working in its sawmill. I later secured a job on a surveying crew on the Oregon Pacific. The road ran west from Albany to Yaquina, and east from

Albany to Detroit in the foothills of the west slope of the Cascades. The road was being surveyed eastward across the mountains to Boise. T. Egerton Hogg was promoting the building of the road. The crew quit because no pay was forthcoming. The chief engineer said to me, 'The men have all quit. All our equipment and supplies will be stolen if we leave them here. Will you stay here all winter and guard them? I will do my best to see that you are paid for your work.'

"I agreed to do so. I stayed up in the Cascades all winter, watching the supplies. The next spring the chief engineer rode out to where I was camped and told me that the plan to extend the road to Boise had been given up. He told me to hire some pack horses and bring the supplies into Albany.

"I delivered the supplies in Albany as ordered, and sent the pack horses back by a man I had hired to help me with the pack outfit. When I got a receipt for the goods from the chief engineer I turned in some cash to him. He looked surprised and said, 'What is this for?'

"I told him I had sold 50 cents worth of sugar and several sacks of flour and this was the money I had received for the supplies.

"He said, 'How long have you been in this country?'

"I said, 'Two years.'

"He said, 'That accounts for it.'

"My beard was down on my chest and my hair was on my shoulders. My clothes were shreds and patches. I registered at the Russ House in Albany and asked the clerk to stand my gun behind the desk for safe-keeping. The chief engineer gave me a note to Mr. Hogg. Mr. Hogg said, 'I am short of money, but inasmuch as you protected our supplies all winter and proved so faithful and responsible I am going to make an exception in your case and pay you.' So he gave me a check for what was due me. I took it to the bank and they offered to cash it if I would let them discount it. I agreed, and got my money in gold coin.

"I bought new shoes, a new suit, and a new outfit complete, went to a barber shop and took a bath and got a clean shave and a haircut. Then I put on my new clothes and went to the hotel and asked for the key to my room. The clerk looked at me and said, 'If you will register I will assign you to a room.'

"I told him I had registered, and I pointed to my signature on the hotel register. He shook his head and said, 'Nothing doing. That fellow is a wild man. He has long hair and a long beard like Santa Claus. That's his gun back of the counter.'

"I signed my name again. The clerk compared the signatures and sized me up, and said, 'One of us is crazy. I don't know which. I saw that fellow an hour or so ago. He is old enough to be your father. I never saw you before in my life.'

"I finally persuaded him that I was the 'wild man', so he gave me the key to my room.

"I went back to Salem and went to work in the sawmill. After a while I was offered a job as guard at the penitentiary. I worked there till 1900, when I resigned to become librarian of the I. O. O. F. I worked for Olive Lodge and when Olive Lodge and Chemeketa Lodge were consolidated I took on the additional duties of custodian. Chemeketa Lodge has never missed a regular weekly meeting since its organization on December 6, 1852."

**Oregon Journal**
December 23, 1925

# First Names

*Recently I invested $35.00 in an old map entitled "Lewis and Clark's Track Across the Western Part of North America From the Mississippi River to the Pacific Ocean by order of the Executive of the United States, Copied by Samuel Lewis From the original Drawing of William Clark: 1804-6".*

*The map shows the winter camp near the mouth of the Columbia River, of Lewis and Clark. It shows the Clatsop village of 200 souls of Indians and on the north bank of the Columbia it shows the Chinook village of 400 souls. North of the Chinooks it shows the Chilts village of 800 souls. Coming up the Columbia River it marks the site of the Cathlamah village of 300 souls. On the north side of the river near the banks of Wowelskee River it shows a village of 2500 souls of Skilute Indians.*

*Near the mouth of the Multnomah River—which we now call the Willamette River—it shows the Clackamas village of 1800 souls. The Snake Indians are located on the upper Willamette showing a population of about 10,000 souls, while the Cal-lah-po-e-wahs are shown just south of the Cal-lah-po-e-wah Mountains as having 3000 souls.*

*Going eastward on the Columbia above the mouth of the Willamette the following tribes are recorded: The Chil-luk-kit-te-quaws, 2400 souls; the E-che-boots, 1000 souls; the E-ne-shurs, 1200 souls; the Wah-how-pums, 1000 souls; the Skad-dals, 400 souls; the Squa-nu-ar-soos, 240 souls; the Pish-quit-pahs, 2600 souls; the Wol-law-wol-lahs, 2600 souls, and near this tribe, the Sel-lo-he-pal-lahs,*

319

*3000 souls. Farther to the eastward are the Cho-pun-nish Indians, 8000 souls.*

*In addition to these villages there are many smaller tribes mentioned and the rivers are hard to identify. For example, between the mouth of the Willamette and The Dalles is the River LaPage. At about where the Cascades are, are two rivers --one called To-war-na-he-wooks; the other, Ki-es-ho-we River. Just east of The Dalles is a river called You-ma-lo-lam, which I rather think is our Umatilla River.*

*There is much quaint information on the map, such as "These mountains are covered with snow," and other similar notes. Our Tillamook River is given as the Killamoucks River. Mount Jefferson, Mount Hood, and Mount St. Helens are all properly named, though Mount Rainier is called Mount Regniere.*

# Elijah C. Hills
# Portland, Oregon

"My father crossed the plains to the Willamette Valley in 1847. Father's name was Cornelius Joel Hills. He was born in New York state in 1818. Father took up a donation land claim of 640 acres at Jasper, in Lane County. Jasper post office was named for my brother, Jasper B. Hills, who was born there in April 19, 1859.

"My father came by way of the Southern Route. Isaac and Elias Briggs, Charles Martin, and Prior Blair took up claims at Pleasant Hill near the claim of Elijah Bristow, who had taken up a claim there the year before. My father settled on the north side of the middle fork of the Willamette River. The following year Elijah Bristow's family took up their residence there. Among others who settled in this neighborhood in the fall of 1848 were James and Caswell Hendricks, Michael and Harrison Shelley, Robert Callison, Abel, William, and E. L. Bristow, William Bowman, and Calvin T. Hale.

"My father went to the gold diggings in California in the fall of 1848. On July 22, 1849, my father, with Charnel Mulligan, Lester Hulin, James H. Chapin, Jason and Leonard Wheeler, William Shively, James Leabo, John Ellenburg, Mr. Walker and his son, with Mr. Churchill, Sexton, Vickers, and some others and seven men of the crew, making 31 in all, sailed from San Francisco for Astoria aboard the schooner W. L. Hackstaff, under command of Captain William White. This schooner registered about 90 tons. It had recently arrived in San Francisco from New York City, where for years it had served as a pilot vessel. Captain White was on his way to the Columbia River to serve with his schooner as a pilot on the Columbia River bar. All of the 24 passengers aboard were from the Willamette Valley. Each of the passengers had paid $100 fare from San Francisco to Astoria.

"Shortly after leaving San Francisco a heavy gale came up, so Captain White headed the schooner northwest. Instead of making the trip in six days, as expected, they were out of sight of land until the 15th day. Part of this time, after the gale had blown itself out, the schooner was becalmed. When they came in sight of the coast the captain could not tell whether they were off California or Oregon. A current set shoreward, which took the schooner close to shore. They had been out of fresh water for several days, so Charnel Mulligan, Lester Hulin and Sexton, with three sailors, took a rowboat with some kegs to see if they could find good drinking water to replenish the vessel's supply.

"When the rowboat approached the shore the men found nearly 100 Indians awaiting them. After one look at the painted Indians, with their bows and arrows ready for action, the men decided they were not as thirsty as they thought they were, so they rowed back to the schooner. Captain White thought they were off Monterey Bay, but the Oregonians believed, from the look of the Indians, that they were off the coast of northern California or southern Oregon. One of the sailors thought they had been blown far south and were off the coast of Mexico. James M. Chapin had been in southern Oregon the year before and was positive that they were off the coast of southern Oregon.

"A breeze sprang up and Captain White got the schooner under way. Seeing an inlet that he believed to be a river, he put a boat overboard and the sailors sounded the channel. They decided to run into the mouth of the river and fill their water casks. The schooner was headed inward for the channel. Before long the Hackstaff grounded. Apparently the vessel was high and dry, so the passengers took their baggage ashore in the boat.

"William Shively and a man named Hughes had laid in a stock of groceries in San Francisco. From the stock of groceries owned by Shively and Hughes each man was furnished flour, raisins and pickled pork. Jim Chapin recognized the river as the Rogue River, for he had been there before. They left the boat on August 8. Vickers was chosen captain of the company and Jim Chapin was elected guide.

"My father left his chest of carpenter tools aboard the boat, as well as his clothing and other things he could not carry. In fact, the passengers and crew brought ashore only what they could carry. Most of the men aboard were bringing home from five to 25 pounds of gold dust apiece. This, of course, they brought ashore with them.

"The Indians went aboard the schooner and carried ashore whatever they wanted. For some reason, game was scarce, and, as the men headed inland on the north side of the Rogue River they saw little or no game. After a few days the men began throwing away everything they did not need. Occasionally they saw a deer but were not able to get any. Finally, on the fifth day, James Leabo went ahead of the company and killed three deer. Some of the men were so hungry that they cut the throats of the deer and drank the blood. Others built a campfire and before long all were feasting on roast venison.

"On the ninth day Leabo and one or two of the other men struck out from the main party and killed nine elk. They camped where the elk had been killed for three days and feasted on the elk meat and jerked a lot of elk meat to carry with them. At times they did not make over four or five miles a day through the heavy brush in the mountains.

"On the 17th day after leaving the schooner they struck Cow Creek. Within an hour or so they had caught a bushel or more of crawfish, on which they made their supper. That same evening they killed three or four deer. The men divided into two companies, Lester Hulin, Jason Wheeler and some others leading the first company.

"On the 21st day after leaving the vessel they met an emigrant train bound for California, from the members of which they secured food and a few days later they reached their homes.

"Father went back across the plains on horseback to marry my mother. My mother's maiden name was Sophrona P. Briggs. She was born in Ohio in 1828. Father and Mother were married on February 19, 1851, in Lee County, Iowa. A few weeks after their marriage they started by ox team and covered wagon for Father's claim on the middle fork of the Willamette River in Lane County.

"My mother's parents, David and Almira Briggs, came across the plains with my father and mother. They settled at Canyonville. My father's brothers, Lije, Rast, and Put, settled near Jasper, in Lane County. My father raised race horses. He had a mile race track on our place.

"My oldest sister, Mary Susannah Hills, was born at Pleasant Hill, in Lane County, on April 8, 1852. She married a man named Powers and after his death she married Will Smith. My next sister,

Henrietta C. Hills, was born on Valentine's Day, 1854, at Jasper. She married D. J. Jacoby. She is now a widow and lives two miles from Jasper. My sister Jessie C. Hills was born on November 19, 1856. She married Charley Humphrey. They live on their farm a mile from Jasper. My brother Jasper B. Hills, for whom Jasper post office was named, was born April 19, 1859. He is a logger and lives at Oak Ridge. My brother John Amos Hills was born January 26, 1862. He died last summer. My brother Philip Sheridan Hills was born at Eugene, July 17, 1865. He lives on Father's old donation land claim at Jasper. My brother Joel Samuel Hills was born on March 15, 1869. He also is living on our old place. I was the next child and was born on June 30, 1872.

"Yes, there was quite a clan of the Hills settled at Pleasant Hill.

"My father was a great hand with horses. He raised some very fine blooded horses on our place. When he went back to get Mother he traveled on horseback, carrying his outfit on a pack horse. Father and Mother started across the plains on April 16, 1851, and arrived in Lane County on September 7.

"When I went to Eugene I had charge of the race track there and also of the city park. Later I put in two years on the police force. I put in the next 12 years as a game warden, part of the time under W. L. Finley, and later under Mr. Shoemaker. I moved to Portland 15 years ago and have been following carpentry ever since."

"I went to school at Jasper till I was 17 years old, at which time I moved to Eugene. I married Sadie Taliaferro of North Carolina. her folks were born in Virginia. We have two children."

**Oregon Journal**
December 30 & 31, 1932

# Urban East Hicks
# Vancouver, Washington

*The histories of the Indian wars of Oregon and Washington record troop movements, battles, and skirmishes, and reproduce proclamations and orders, but there are scores of minor incidents that never find their way into the histories.*

*Mr. Hicks was commissioned captain on May 24, 1856. His company at its highest enrollment consisted of 46 men. They were in the service six months, during which time they erected nine blockhouses for the settlers and did considerable road work.*

After completing a blockhouse on South Prairie, with 25 men, Mr. Hicks started out on a scouting trip toward Mount Rainier. Each man carried a gun, 21 rounds of ammunition, two days' provisions and a blanket. They took with them a young Indian as guide. They camped just below snowline on Mount Rainier at dusk of the first day out. The following day, on their way back to South Prairie, the guide found Indian signs and followed the trail till they came to where the Indians were camped close to a stream of water. Most of the Indians were in a long building formed of cedar planks. As the Indians came out of the narrow doorway, the soldiers shot them down--men, women and children--only one buck and one squaw of the entire party escaping. They burned the Indians' house and left the Indians where they had fallen.

A few days later a lieutenant belonging to Colonel Casey's command of regulars came to South Prairie with a squad of about a dozen soldiers. An equal number of volunteers from Captain Hicks' company joined them and they went to the headwaters of the Nisqually, where another Indian ranch was located. They took the Indians by surprise, killing a number of them and taking the rest prisoners.

They returned with their prisoners to Montgomery's place. A trial was held and it was decided to shoot two of the Indians and hang one, as an example to the other Indians of the might of the white man. They gave the Indians a night to think it over, and next morning the two Indians to be shot walked calmly forth and faced the firing squad.

The Indian who was to be hung begged to be shot. He told the soldiers that his Ta-mah-na-wis--his protecting spirit--had told him during the night that if he was hung the rope would break. The soldiers led him out under an oak tree, fastened a good strong rope around his neck, and pulled the Indian up till his feet were about six feet above the ground. The Indian raised himself, gave a lurch, and the rope broke. He was nearly strangled, but they allowed him to come to, and one of the soldiers went back to the camp and secured a rawhide lariat, with which they hung him.

The company of men commanded by Captain Hicks was recruited in and about Steilacoom and many of them were old army men, while others were sailors or old-time whalers, and there were some Kanakas. In Captain Hicks' company was a man named Lake, some of whose relatives had been killed by the Indians. Dr. Tolmie obtained permission from Governor Stevens to keep a few Indians who were company servants, at his place at Nisqually, the doctor promising to be responsible for the Indians. Lake obtained a furlough to go to Steilacoom, 118 miles from Montgomery's. Upon his return next day, just at dusk, he saw one of Dr. Tolmie's friendly Indians. The temptation was too great for him, so he shot and killed the Indian. Returning to camp, he hid in his tent and later sent for Captain Hicks and told him what he had done.

Next morning Dr. Tolmie, accompanied by three squaws, came to the camp and reported to Colonel Shaw that one of his volunteers had killed a friendly Indian without provocation. The squaws identified Lake as the man who had killed the Indian. The volunteers broke ranks, rushed to their guns, and threatened to kill Dr. Tolmie and the squaws. They took refuge in Colonel Shaw's tent, which was at once surrounded by officers to protect Dr. Tolmie and the squaws from being killed. The squaws agreed to take no further action if the soldiers would let them off with their lives, so they were allowed to go.

*Oregon Journal*
*October 5, 1928*

# J. D. Matlock
# Pioneer of 1853
# Eugene, Oregon

"When I was a youngster of 12 or 14, in Dade County, Missouri, any time you chanced to look out on the hillside from our house you could see from a dozen to 100 deer grazing. Wild turkeys were abundant. We raised, killed, or caught all we ate, for there was no market for our goods and no corner grocery to go to, with its canned goods, as there is today. We lived on deer or turkey meat, bacon and pork. Sometimes we ate pigeons, cottontail rabbits, or squirrels. Once in a while we would have catfish or bass. A bee tree furnished our honey. Wild fox grapes were abundant and delicious. Pawpaws and persimmons, wild berries and black walnuts, corn and sweet potatoes added variety to our diet.

"Labor was cheap. Father got one of the best farm hands in the county at eight dollars a month. Mother made the soap and spun and wove the cloth, dyed it and made our clothing. We raised a patch of cotton and ran a band of sheep. We children used to sit of nights in front of the fireplace, in which there would be a supply of pitch pine burning to make a good light, and pick the seeds out of the cotton. Later Father bought a machine with rollers, that looked like a clothes wringer, to take the seeds out. Cass, my oldest brother, did the spinning. Mother did the weaving. I wouldn't do what I termed girls' work, so I had to work hard splitting rails or putting up fence. There were no girls for the first 15 years or so in our family, so the boys had to help Mother.

"I remember the great bluffs along the Missouri and the lofty mountain peaks of the Ozarks, in my boyhood. Half a century later I revisited my childhood home and was shocked to find the high bluffs along the river were about 20 feet high and the lofty mountains were low, rolling hills.

"We started from our Ozark farm for Oregon in the spring of 1853, when I was coming 15. We had three wagons and plenty of oxen, with some milch cows. Before we reached the Willamette Valley our milch cows were yoked to the wagons. I had determined to walk all the way to Oregon, so no coaxing would induce me to ride a foot of the way. We got lost on the headwaters of the Malheur and had a hard time wandering around to find a way across the mountains. We went as far south as the lakes in Klamath County, and then drifted back to the headwaters of the Deschutes. From there Martin Blanding and Pleas Nolan struck out afoot to find a way across the Cascades.

"When we at last got across the mountains, near the base of the Three Sisters, we crossed the Willamette River 19 times before reaching Disappointment Butte near what is now Eugene, October 27, 1853, and Father took up a place seven miles from here in a district he named Land of Goshen. They called the school the Goshen school house and the post office took its name from the school district.

"The first time I was ever in a school house was at the school at Goshen. I was 15 years old and was in the a-b-c class. I had gone barefoot all my life, but Mother made me put on shoes to go to school. The teacher, John Winters, told us not to take our shoes off at noon for fear we might catch cold. I got the whole bunch to shed their shoes and go barefoot, for how could you run fast with shoes on?

"The teacher, to punish me, made me sit on a bench in the corner. This didn't worry me any, so he made me sit on his writing desk. He said, 'How do you like that?'

"I said, 'It's pretty hard. You might let me take your coat to sit on.'

"He jerked me off the bench and whaled me till he was nearly worn out. I discovered when I started teaching that you do not have to use a club to control children.

"After going to Columbia College, here at Eugene, I was asked to teach a school where every teacher had been run off by the big boys. The first day I heard someone hooting like a grouse. I spotted one of the larger boys, George Swaggart, doing it, so, instead of whipping him, I said, 'George, that's the best imitation of a grouse I ever heard. Come on up to my desk and show the children how you do it.'

"He looked astonished, but came up and I told him to hoot. He hooted, and for quite a while the children thought it funny, and laughed. Presently they tired of it, so I said, 'George, our show isn't working very well. Get up on my desk and roost there, and keep on hooting.' He saw I meant business, so he roosted on my desk. I made him keep on hooting till he was so sick of it he was good and ready to quit. Finally I let him go back to his desk. He was permanently cured.

"I taught there for a term, till the school was perfectly tamed, when the directors of Knox School sent for me. They couldn't keep their teachers. The children ran them all out. A boy named Billy Kelly there could move his scalp and wiggle his ears, and did so to the utter destruction of discipline. I dismissed the classes and told the children we would have a show—that we had one pupil who must be part monkey and he would entertain us by wiggling his ears. I made him wiggle his ears till he begged me to let him quit making a fool of himself.

"A boy named Vaughan stayed overnight with a boy named Southwell and the Vaughan boy's father sent word for me to punish his boy. I had him get a big stick and then I started to talk to him, telling him how I had counted on him to help me make this a model school. I threw the stick away and sent him to his father to be punished. I went with him to his home and asked his father not to punish him. He was the best boy in the school after that. I had won him by love and he saw to it that no one else started anything in that school.

"From there I went to the Harper School, which had also been unable to keep a teacher because of the unruly conduct of the boys. I soon had that a model school, and quit there to serve as county school superintendent.

"On October 26, 1862, I married Elizabeth Millicent Rutledge. She died on August 22, 1864, shortly after the birth of our daughter.

"I went into partnership with my father-in-law, Blassingham Rutledge, buying and selling hams and bacon. I lost $700 in short order, so retired from the firm.

"I started a store in Rattlesnake Precinct, and in 19 months cleaned up $4000. With this start I got a farm and married Louise Rutledge, the half-sister of my first wife. For many years I farmed at Pleasant Hill. We had 12 children--four boys and eight girls--which, with the daughter of my first wife, made 13 children in our family."

Oregon Journal
April 11, 1920

# Thomas H. Cooper
# Corvallis, Oregon

"My father died in 1891. He would not recognize the world we are now living in. It isn't the change from ox team to airplanes that I mean. It's the change in people themselves. Sunday observance and law observance mean nothing to the children of today. They don't respect the authority of their parents, because the parents give them no home training. Many of the children are receiving no religious instruction whatever. They are not trained to respect the rights of others, nor do they receive any training in the building of character. People are less friendly, more restless, and less happy than when I was a boy."

Oregon Journal
August 8, 1934

# J. A. Baker
# Salem, Oregon

"In 1846 we lived at Oskaloosa, Iowa. A blacksmith near our home used to go out near the creek and pick up a basket of coal every day for his forge. He was the only one that burned coal around there. We and all our neighbors burned hickory. Later an extensive coal mine was opened up on my father's place, the shaft house being put where our home stood.

"In 1846 my father got Oregon fever. He sold his farm, bought two wagons at Oskaloosa and four yoke of oxen and early in the spring of 1847 we assembled with the other emigrants and started for Oregon.

"Our company was called the Oskaloosa Company. Wylie Chapman, father of Mrs. Eades and of Mrs. M. N. Chapman of Salem, was our captain, and, by the way, Mrs. Mem Chapman, who lives near

Peter D'Arcy's house on Church Street, is one of the early pioneers of Salem. There were about 40 families in our party.

"Part way across the plains we separated on account of some wanting to travel faster than others. I remember our train had to separate once to let a big herd of buffalo pass through. This herd scared our loose horses and 16 of them ran off with the buffalo. We stopped a day to hunt them up, but could find only one of them, an old mare that could not keep up with the rest.

"The Saunderses, Canfields, Sawyers and others stopped at Whitman's mission, just a few weeks before the Whitman Massacre. The rest of us went on to The Dalles.

"There was so much snow on the mountains that Father decided to leave his cattle there and go back and get them in the spring. He left 12 head. The next spring when he went back there were only three of them left. The soldiers from the Willamette Valley who had gone up to punish the murderers of Dr. Whitman had been compelled to kill loose stock for food, and it happened they killed nine of my father's 12 cattle. Father never regretted it, as he said if they were willing to give their time and risk their lives he was willing to give his cattle.

"We stopped for a day or two at Linnton. From there we went on to Oregon City. Father got work at Clackamas chopping wood. I went to school to a man named Brush. In the spring of 1848 my father went to a place known as Cutting's Mill and took up a donation land claim. After Father had built a cabin and put in a summer's work, another man turned up and claimed he had taken up the claim first. He told Father he would give him a yoke of cattle and a horse in payment for the summer's work he had done on the place. Father accepted the offer and joined a party of men at Oregon City who were going to the California gold fields.

"My father had not been there long when he began to make a good deal of money. One day a man dropped into his place who said he was going to the Willamette Valley. My father put about $400 worth of gold dust into a buckskin sack and said, 'When you get up to Clackamas look up my wife and hand her this sack of gold dust.' My mother was very much astonished to have a total stranger hand her this sack.

"After mining awhile Father decided to run a store. Everything sold for a dollar a pound. Sugar, flour, tobacco, whatever it was, he charged a dollar a pound. He brought in a big barrel of sauerkraut one day and it happened that some German miners dropped into his store. They weighed out their gold dust and bought the whole barrel at the rate of a dollar a pound.

"One day Father bought a pair of boots in Stockton for himself, paying $20. While driving his ox team to his store in the gold diggings a miner by the side of the road signaled for him to stop. Pointing to the new boots Father was wearing, he said, 'I will give you $75 for your boots if they fit me.' Father pulled off his boots, tossed them to the miner in the road, who took off his own wornout boots and put Father's on and said: 'They fit me fine. Here is your money,' and he handed Father $75 in gold dust. Gold dust was so plentiful in those days they were not particular about a few dollars one way or the other.

"While Father was gone I dug potatoes on shares. We were living in a little log cabin. Every other row of potatoes was mine, so each night I would bring home my share of potatoes. Mother poured them out in a corner of the cabin and next morning, to her astonishment, every potato was gone. This happened several nights in succession. We couldn't solve the mystery of who was stealing our potatoes. Finally I crawled under the house and discovered that the woodrats were caching them away for their winter supplies."

Oregon Journal
May 16, 1922

# Theophilus E. Hills
# Garden Home, Oregon

"I was 17 when I enlisted in Company I, 34th Illinois, as a drummer. We were with the 2nd Division of the 14th Corps and I went with Sherman to the sea. I enlisted in August, 1861, for three years, and reenlisted at the end of that period. Shiloh was our first battle. Most of the members of our company were young chaps--from 17 to about 21 years of age.

"At the Battle of Stone River, which started on December 31, 1862, our company was on the extreme right. General Braxton Bragg moved up from Murfreesboro and planned to fold up our right and enfilade our forces. Just at daylight our pickets began firing, and soon came back on the run. I was frying bacon and watching the pot of coffee over the campfire. I looked up and saw a line of gray three feet deep. We fell back about as fast as we could fall. A bayonet lying on the ground ran into my shoe and tripped me. While I was freeing my foot from the bayonet I could hear the bullets singing around my ears and I saw numerous spurts of dust all around me. All of which encouraged me to a burst of speed when I got free from the bayonet. But I had waited too long and was taken prisoner. The sergeant major of our regiment and myself were detailed by the Confederates to care for the wounded. We watched our chance and got into a plum thicket, so we were not paroled.

"On January 2 the Confederates again attacked our forces but met with little success, and the next day they retired. There were over 37,000 Confederates engaged and about 44,000 of our forces. We lost nearly 1700 killed and over 3500 of our men were reported missing, which means that most of them were taken prisoners.

"After I had gone over the battlefield I decided to take one more look. Between two boulders I saw a wounded man, and, to my surprise, found he was Joe Teeter, my bunkie. He was shot through the lower part of the abdomen. I got help and carried him to an ambulance. He was unconscious. I never expected to see him again, but he recovered, rejoined our company, and became captain of the company. He and I were in the grand review at Washington."

Oregon Journal
August 9, 1933

# C. C. Masiker
## Pioneer of 1853
## Elmira, Oregon

"No, I have no recollection of our trip across the plains, for we started when I was only two weeks old. Our train was made up at Elgin, Illinois. There were 40 wagons. My father had two wagons --one of them pulled by four horses, the other by two horses.

"Our train was nearly wiped out by cholera. My mother and my sister had the cholera and were not expected to live, but both lived. Many a family in the train, however, was completely wiped out. The captain of the wagon train died on the Platte. Many of the wagons were abandoned, and out of the 40 wagons that started, only six reached Salt Lake City, late in that fall.

"Our family and five others decided to winter at what was then known as Box Elder, Utah, but is now known as Brigham City. Father and the others met and decided to send a delegation to Salt Lake City to secure permission from Brigham

Young to winter there. Brigham Young said, 'I suppose your teams are badly jaded on account of the long trip. I will send out fresh teams to do the hauling. Your men can cut down trees and put up substantial log buildings in which to live this winter. Put up about twice as many cabins as you need, and I will send settlers out to occupy them, which will make it safer for you, on account of the Indians. When you leave next spring I will send other settlers there to occupy your cabins.'

"Father and the other men of our party built about a dozen log cabins. Not wanting to offend Brigham Young, when the tithe gatherer came round they paid the regular tithes of one tenth of all they had."

**Oregon Journal**
July 5, 1934

# Verd Hill
# Independence, Oregon

"Father had an old-fashioned Kentucky flintlock gun. When the party landed at San Francisco they decided to celebrate their safe arrival by hunting up the nearest saloon. As Father didn't drink, and had a gun, they told him to take charge of their supplies.

"An Irish sailor, who was half seas over, came up to my father and in a very domineering voice, said, 'Here, boy, load my pipe, and see that you put good tobacco in it, too.'

"My father put in a little tobacco and on this he slipped in about half a spoonful of powder from his powderhorn and then put a little more tobacco on top of it. The sailor lit his pipe, and a moment later the powder caught fire. There was a flash, which singed the sailor's eyebrows, shattered his pipe, and completely ruined his disposition and temper. He started for my father, and if his language was any criterion of what his actions were going to be, he would have wiped the wharf up with him.

"Father pointed his long Kentucky rifle at him and told him if he came any nearer he would bore a hole clean through him, so the sailor thought better of it and decided to wait for a more convenient season to trim my father."

**Oregon Journal**
May 11, 1923

# Edwin Markham
## Oregon City, Oregon

"I came very near not having any boyhood. My father and mother, with their family, came across the plains to Oregon by ox team in 1847. They had heard of the land of promise by the shores of the western sea and started out with a number of neighbors for the 2000-mile trip across the desert to the far-famed Willamette Valley.

"The party camped one night not far from a stream and drew their wagons into a circle to be prepared in case of an attack by Indians. My mother, taking two pails, went to the spring nearby to get some water. Hearing a noise like subdued thunder, she looked up and saw a herd of buffaloes, which had been alarmed and were charging toward the river. She started to run toward the river, but, seeing she would be cut off, she turned and ran toward the wagons. Before she could reach the circle of wagons the buffaloes were upon her. She was knocked down and the buffaloes at the edge of the herd ran over her.

"Father and the other men ran down to where she lay. Her clothes were almost torn from her. She was unconscious. Her right shoulder blade and a number of ribs were broken. They fixed up a mattress in one of the wagons, and for the next six or eight weeks, my mother directed the household and camping activities from her bed in the wagon."

Oregon Journal
December 14, 192?
(last digit illegible)

# Son of Andrew Jackson Masters
## Hillsboro, Oregon

*While walking along one of the residence streets in Hillsboro a day or so ago I stopped to admire a large front yard in which was a profusion of old-fashioned flowers. On each side of the walk were huge beds of Oriental poppies whose crinkly flame-red petals looked as if made of tissue paper. I stopped to pass the time of day with the owner of this place.*

"I have been sick this spring, so my place doesn't look as good as it should. I have lived in Washington County for more than 80 years, and this spring is the first time in all my life that I was ever sick. I had the flu a couple of months

333

ago, and I still feel a little run down from it. No, I never had a doctor during the past 80 years. I have been in runaways, been kicked by horses and met with occasional accidents, but I never had a doctor for such trifles.

"Yes, I was born in Washington County, on March 5, 1845, on Squire Ebberts' place. The Orenco Nursery now owns the old Ebberts donation land claim. The old squire was an old-time trapper and mountain man. He and Joe Meek came to this county together. Like Joe Meek, he had an Indian wife.

"My father, Andrew Jackson Masters, was born in Kentucky in 1816, and in 1843, when he was 27 years old, he went to Elm Grove, near Independence, Missouri, where Oregon emigrants met to organize for the trip across the plains. They elected Peter H. Burnett captain of the wagon train. When he resigned they elected Captain William Martin.

"My mother, Sarah Jenkins Masters, was born in Kentucky in 1826. She and my father were married at Weston, Missouri, October 4, 1842, when Mother was 16 and Father 26 years old. The next spring they were on their way to the Willamette Valley. When they got to the Blue Mountains Mother was expecting her baby most any day, so the rest of the wagon train hurried on to The Dalles, while Father and Mother, on horseback, came on more slowly. The day after they reached The Dalles Mother's first baby was born. They named it for Dr. Marcus Whitman, who had served as guide till he left a Cayuse Indian named Stickas to serve in that capacity. The baby was named Marcus Gilliam Masters. Mother stayed that winter with the Methodist missionaries at The Dalles. Father went on to the Willamette Valley. The next spring he went up to The Dalles to get mother and the baby. They hired some Indians to take them down the Columbia. In the swift water of the Cascades the canoe was overturned and they lost all their baggage and narrowly escaped with their lives. They moved onto the Ebberts place, where I was born in the spring of 1845.

"In 1852 Jane Gray came out from Boston and taught school on the Robinson place, on which Reedville was later located. I went to school to her. In 1854-55 I went to school at Farmington, four miles south of Hillsboro.

"In the spring of 1849 we went to Suttersville, California, by wagon. It is now called Sacramento. Father mined one day and didn't like it. He told Mother they would yoke up the oxen and start right back for the Willamette Valley. Mother said, 'You have dragged me clear down here to make a fortune in the mines. I won't go back till we have made our fortune. Sell our wagon and oxen and buy me a house here and I will run a boarding house. When we have saved $10,000 I will go back, but not before.'

"Father sold his outfit and bought a boarding house. Mother charged a dollar a meal for regulars and $1.25 a meal for comers and goers. Inside of a year she had $10,000 in gold coin, so they sold the boarding house and we came back to our farm in Washington County. We came back on a sailing vessel. It was wrecked while crossing the bar coming into the Columbia River. The passengers were all saved, but the boat broke up and was a total loss.

"By 1856 there were five children in our family. Father was 40 and Mother was 30. Father was killed that year. A man named J. H. McMillan took up the place next to ours. He claimed our cattle got on his place. Our cattle were poisoned, and Father thought this man had poisoned them, and accused him of it. He threatened to shoot Father if he ever came on his place. They went to law about their boundary line. One time Father was riding along the road and he passed McMillan, who was working in the timber. McMillan shot and killed Father.

"There are always two sides to every quarrel, so I don't know who was most to blame, except that I do know that McMillan interfered with my father and talked about him to the neighbors. At the trial of McMillan for murdering my father he claimed my father, who, being a Kentuckian, was a dead shot, as most Kentuckians were, had threatened him and he had killed him through fear of losing his own life. No one witnessed the shooting, and as my father was dead the jury failed to convict McMillan of murder, so he was turned loose.

"My father's death ended my schooling, for my brother Marcus had died and I was the oldest boy and had to do the plowing with two yoke of oxen and attend to the farm work. I was 11 years old, but I was large for my age. Mother later married Henry Willoughby and had three children by him.

"I worked on my mother's place till I was 21, when I struck out for myself. I went up into Klickitat County and got a job in a logging camp near the old Fort Simcoe blockhouse. I worked a couple of years there and then bought a farm near Reedville. I married Clarinda Harris on October 10, 1867. Her father came to Oregon in 1847. All but five acres of my place was in timber. During the next 21 years I cleared the place and got it into crops. I sold it in 1888 and moved to Hillsboro.

"When I was a boy all I knew was to work from sunrise to sunset and mind my parents. It never occurred to me not to obey them. In those days the parents, not the children, were the heads of the family.

"No, I never had time to go fishing when I was a boy. We could buy a 40-pound salmon from the Indians for two bits to four bits, and when you can buy fish for a cent a pound it doesn't pay to fish. Whenever we needed meat I would kill a deer, for the country was alive with game when I was a boy. I have seen the wheat fields dark with wild geese and brants.

"I have seen the pack train and the ox team pass and the day of paved highways and auto stages come. The next generation will probably see the passenger and freight traffic carried on in the air."

Oregon Journal
May 23, 1925

# J. C. Mason
# Talent, Oregon

"I was 85 years old on the third of last April. I was born at Kinderhook, in Pike County, Illinois. Kinderhook is just east of Hannibal, Missouri, the boyhood home of Mark Twain, and Pike County, Illinois, is across the Mississippi from Pike County, Missouri.

"I was five years old when we came across the plains. My father was a great hand to trade, so you couldn't really say he settled anywhere, for he would buy a farm, fix it up a little, sell it at a profit, and be on the wing.

"In the fall of 1853 he bought a place on French Prairie, about 15 miles north of Salem. He put in a crop and sold it in the spring of 1854 and we started for Yreka, California. He hired a man to drive the wagon, while he rode on horseback. I was only six years old, but Father let me ride back of him on the horse. I can remember our constant fording and crossing of Cow Creek in southern Oregon. We crossed this stream over 30 times, for in those days the road followed the bed of the stream through the canyon. In places south of Canyonville the mud was hub-deep and the oxen nearly mired.

"Father mined at Yreka a few months and then went up the Shasta Valley and bought a farm near his sister. Everyone called her Mammy Ray. Money was plentiful in those days. In 1858 a man came to our place and bought four cows, giving Father 50 20-dollar gold pieces for them—that means $250 apiece.

"Our place was near Bummerville. Pack trains

between Sacramento and Yreka frequently put up at our place. Sometimes there would be 75 to 100 pack horses or pack mules grazing on our place. Father charged so much a head, so he made good money. In 1859 Father sold this place and went to Dayton, in Yamhill County, Oregon."

Oregon Journal<br>
August 14, 1933

# J. B. "Dad" Hoss
## Salem, Oregon

"My father believed in discipline with a capital D, and when he wanted to whip me he grabbed the first thing handy. He believed in doing with his might what his hand found to do. He probably meant well but he had a heavy hand and a quick-trigger temper, so when I was 14 I lit out. I took one of Father's saddle horses, leaving a note that I would send the money for it later.

"I struck south, not knowing or caring where I was going. I had not traveled over a day or two before I fell in with a man named Vaughn Smith. I didn't know at the time just what was the matter with him, but now I realize that he was locoed. He had an eye like a mean mustang. His eyes would roll and he would show the whites of his eyes and sometimes I got pretty nervous about the way he acted.

"One of his favorite expressions was, 'I have more money than most folks have hay.' He had a diamond about the size of a hazelnut, which he wore in a buckskin bag tied around his neck. There seemed to be some great mystery about this diamond and he was constantly afraid that someone would learn about it. He used to walk back and forth like a caged animal, with the whites of his eyes showing, cracking his knuckles or striking one fist in the palm of his other hand and saying, 'It serves her right. It serves her right.'

"One day I incautiously said, 'It serves her right. What did she do?'

"He turned on me like a trapped wolf, glared at me and said, 'It's none of your damn business. You keep your mouth shut.'

"I never found out who she was nor what she had done, and I never asked again.

"Smith seemed to have plenty of money and he paid all of our expenses to Yuma, Arizona, where I quit him. Sometime later I heard that a man answering his description and who was supposed to be demented had been drowned while crossing a river.

I never knew what became of the diamond he wore around his neck, though I have always been curious to know more about him.

"The year 1872 found me in Eugene. That same year I went east of the mountains and stopped at Pendleton. Pendleton in 1872 was a cowboy town. It was sure wide open and you could get action on your money. The principal places of business were saloons.

"Pendleton was about three years old when I hit there. In the spring of 1869 there was only a log store, which was run by Lot Livermore, a small hotel run by M. E. Goodwin, and Judge G. W. Bailey's house. Although there were only two or three buildings there the county commissioners selected it as the county seat and named the town Pendleton.

"I was there when the Indian trouble occurred. Buffalo Horn was killed and Chief Egan took over command of the Indians. The settlers hurried pell-mell into Pendleton. They dug a trench around the courthouse and banked the dirt up and a lot of the citizens formed a volunteer company and started for southern Umatilla County to fight the Indians.

"I was in Pendleton when White Owl, Quit-a-tunips and Aps were sentenced to be hung. White Owl and Quit-a-tunips were hung in the jail yard of the courthouse on January 10, 1879, and Aps was hung a week later in the same place.

"Do you remember Cal Young, early-day stage driver, who later drove the mail hack from the depot to the Salem post office? When I was up in Pendleton in the late '70s I met Cal Young's daughter Millie. I was doing carpenter work there. Millie and I were married 50 years ago."

Oregon Journal
July 24, 1931

# Thomas M. Miller
# Pioneer of 1850
# Oregon City, Oregon

*Thomas M. Miller has been bailiff of the court of Oregon City 55 years. I doubt if another bailiff in the West has such a record of continuous service. When I visited him recently he said:*

"I have lived in Oregon City 75 years. I was born in Indiana, October 10, 1839. My father, Samuel Miller, was born in New Jersey and my mother, whose maiden name was Rachel Hart, was born in Maryland. They were married in Delaware. My father and his brother decided to come West when the discovery of gold in California became known. They started in the spring of 1849. We traveled by ox team to St. Joe, Missouri. There were five children of us, and while we were waiting at St. Joe several of the children got sick. My uncle started on with other emigrants, but Father decided to wait till the chidren were well. It was then too late to start, so we stayed at Savannah, Missouri, not far from St. Joe, till the spring of 1850.

"It wasn't the discovery of gold that principally decided my father to go west, but disgust with conditions in Indiana. He had a water power sawmill, which was washed away by high water. Everybody said such high water was unusual and probably would not occur again in 20 years, so Father spent most of his money in fixing up a better mill than he had lost, when along came the high water the next spring, washed this mill away, and left him broke and disgusted. He had just about enough money left to buy our outfit to go to Oregon.

"My father's favorite brother reached Oregon City in the fall of 1849 and took up a place two miles west. Willamette Valley farmers came back late that fall from California with glowing reports, so he decided to try the gold fields and went to California with his two boys, Jim and Jeff. They struck a rich claim and cleaned up a good bunch of money. The next spring they sold their claim, but just as they were about to start home my uncle took sick and died. His sons buried him near their claim and returned to Oregon City.

"I was 11 when we left St. Joe. There were 15 wagons in our train. There was so much travel in 1850 that we had no trouble from Indians. Most of those who visited our camp carried papers that they carefully treasured, to prove that they were good Indians. Some of the 'recommendations' were very curious. An Indian would gravely hand out a 'recommendation' reading 'This is a bad Indian. Look out for him. He will steal your eyeteeth if you don't watch him.'

"We started out with plenty of provisions, but a good many that year ran short, so we shared ours till we also were out of food. From Fort Hall on we lived pretty much on corn bread, sage hens and jackrabbits. My cousins, who had come back from California that spring had an idea that we might be out of supplies, so they packed some horses with bacon, flour, potatoes, and other supplies, and had come to meet us. They met us in the Grand Ronde Valley, and I needn't tell you we were mighty glad to see them.

"One reason why we were so late was that the travel was so heavy in 1850 that the grass on both sides of the Old Oregon Trail was pretty well eaten off, so we had to drive our cattle a mile or two back from the trail to get any grass. We laid over a day each week to let them feed up and rest up.

"In coming across the plains I ran across a blue ox that somebody had abandoned. I called him Old Bull and brought him along. In the Blue Mountains, near Lee's Encampment, not far from where Meacham is now, the timber wolves killed my old blue ox, to my great sorrow. I heard him bawling and the bells of the other cattle jingling as they ran, but before we could get there the wolves had dragged Old Bull down and torn his throat so badly that he bled to death.

"We reached Laurel Hill about October 20, with all 12 of our cattle that we had started from St. Joe with. The night we camped at Laurel Hill a cold sleet storm set in that was something like the silver thaws we occasionally have here in Portland. The next morning six of our 12 oxen were dead. They were thin and gaunt and had chilled to death.

"My father bought a place of 640 acres near our cousins', for which he paid $250. I spent my boyhood working on this farm."

**Oregon Journal**
January 25, 1926

# The End

"Don't you ever run out of material
for your articles?" inquired an acquaintance
a day or so ago.
    As long as there are any people
left in the world I shan't run out of
material, for if you are interested in
humanity, everyone you meet is a story."

Fred Lockley
1871–1958

# Index

344

356

Illustrations in this book and in **Conversations with Pioneer Women** were taken from the **Dover Pictorial Archive Series.**

# What they say
# About the
# Oregon Country Library:

## Conversations
## with
## Pioneer Women
by Fred Lockley
Compiled and Edited by Mike Helm

"...riveting...a book to treasure."
**Willamette Valley Observer**

"These oral histories of Pacific Northwest women...are action-packed, adventurous love stories of our forebears who trudged to the Oregon Territory in the mid-1800s. This one is a diamond."
**Los Angeles Times**

"...an engaging, meaningful documentation of women's experiences on the frontier."
**Seattle Post Intelligencer**

"The trials of crossing the plains in a wagon and establishing a home in the Northwest wilderness are brought into sharp clarity."
**Walla Walla Union Bulletin**

"...of great use to history teachers, those who teach women's studies, and readers who enjoy the true flavor of frontier life."
**Oregon Journal**

"...so fascinating..."
*Eugene Register Guard*

"...a rare treasure..."
*Corvallis Gazette-Times*

"...fascinating reading..."
*The Delta Paper*
Delta Junction, Alaska

**Conversations with Pioneer Women** is recommended by *Booklist* and *Choice*, publications of the American Library Association.

**Conversations with Pioneer Women** is a Small Press Book Club Selection.

**Conversations with Pioneer Women** received the Pacific Northwest Booksellers Award for Literary Excellence.

ISBN 0-931742-08-0

# Tracking Down Coyote
by Mike Helm

"**Tracking Down Coyote** is a wonderful book...Many have walked, stomped, hiked, biked, or horsed their way across Oregon, and some have written about it, but none yet with quite the personal approach taken by Helm, a man of 47 who has tender feet as well as a tender, romantic heart...Helm is a storyteller, historian, and writer of worth. His Coyote tales are delightful, depictive of the Indians' interpretations of the mysteries of this beautiful country."
*The Oregonian*

"In **Tracking Down Coyote**...Mike Helm recounts a personal odyssey in search of the soul of his territory. His predecessors are Edward Abbey, Edward S. Curtis, John Muir, Henry Thoreau, W. P. Kinsella, with an echo of Carlos Castaneda...his scholarship approaches the religious..his best writing recreates journeys into the mind and legends of Coyote and his fellow Oregon deities, bringing ancient stories to life..."
*San Francisco Chronicle*

"**Tracking Down Coyote** (is Mike Helm's) heartfelt, roughhewn and lyrical ode to his native state...Helm's journeys to the outback of Oregon are also Coyote tales. His search for the spirit of Oregon's wild places is metaphorically a hunt for the totem figure that personifies that spirit.
"**Tracking Down Coyote**...is a unique, flavorful mix of inner quests, outer struggle, and recaps of local lore.
"Coyote would dig it. He likes it when we let go with a few howls of our own."
*What's Happening*

"**Tracking Down Coyote** is one of the best books of its kind I have ever read. Mike Helm is an excellent teller of tales and a fine hand at weaving experience, fact, legend and myth into an engrossing whole.

"...it is an honest, clear-sighted and in some places angry book. It sounds a warning we will ignore to our sorrow."
*Eugene Register Guard*
*Salem Statesman-Journal*

ISBN 0-931742-16-1

# Visionaries, Mountain Men & Empire Builders They Made a Difference

by Fred Lockley
Compiled and Edited by Mike Helm

"A treasury of intriguing tales about not-too-remote pioneer citizens..."
*Eugene Register Guard*

"...profiles of such legendary figures as Dr. John McLoughlin, Joe and Stephen Meek, Ewing Young, Abigail Scott Duniway, Simon Benson, Sam Jackson, and Lockley himself, to name only a few included in this biographical pantheon."
*Northwest Magazine*
Sunday magazine of *The Oregonian*

"A more colorful cast of characters would be hard to find..."
*Salem Statesman-Journal*

"I doubt if Fred Lockley ever met a stranger. The people he writes about were his friends and he simply expects you too will want to meet them."
*The CorvallisGazette-Times*

ISBN 9 0-931742-09-9

<hr>

# Oregon's Ghosts and Monsters
## by Mike Helm

"...familiar tales of regional phantoms and haunted buildings...(and) some bloodcurdling newer ones that sent shivers down the spine of at least one late-night reader."
*The Register Guard*

"For readers fascinated by Oregon lore, the book will be hard to resist."
*The La Grande Observer*

ISBN 0-931742-03-X

# The Oregon Country Library

**1. Conversations with Pioneer Women**
By Fred Lockley, compiled and edited by Mike Helm. 310 pages.
ISBN 0-931742-08-0

**2. Conversations with Bullwhackers, Muleskinners, Pioneers, Prospectors, '49ers, Indian Fighters, Trappers, Ex-Barkeepers, Authors, Preachers, Poets & Near Poets & All Sorts & Conditions of Men**
By Fred Lockley, compiled and edited by Mike Helm. 358 pages.
ISBN 0-931742-09-0

**3. Visionaries, Mountain Men and Empire Builders**
By Fred Lockley, compiled and edited by Mike Helm. 395 pages.
ISBN 0-931742-10-2

**4. A Bit of Verse: Poetry (&Etc.) from the Lockley Files**
By Fred Lockley, compiled and edited by Mike Helm. 165 pages.
ISBN 0-931742-10-2

**5. Oregon's Ghosts and Monsters**
By Mike Helm. 158 pages.
ISBN 0-931742-03-X

**6. Tracking Down Coyote**
By Mike Helm. 218 pages.
ISBN 0-931742-16-1


What they say about the Oregon Country Library:
"...an amazing oral history collection..."
**Small Press Review**
"...engaging, meaningful documentation of women's experiences on the frontier..."
**Seattle Post Intelligencer**
"...preserves something today's Oregonians forget at their peril—the human dimension."
**Corvallis Gazette-Times**
"...enough colorful wind to sail a ship."
**Portland Oregonian**
"...highly recommended."
**Kliatt Paperback Book Guide**
"...a rare treasure..."
**Corvallis Gazette Times**
"I highly recommend this book."
**Wyoming Library Roundup**
"...vivid view of those obscure lives..."
**Western Humanities Review**

## A special offer for lovers
## of Pacific Northwest Literature--
## The Oregon Country Library

Please send me:

____copies of **Conversations with Pioneer Women**
      @ $17.95 each                    $_____
____copies of **Conversations with Pioneer Men**
      @ $22.00 each                    $_____
____copies of **Visionaries, Mountain Men & Empire Builders**
      @ $20.00 each (This book is temporarily out of print.)
____copies of **A Bit of Verse: Poems (& Etc.) from the Lockley**
      **Files** @ $7.95 each           $_____
____copies of **Oregon's Ghosts and Monsters**
      @ $9.95 each                     $_____
____copies of **Tracking Down Coyote**
      @ $14.95 each                    $_____

            Subtotal                   $_____

            Less discount of 10%       $_____

            Plus postage & handling ($1.50 for the first book,
$.50 for each additional book)
                                       $_____

            Total                      $_____

Name_____Address_____

City_____State_____Zip_____

**One Horse Press**
**PO Box 3035**
**Eugene, OR 97403**

The Lockley Files
# Conversations
# with
# Pioneer Women

*". . .riveting. . .a book to treasure. . ."*
**Willamette Valley Observer**

*". . .an engaging, meaningful documentation
of women's experiences on the frontier."*
**Seattle Post-Intelligencer**

*". . .a rare treasure. . ."*
**Corvallis Gazette-Times**

*". . .so fascinating. . ."*
**Eugene Register Guard**

*"The trials of crossing the plains in a wagon
and establishing a home in the Northwest wilderness
are brought into sharp clarity. . ."*
**Walla Walla Union Bulletin**

*". . .revealing information on what it was like
for women in early Oregon. . ."*
**Portland Oregonian**

ISBN 0-931742-08-0
LOC #81-50845
6x9 paperback
248 pages

By Fred Lockley
Compiled by Mike Helm